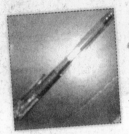

> This is a pen.
> —Tsugumi Ohba

> I spill more than just ink on my manuscripts. The most common mishaps are with coffee and for some reason, blood from my nose...
> —Takeshi Obata

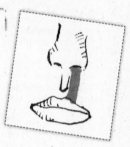

Tsugumi Ohba

Born in Tokyo, Tsugumi Ohba is the author of the hit series *Death Note*. His current series *Bakuman。* is serialized in *Weekly Shonen Jump*.

Takeshi Obata

Takeshi Obata was born in 1969 in Niigata, Japan, and is the artist of the wildly popular SHONEN JUMP title *Hikaru no Go*, which won the 2003 Tezuka Osamu Cultural Prize: Shinsei "New Hope" award and the 2000 Shogakukan Manga award. Obata is also the artist of *Arabian Majin Bokentan Lamp Lamp*, *Ayatsuri Sakon*, *Cyborg Jichan G.*, and the smash hit manga *Death Note*. His current series *Bakuman。* is serialized in *Weekly Shonen Jump*.

BAKUMAN。

Volume 5

SHONEN JUMP Manga Edition

Story by **TSUGUMI OHBA**
Art by **TAKESHI OBATA**

Translation | **Tetsuichiro Miyaki**
English Adaptation | **Hope Donovan**
Touch-up Art & Lettering | **James Gaubatz**
Design | **Fawn Lau**
Editor | **Alexis Kirsch**

BAKUMAN。© 2008 by Tsugumi Ohba, Takeshi Obata
All rights reserved.
First published in Japan in 2008 by SHUEISHA Inc., Tokyo.
English translation rights arranged by SHUEISHA Inc.

Printed in the U.S.A.

Published by VIZ Media, LLC
P.O. Box 77010
San Francisco, CA 94107

10 9 8 7 6 5 4 3 2 1
First printing, June 2011

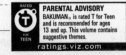
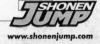

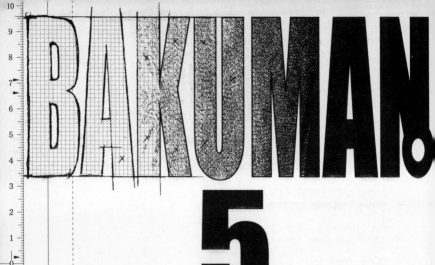

BAKUMAN.

5

YEARBOOK
and
PHOTOBOOK

STORY BY
TSUGUMI OHBA

ART BY
TAKESHI OBATA

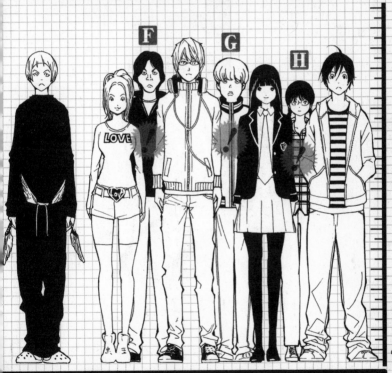

EIJI Nizuma	KAYA Miyoshi	AKITO Takagi	MIHO Azuki	MORITAKA Mashiro
A manga prodigy and Tezuka Award winner at the age of 15. He's in high school and already has a series running in *Jump*.	Miho's friend and Akito's girlfriend. A nice girl who actively works as the interceder between Moritaka and Azuki.	Aspiring manga writer. An extremely smart guy who gets the best grades in his class. A cool guy who becomes very passionate when it comes to manga.	A girl who dreams of becoming a voice actress. She promised to marry Moritaka under the condition that they not see each other until their dreams come true.	Aspiring manga artist. An extreme romantic who believes that he will marry Miho Azuki once their dreams come true.
Age: 18	Age: 17	Age: 16	Age: 17	Age: 16

*These ages are from December 2010.

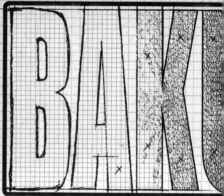

STORY In order to attain the glory that only a handful of people can, two young men decide to walk the rough "path of manga" and become professional manga creators. This is the story of a great artist, Moritaka Mashiro, a talented writer, Akito Takagi, and their quest to become manga legends!

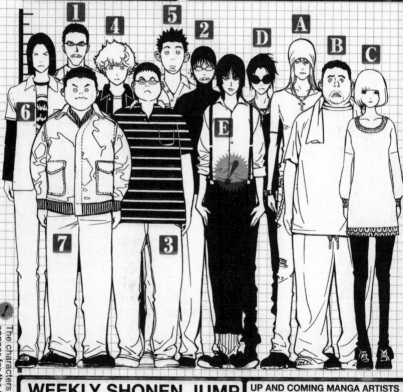

The characters with this mark ✦ appear for the first time in volume 5.

WEEKLY SHONEN JUMP
Editorial Office

1 Editor in Chief Sasaki	Age: 47
2 Deputy Editor in Chief Heishi	Age: 42
3 Soichi Aida	Age: 35
4 Yujiro Hattori	Age: 28
5 Akira Hattori	Age: 30
6 Koji Yoshida	Age: 32
7 Goro Miura	Age: 23

UP AND COMING MANGA ARTISTS

A SHINTA FUKUDA	Age: 20	
B TAKURO NAKAI	Age: 34	
C KO AOKI	Age: 20	
D KOJI MAKAINO	Age: 30	
E KAZUYA HIRAMARU	Age: 26	
F Ogawa	**G** Takahama	**H** Kato
	Muto Ashirogi's Assistants	

BAKUMAN。 Vol.5 CONTENTS

(YEARBOOK AND PHOTOBOOK)

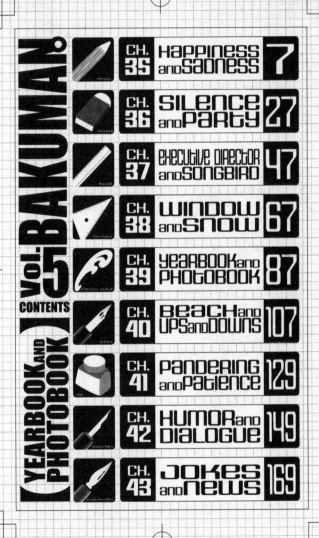

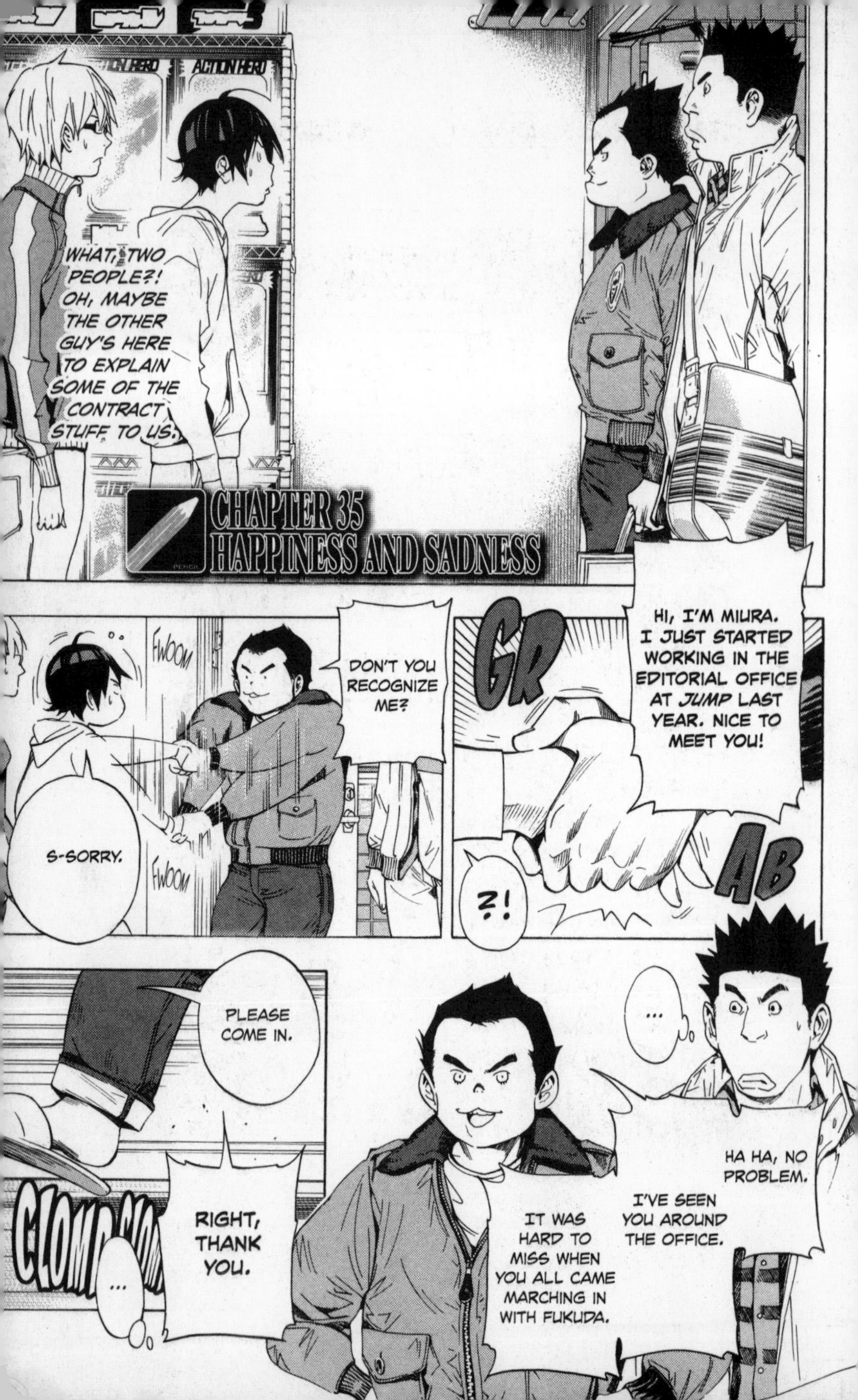
WHAT, TWO PEOPLE?! OH, MAYBE THE OTHER GUY'S HERE TO EXPLAIN SOME OF THE CONTRACT STUFF TO US.
CHAPTER 35 HAPPINESS AND SADNESS
HI, I'M MIURA. I JUST STARTED WORKING IN THE EDITORIAL OFFICE AT *JUMP* LAST YEAR. NICE TO MEET YOU!
GR
AB
?!
DON'T YOU RECOGNIZE ME?
FWOOM
FWOOM
S-SORRY.
...
HA HA, NO PROBLEM.
I'VE SEEN YOU AROUND THE OFFICE.
IT WAS HARD TO MISS WHEN YOU ALL CAME MARCHING IN WITH FUKUDA.
PLEASE COME IN.
RIGHT, THANK YOU.
...
CLOMP

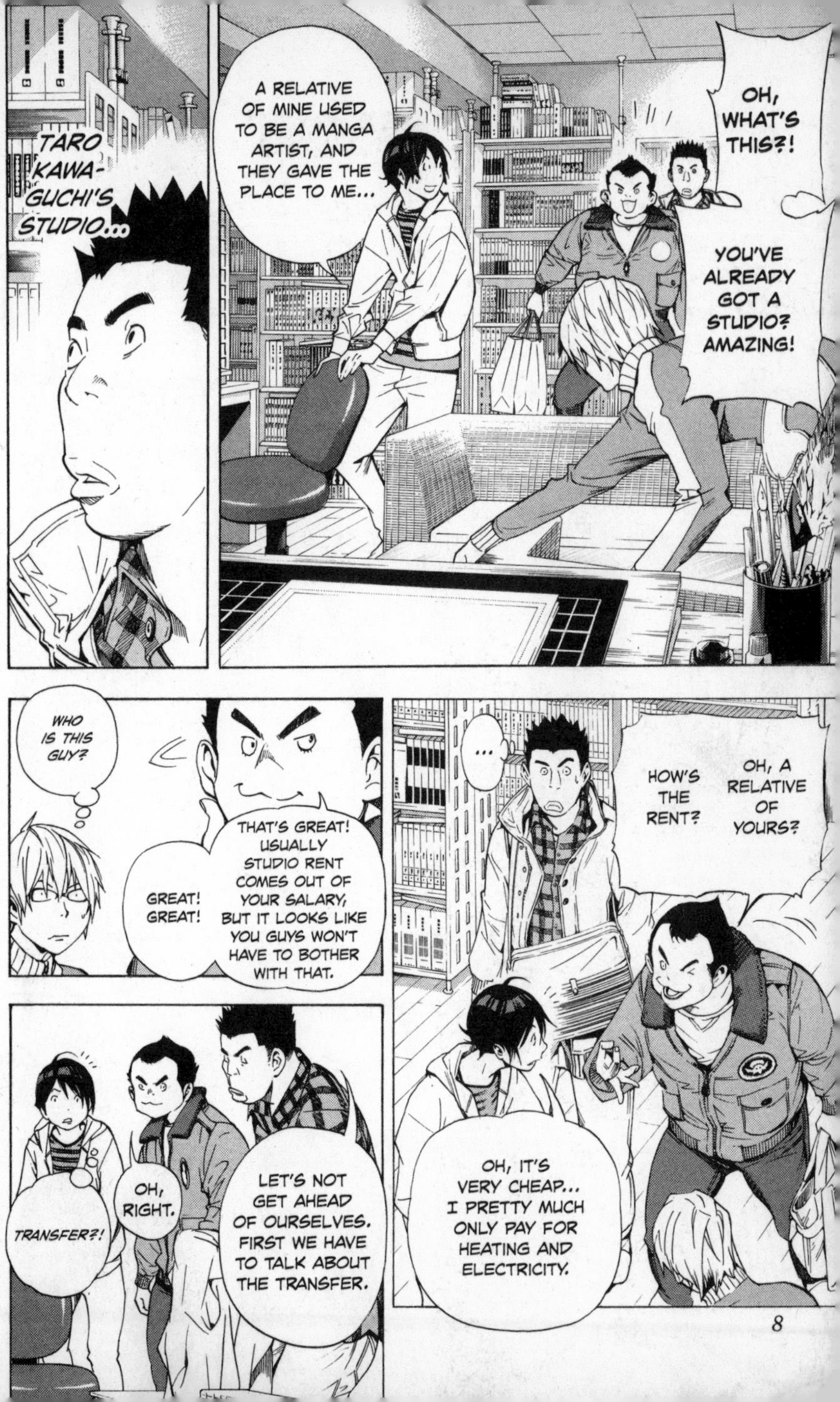
OH, WHAT'S THIS?!
YOU'VE ALREADY GOT A STUDIO? AMAZING!
A RELATIVE OF MINE USED TO BE A MANGA ARTIST, AND THEY GAVE THE PLACE TO ME...
TARO KAWA-GUCHI'S STUDIO...
OH, A RELATIVE OF YOURS?
HOW'S THE RENT?
...
OH, IT'S VERY CHEAP... I PRETTY MUCH ONLY PAY FOR HEATING AND ELECTRICITY.
THAT'S GREAT! USUALLY STUDIO RENT COMES OUT OF YOUR SALARY, BUT IT LOOKS LIKE YOU GUYS WON'T HAVE TO BOTHER WITH THAT.
GREAT! GREAT!
WHO IS THIS GUY?
LET'S NOT GET AHEAD OF OURSELVES. FIRST WE HAVE TO TALK ABOUT THE TRANSFER.
OH, RIGHT.
TRANSFER?!

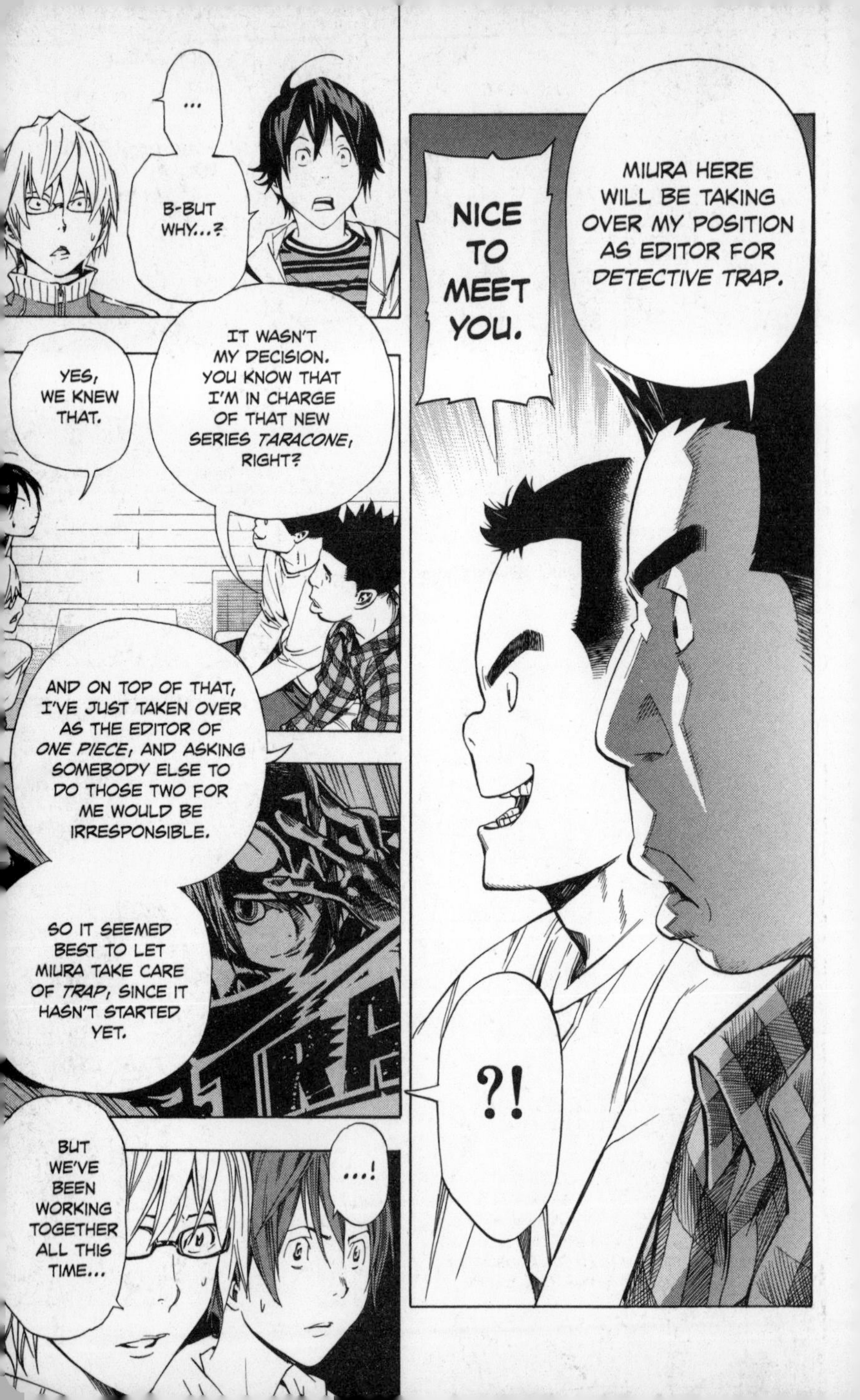
MIURA HERE WILL BE TAKING OVER MY POSITION AS EDITOR FOR DETECTIVE TRAP.
NICE TO MEET YOU.
?!
...
B-BUT WHY...?
IT WASN'T MY DECISION. YOU KNOW THAT I'M IN CHARGE OF THAT NEW SERIES *TARACONE*, RIGHT?
YES, WE KNEW THAT.
AND ON TOP OF THAT, I'VE JUST TAKEN OVER AS THE EDITOR OF *ONE PIECE*, AND ASKING SOMEBODY ELSE TO DO THOSE TWO FOR ME WOULD BE IRRESPONSIBLE.
SO IT SEEMED BEST TO LET MIURA TAKE CARE OF *TRAP*, SINCE IT HASN'T STARTED YET.
...!
BUT WE'VE BEEN WORKING TOGETHER ALL THIS TIME...

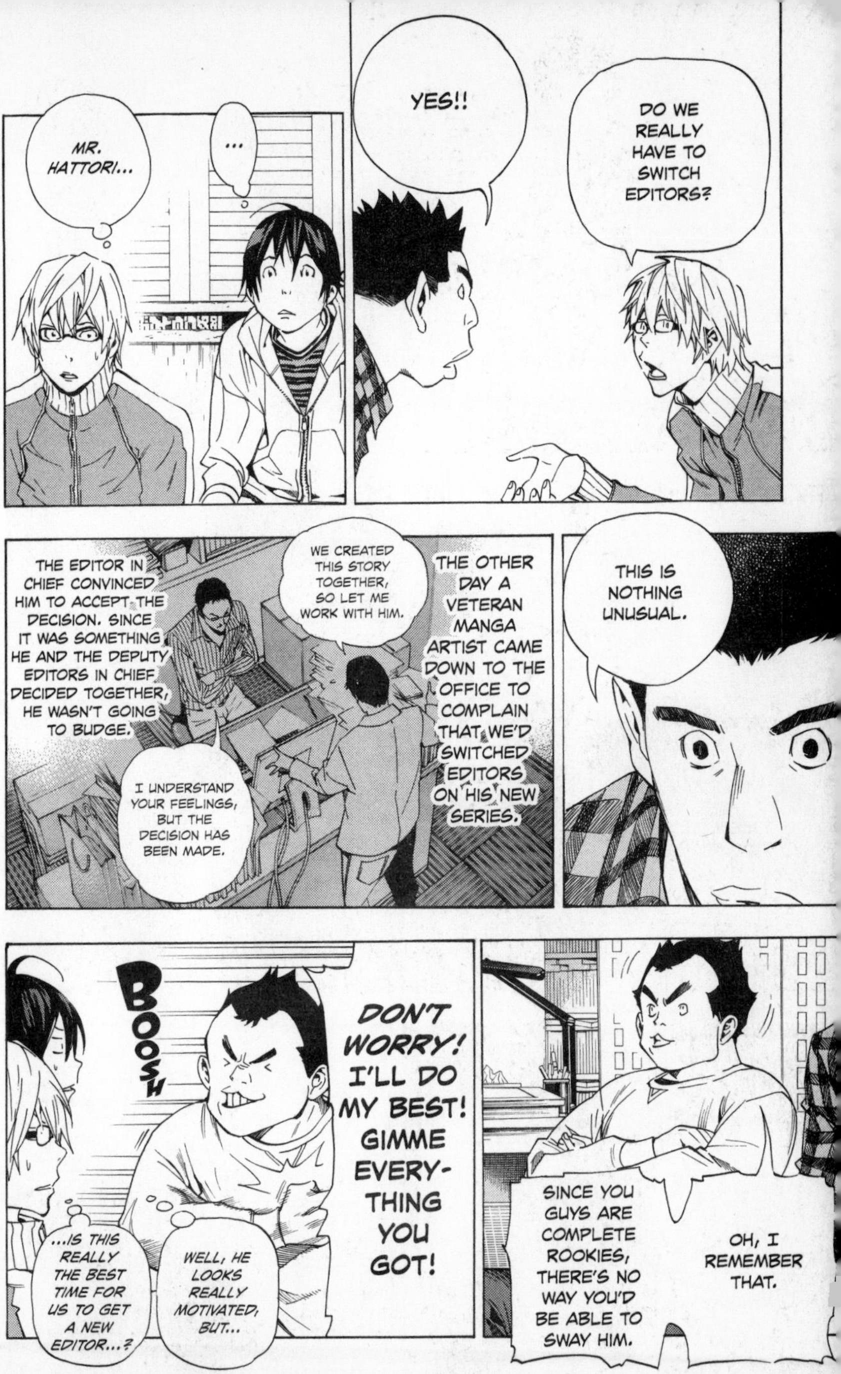
DO WE REALLY HAVE TO SWITCH EDITORS?
YES!!
...
MR. HATTORI...
THIS IS NOTHING UNUSUAL.
THE OTHER DAY A VETERAN MANGA ARTIST CAME DOWN TO THE OFFICE TO COMPLAIN THAT WE'D SWITCHED EDITORS ON HIS NEW SERIES.
WE CREATED THIS STORY TOGETHER, SO LET ME WORK WITH HIM.
I UNDERSTAND YOUR FEELINGS, BUT THE DECISION HAS BEEN MADE.
THE EDITOR IN CHIEF CONVINCED HIM TO ACCEPT THE DECISION. SINCE IT WAS SOMETHING HE AND THE DEPUTY EDITORS IN CHIEF DECIDED TOGETHER, HE WASN'T GOING TO BUDGE.
OH, I REMEMBER THAT.
SINCE YOU GUYS ARE COMPLETE ROOKIES, THERE'S NO WAY YOU'D BE ABLE TO SWAY HIM.
DON'T WORRY! I'LL DO MY BEST! GIMME EVERYTHING YOU GOT!
BOOSH
WELL, HE LOOKS REALLY MOTIVATED, BUT...
...IS THIS REALLY THE BEST TIME FOR US TO GET A NEW EDITOR...?

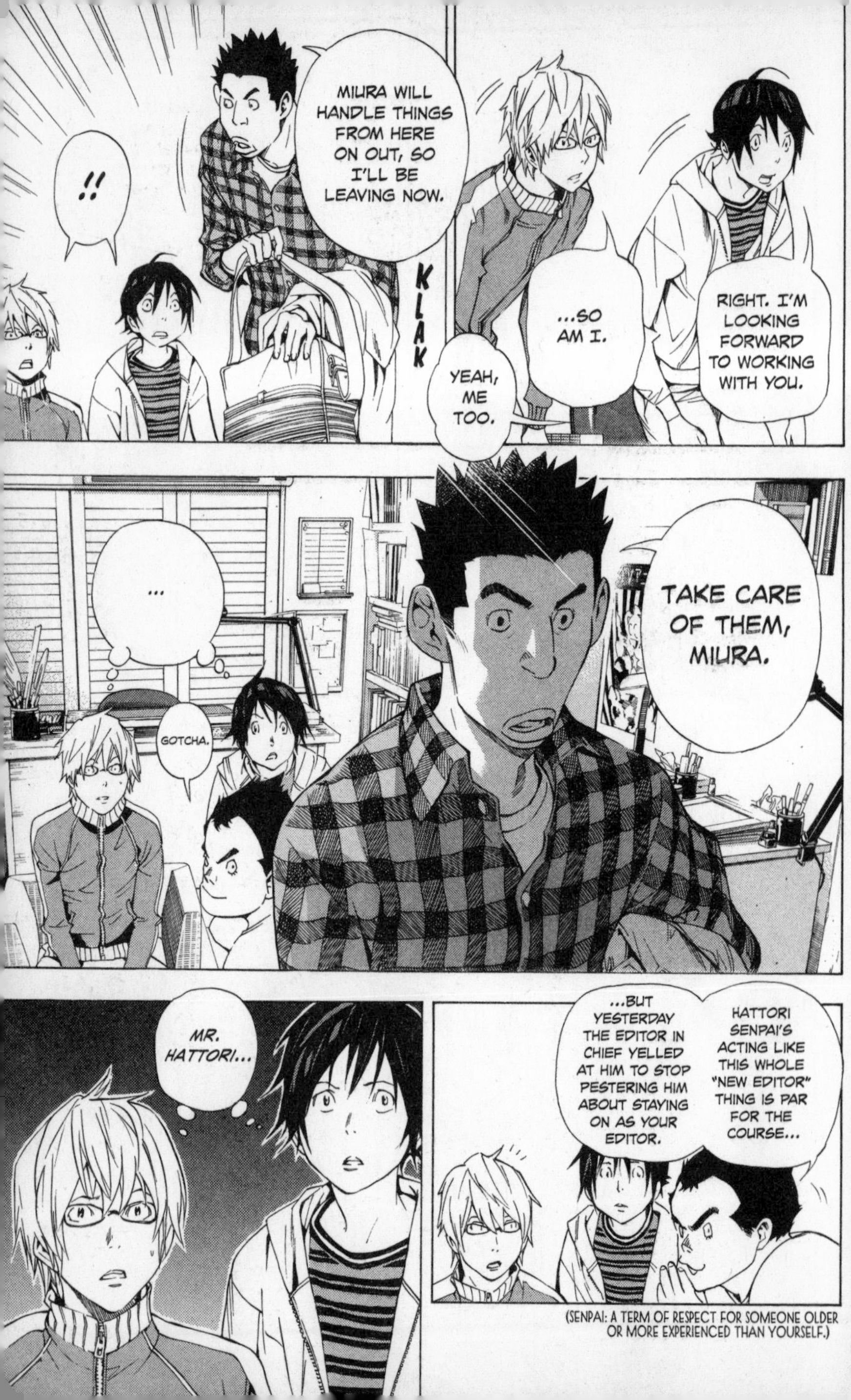
RIGHT. I'M LOOKING FORWARD TO WORKING WITH YOU.
...SO AM I.
YEAH, ME TOO.
MIURA WILL HANDLE THINGS FROM HERE ON OUT, SO I'LL BE LEAVING NOW.
KLAK
!!
TAKE CARE OF THEM, MIURA.
...
GOTCHA.
HATTORI SENPAI'S ACTING LIKE THIS WHOLE "NEW EDITOR" THING IS PAR FOR THE COURSE...
...BUT YESTERDAY THE EDITOR IN CHIEF YELLED AT HIM TO STOP PESTERING HIM ABOUT STAYING ON AS YOUR EDITOR.
MR. HATTORI...

(SENPAI: A TERM OF RESPECT FOR SOMEONE OLDER OR MORE EXPERIENCED THAN YOURSELF.)

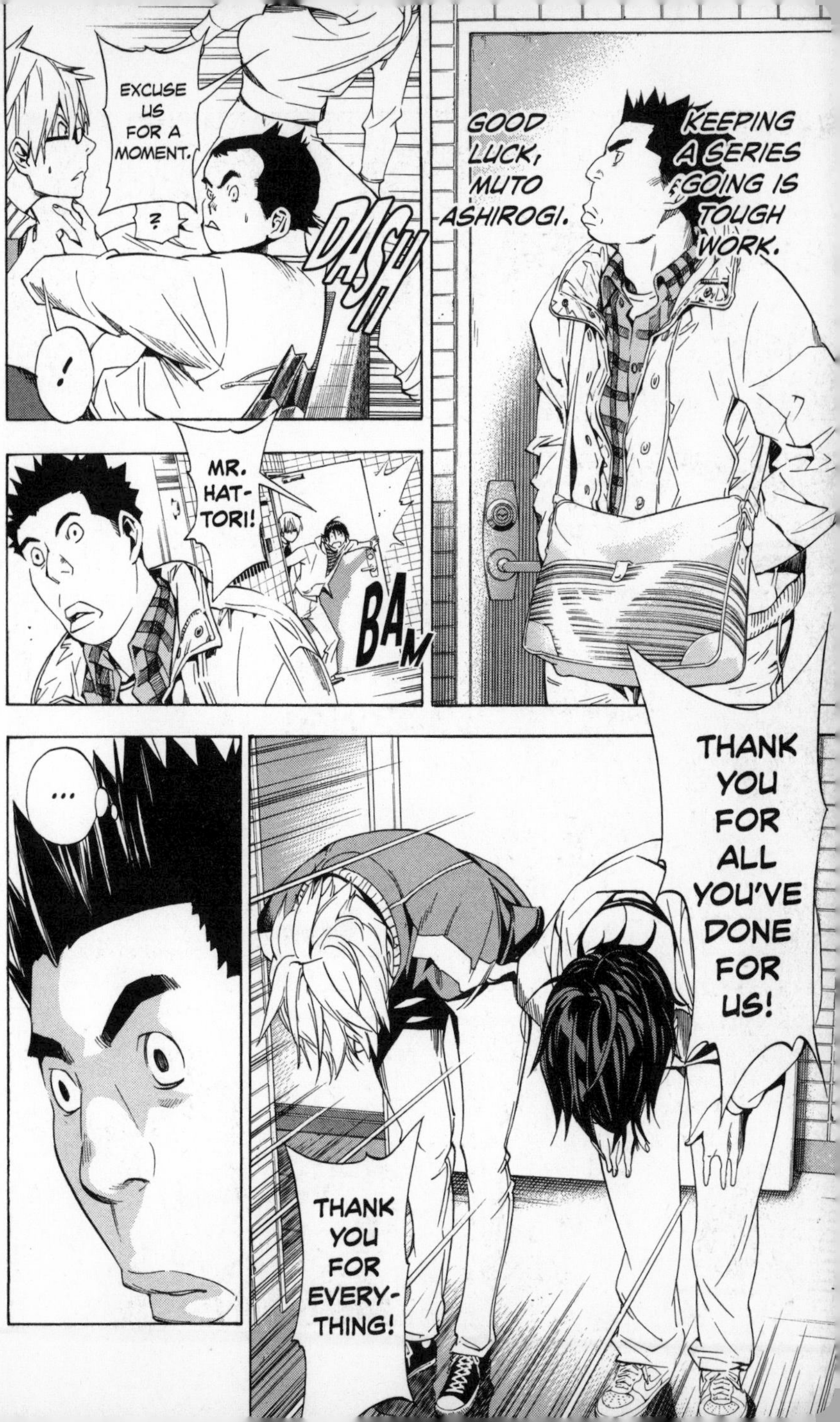
KEEPING A SERIES GOING IS TOUGH WORK.
GOOD LUCK, MUTO ASHIROGI.
EXCUSE US FOR A MOMENT.
?
DASH
!
MR. HAT-TORI!
BAM
THANK YOU FOR ALL YOU'VE DONE FOR US!
THANK YOU FOR EVERY-THING!
...

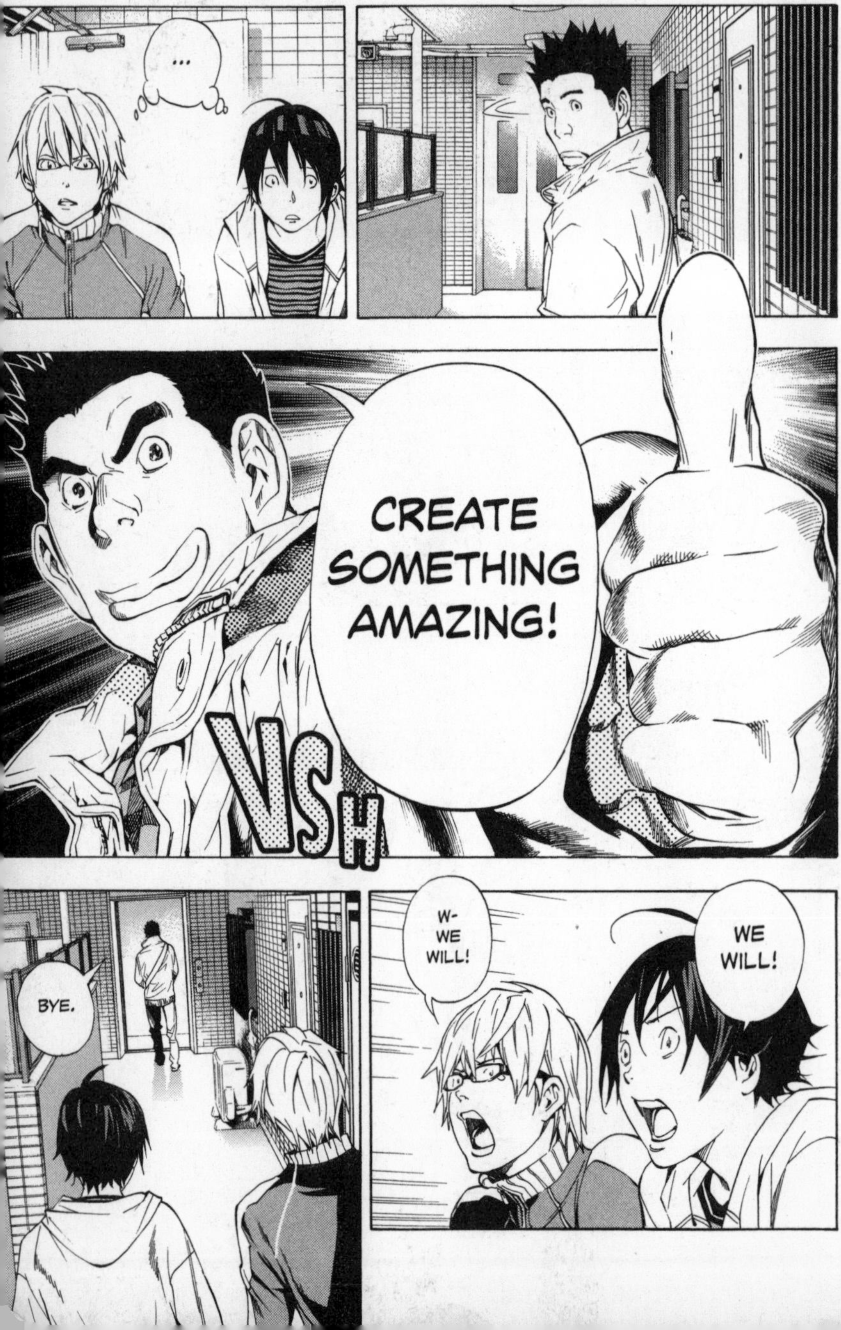
...
CREATE SOMETHING AMAZING!
VSH
WE WILL!
W-WE WILL!
BYE.

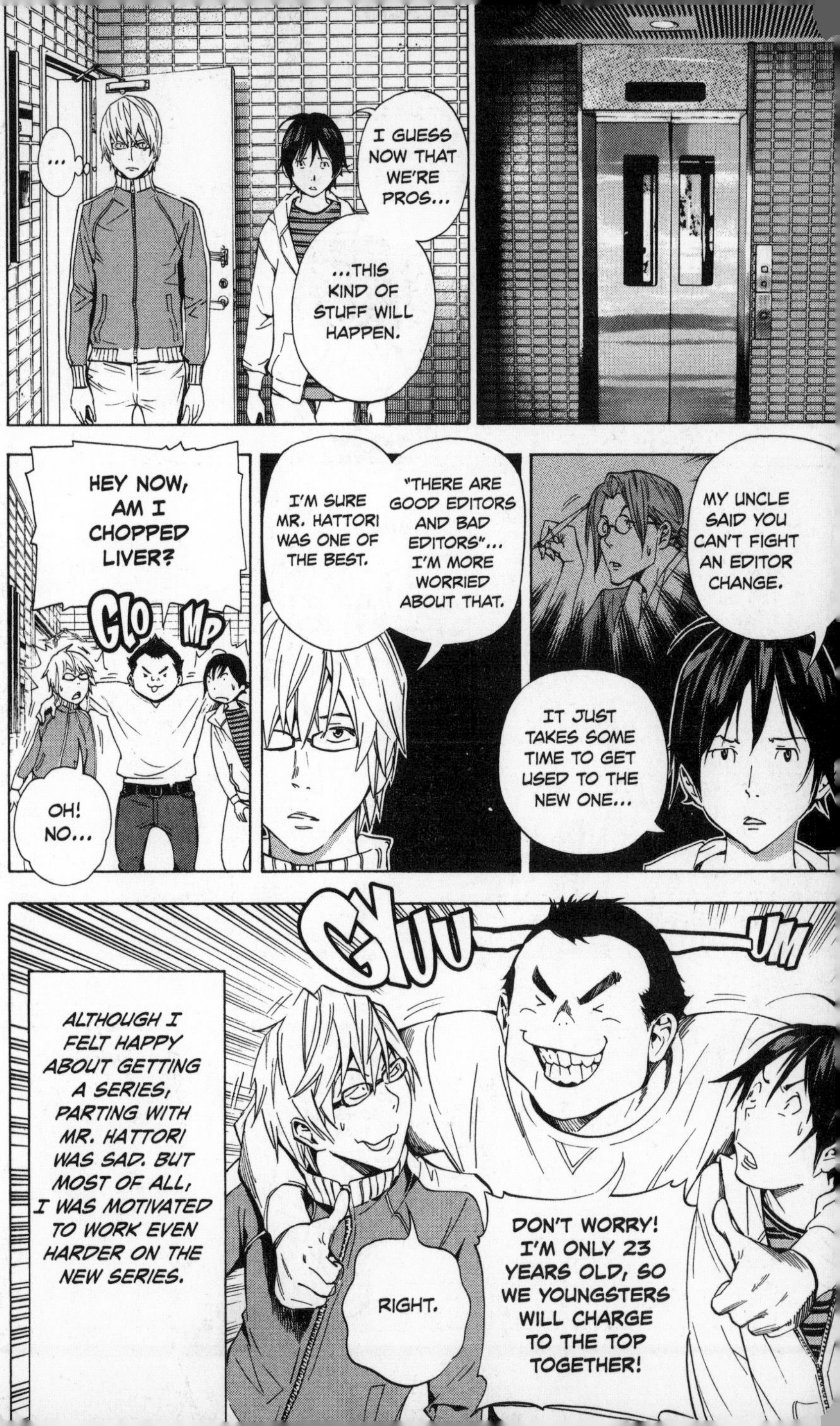
I GUESS NOW THAT WE'RE PROS...
...THIS KIND OF STUFF WILL HAPPEN.
...
MY UNCLE SAID YOU CAN'T FIGHT AN EDITOR CHANGE.
IT JUST TAKES SOME TIME TO GET USED TO THE NEW ONE...
"THERE ARE GOOD EDITORS AND BAD EDITORS"... I'M MORE WORRIED ABOUT THAT.
I'M SURE MR. HATTORI WAS ONE OF THE BEST.
HEY NOW, AM I CHOPPED LIVER?
GLO
MP
OH! NO...
GYUU
UM
DON'T WORRY! I'M ONLY 23 YEARS OLD, SO WE YOUNGSTERS WILL CHARGE TO THE TOP TOGETHER!
RIGHT.
ALTHOUGH I FELT HAPPY ABOUT GETTING A SERIES, PARTING WITH MR. HATTORI WAS SAD. BUT MOST OF ALL, I WAS MOTIVATED TO WORK EVEN HARDER ON THE NEW SERIES.

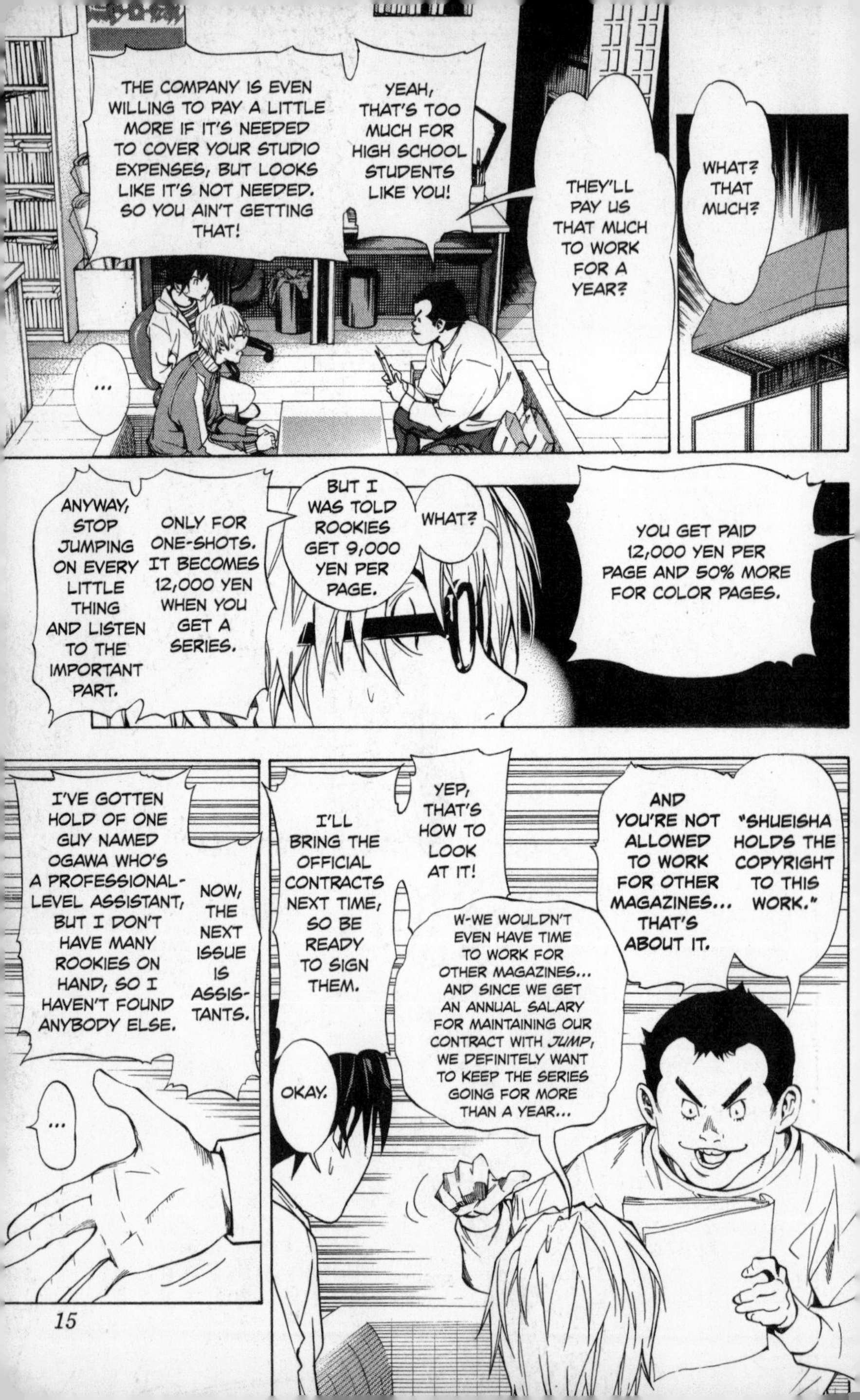
WHAT? THAT MUCH?
THEY'LL PAY US THAT MUCH TO WORK FOR A YEAR?
YEAH, THAT'S TOO MUCH FOR HIGH SCHOOL STUDENTS LIKE YOU!
THE COMPANY IS EVEN WILLING TO PAY A LITTLE MORE IF IT'S NEEDED TO COVER YOUR STUDIO EXPENSES, BUT LOOKS LIKE IT'S NOT NEEDED. SO YOU AIN'T GETTING THAT!
...
YOU GET PAID 12,000 YEN PER PAGE AND 50% MORE FOR COLOR PAGES.
WHAT?
BUT I WAS TOLD ROOKIES GET 9,000 YEN PER PAGE.
ONLY FOR ONE-SHOTS. IT BECOMES 12,000 YEN WHEN YOU GET A SERIES.
ANYWAY, STOP JUMPING ON EVERY LITTLE THING AND LISTEN TO THE IMPORTANT PART.
"SHUEISHA HOLDS THE COPYRIGHT TO THIS WORK."
AND YOU'RE NOT ALLOWED TO WORK FOR OTHER MAGAZINES... THAT'S ABOUT IT.
W-WE WOULDN'T EVEN HAVE TIME TO WORK FOR OTHER MAGAZINES... AND SINCE WE GET AN ANNUAL SALARY FOR MAINTAINING OUR CONTRACT WITH *JUMP*, WE DEFINITELY WANT TO KEEP THE SERIES GOING FOR MORE THAN A YEAR...
YEP, THAT'S HOW TO LOOK AT IT!
I'LL BRING THE OFFICIAL CONTRACTS NEXT TIME, SO BE READY TO SIGN THEM.
OKAY.
NOW, THE NEXT ISSUE IS ASSIS-TANTS.
I'VE GOTTEN HOLD OF ONE GUY NAMED OGAWA WHO'S A PROFESSIONAL-LEVEL ASSISTANT, BUT I DON'T HAVE MANY ROOKIES ON HAND, SO I HAVEN'T FOUND ANYBODY ELSE.
...

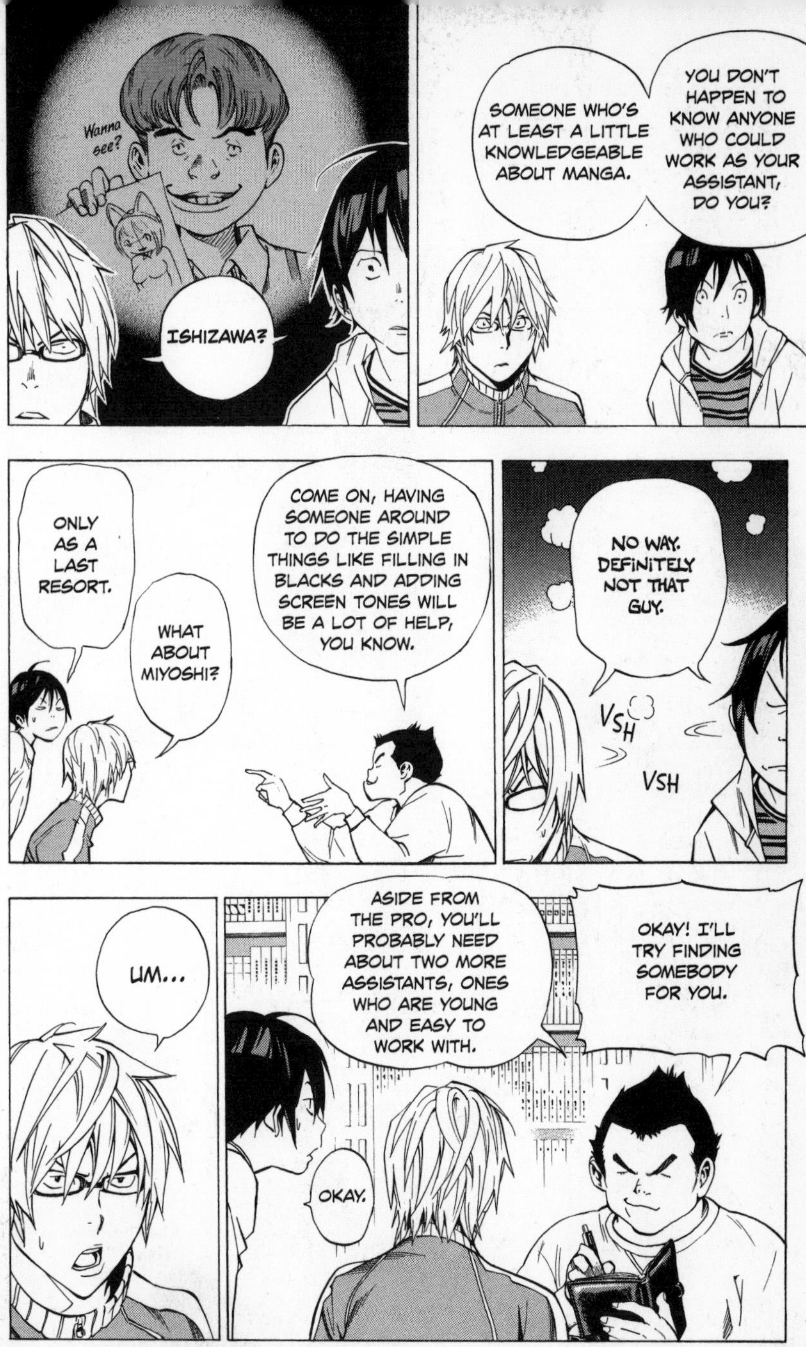
YOU DON'T HAPPEN TO KNOW ANYONE WHO COULD WORK AS YOUR ASSISTANT, DO YOU?
SOMEONE WHO'S AT LEAST A LITTLE KNOWLEDGEABLE ABOUT MANGA.
Wanna see?
ISHIZAWA?
NO WAY. DEFINITELY NOT THAT GUY.
VSH
VSH
COME ON, HAVING SOMEONE AROUND TO DO THE SIMPLE THINGS LIKE FILLING IN BLACKS AND ADDING SCREEN TONES WILL BE A LOT OF HELP, YOU KNOW.
WHAT ABOUT MIYOSHI?
ONLY AS A LAST RESORT.
OKAY! I'LL TRY FINDING SOMEBODY FOR YOU.
ASIDE FROM THE PRO, YOU'LL PROBABLY NEED ABOUT TWO MORE ASSISTANTS, ONES WHO ARE YOUNG AND EASY TO WORK WITH.
OKAY.
UM...

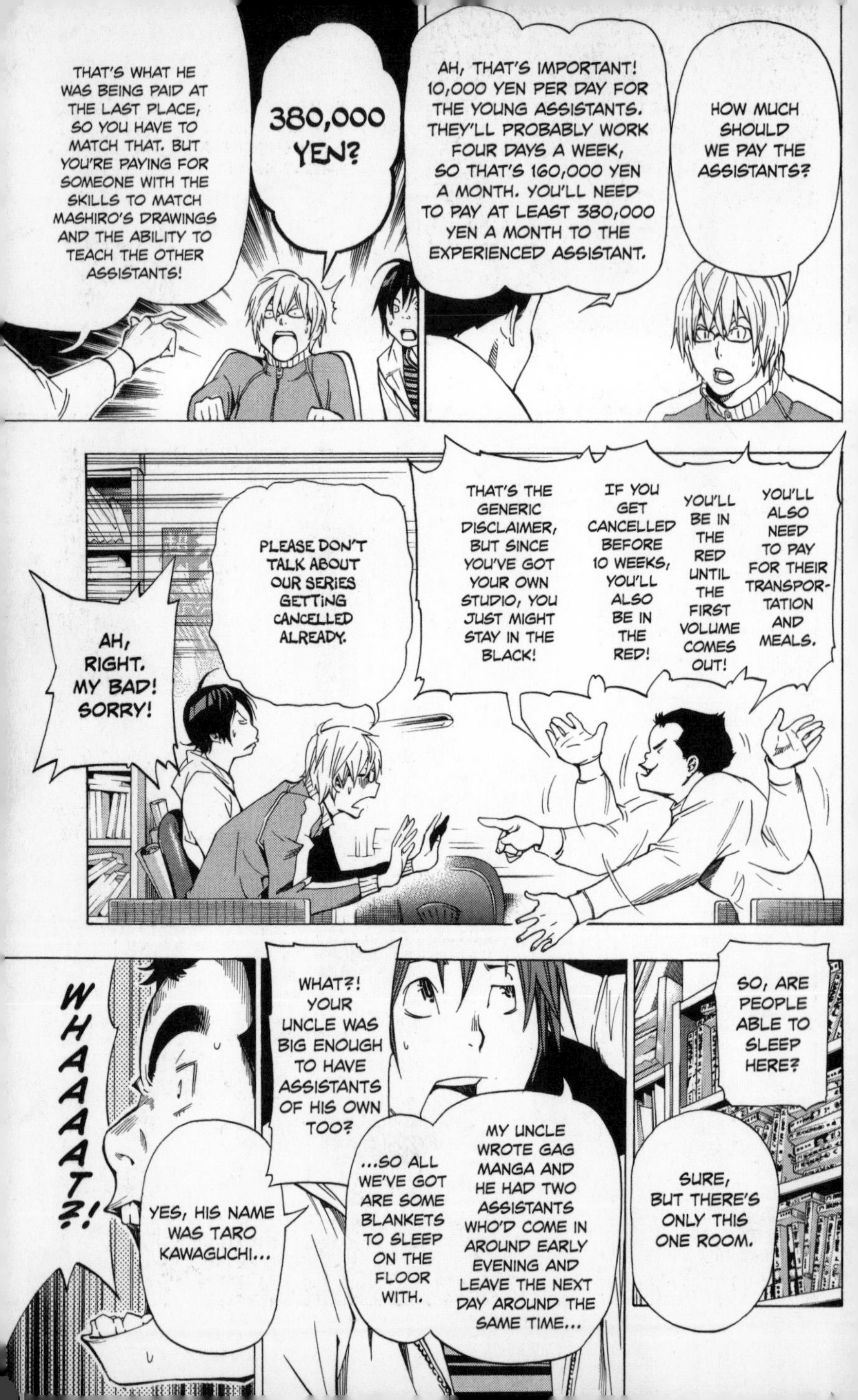
HOW MUCH SHOULD WE PAY THE ASSISTANTS?
AH, THAT'S IMPORTANT! 10,000 YEN PER DAY FOR THE YOUNG ASSISTANTS. THEY'LL PROBABLY WORK FOUR DAYS A WEEK, SO THAT'S 160,000 YEN A MONTH. YOU'LL NEED TO PAY AT LEAST 380,000 YEN A MONTH TO THE EXPERIENCED ASSISTANT.
380,000 YEN?
THAT'S WHAT HE WAS BEING PAID AT THE LAST PLACE, SO YOU HAVE TO MATCH THAT. BUT YOU'RE PAYING FOR SOMEONE WITH THE SKILLS TO MATCH MASHIRO'S DRAWINGS AND THE ABILITY TO TEACH THE OTHER ASSISTANTS!
YOU'LL ALSO NEED TO PAY FOR THEIR TRANSPORTATION AND MEALS.
YOU'LL BE IN THE RED UNTIL THE FIRST VOLUME COMES OUT!
IF YOU GET CANCELLED BEFORE 10 WEEKS, YOU'LL ALSO BE IN THE RED!
THAT'S THE GENERIC DISCLAIMER, BUT SINCE YOU'VE GOT YOUR OWN STUDIO, YOU JUST MIGHT STAY IN THE BLACK!
PLEASE DON'T TALK ABOUT OUR SERIES GETTING CANCELLED ALREADY.
AH, RIGHT. MY BAD! SORRY!
SO, ARE PEOPLE ABLE TO SLEEP HERE?
SURE, BUT THERE'S ONLY THIS ONE ROOM.
...SO ALL WE'VE GOT ARE SOME BLANKETS TO SLEEP ON THE FLOOR WITH.
MY UNCLE WROTE GAG MANGA AND HE HAD TWO ASSISTANTS WHO'D COME IN AROUND EARLY EVENING AND LEAVE THE NEXT DAY AROUND THE SAME TIME...
WHAT?! YOUR UNCLE WAS BIG ENOUGH TO HAVE ASSISTANTS OF HIS OWN TOO?
YES, HIS NAME WAS TARO KAWAGUCHI...
WHAAAAAT?!

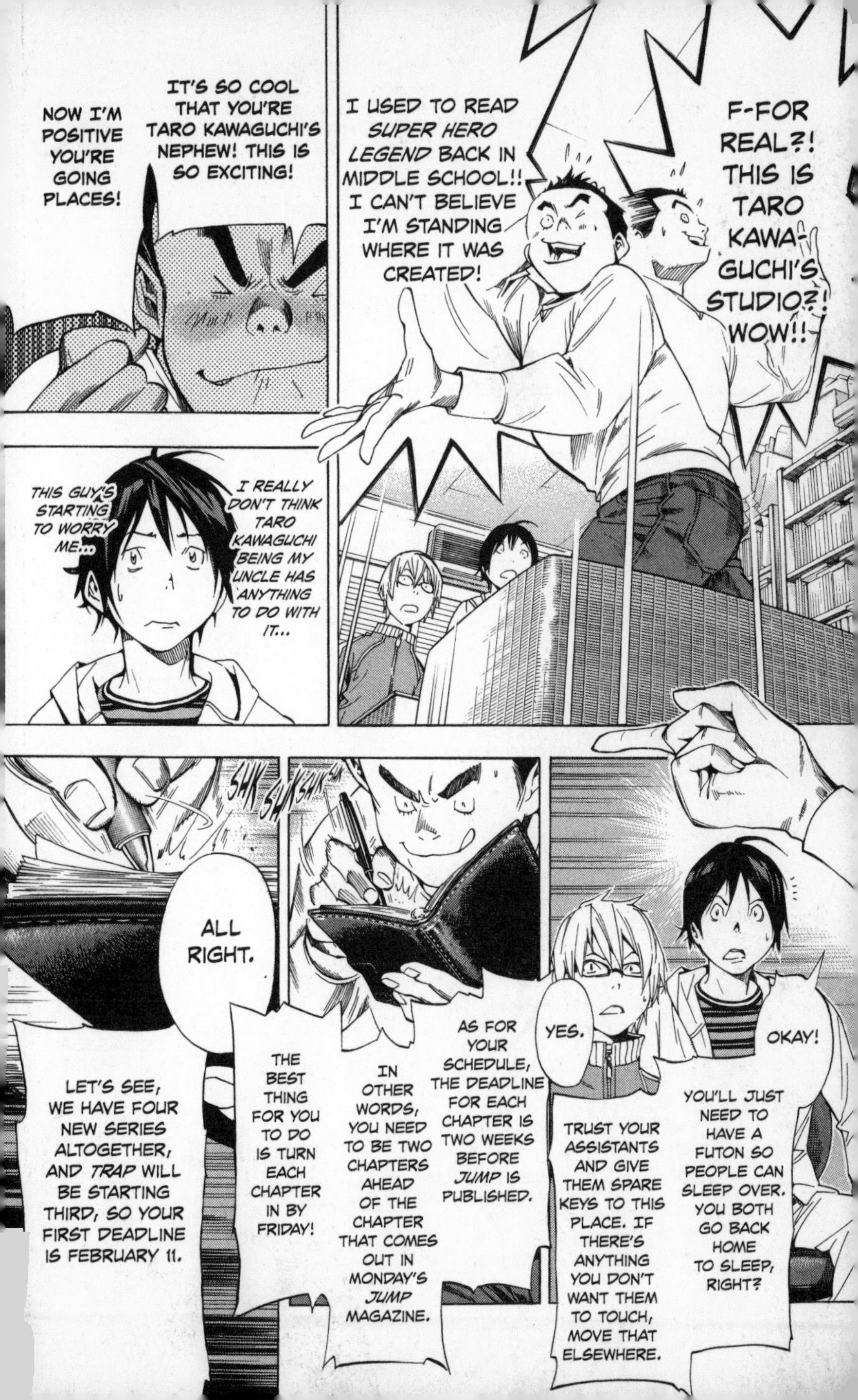
F-FOR REAL?! THIS IS TARO KAWAGUCHI'S STUDIO?! WOW!!
I USED TO READ *SUPER HERO LEGEND* BACK IN MIDDLE SCHOOL!! I CAN'T BELIEVE I'M STANDING WHERE IT WAS CREATED!
IT'S SO COOL THAT YOU'RE TARO KAWAGUCHI'S NEPHEW! THIS IS SO EXCITING!
NOW I'M POSITIVE YOU'RE GOING PLACES!
I REALLY DON'T THINK TARO KAWAGUCHI BEING MY UNCLE HAS ANYTHING TO DO WITH IT...
THIS GUY'S STARTING TO WORRY ME...
YOU'LL JUST NEED TO HAVE A FUTON SO PEOPLE CAN SLEEP OVER. YOU BOTH GO BACK HOME TO SLEEP, RIGHT?
OKAY!
TRUST YOUR ASSISTANTS AND GIVE THEM SPARE KEYS TO THIS PLACE. IF THERE'S ANYTHING YOU DON'T WANT THEM TO TOUCH, MOVE THAT ELSEWHERE.
YES.
SHK SHK SHK
AS FOR YOUR SCHEDULE, THE DEADLINE FOR EACH CHAPTER IS TWO WEEKS BEFORE *JUMP* IS PUBLISHED.
IN OTHER WORDS, YOU NEED TO BE TWO CHAPTERS AHEAD OF THE CHAPTER THAT COMES OUT IN MONDAY'S *JUMP* MAGAZINE.
THE BEST THING FOR YOU TO DO IS TURN EACH CHAPTER IN BY FRIDAY!
ALL RIGHT.
LET'S SEE, WE HAVE FOUR NEW SERIES ALTOGETHER, AND *TRAP* WILL BE STARTING THIRD, SO YOUR FIRST DEADLINE IS FEBRUARY 11.

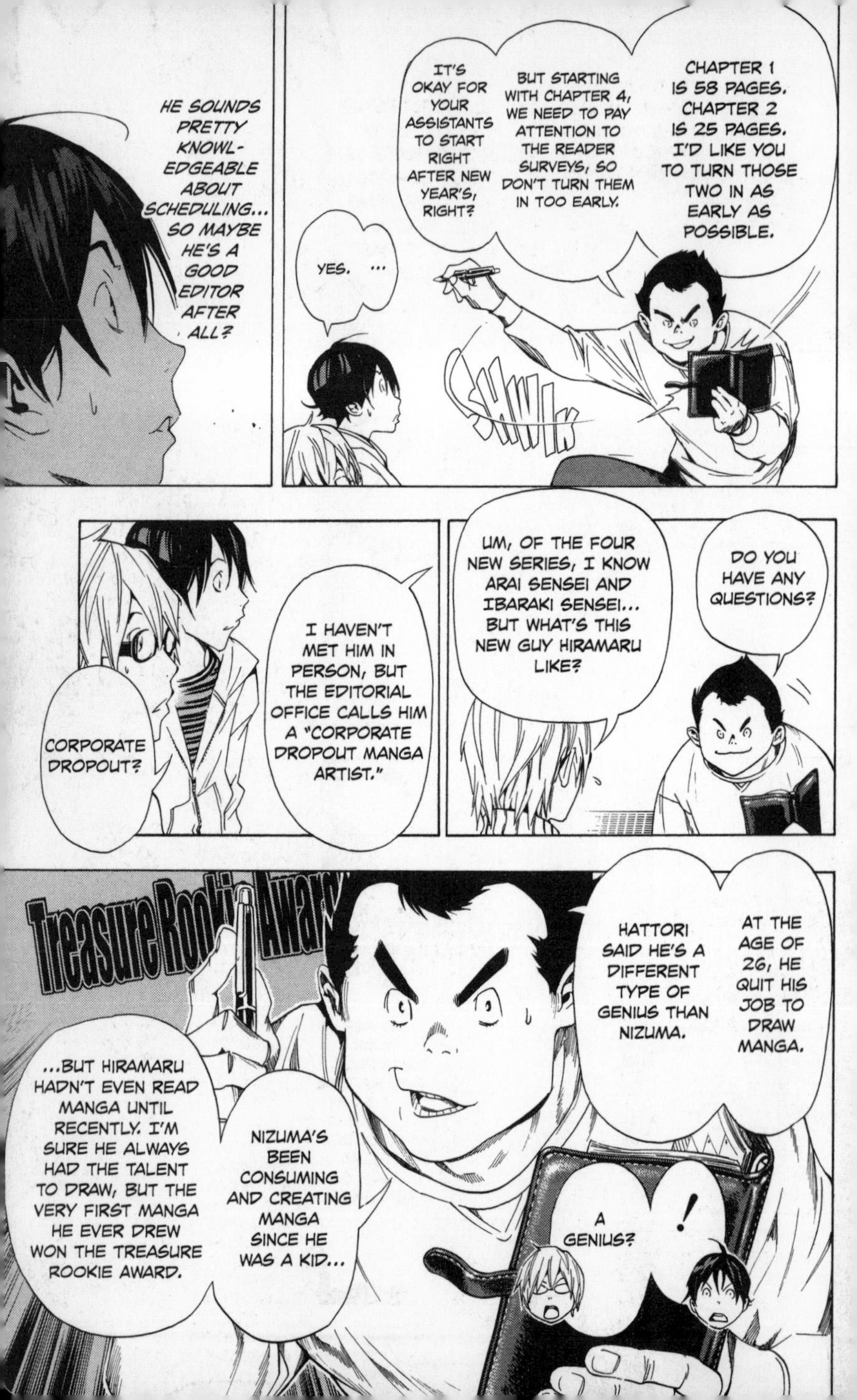
CHAPTER 1 IS 58 PAGES. CHAPTER 2 IS 25 PAGES. I'D LIKE YOU TO TURN THOSE TWO IN AS EARLY AS POSSIBLE.
BUT STARTING WITH CHAPTER 4, WE NEED TO PAY ATTENTION TO THE READER SURVEYS, SO DON'T TURN THEM IN TOO EARLY.
IT'S OKAY FOR YOUR ASSISTANTS TO START RIGHT AFTER NEW YEAR'S, RIGHT?
YES. ...
HE SOUNDS PRETTY KNOWL-EDGEABLE ABOUT SCHEDULING... SO MAYBE HE'S A GOOD EDITOR AFTER ALL?
DO YOU HAVE ANY QUESTIONS?
UM, OF THE FOUR NEW SERIES, I KNOW ARAI SENSEI AND IBARAKI SENSEI... BUT WHAT'S THIS NEW GUY HIRAMARU LIKE?
I HAVEN'T MET HIM IN PERSON, BUT THE EDITORIAL OFFICE CALLS HIM A "CORPORATE DROPOUT MANGA ARTIST."
CORPORATE DROPOUT?
AT THE AGE OF 26, HE QUIT HIS JOB TO DRAW MANGA.
HATTORI SAID HE'S A DIFFERENT TYPE OF GENIUS THAN NIZUMA.
A GENIUS?
!
NIZUMA'S BEEN CONSUMING AND CREATING MANGA SINCE HE WAS A KID...
...BUT HIRAMARU HADN'T EVEN READ MANGA UNTIL RECENTLY. I'M SURE HE ALWAYS HAD THE TALENT TO DRAW, BUT THE VERY FIRST MANGA HE EVER DREW WON THE TREASURE ROOKIE AWARD.

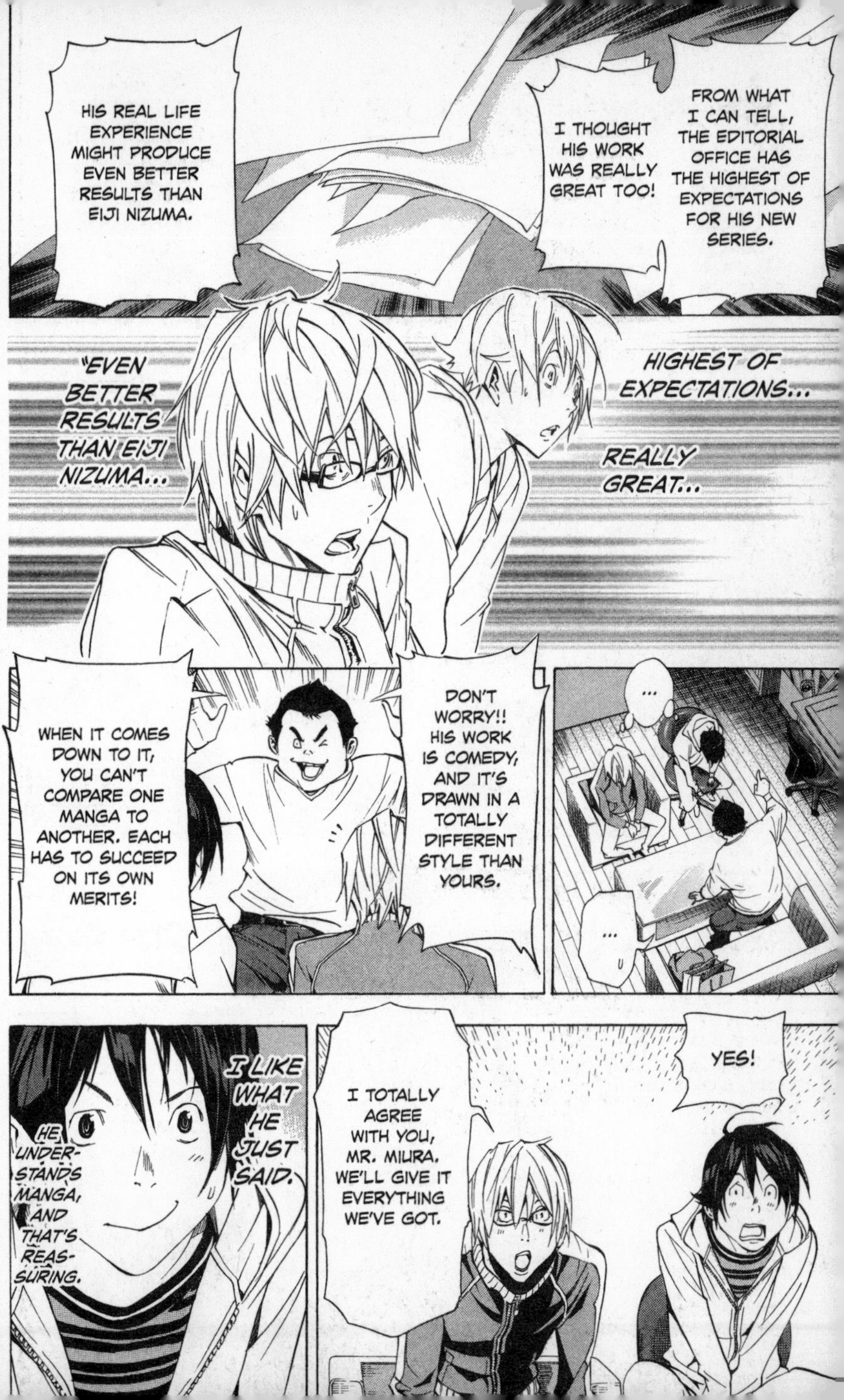
FROM WHAT I CAN TELL, THE EDITORIAL OFFICE HAS THE HIGHEST OF EXPECTATIONS FOR HIS NEW SERIES.
I THOUGHT HIS WORK WAS REALLY GREAT TOO!
HIS REAL LIFE EXPERIENCE MIGHT PRODUCE EVEN BETTER RESULTS THAN EIJI NIZUMA.
HIGHEST OF EXPECTATIONS...
REALLY GREAT...
"EVEN BETTER RESULTS THAN EIJI NIZUMA...
...
...
DON'T WORRY!! HIS WORK IS COMEDY, AND IT'S DRAWN IN A TOTALLY DIFFERENT STYLE THAN YOURS.
WHEN IT COMES DOWN TO IT, YOU CAN'T COMPARE ONE MANGA TO ANOTHER. EACH HAS TO SUCCEED ON ITS OWN MERITS!
YES!
I TOTALLY AGREE WITH YOU, MR. MIURA. WE'LL GIVE IT EVERYTHING WE'VE GOT.
I LIKE WHAT HE JUST SAID.
HE UNDERSTANDS MANGA, AND THAT'S REASSURING.

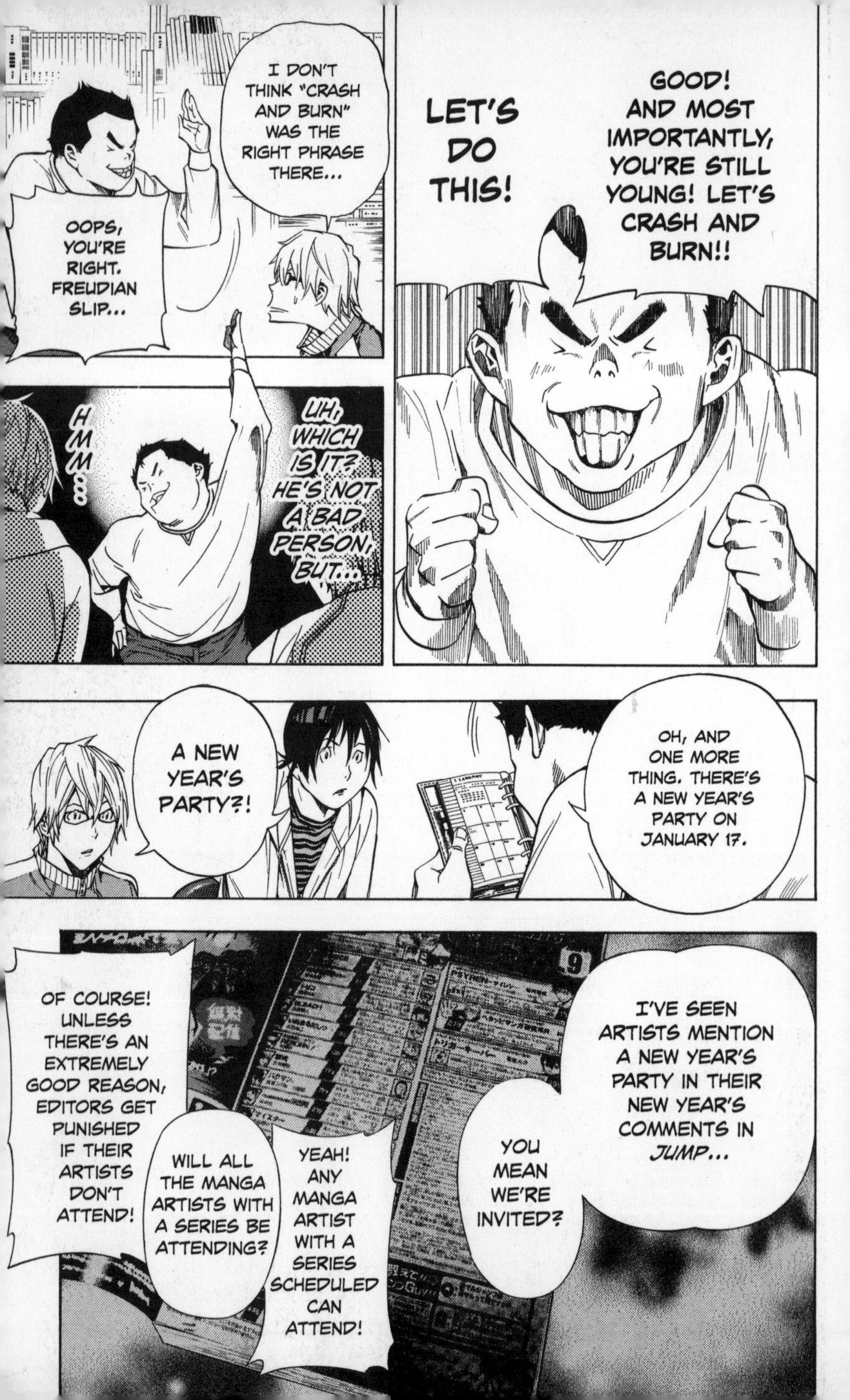
GOOD! AND MOST IMPORTANTLY, YOU'RE STILL YOUNG! LET'S CRASH AND BURN!!
LET'S DO THIS!
I DON'T THINK "CRASH AND BURN" WAS THE RIGHT PHRASE THERE...
OOPS, YOU'RE RIGHT. FREUDIAN SLIP...
UH, WHICH IS IT? HE'S NOT A BAD PERSON, BUT...
HMM...
OH, AND ONE MORE THING. THERE'S A NEW YEAR'S PARTY ON JANUARY 17.
A NEW YEAR'S PARTY?!
I'VE SEEN ARTISTS MENTION A NEW YEAR'S PARTY IN THEIR NEW YEAR'S COMMENTS IN *JUMP*...
YOU MEAN WE'RE INVITED?
YEAH! ANY MANGA ARTIST WITH A SERIES SCHEDULED CAN ATTEND!
WILL ALL THE MANGA ARTISTS WITH A SERIES BE ATTENDING?
OF COURSE! UNLESS THERE'S AN EXTREMELY GOOD REASON, EDITORS GET PUNISHED IF THEIR ARTISTS DON'T ATTEND!

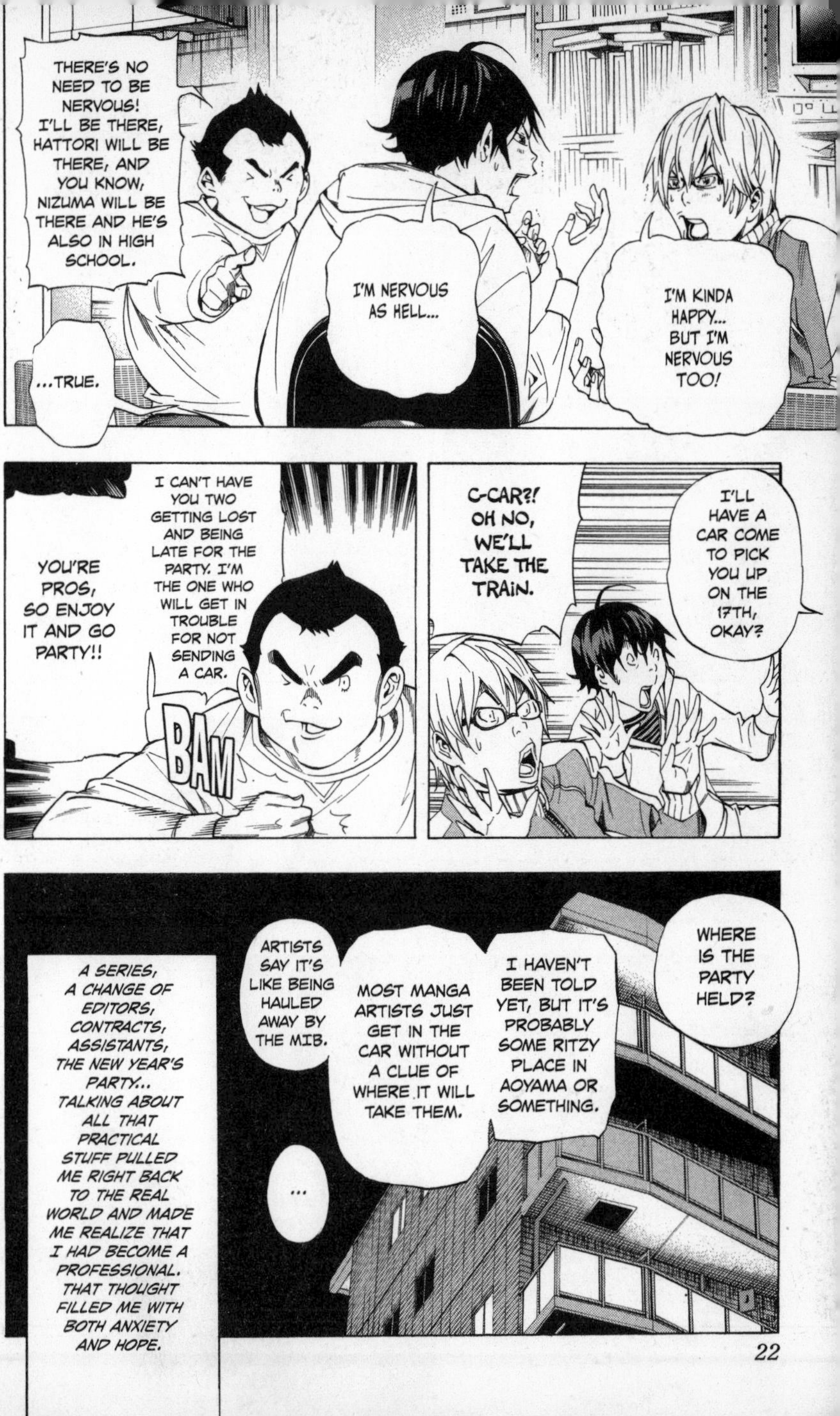
I'M KINDA HAPPY... BUT I'M NERVOUS TOO!
I'M NERVOUS AS HELL...
THERE'S NO NEED TO BE NERVOUS! I'LL BE THERE, HATTORI WILL BE THERE, AND YOU KNOW, NIZUMA WILL BE THERE AND HE'S ALSO IN HIGH SCHOOL.
...TRUE.
I'LL HAVE A CAR COME TO PICK YOU UP ON THE 17TH, OKAY?
C-CAR?! OH NO, WE'LL TAKE THE TRAIN.
I CAN'T HAVE YOU TWO GETTING LOST AND BEING LATE FOR THE PARTY. I'M THE ONE WHO WILL GET IN TROUBLE FOR NOT SENDING A CAR.
YOU'RE PROS, SO ENJOY IT AND GO PARTY!!
BAM
WHERE IS THE PARTY HELD?
I HAVEN'T BEEN TOLD YET, BUT IT'S PROBABLY SOME RITZY PLACE IN AOYAMA OR SOMETHING.
MOST MANGA ARTISTS JUST GET IN THE CAR WITHOUT A CLUE OF WHERE IT WILL TAKE THEM.
ARTISTS SAY IT'S LIKE BEING HAULED AWAY BY THE MIB.
...
A SERIES, A CHANGE OF EDITORS, CONTRACTS, ASSISTANTS, THE NEW YEAR'S PARTY... TALKING ABOUT ALL THAT PRACTICAL STUFF PULLED ME RIGHT BACK TO THE REAL WORLD AND MADE ME REALIZE THAT I HAD BECOME A PROFESSIONAL. THAT THOUGHT FILLED ME WITH BOTH ANXIETY AND HOPE.

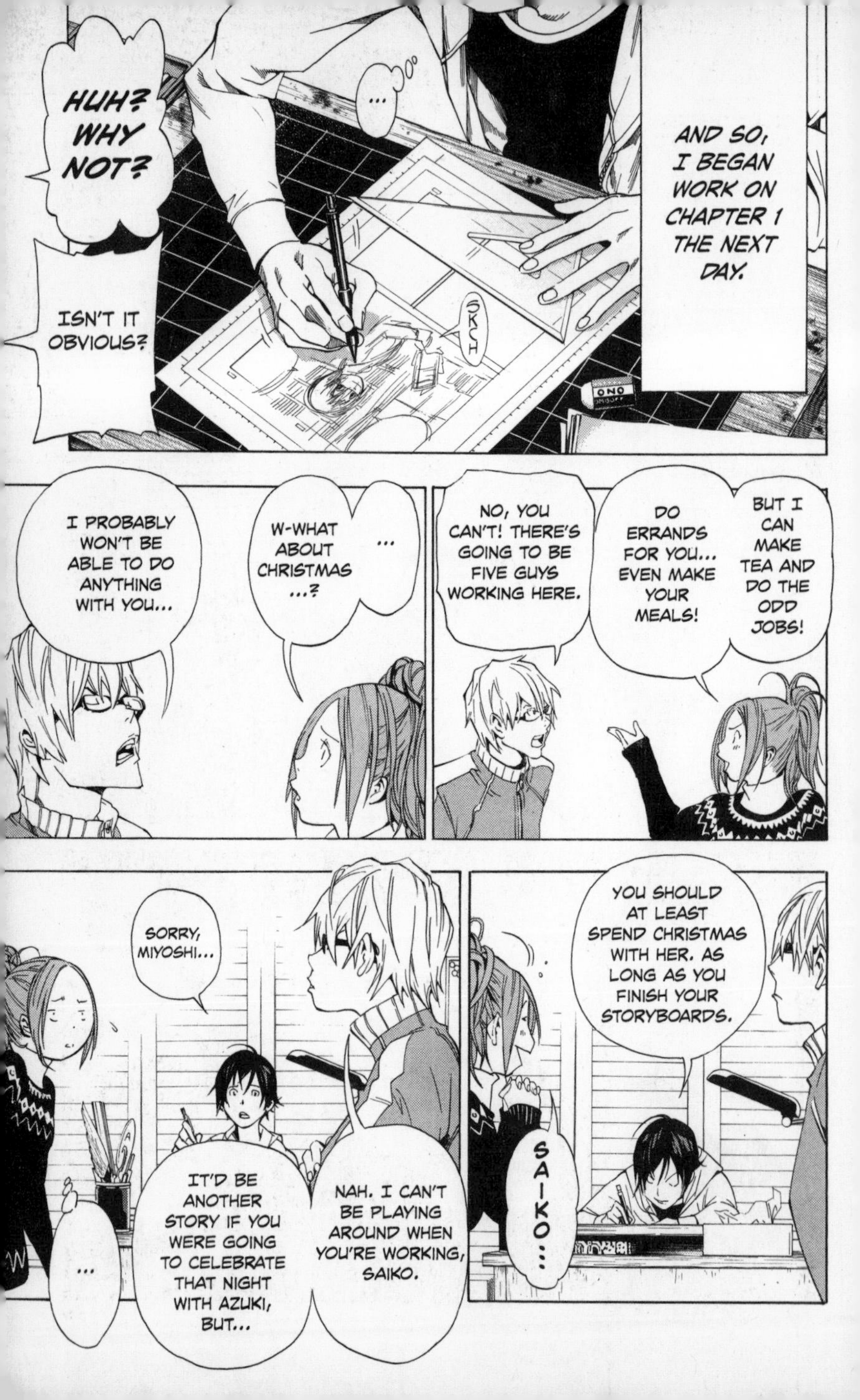

AND SO, I BEGAN WORK ON CHAPTER 1 THE NEXT DAY.
...
SKCH
HUH? WHY NOT?
ISN'T IT OBVIOUS?
BUT I CAN MAKE TEA AND DO THE ODD JOBS!
DO ERRANDS FOR YOU... EVEN MAKE YOUR MEALS!
NO, YOU CAN'T! THERE'S GOING TO BE FIVE GUYS WORKING HERE.
...
W-WHAT ABOUT CHRISTMAS ...?
I PROBABLY WON'T BE ABLE TO DO ANYTHING WITH YOU...
YOU SHOULD AT LEAST SPEND CHRISTMAS WITH HER. AS LONG AS YOU FINISH YOUR STORYBOARDS.
SAIKO...
SORRY, MIYOSHI...
NAH. I CAN'T BE PLAYING AROUND WHEN YOU'RE WORKING, SAIKO.
IT'D BE ANOTHER STORY IF YOU WERE GOING TO CELEBRATE THAT NIGHT WITH AZUKI, BUT...
...

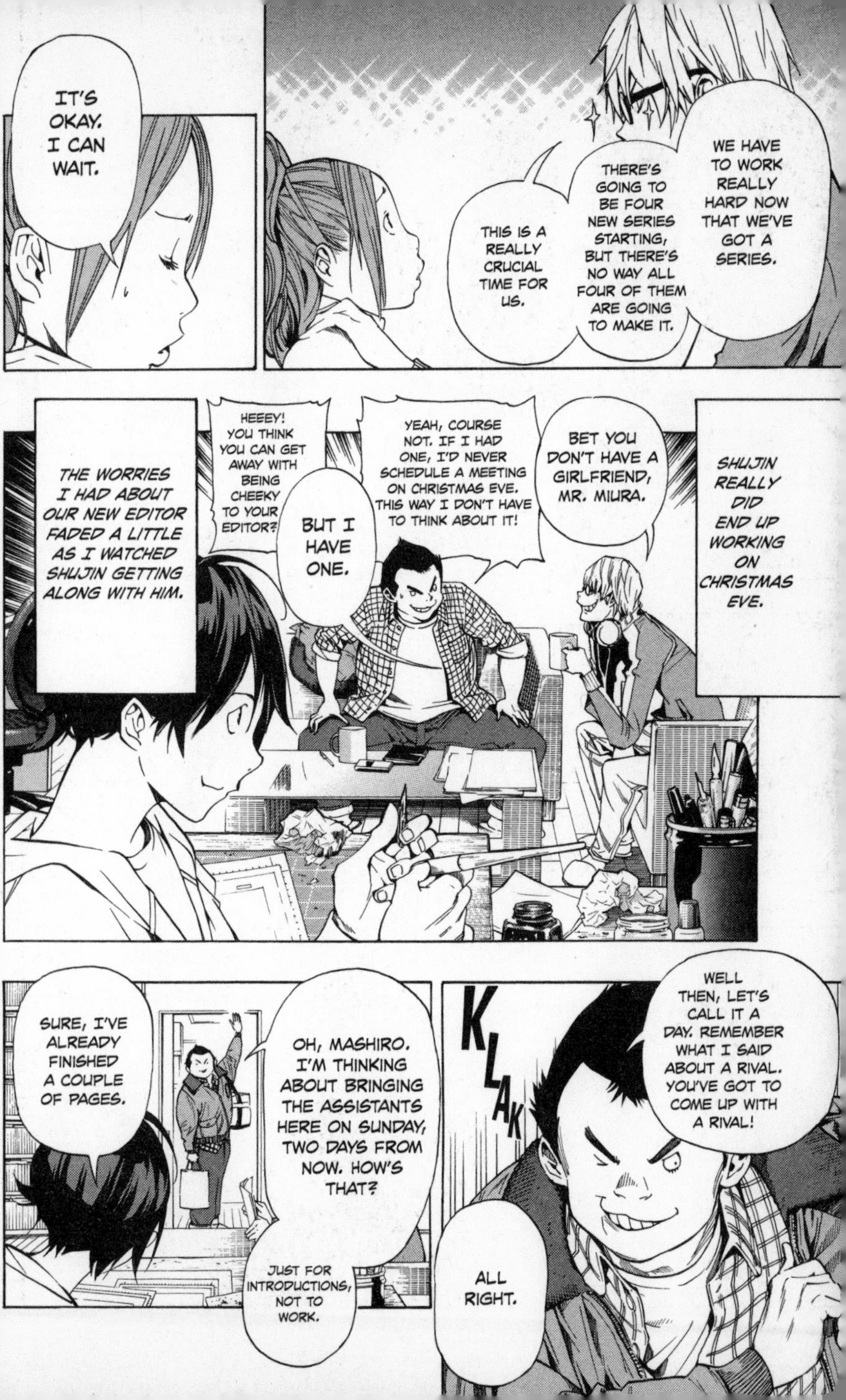
WE HAVE TO WORK REALLY HARD NOW THAT WE'VE GOT A SERIES.
THERE'S GOING TO BE FOUR NEW SERIES STARTING, BUT THERE'S NO WAY ALL FOUR OF THEM ARE GOING TO MAKE IT.
THIS IS A REALLY CRUCIAL TIME FOR US.
IT'S OKAY. I CAN WAIT.
SHUJIN REALLY DID END UP WORKING ON CHRISTMAS EVE.
BET YOU DON'T HAVE A GIRLFRIEND, MR. MIURA.
YEAH, COURSE NOT. IF I HAD ONE, I'D NEVER SCHEDULE A MEETING ON CHRISTMAS EVE. THIS WAY I DON'T HAVE TO THINK ABOUT IT!
HEEEY! YOU THINK YOU CAN GET AWAY WITH BEING CHEEKY TO YOUR EDITOR?
BUT I HAVE ONE.
THE WORRIES I HAD ABOUT OUR NEW EDITOR FADED A LITTLE AS I WATCHED SHUJIN GETTING ALONG WITH HIM.
KLAK
WELL THEN, LET'S CALL IT A DAY. REMEMBER WHAT I SAID ABOUT A RIVAL. YOU'VE GOT TO COME UP WITH A RIVAL!
ALL RIGHT.
OH, MASHIRO. I'M THINKING ABOUT BRINGING THE ASSISTANTS HERE ON SUNDAY, TWO DAYS FROM NOW. HOW'S THAT?
JUST FOR INTRODUCTIONS, NOT TO WORK.
SURE, I'VE ALREADY FINISHED A COUPLE OF PAGES.

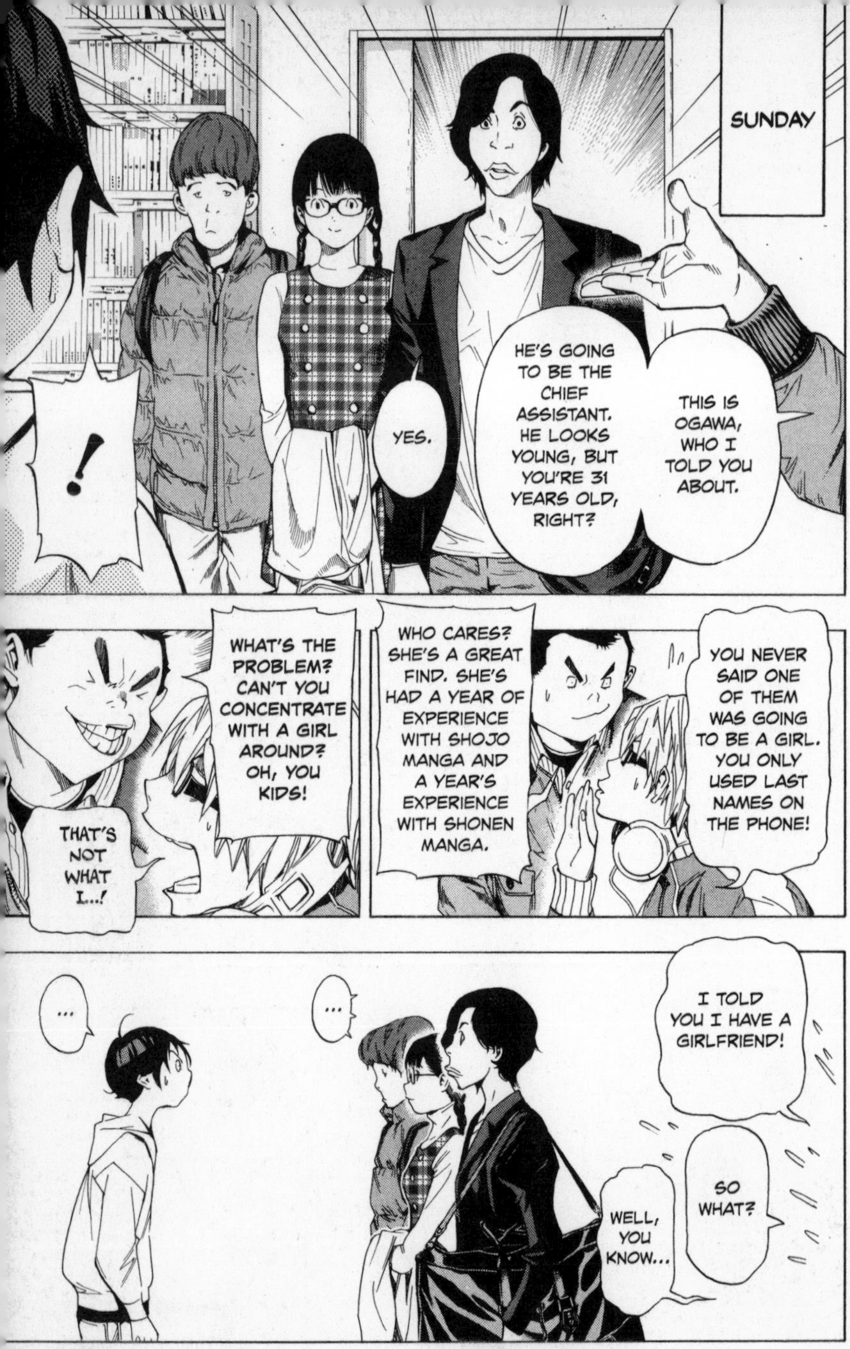
SUNDAY
THIS IS OGAWA, WHO I TOLD YOU ABOUT.
HE'S GOING TO BE THE CHIEF ASSISTANT. HE LOOKS YOUNG, BUT YOU'RE 31 YEARS OLD, RIGHT?
YES.
!
YOU NEVER SAID ONE OF THEM WAS GOING TO BE A GIRL. YOU ONLY USED LAST NAMES ON THE PHONE!
WHO CARES? SHE'S A GREAT FIND. SHE'S HAD A YEAR OF EXPERIENCE WITH SHOJO MANGA AND A YEAR'S EXPERIENCE WITH SHONEN MANGA.
WHAT'S THE PROBLEM? CAN'T YOU CONCENTRATE WITH A GIRL AROUND? OH, YOU KIDS!
THAT'S NOT WHAT I...!
I TOLD YOU I HAVE A GIRLFRIEND!
SO WHAT?
WELL, YOU KNOW...
...
...

OHBA'S STORYBOARD

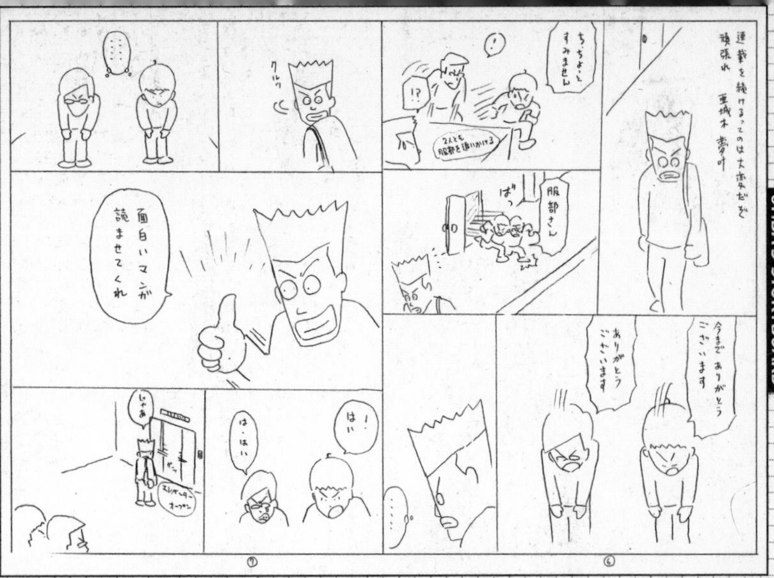
連載を続けるってのは大変だぞ
頑張れ 亜城木夢叶
ちょっとすみません
!
!?
2人とも服部を追いかける
服部さん
ばっ
今まで ありがとうございます
ありがとうございます
……
クルッ
……
面白いマンガ読ませてくれ
はい!
は・はい
じゃあ
エレベーターオープン

OBATA'S STORYBOARD

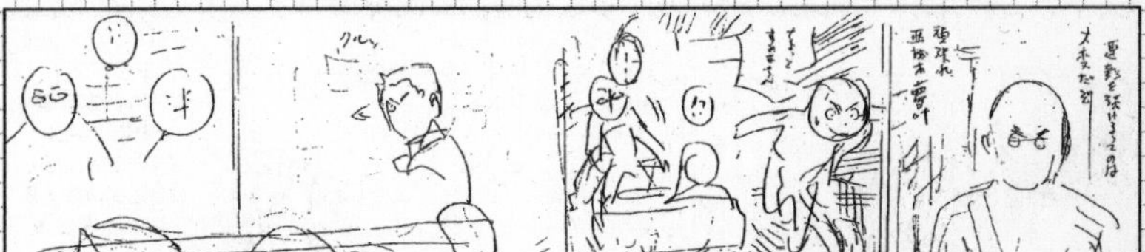
連載を続けるってのは大変だぞ
頑張れ 亜城木夢叶
ちょっとすみません
服部さん
今まで ありがとうございます
ありがとうございます
クルッ
面白いマンガ読ませてくれ
はい!
は・はい

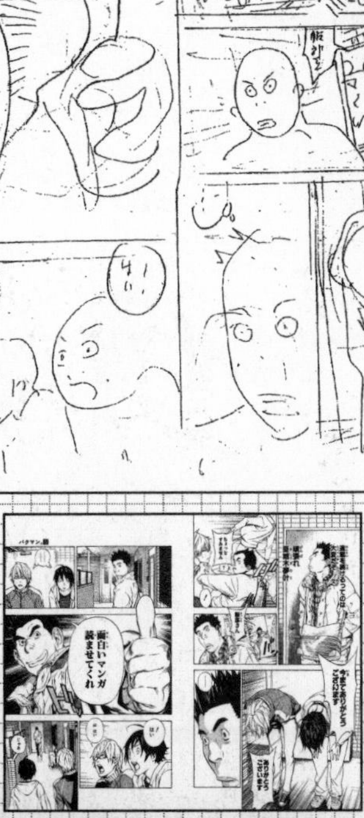
面白いマンガ読ませてくれ

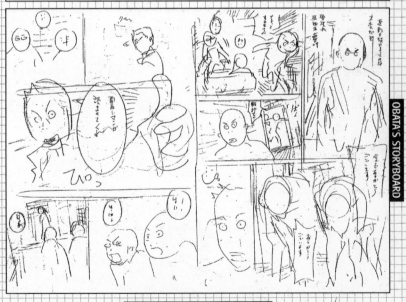

COMPLETE!

*CREATOR STORYBOARDS AND FINISHED PAGES IN JAPANESE

BAKUMAN。 vol. 5

"Until the Final Draft Is Complete"

Chapter 35, pp. 12-13

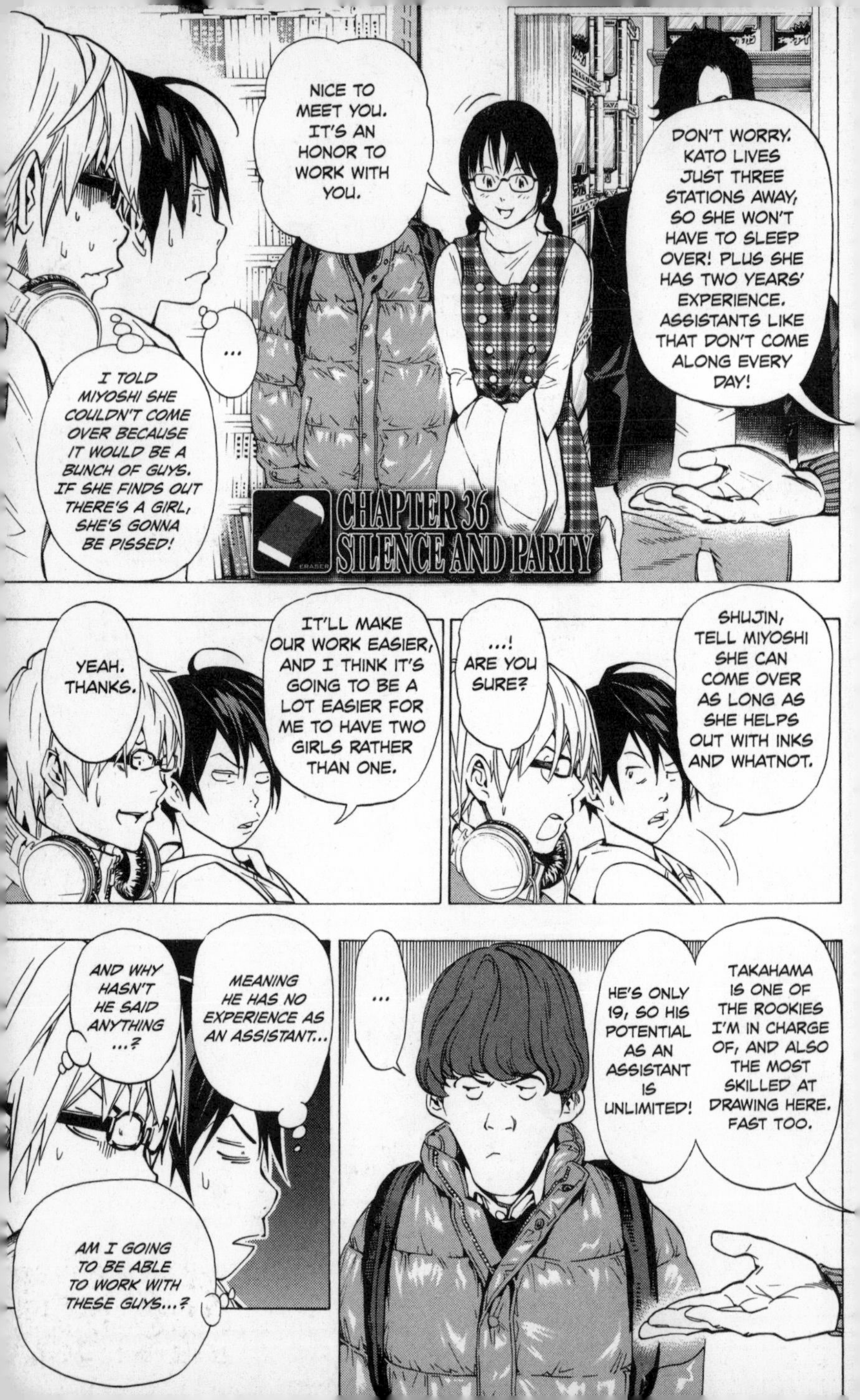
DON'T WORRY. KATO LIVES JUST THREE STATIONS AWAY, SO SHE WON'T HAVE TO SLEEP OVER! PLUS SHE HAS TWO YEARS' EXPERIENCE. ASSISTANTS LIKE THAT DON'T COME ALONG EVERY DAY!
NICE TO MEET YOU. IT'S AN HONOR TO WORK WITH YOU.
...
I TOLD MIYOSHI SHE COULDN'T COME OVER BECAUSE IT WOULD BE A BUNCH OF GUYS. IF SHE FINDS OUT THERE'S A GIRL, SHE'S GONNA BE PISSED!
ERASER
CHAPTER 36 SILENCE AND PARTY
SHUJIN, TELL MIYOSHI SHE CAN COME OVER AS LONG AS SHE HELPS OUT WITH INKS AND WHATNOT.
...! ARE YOU SURE?
IT'LL MAKE OUR WORK EASIER, AND I THINK IT'S GOING TO BE A LOT EASIER FOR ME TO HAVE TWO GIRLS RATHER THAN ONE.
YEAH. THANKS.
TAKAHAMA IS ONE OF THE ROOKIES I'M IN CHARGE OF, AND ALSO THE MOST SKILLED AT DRAWING HERE. FAST TOO.
HE'S ONLY 19, SO HIS POTENTIAL AS AN ASSISTANT IS UNLIMITED!
...
MEANING HE HAS NO EXPERIENCE AS AN ASSISTANT...
AND WHY HASN'T HE SAID ANYTHING ...?
AM I GOING TO BE ABLE TO WORK WITH THESE GUYS...?

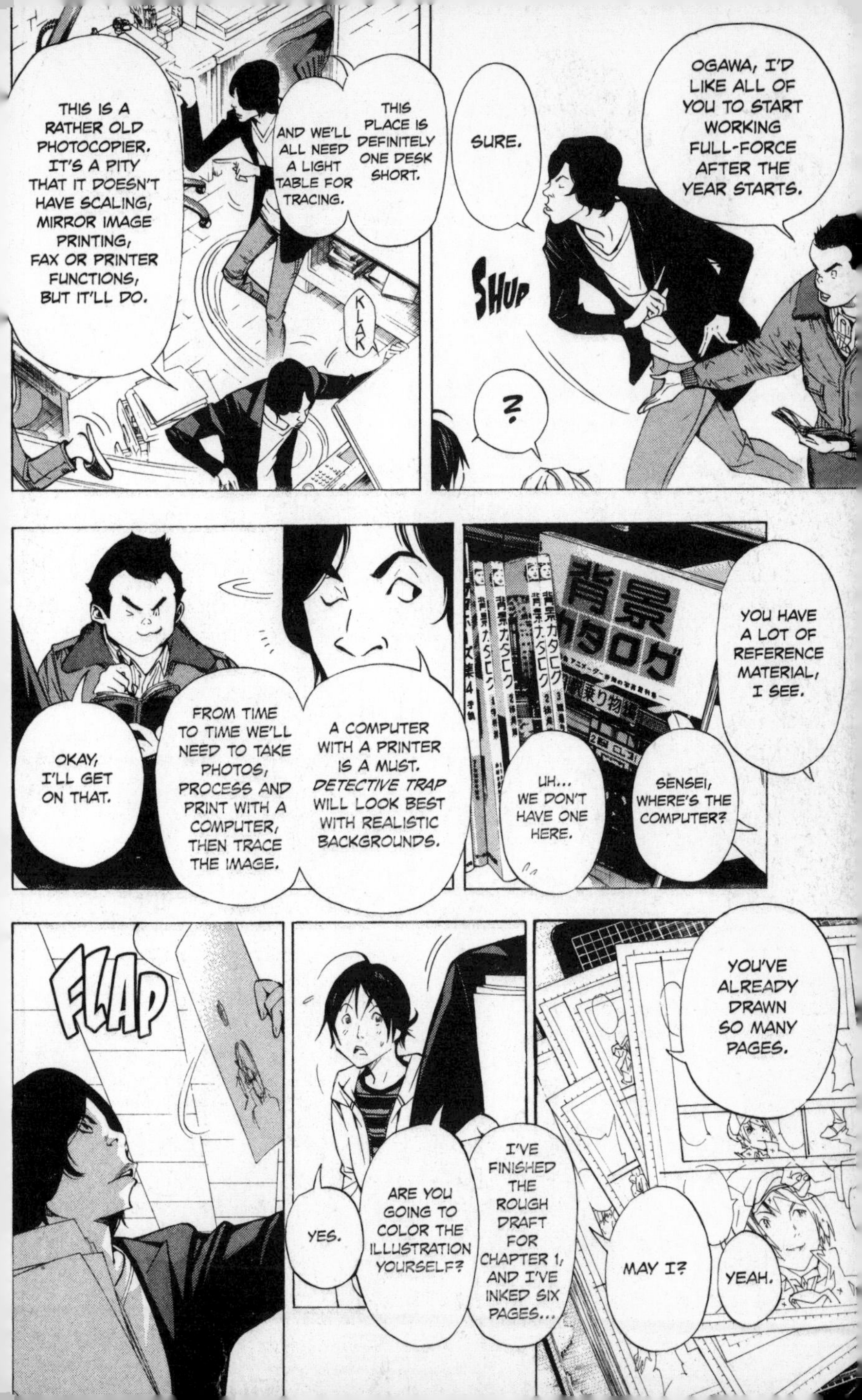
OGAWA, I'D LIKE ALL OF YOU TO START WORKING FULL-FORCE AFTER THE YEAR STARTS.
SURE.
SHUP
?
THIS PLACE IS DEFINITELY ONE DESK SHORT.
AND WE'LL ALL NEED A LIGHT TABLE FOR TRACING.
KLAK
THIS IS A RATHER OLD PHOTOCOPIER. IT'S A PITY THAT IT DOESN'T HAVE SCALING, MIRROR IMAGE PRINTING, FAX OR PRINTER FUNCTIONS, BUT IT'LL DO.
背景カタログ
YOU HAVE A LOT OF REFERENCE MATERIAL, I SEE.
SENSEI, WHERE'S THE COMPUTER?
UH... WE DON'T HAVE ONE HERE.
A COMPUTER WITH A PRINTER IS A MUST. *DETECTIVE TRAP* WILL LOOK BEST WITH REALISTIC BACKGROUNDS.
FROM TIME TO TIME WE'LL NEED TO TAKE PHOTOS, PROCESS AND PRINT WITH A COMPUTER, THEN TRACE THE IMAGE.
OKAY, I'LL GET ON THAT.
YOU'VE ALREADY DRAWN SO MANY PAGES.
YEAH.
MAY I?
I'VE FINISHED THE ROUGH DRAFT FOR CHAPTER 1, AND I'VE INKED SIX PAGES...
ARE YOU GOING TO COLOR THE ILLUSTRATION YOURSELF?
YES.
FLAP

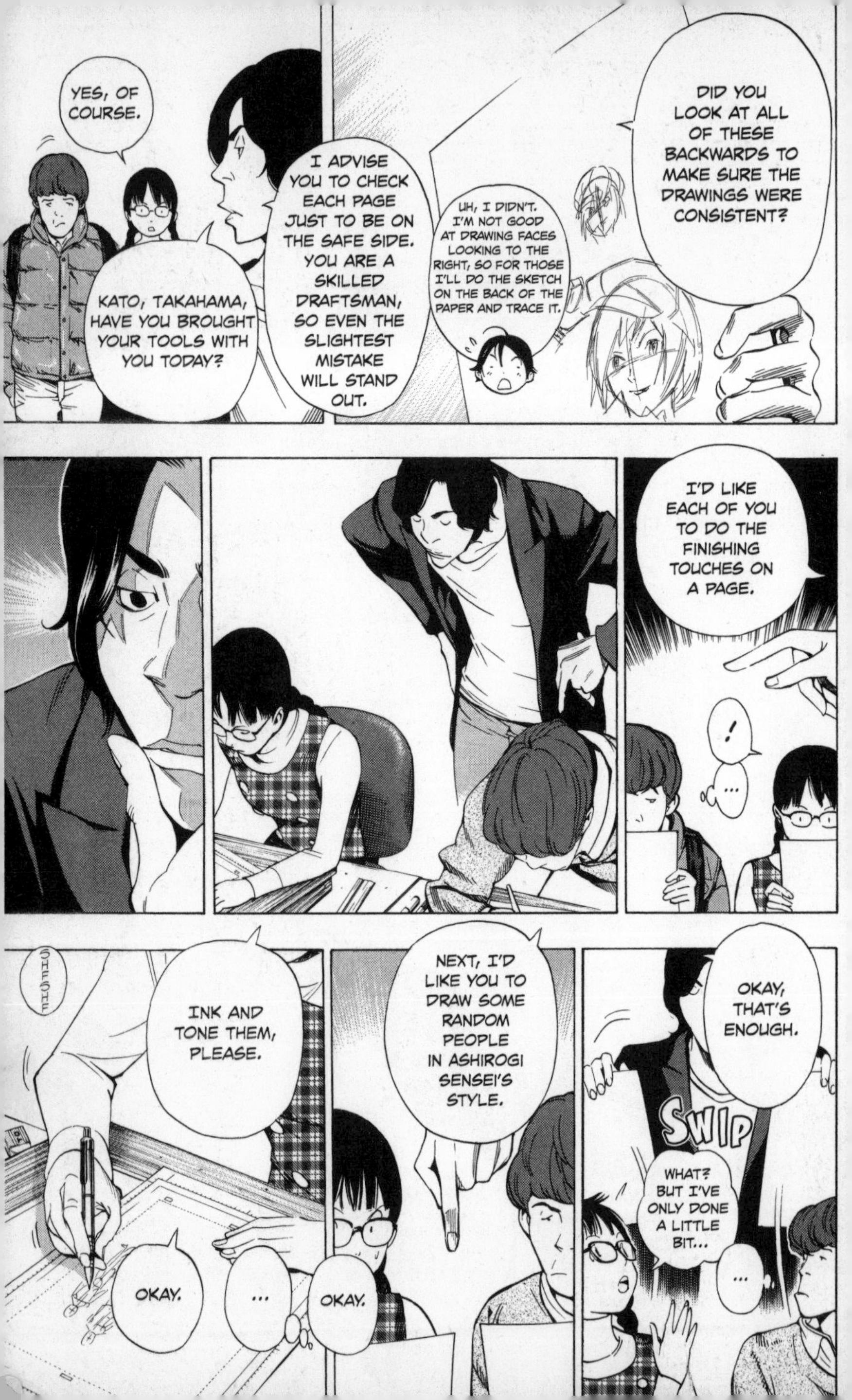
DID YOU LOOK AT ALL OF THESE BACKWARDS TO MAKE SURE THE DRAWINGS WERE CONSISTENT?
UH, I DIDN'T. I'M NOT GOOD AT DRAWING FACES LOOKING TO THE RIGHT, SO FOR THOSE I'LL DO THE SKETCH ON THE BACK OF THE PAPER AND TRACE IT.
I ADVISE YOU TO CHECK EACH PAGE JUST TO BE ON THE SAFE SIDE. YOU ARE A SKILLED DRAFTSMAN, SO EVEN THE SLIGHTEST MISTAKE WILL STAND OUT.
KATO, TAKAHAMA, HAVE YOU BROUGHT YOUR TOOLS WITH YOU TODAY?
YES, OF COURSE.
I'D LIKE EACH OF YOU TO DO THE FINISHING TOUCHES ON A PAGE.
!
...
OKAY, THAT'S ENOUGH.
SWIP
WHAT? BUT I'VE ONLY DONE A LITTLE BIT...
...
NEXT, I'D LIKE YOU TO DRAW SOME RANDOM PEOPLE IN ASHIROGI SENSEI'S STYLE.
OKAY.
INK AND TONE THEM, PLEASE.
SHF SHF
...
OKAY.

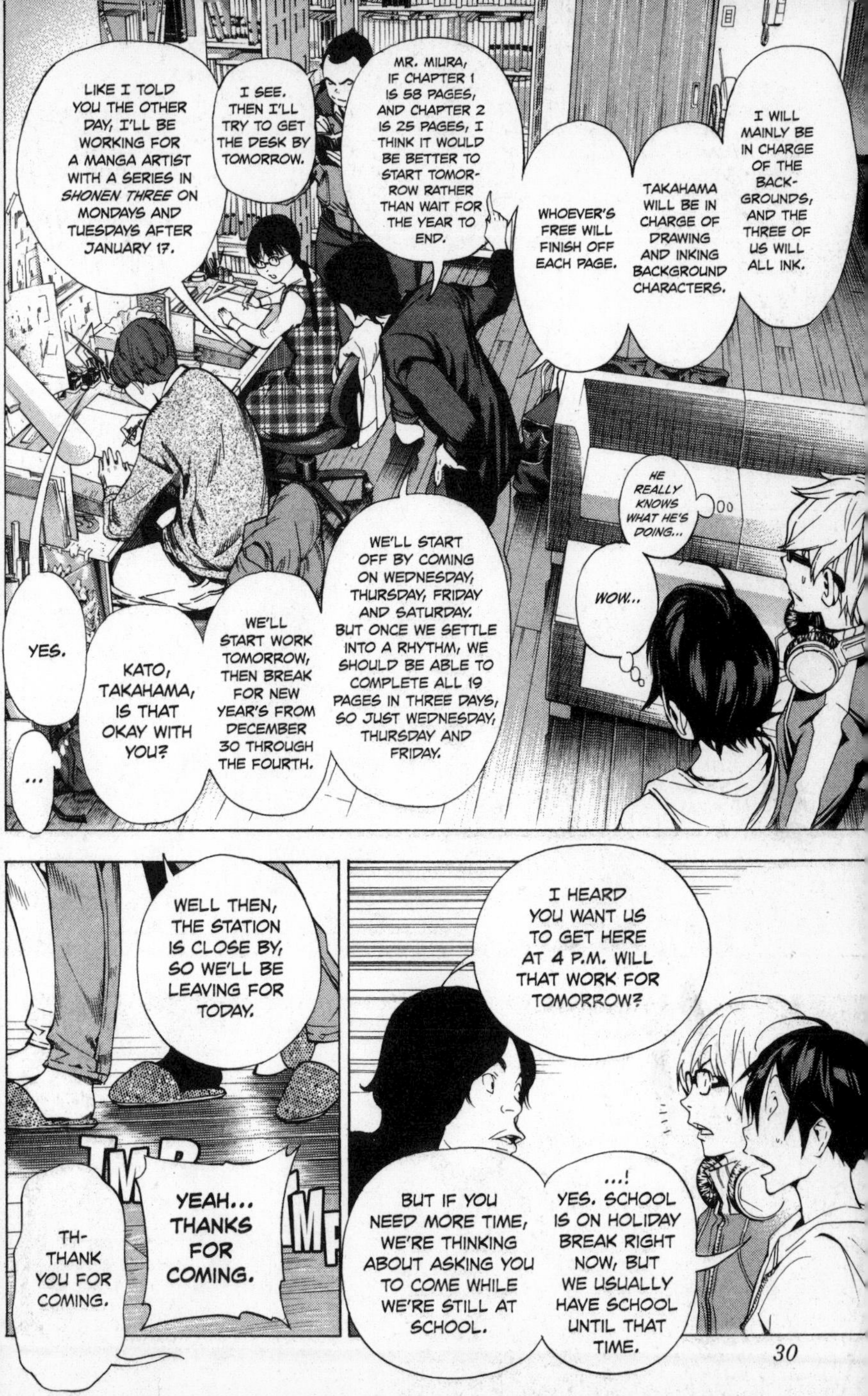
I WILL MAINLY BE IN CHARGE OF THE BACK-GROUNDS, AND THE THREE OF US WILL ALL INK.
TAKAHAMA WILL BE IN CHARGE OF DRAWING AND INKING BACKGROUND CHARACTERS.
WHOEVER'S FREE WILL FINISH OFF EACH PAGE.
MR. MIURA, IF CHAPTER 1 IS 58 PAGES, AND CHAPTER 2 IS 25 PAGES, I THINK IT WOULD BE BETTER TO START TOMOR-ROW RATHER THAN WAIT FOR THE YEAR TO END.
I SEE. THEN I'LL TRY TO GET THE DESK BY TOMORROW.
LIKE I TOLD YOU THE OTHER DAY, I'LL BE WORKING FOR A MANGA ARTIST WITH A SERIES IN *SHONEN THREE* ON MONDAYS AND TUESDAYS AFTER JANUARY 17.
HE REALLY KNOWS WHAT HE'S DOING...
WOW...
WE'LL START OFF BY COMING ON WEDNESDAY, THURSDAY, FRIDAY AND SATURDAY. BUT ONCE WE SETTLE INTO A RHYTHM, WE SHOULD BE ABLE TO COMPLETE ALL 19 PAGES IN THREE DAYS, SO JUST WEDNESDAY, THURSDAY AND FRIDAY.
WE'LL START WORK TOMORROW, THEN BREAK FOR NEW YEAR'S FROM DECEMBER 30 THROUGH THE FOURTH.
KATO, TAKAHAMA, IS THAT OKAY WITH YOU?
YES.
...
I HEARD YOU WANT US TO GET HERE AT 4 P.M. WILL THAT WORK FOR TOMORROW?
...! YES. SCHOOL IS ON HOLIDAY BREAK RIGHT NOW, BUT WE USUALLY HAVE SCHOOL UNTIL THAT TIME.
BUT IF YOU NEED MORE TIME, WE'RE THINKING ABOUT ASKING YOU TO COME WHILE WE'RE STILL AT SCHOOL.
WELL THEN, THE STATION IS CLOSE BY, SO WE'LL BE LEAVING FOR TODAY.
YEAH... THANKS FOR COMING.
TH-THANK YOU FOR COMING.

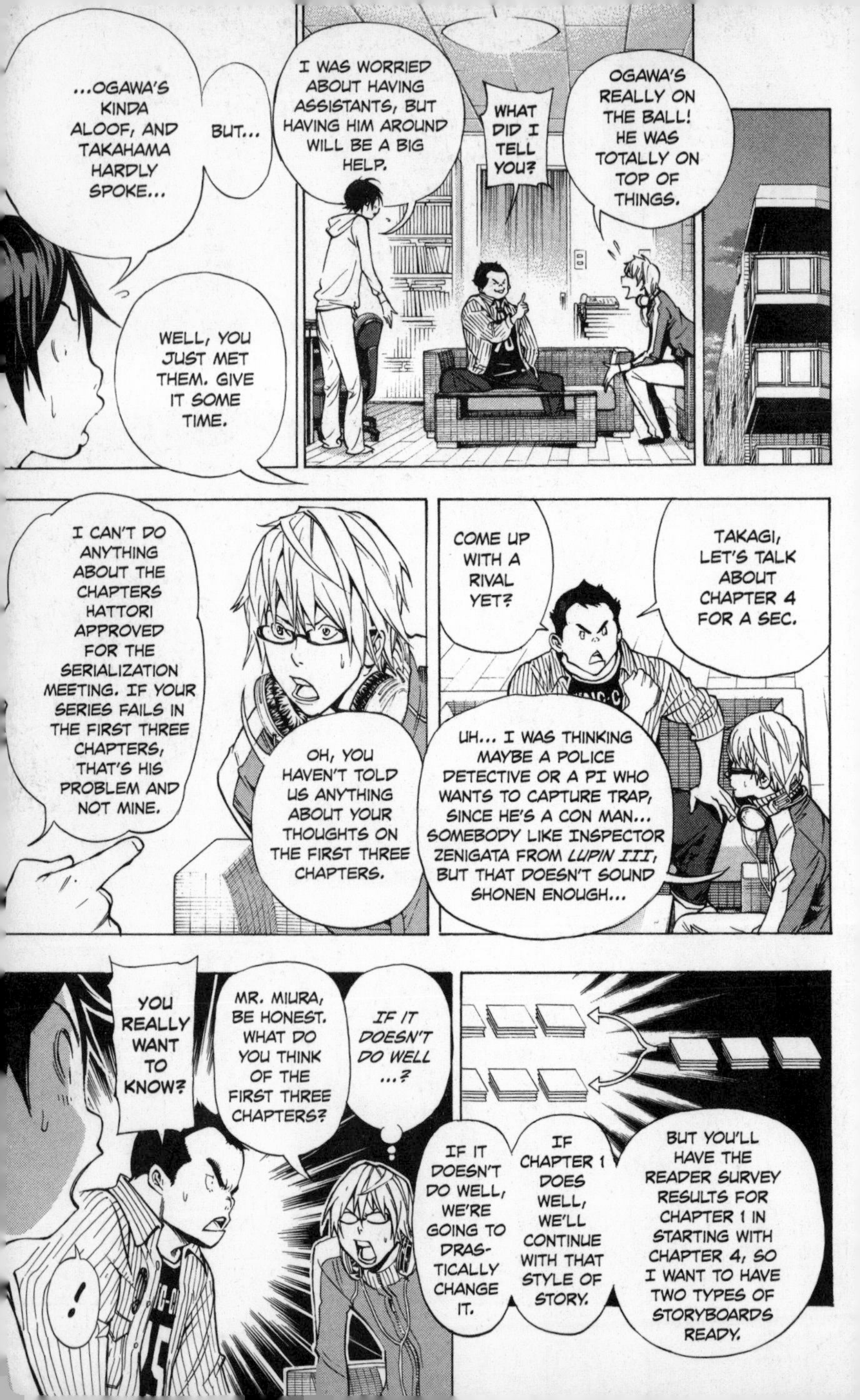
OGAWA'S REALLY ON THE BALL! HE WAS TOTALLY ON TOP OF THINGS.
WHAT DID I TELL YOU?
I WAS WORRIED ABOUT HAVING ASSISTANTS, BUT HAVING HIM AROUND WILL BE A BIG HELP.
BUT...
...OGAWA'S KINDA ALOOF, AND TAKAHAMA HARDLY SPOKE...
WELL, YOU JUST MET THEM. GIVE IT SOME TIME.
TAKAGI, LET'S TALK ABOUT CHAPTER 4 FOR A SEC.
COME UP WITH A RIVAL YET?
UH... I WAS THINKING MAYBE A POLICE DETECTIVE OR A PI WHO WANTS TO CAPTURE TRAP, SINCE HE'S A CON MAN... SOMEBODY LIKE INSPECTOR ZENIGATA FROM *LUPIN III*, BUT THAT DOESN'T SOUND SHONEN ENOUGH...
OH, YOU HAVEN'T TOLD US ANYTHING ABOUT YOUR THOUGHTS ON THE FIRST THREE CHAPTERS.
I CAN'T DO ANYTHING ABOUT THE CHAPTERS HATTORI APPROVED FOR THE SERIALIZATION MEETING. IF YOUR SERIES FAILS IN THE FIRST THREE CHAPTERS, THAT'S HIS PROBLEM AND NOT MINE.
BUT YOU'LL HAVE THE READER SURVEY RESULTS FOR CHAPTER 1 IN STARTING WITH CHAPTER 4, SO I WANT TO HAVE TWO TYPES OF STORYBOARDS READY.
IF CHAPTER 1 DOES WELL, WE'LL CONTINUE WITH THAT STYLE OF STORY.
IF IT DOESN'T DO WELL, WE'RE GOING TO DRAS-TICALLY CHANGE IT.
IF IT DOESN'T DO WELL ...?
MR. MIURA, BE HONEST. WHAT DO YOU THINK OF THE FIRST THREE CHAPTERS?
YOU REALLY WANT TO KNOW?
!

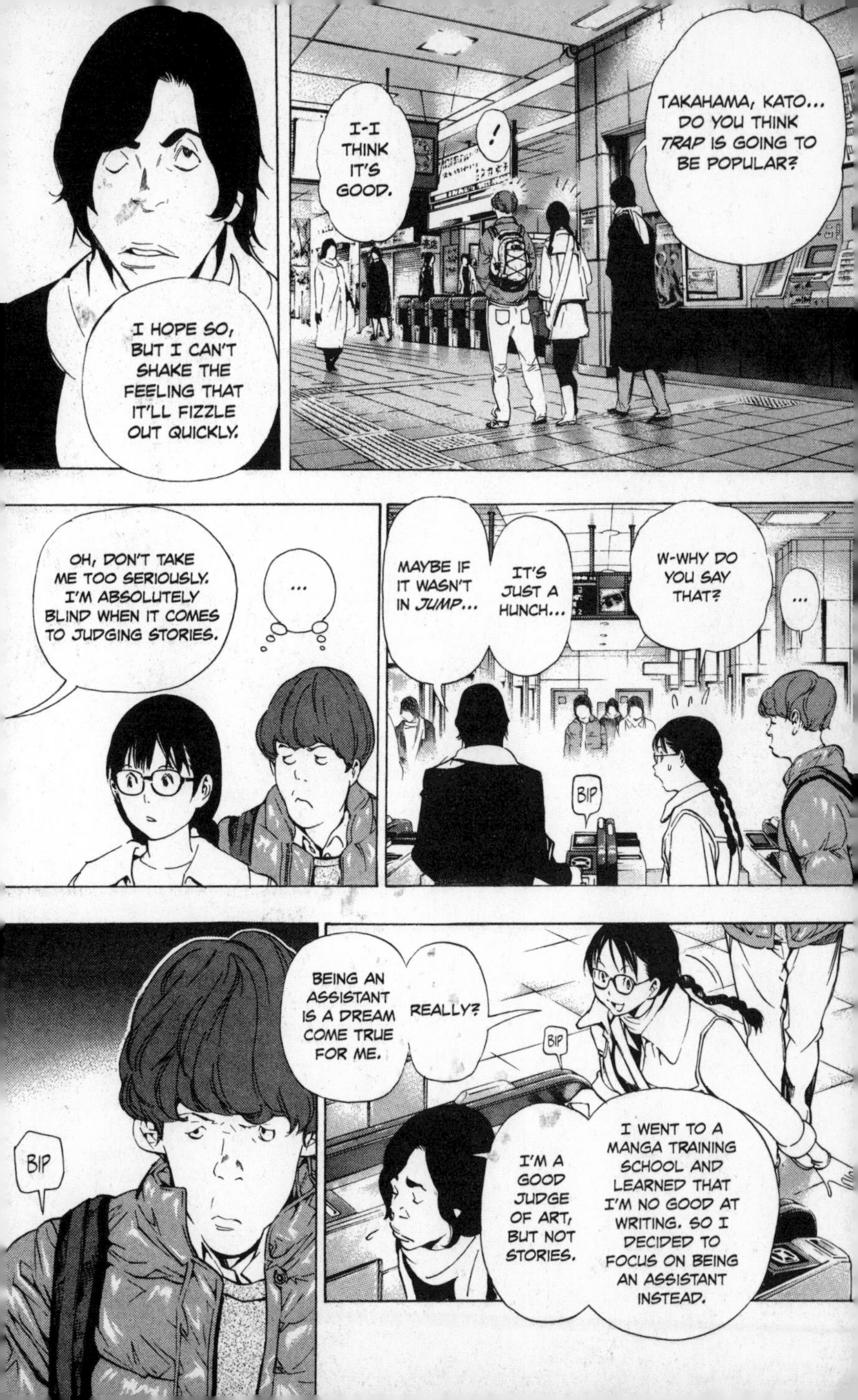
TAKAHAMA, KATO... DO YOU THINK *TRAP* IS GOING TO BE POPULAR?
!
I-I THINK IT'S GOOD.
I HOPE SO, BUT I CAN'T SHAKE THE FEELING THAT IT'LL FIZZLE OUT QUICKLY.
...
W-WHY DO YOU SAY THAT?
IT'S JUST A HUNCH...
MAYBE IF IT WASN'T IN *JUMP*...
BIP
...
OH, DON'T TAKE ME TOO SERIOUSLY. I'M ABSOLUTELY BLIND WHEN IT COMES TO JUDGING STORIES.
REALLY?
BEING AN ASSISTANT IS A DREAM COME TRUE FOR ME.
BIP
I WENT TO A MANGA TRAINING SCHOOL AND LEARNED THAT I'M NO GOOD AT WRITING. SO I DECIDED TO FOCUS ON BEING AN ASSISTANT INSTEAD.
I'M A GOOD JUDGE OF ART, BUT NOT STORIES.
BIP

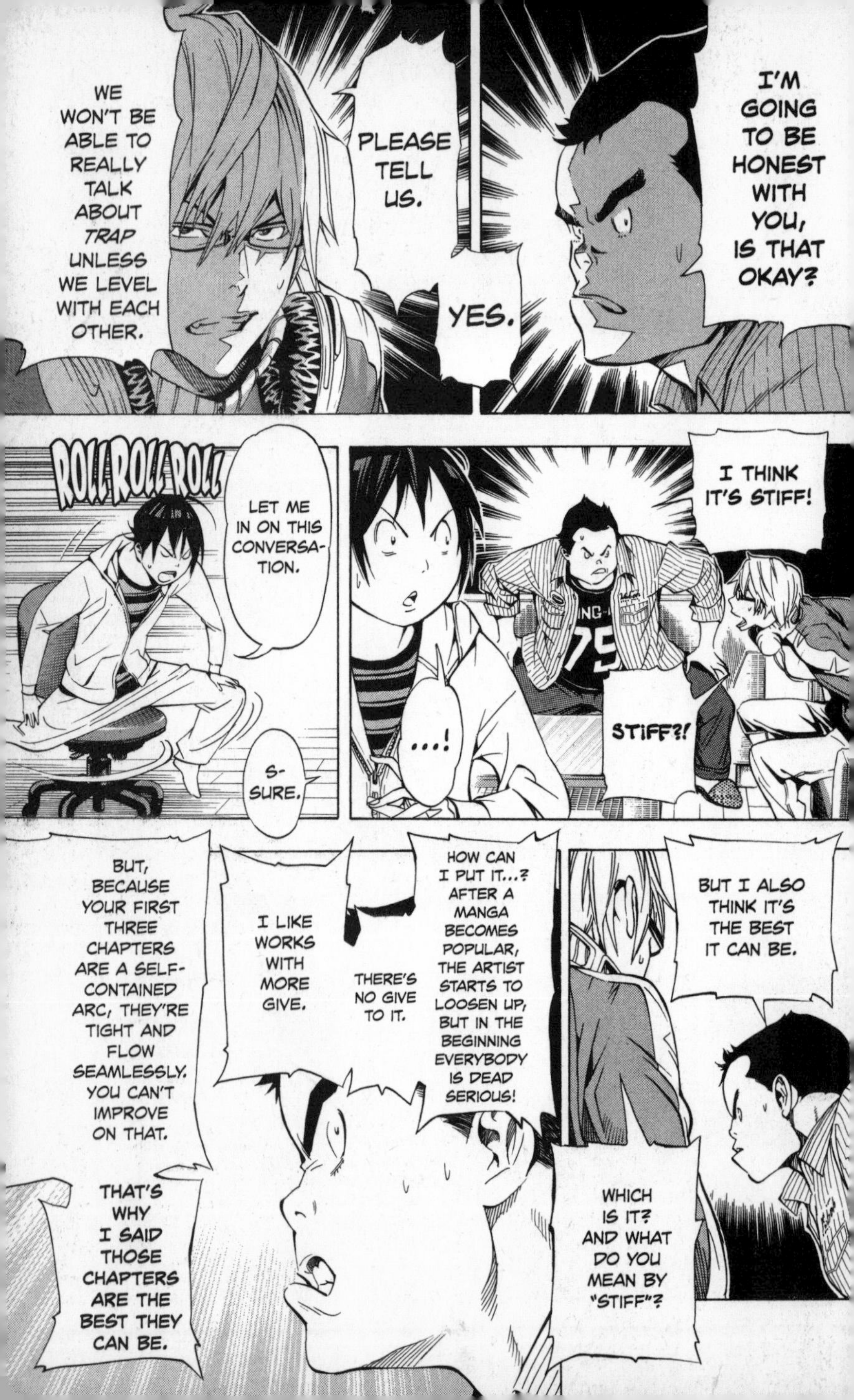
I'M GOING TO BE HONEST WITH YOU, IS THAT OKAY?
YES.
PLEASE TELL US.
WE WON'T BE ABLE TO REALLY TALK ABOUT *TRAP* UNLESS WE LEVEL WITH EACH OTHER.
I THINK IT'S STIFF!
STIFF?!
...!
ROLL ROLL ROLL
LET ME IN ON THIS CONVERSATION.
S-SURE.
BUT I ALSO THINK IT'S THE BEST IT CAN BE.
WHICH IS IT? AND WHAT DO YOU MEAN BY "STIFF"?
HOW CAN I PUT IT...? AFTER A MANGA BECOMES POPULAR, THE ARTIST STARTS TO LOOSEN UP, BUT IN THE BEGINNING EVERYBODY IS DEAD SERIOUS!
THERE'S NO GIVE TO IT.
I LIKE WORKS WITH MORE GIVE.
BUT, BECAUSE YOUR FIRST THREE CHAPTERS ARE A SELF-CONTAINED ARC, THEY'RE TIGHT AND FLOW SEAMLESSLY. YOU CAN'T IMPROVE ON THAT.
THAT'S WHY I SAID THOSE CHAPTERS ARE THE BEST THEY CAN BE.

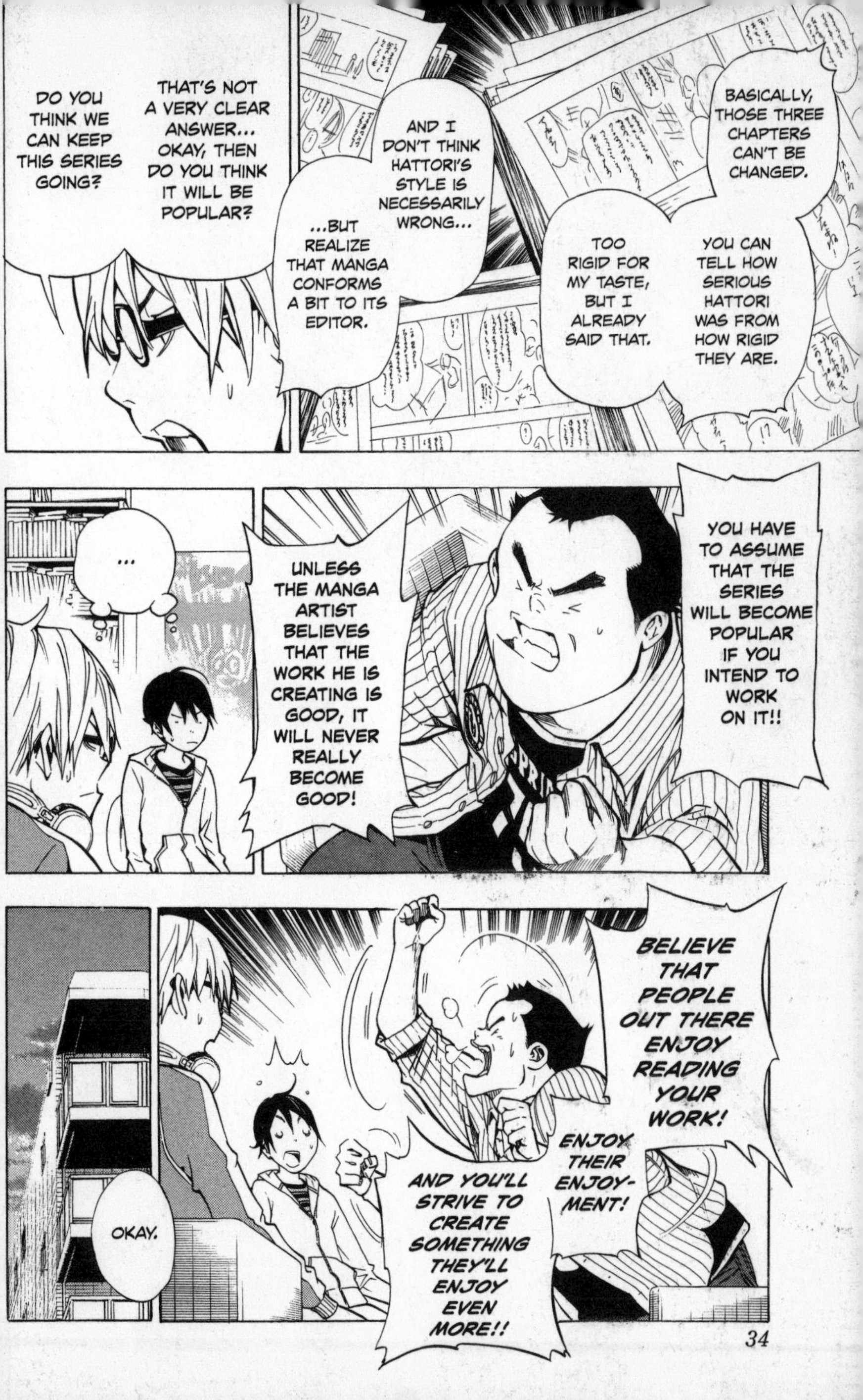

BASICALLY, THOSE THREE CHAPTERS CAN'T BE CHANGED.
YOU CAN TELL HOW SERIOUS HATTORI WAS FROM HOW RIGID THEY ARE.
TOO RIGID FOR MY TASTE, BUT I ALREADY SAID THAT.
AND I DON'T THINK HATTORI'S STYLE IS NECESSARILY WRONG...
...BUT REALIZE THAT MANGA CONFORMS A BIT TO ITS EDITOR.
THAT'S NOT A VERY CLEAR ANSWER... OKAY, THEN DO YOU THINK IT WILL BE POPULAR?
DO YOU THINK WE CAN KEEP THIS SERIES GOING?
YOU HAVE TO ASSUME THAT THE SERIES WILL BECOME POPULAR IF YOU INTEND TO WORK ON IT!!
UNLESS THE MANGA ARTIST BELIEVES THAT THE WORK HE IS CREATING IS GOOD, IT WILL NEVER REALLY BECOME GOOD!
...
BELIEVE THAT PEOPLE OUT THERE ENJOY READING YOUR WORK!
ENJOY THEIR ENJOYMENT!
AND YOU'LL STRIVE TO CREATE SOMETHING THEY'LL ENJOY EVEN MORE!!
OKAY.

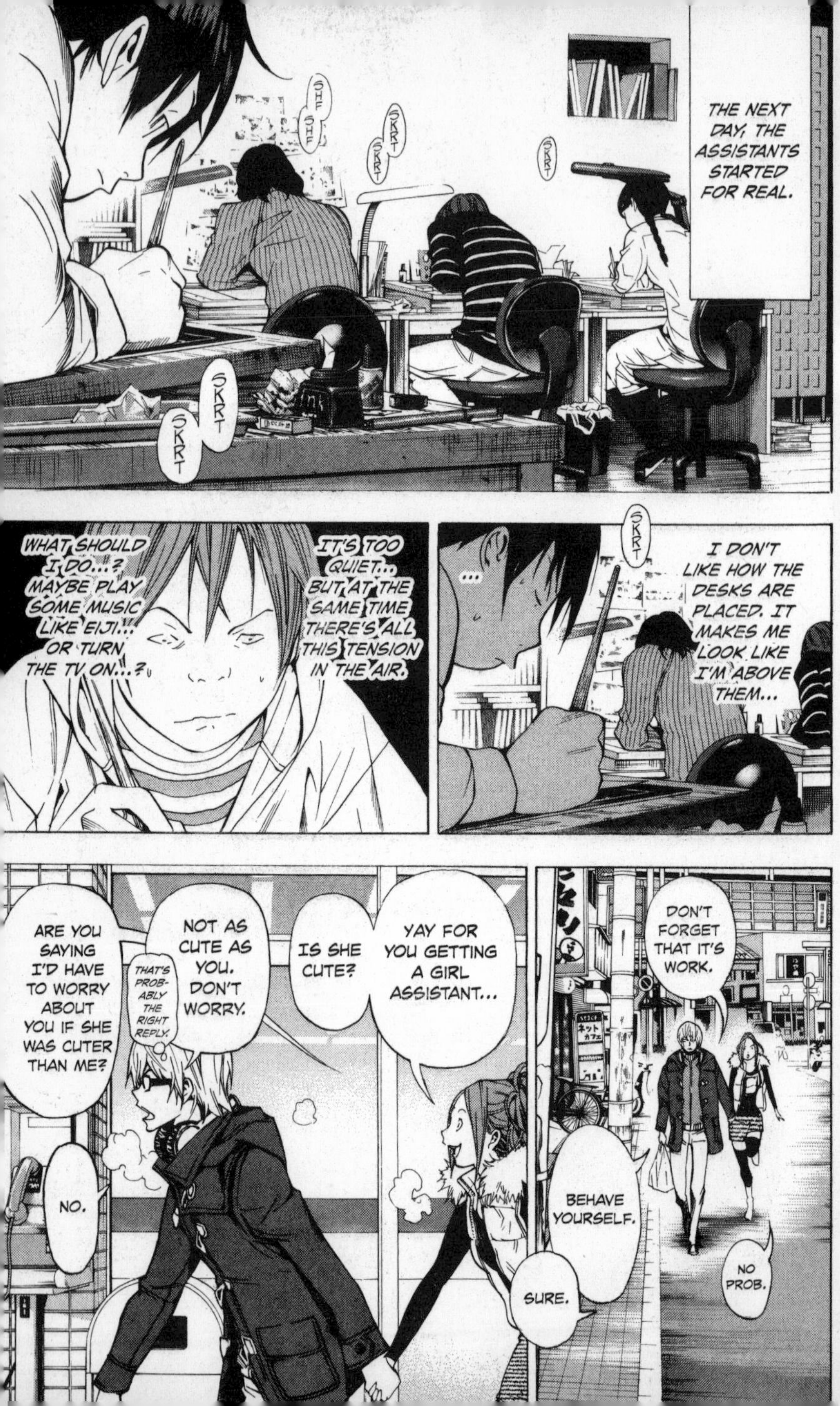
THE NEXT DAY, THE ASSISTANTS STARTED FOR REAL.
SKRT
SKRT SKRT
SHF SHF
SKRT
SKRT
SKRT
I DON'T LIKE HOW THE DESKS ARE PLACED. IT MAKES ME LOOK LIKE I'M ABOVE THEM...
...
IT'S TOO QUIET... BUT AT THE SAME TIME THERE'S ALL THIS TENSION IN THE AIR.
WHAT SHOULD I DO...? MAYBE PLAY SOME MUSIC LIKE EIJI... OR TURN THE TV ON...?
DON'T FORGET THAT IT'S WORK.
NO PROB.
BEHAVE YOURSELF.
SURE.
YAY FOR YOU GETTING A GIRL ASSISTANT...
IS SHE CUTE?
NOT AS CUTE AS YOU. DON'T WORRY.
THAT'S PROBABLY THE RIGHT REPLY.
ARE YOU SAYING I'D HAVE TO WORRY ABOUT YOU IF SHE WAS CUTER THAN ME?
NO.

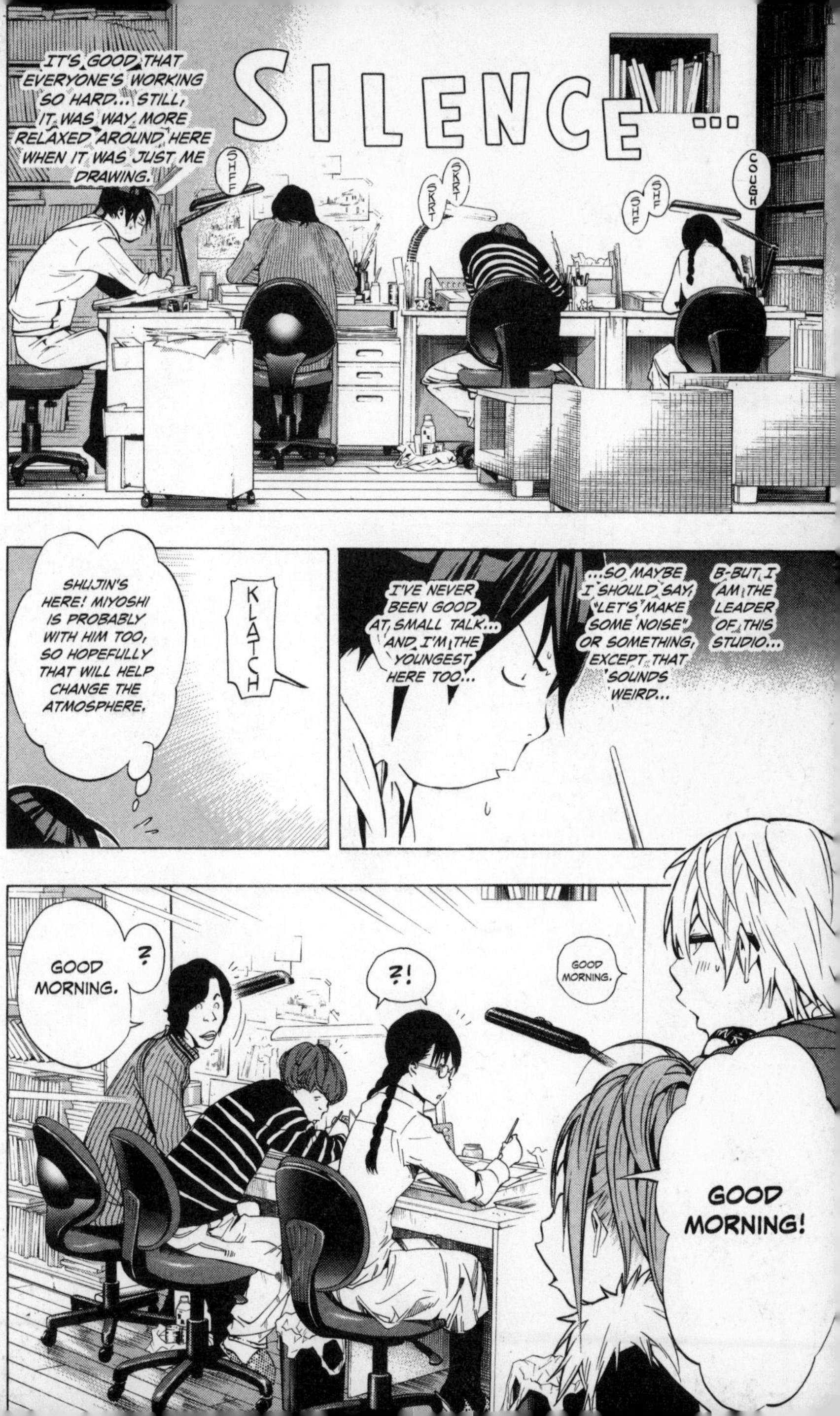
SILENCE...
COUGH
SHF
SHF
SKRT
SKRT
SHFF
IT'S GOOD THAT EVERYONE'S WORKING SO HARD... STILL, IT WAS WAY MORE RELAXED AROUND HERE WHEN IT WAS JUST ME DRAWING.
B-BUT I AM THE LEADER OF THIS STUDIO...
...SO MAYBE I SHOULD SAY, "LET'S MAKE SOME NOISE" OR SOMETHING, EXCEPT THAT SOUNDS WEIRD...
I'VE NEVER BEEN GOOD AT SMALL TALK... AND I'M THE YOUNGEST HERE TOO...
KLATCH
SHUJIN'S HERE! MIYOSHI IS PROBABLY WITH HIM TOO, SO HOPEFULLY THAT WILL HELP CHANGE THE ATMOSPHERE.
GOOD MORNING!
GOOD MORNING.
?!
?
GOOD MORNING.

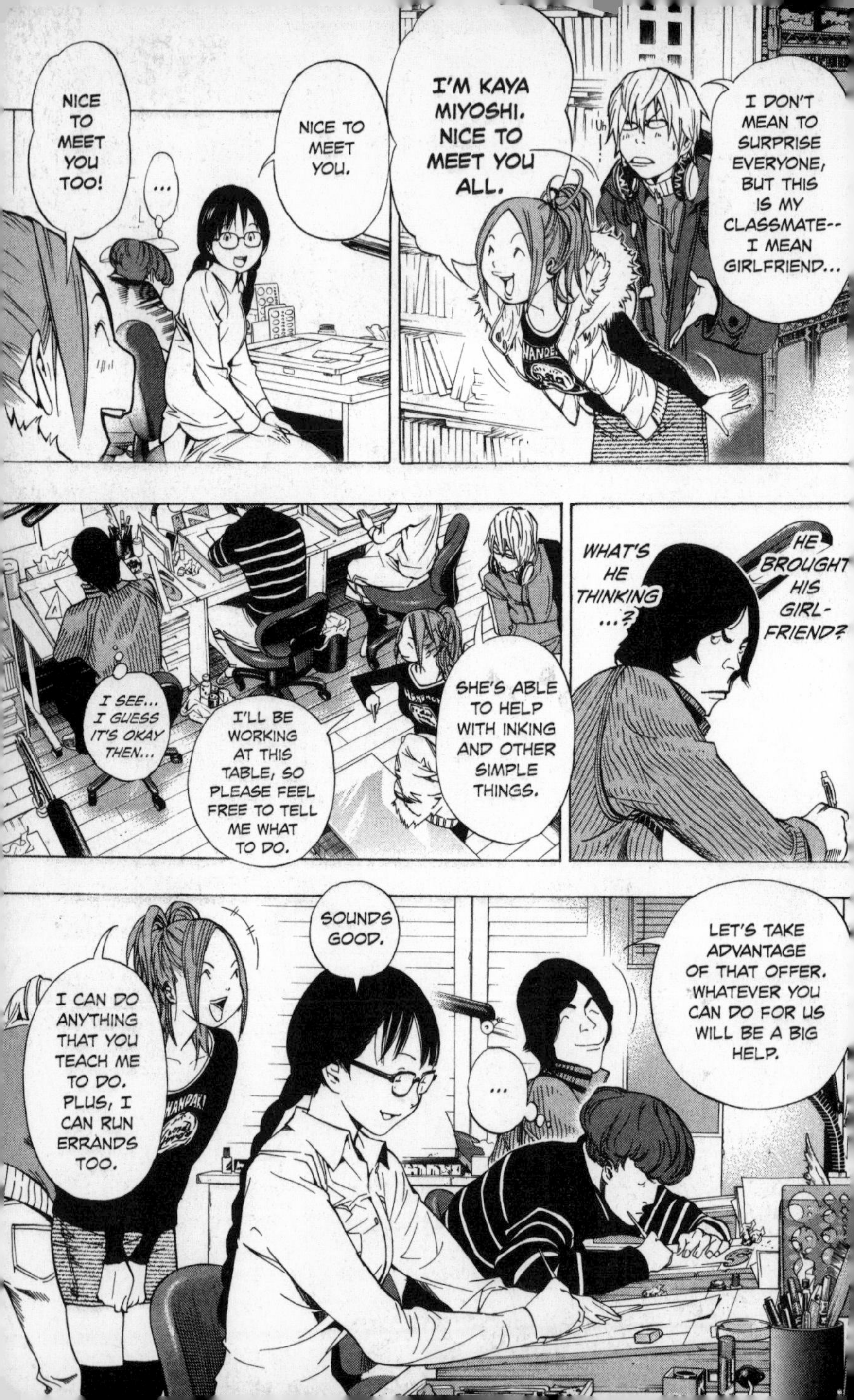
I DON'T MEAN TO SURPRISE EVERYONE, BUT THIS IS MY CLASSMATE-- I MEAN GIRLFRIEND...
I'M KAYA MIYOSHI. NICE TO MEET YOU ALL.
NICE TO MEET YOU.
...
NICE TO MEET YOU TOO!
HE BROUGHT HIS GIRLFRIEND?
WHAT'S HE THINKING...?
SHE'S ABLE TO HELP WITH INKING AND OTHER SIMPLE THINGS.
I'LL BE WORKING AT THIS TABLE, SO PLEASE FEEL FREE TO TELL ME WHAT TO DO.
I SEE... I GUESS IT'S OKAY THEN...
LET'S TAKE ADVANTAGE OF THAT OFFER. WHATEVER YOU CAN DO FOR US WILL BE A BIG HELP.
SOUNDS GOOD.
...
I CAN DO ANYTHING THAT YOU TEACH ME TO DO. PLUS, I CAN RUN ERRANDS TOO.

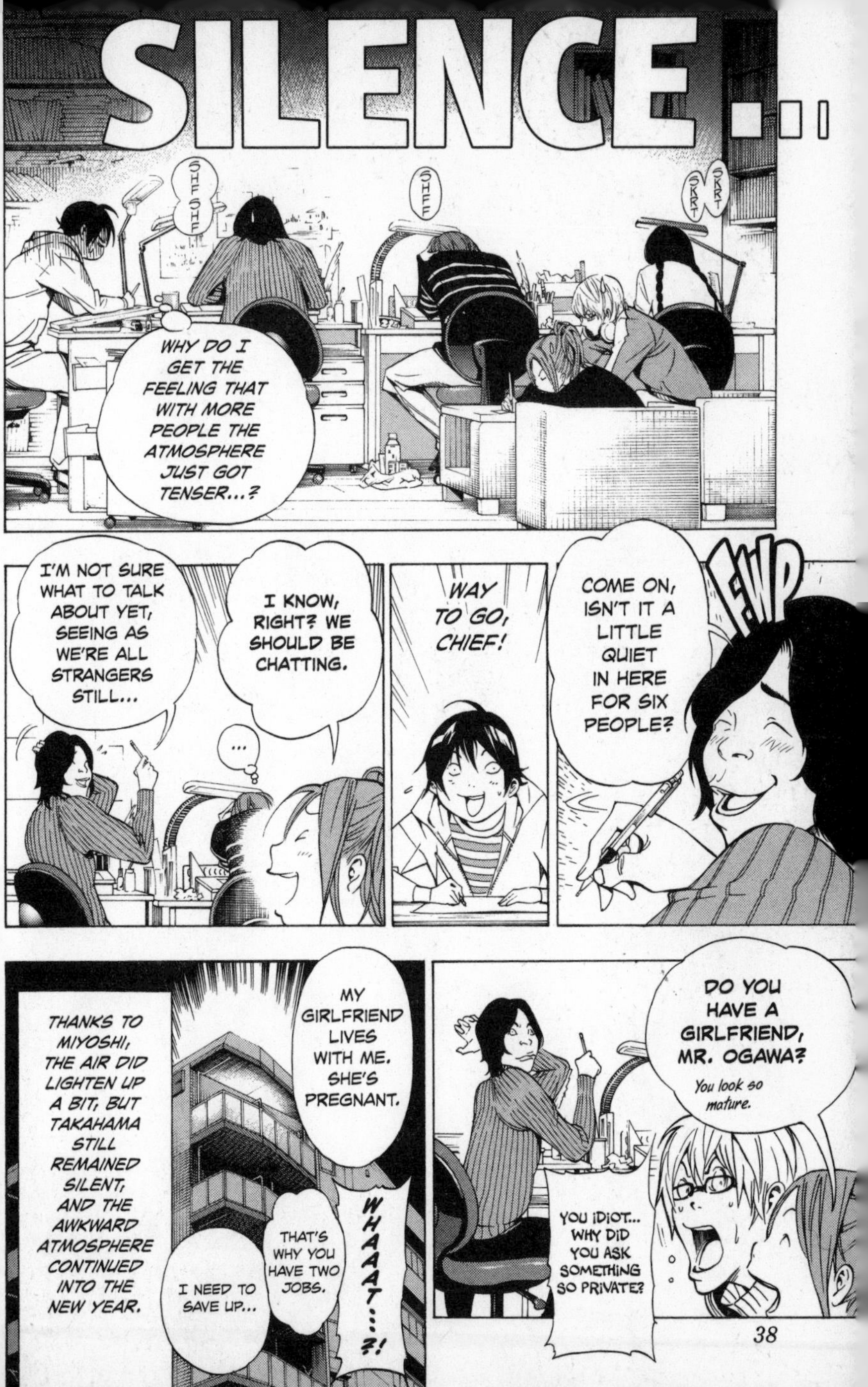
SILENCE...
SHF SHF
SHFF
SKRT SKRT
WHY DO I GET THE FEELING THAT WITH MORE PEOPLE THE ATMOSPHERE JUST GOT TENSER...?
COME ON, ISN'T IT A LITTLE QUIET IN HERE FOR SIX PEOPLE?
WAY TO GO, CHIEF!
I KNOW, RIGHT? WE SHOULD BE CHATTING.
I'M NOT SURE WHAT TO TALK ABOUT YET, SEEING AS WE'RE ALL STRANGERS STILL...
...
DO YOU HAVE A GIRLFRIEND, MR. OGAWA?
You look so mature.
YOU IDIOT... WHY DID YOU ASK SOMETHING SO PRIVATE?
MY GIRLFRIEND LIVES WITH ME. SHE'S PREGNANT.
WHAAAAT...?!
THAT'S WHY YOU HAVE TWO JOBS.
I NEED TO SAVE UP...
THANKS TO MIYOSHI, THE AIR DID LIGHTEN UP A BIT, BUT TAKAHAMA STILL REMAINED SILENT, AND THE AWKWARD ATMOSPHERE CONTINUED INTO THE NEW YEAR.

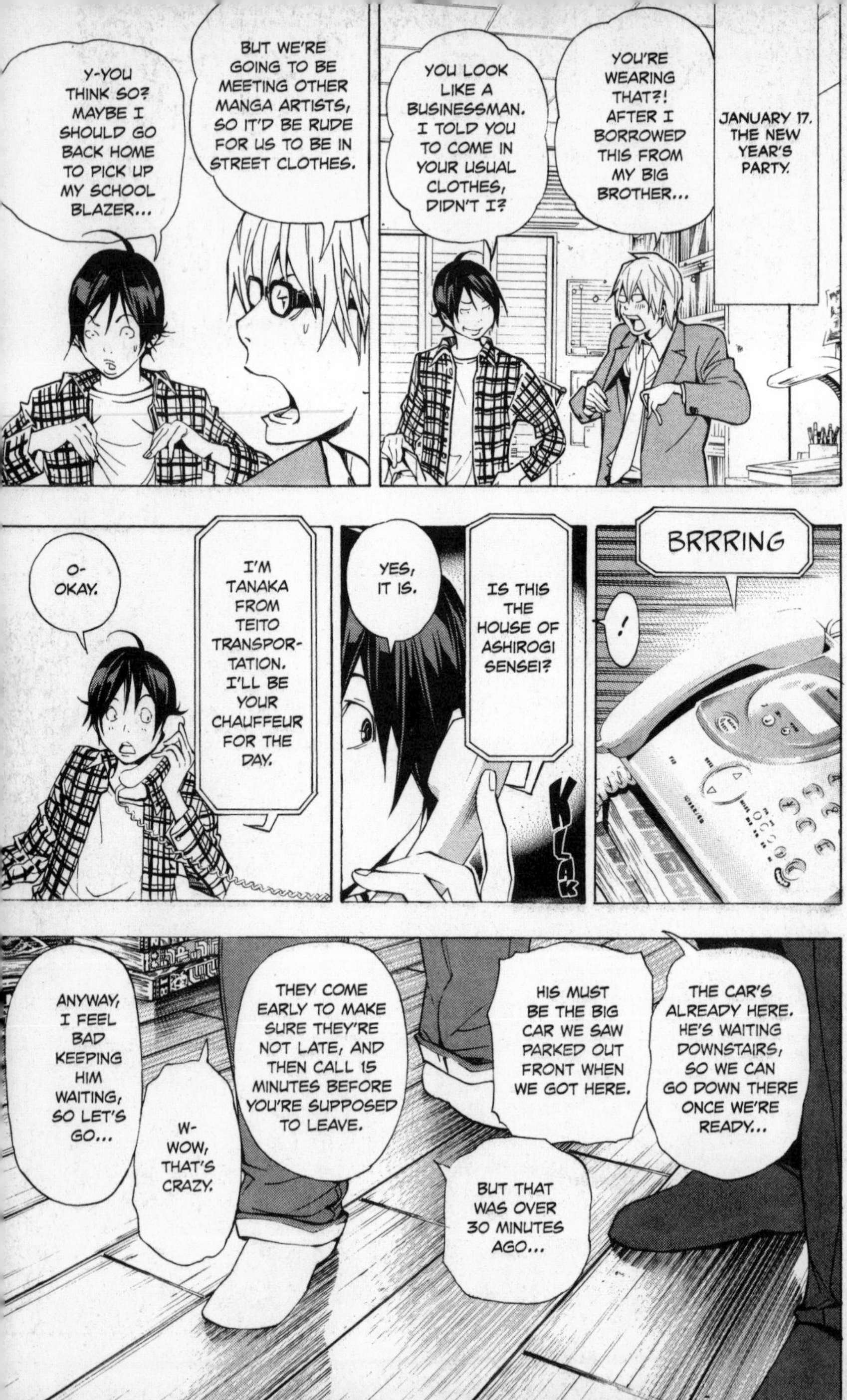
JANUARY 17. THE NEW YEAR'S PARTY.
YOU'RE WEARING THAT?! AFTER I BORROWED THIS FROM MY BIG BROTHER...
YOU LOOK LIKE A BUSINESSMAN. I TOLD YOU TO COME IN YOUR USUAL CLOTHES, DIDN'T I?
BUT WE'RE GOING TO BE MEETING OTHER MANGA ARTISTS, SO IT'D BE RUDE FOR US TO BE IN STREET CLOTHES.
Y-YOU THINK SO? MAYBE I SHOULD GO BACK HOME TO PICK UP MY SCHOOL BLAZER...
BRRRING
!
IS THIS THE HOUSE OF ASHIROGI SENSEI?
YES, IT IS.
KLAK
I'M TANAKA FROM TEITO TRANSPORTATION. I'LL BE YOUR CHAUFFEUR FOR THE DAY.
O-OKAY.
THE CAR'S ALREADY HERE. HE'S WAITING DOWNSTAIRS, SO WE CAN GO DOWN THERE ONCE WE'RE READY...
HIS MUST BE THE BIG CAR WE SAW PARKED OUT FRONT WHEN WE GOT HERE.
BUT THAT WAS OVER 30 MINUTES AGO...
THEY COME EARLY TO MAKE SURE THEY'RE NOT LATE, AND THEN CALL 15 MINUTES BEFORE YOU'RE SUPPOSED TO LEAVE.
W-WOW, THAT'S CRAZY.
ANYWAY, I FEEL BAD KEEPING HIM WAITING, SO LET'S GO...

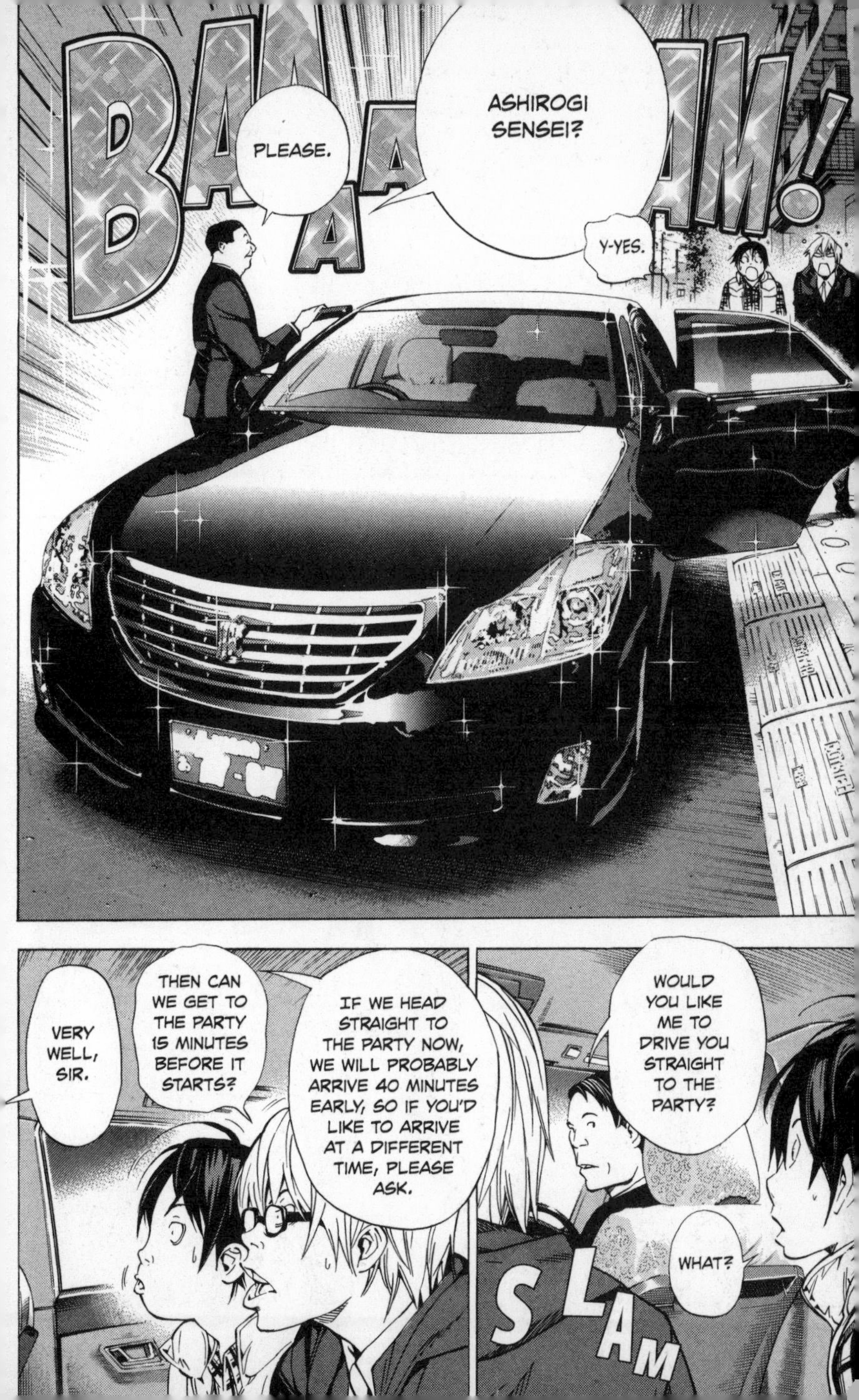
BADAAAM!
ASHIROGI SENSEI?
Y-YES.
PLEASE.
WOULD YOU LIKE ME TO DRIVE YOU STRAIGHT TO THE PARTY?
WHAT?
SLAM
IF WE HEAD STRAIGHT TO THE PARTY NOW, WE WILL PROBABLY ARRIVE 40 MINUTES EARLY, SO IF YOU'D LIKE TO ARRIVE AT A DIFFERENT TIME, PLEASE ASK.
THEN CAN WE GET TO THE PARTY 15 MINUTES BEFORE IT STARTS?
VERY WELL, SIR.

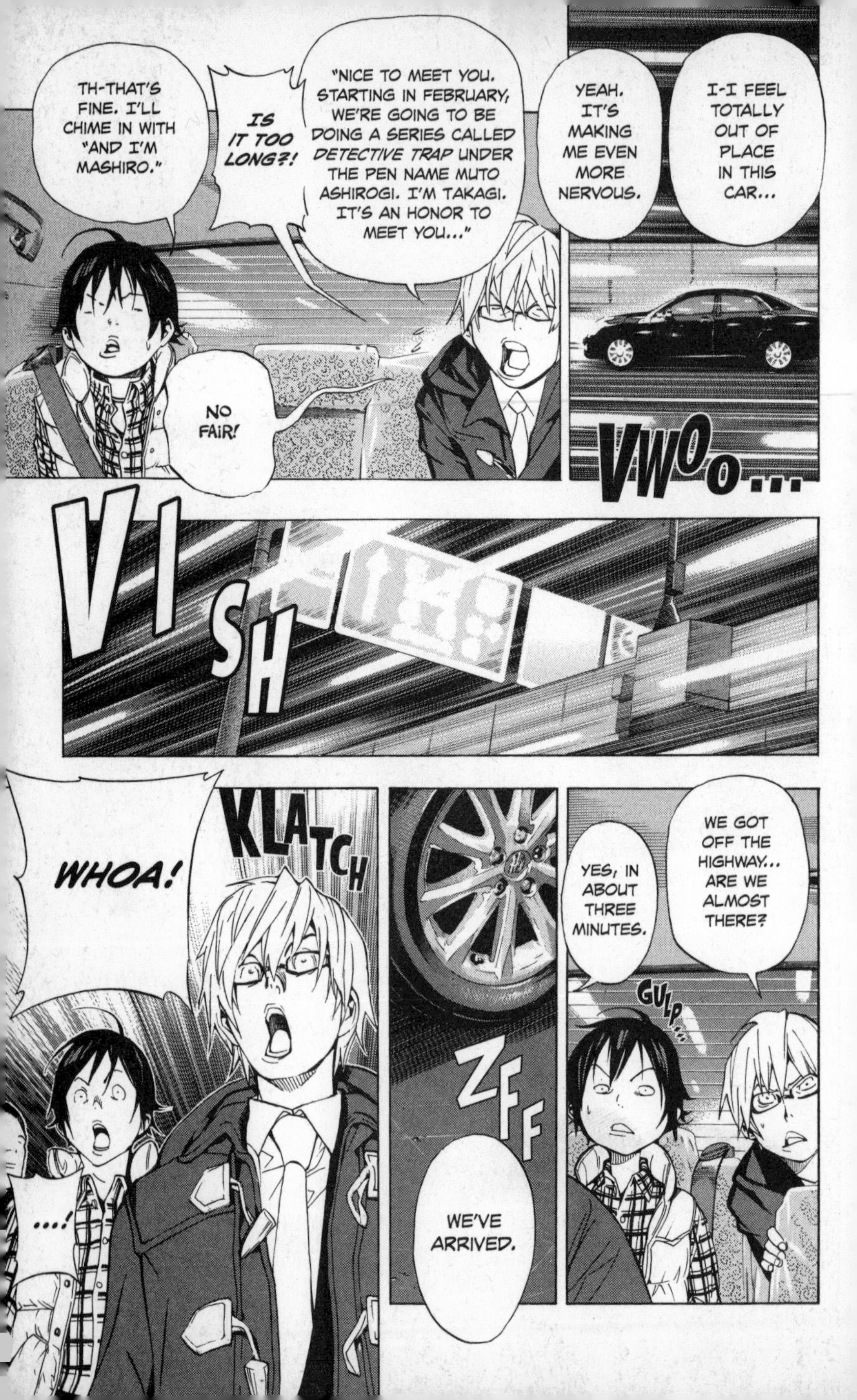
I-I FEEL TOTALLY OUT OF PLACE IN THIS CAR...
YEAH. IT'S MAKING ME EVEN MORE NERVOUS.
VWOO...
"NICE TO MEET YOU. STARTING IN FEBRUARY, WE'RE GOING TO BE DOING A SERIES CALLED *DETECTIVE TRAP* UNDER THE PEN NAME MUTO ASHIROGI. I'M TAKAGI. IT'S AN HONOR TO MEET YOU..."
IS IT TOO LONG?!
TH-THAT'S FINE. I'LL CHIME IN WITH "AND I'M MASHIRO."
NO FAIR!
VISH
WE GOT OFF THE HIGHWAY... ARE WE ALMOST THERE?
YES, IN ABOUT THREE MINUTES.
GULP...
ZFF
WE'VE ARRIVED.
KLATCH
WHOA!
...!

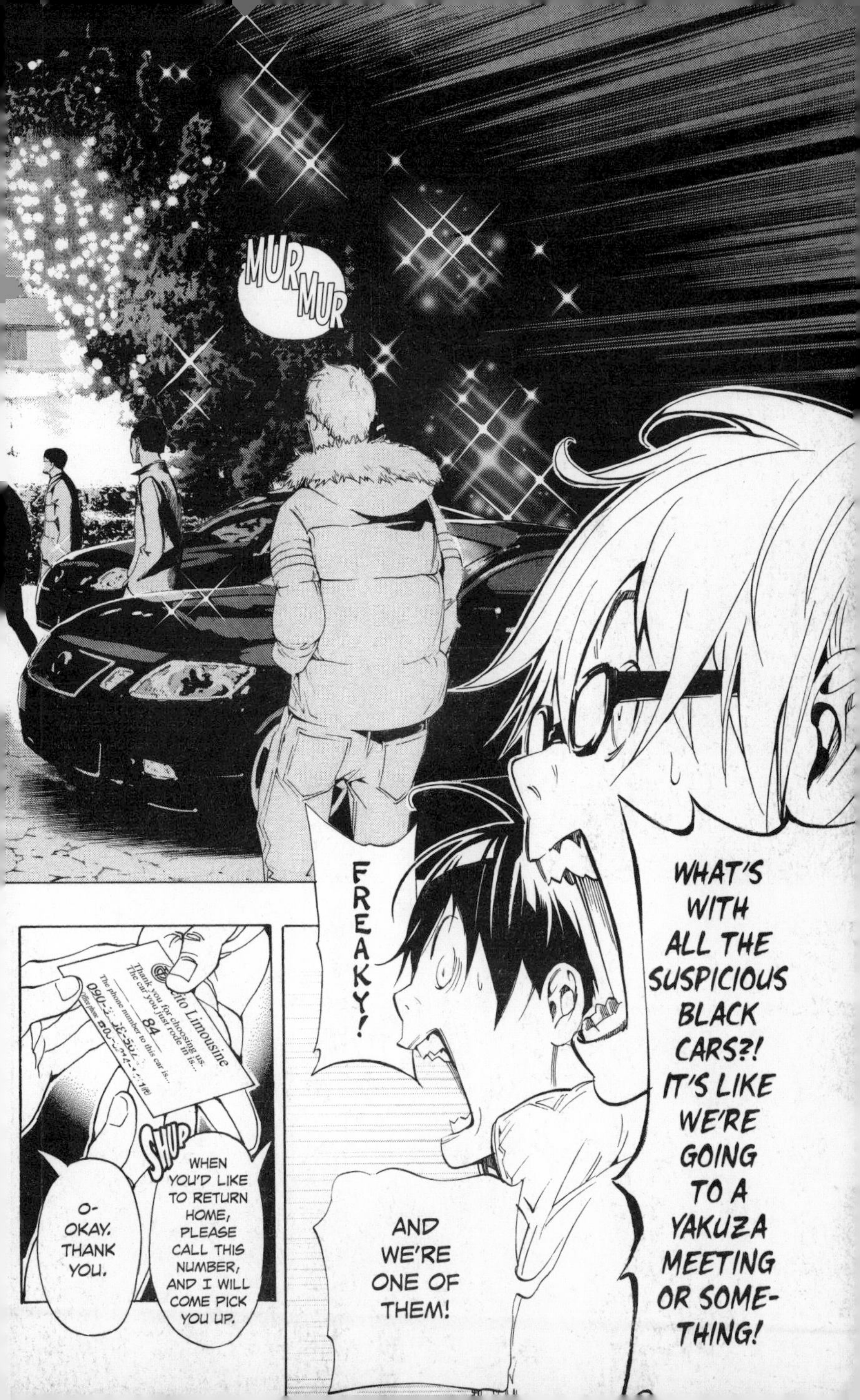
MURMUR MURMUR
WHAT'S WITH ALL THE SUSPICIOUS BLACK CARS?! IT'S LIKE WE'RE GOING TO A YAKUZA MEETING OR SOMETHING!
FREAKY!
AND WE'RE ONE OF THEM!
SHUP
WHEN YOU'D LIKE TO RETURN HOME, PLEASE CALL THIS NUMBER, AND I WILL COME PICK YOU UP.
O-OKAY. THANK YOU.

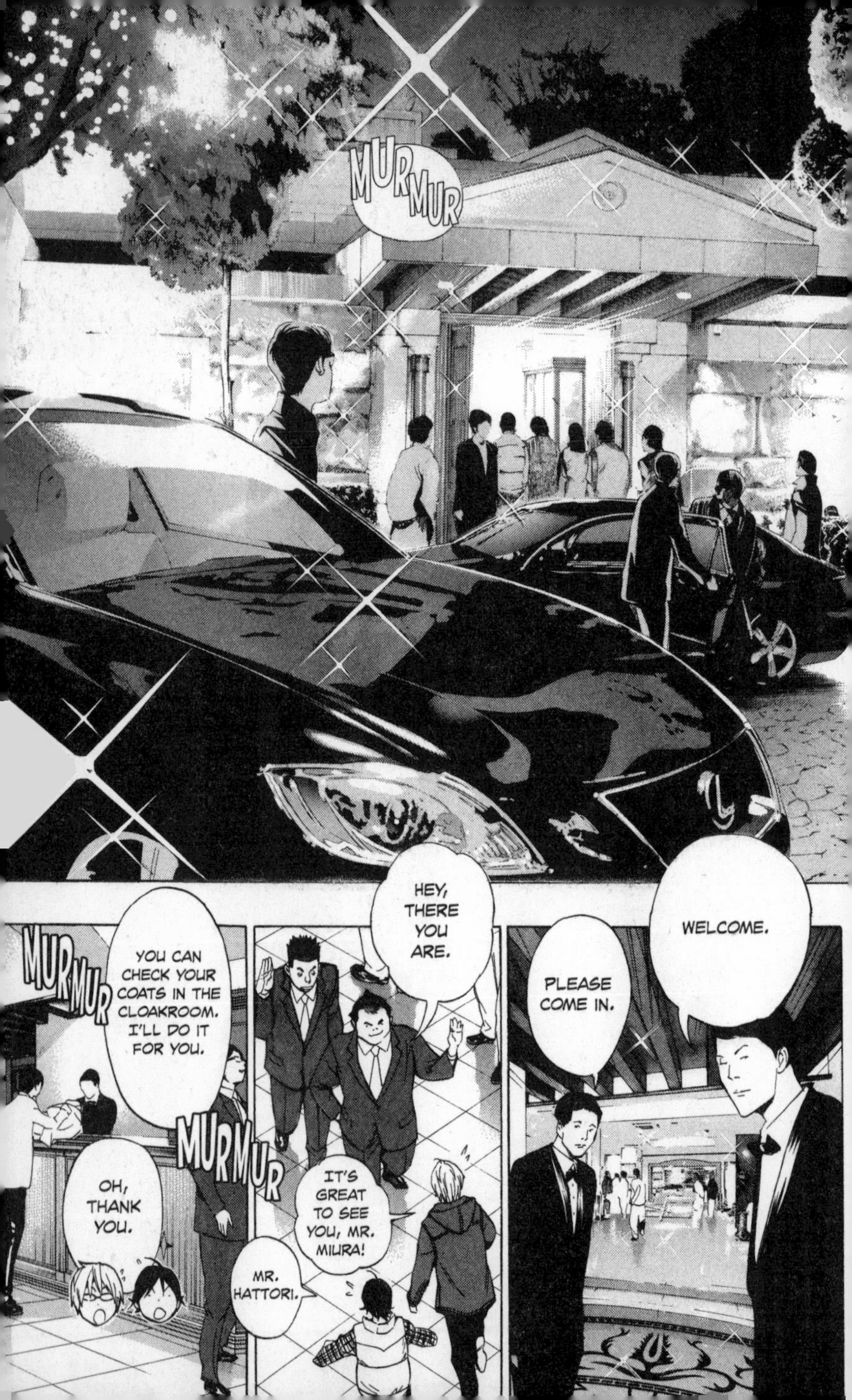
MURMUR
WELCOME.
PLEASE COME IN.
HEY, THERE YOU ARE.
IT'S GREAT TO SEE YOU, MR. MIURA!
MR. HATTORI.
MURMUR
YOU CAN CHECK YOUR COATS IN THE CLOAKROOM. I'LL DO IT FOR YOU.
MURMUR
OH, THANK YOU.

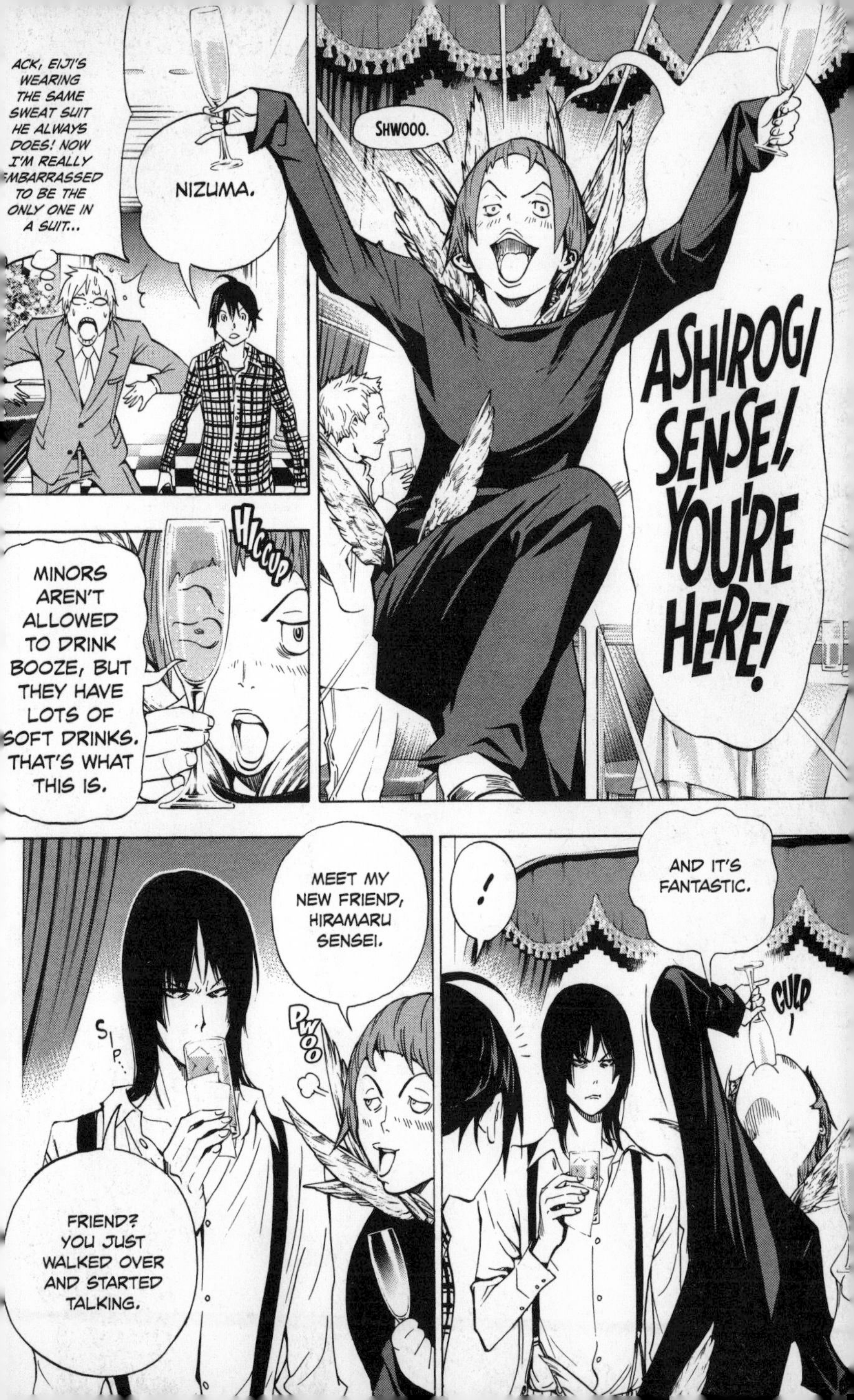
ASHIROGI SENSEI, YOU'RE HERE!
SHWOOO.
NIZUMA.
ACK, EIJI'S WEARING THE SAME SWEAT SUIT HE ALWAYS DOES! NOW I'M REALLY EMBARRASSED TO BE THE ONLY ONE IN A SUIT...
HICCUP
MINORS AREN'T ALLOWED TO DRINK BOOZE, BUT THEY HAVE LOTS OF SOFT DRINKS. THAT'S WHAT THIS IS.
AND IT'S FANTASTIC.
!
GULP
MEET MY NEW FRIEND, HIRAMARU SENSEI.
PWOO
SIP...
FRIEND? YOU JUST WALKED OVER AND STARTED TALKING.

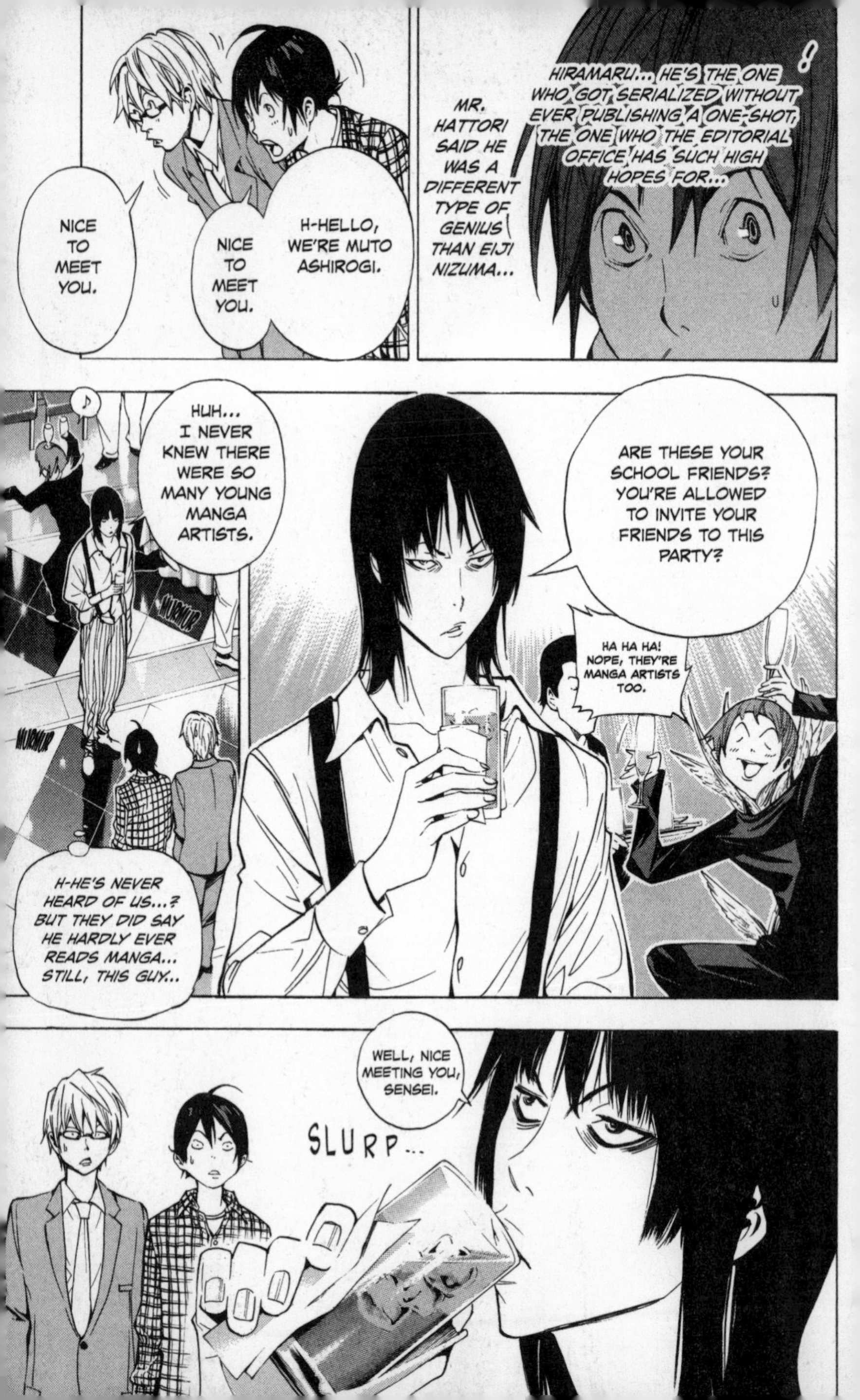
HIRAMARU... HE'S THE ONE WHO GOT SERIALIZED WITHOUT EVER PUBLISHING A ONE-SHOT, THE ONE WHO THE EDITORIAL OFFICE HAS SUCH HIGH HOPES FOR...
MR. HATTORI SAID HE WAS A DIFFERENT TYPE OF GENIUS THAN EIJI NIZUMA...
H-HELLO, WE'RE MUTO ASHIROGI.
NICE TO MEET YOU.
NICE TO MEET YOU.
ARE THESE YOUR SCHOOL FRIENDS? YOU'RE ALLOWED TO INVITE YOUR FRIENDS TO THIS PARTY?
HA HA HA! NOPE, THEY'RE MANGA ARTISTS TOO.
HUH... I NEVER KNEW THERE WERE SO MANY YOUNG MANGA ARTISTS.
MURMUR
MURMUR
H-HE'S NEVER HEARD OF US...? BUT THEY DID SAY HE HARDLY EVER READS MANGA... STILL, THIS GUY...
WELL, NICE MEETING YOU, SENSEI.
SLURP...

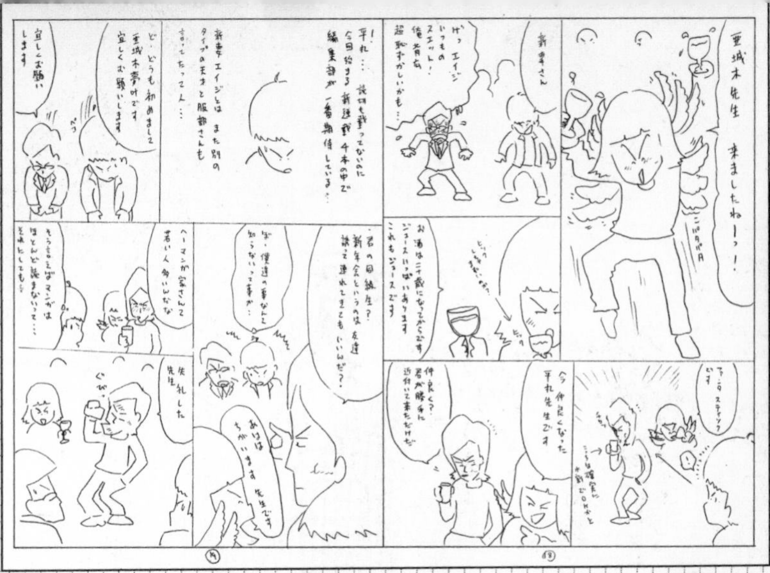
亜城木先生 来ましたねーっ!
新妻さん
げっ エイジ いつものスエット! 俺 背広 超恥ずかしいかも…
お酒は二十歳になってからです ジュースいっぱいあります これもジュースです
今仲良くなった平丸先生です
仲良く? 君が勝手に近付いて来ただけだ
平丸… 読切も載ってないのに 今回始まる新連載4本の中で 編集部が一番期待している…
新妻エイジとはまた別のタイプの天才と服部さんも言ってたっけ…
ど・どうも初めまして 亜城木夢叶です 宜しくお願いします
宜しくお願いします
君の同級生? 新年会というのは友達誘って連れてきてもいいんだ?
ぼ・僕達の事なんて知らないって事か…
あはは ちがいます 先生です
へーマンガ家さんて若い人多いんだな
そう言えばマンガはほとんど読まないって… それにしても…
失礼した先生
ぐびっ

OHBA'S STORYBOARD

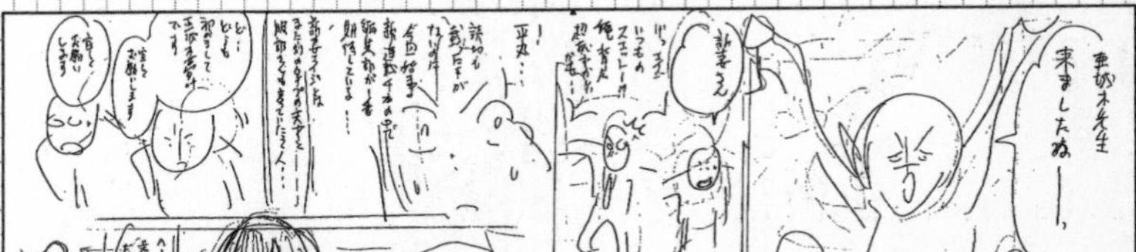

OBATA'S STORYBOARD

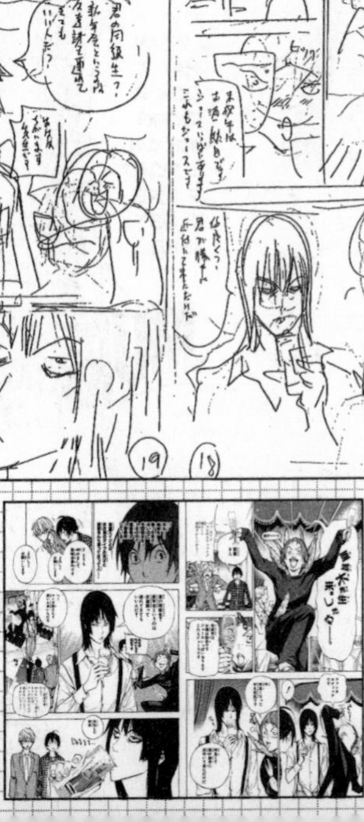

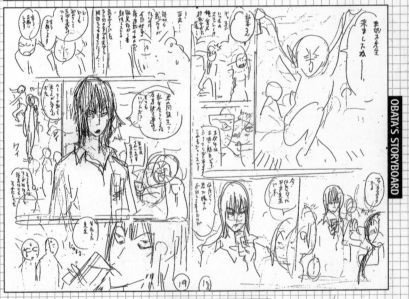

COMPLETE!

※CREATOR STORYBOARDS AND FINISHED PAGES IN JAPANESE

BAKUMAN。 vol.5

"Until the Final Draft Is Complete"

Chapter 36, pp. 44-45

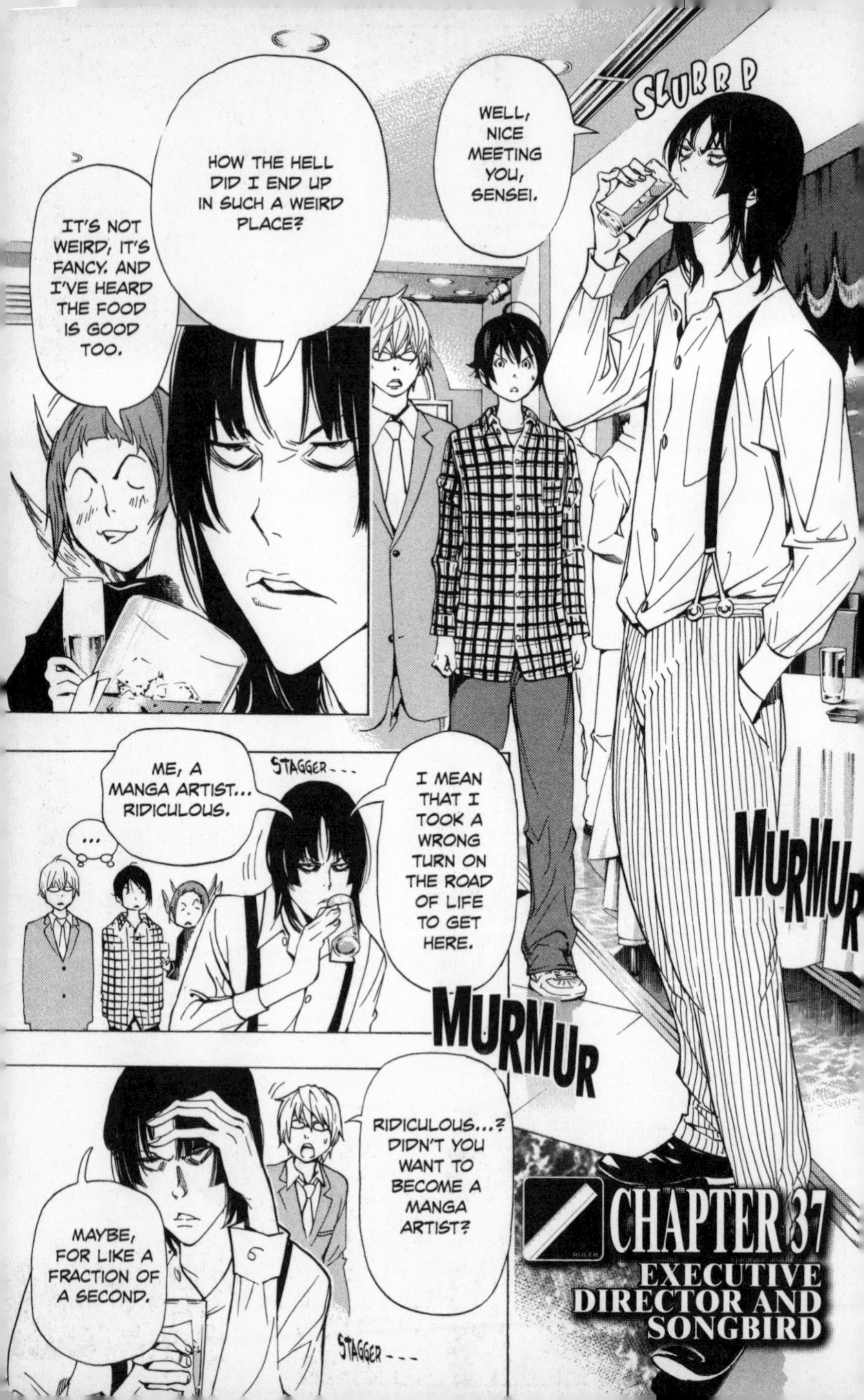
SLURRP
WELL, NICE MEETING YOU, SENSEI.
MURMUR
MURMUR
CHAPTER 37
EXECUTIVE DIRECTOR AND SONGBIRD
HOW THE HELL DID I END UP IN SUCH A WEIRD PLACE?
IT'S NOT WEIRD, IT'S FANCY. AND I'VE HEARD THE FOOD IS GOOD TOO.
STAGGER...
I MEAN THAT I TOOK A WRONG TURN ON THE ROAD OF LIFE TO GET HERE.
ME, A MANGA ARTIST... RIDICULOUS.
...
RIDICULOUS...? DIDN'T YOU WANT TO BECOME A MANGA ARTIST?
MAYBE, FOR LIKE A FRACTION OF A SECOND.
STAGGER...

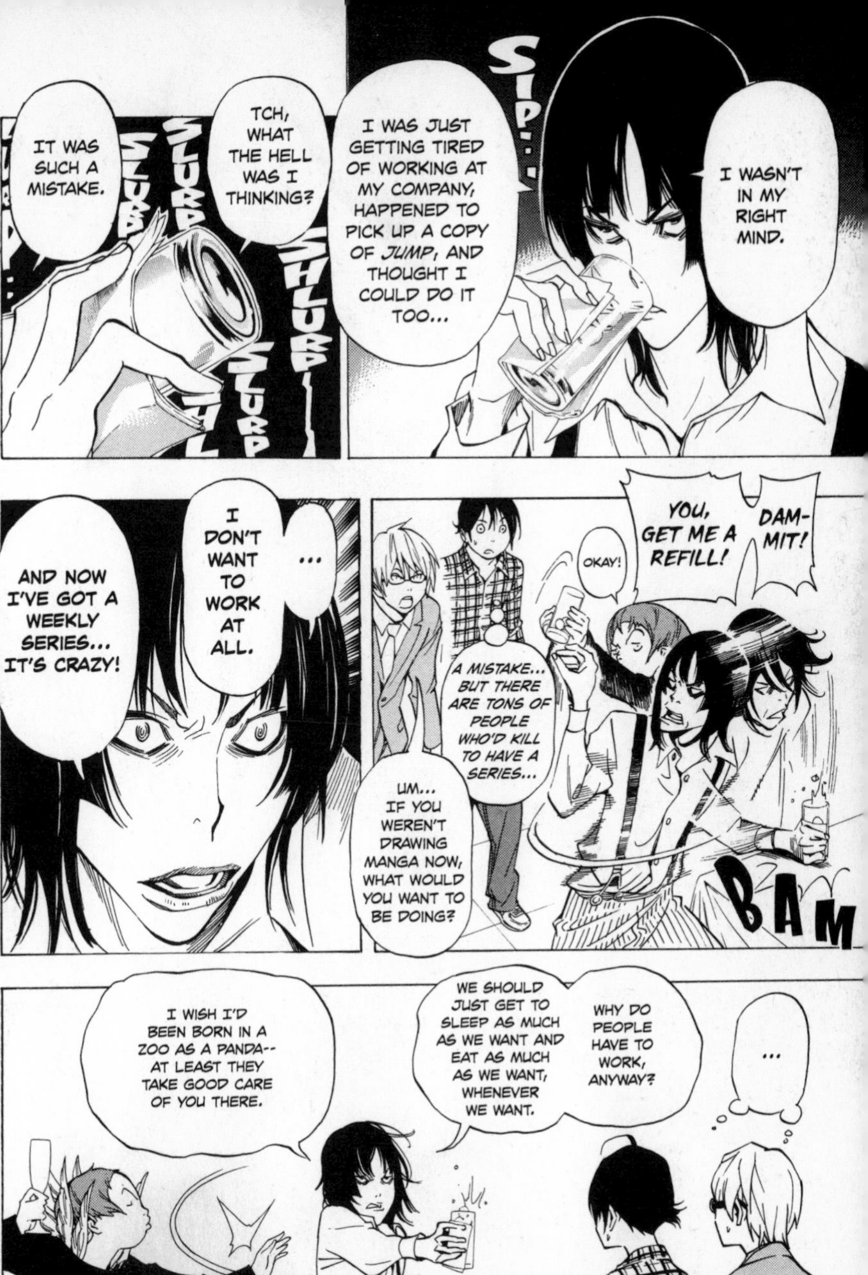
I WASN'T IN MY RIGHT MIND.
SIP...
I WAS JUST GETTING TIRED OF WORKING AT MY COMPANY, HAPPENED TO PICK UP A COPY OF *JUMP*, AND THOUGHT I COULD DO IT TOO...
SHLURP
SLURP
TCH, WHAT THE HELL WAS I THINKING?
SLURP
SLURP
SHL
IT WAS SUCH A MISTAKE.
DAM-MIT!
YOU, GET ME A REFILL!
OKAY!
A MISTAKE... BUT THERE ARE TONS OF PEOPLE WHO'D KILL TO HAVE A SERIES...
UM... IF YOU WEREN'T DRAWING MANGA NOW, WHAT WOULD YOU WANT TO BE DOING?
BAM
...
I DON'T WANT TO WORK AT ALL.
AND NOW I'VE GOT A WEEKLY SERIES... IT'S CRAZY!
...
WHY DO PEOPLE HAVE TO WORK, ANYWAY?
WE SHOULD JUST GET TO SLEEP AS MUCH AS WE WANT AND EAT AS MUCH AS WE WANT, WHENEVER WE WANT.
I WISH I'D BEEN BORN IN A ZOO AS A PANDA--AT LEAST THEY TAKE GOOD CARE OF YOU THERE.

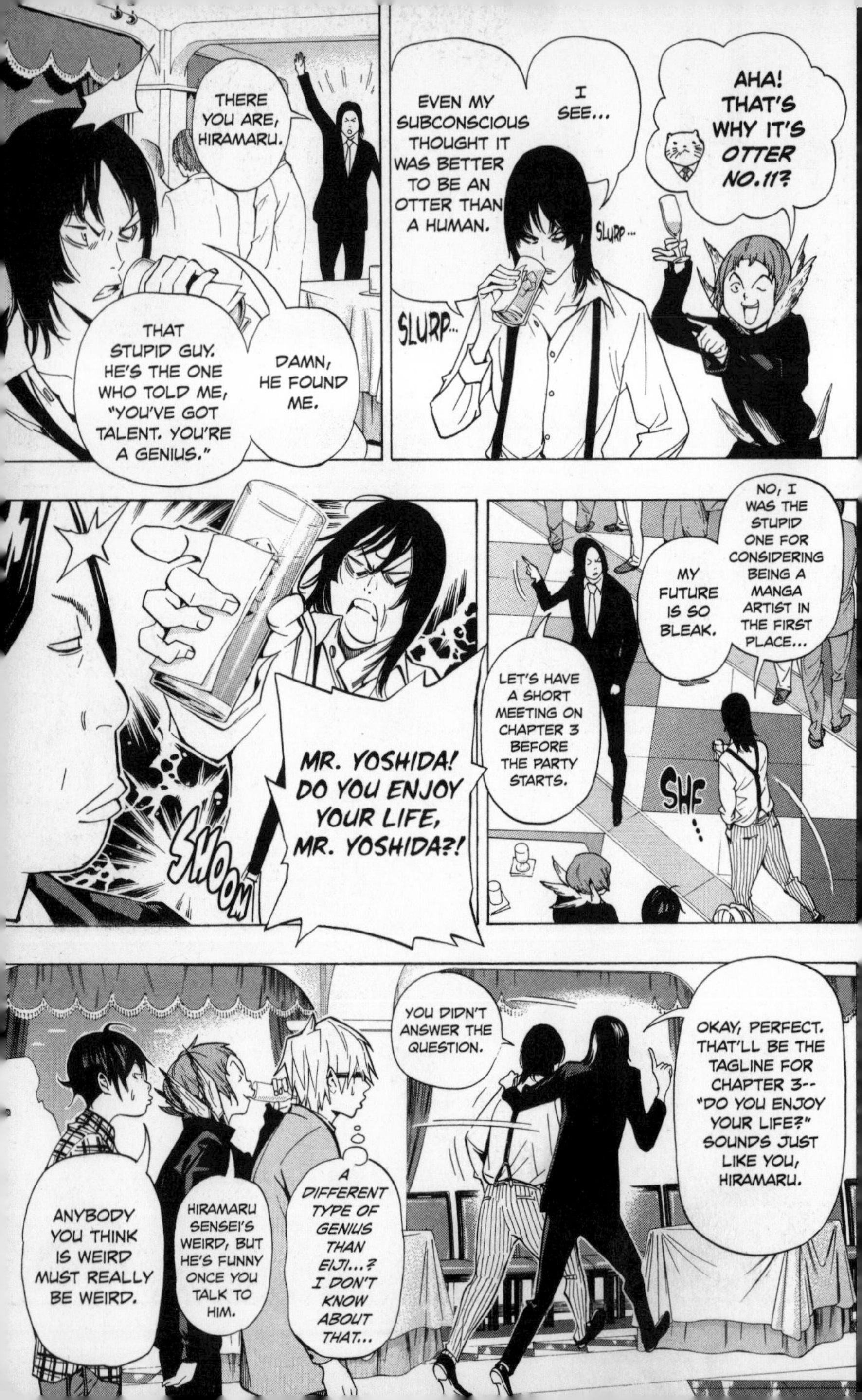
AHA! THAT'S WHY IT'S *OTTER NO.11?*
I SEE...
EVEN MY SUBCONSCIOUS THOUGHT IT WAS BETTER TO BE AN OTTER THAN A HUMAN.
SLURP...
SLURP...
THERE YOU ARE, HIRAMARU.
DAMN, HE FOUND ME.
THAT STUPID GUY. HE'S THE ONE WHO TOLD ME, "YOU'VE GOT TALENT. YOU'RE A GENIUS."
NO, I WAS THE STUPID ONE FOR CONSIDERING BEING A MANGA ARTIST IN THE FIRST PLACE...
MY FUTURE IS SO BLEAK.
LET'S HAVE A SHORT MEETING ON CHAPTER 3 BEFORE THE PARTY STARTS.
SHF...
MR. YOSHIDA! DO YOU ENJOY YOUR LIFE, MR. YOSHIDA?!
SHOOM
OKAY, PERFECT. THAT'LL BE THE TAGLINE FOR CHAPTER 3-- "DO YOU ENJOY YOUR LIFE?" SOUNDS JUST LIKE YOU, HIRAMARU.
YOU DIDN'T ANSWER THE QUESTION.
A DIFFERENT TYPE OF GENIUS THAN EIJI...? I DON'T KNOW ABOUT THAT...
HIRAMARU SENSEI'S WEIRD, BUT HE'S FUNNY ONCE YOU TALK TO HIM.
ANYBODY YOU THINK IS WEIRD MUST REALLY BE WEIRD.

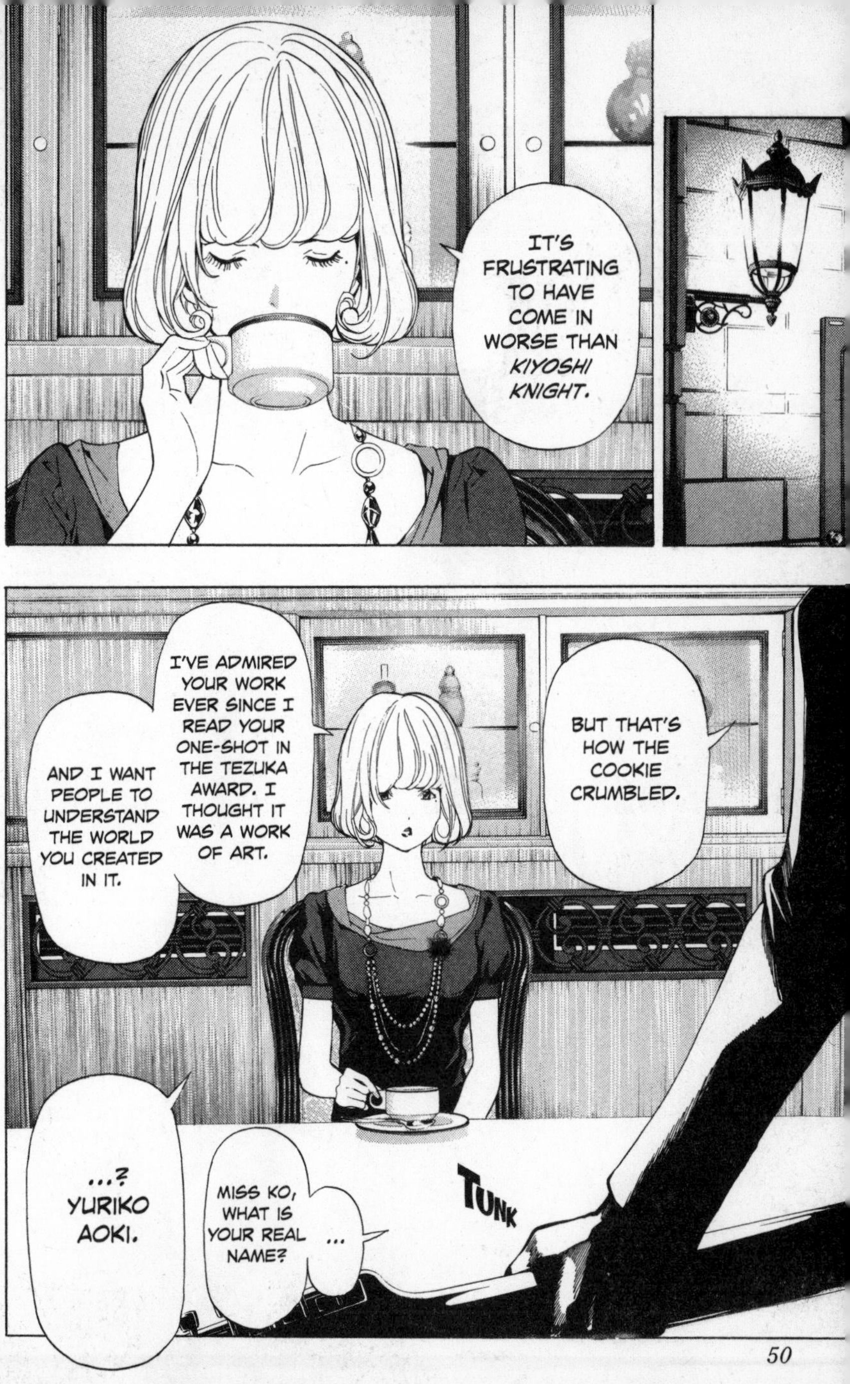
IT'S FRUSTRATING TO HAVE COME IN WORSE THAN *KIYOSHI KNIGHT*.
BUT THAT'S HOW THE COOKIE CRUMBLED.
I'VE ADMIRED YOUR WORK EVER SINCE I READ YOUR ONE-SHOT IN THE TEZUKA AWARD. I THOUGHT IT WAS A WORK OF ART.
AND I WANT PEOPLE TO UNDERSTAND THE WORLD YOU CREATED IN IT.
TUNK
...
MISS KO, WHAT IS YOUR REAL NAME?
...? YURIKO AOKI.

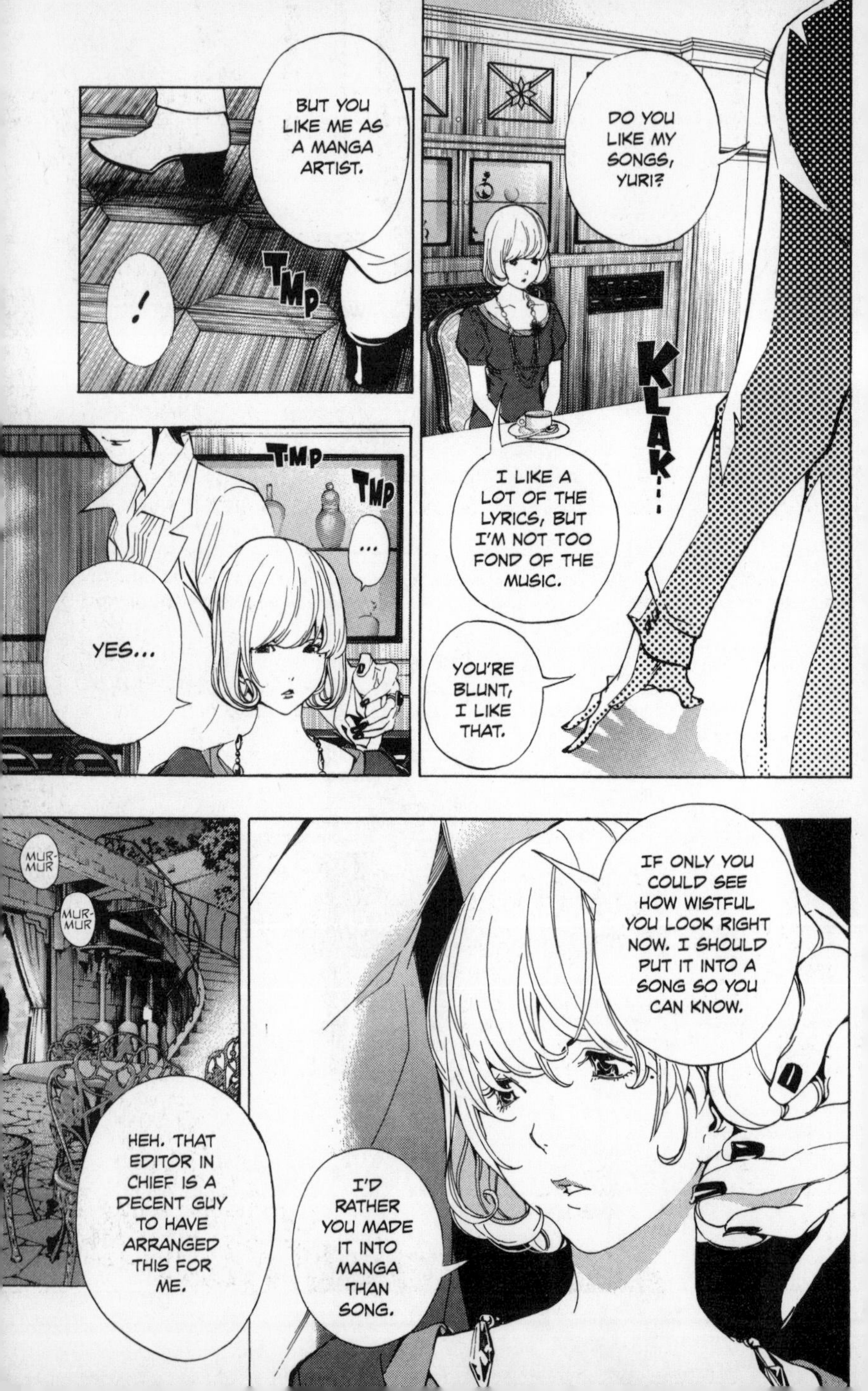
DO YOU LIKE MY SONGS, YURI?
KLAK...
I LIKE A LOT OF THE LYRICS, BUT I'M NOT TOO FOND OF THE MUSIC.
YOU'RE BLUNT, I LIKE THAT.
BUT YOU LIKE ME AS A MANGA ARTIST.
TMP
!
TMP
TMP
...
YES...
IF ONLY YOU COULD SEE HOW WISTFUL YOU LOOK RIGHT NOW. I SHOULD PUT IT INTO A SONG SO YOU CAN KNOW.
I'D RATHER YOU MADE IT INTO MANGA THAN SONG.
MUR-MUR
MUR-MUR
HEH. THAT EDITOR IN CHIEF IS A DECENT GUY TO HAVE ARRANGED THIS FOR ME.

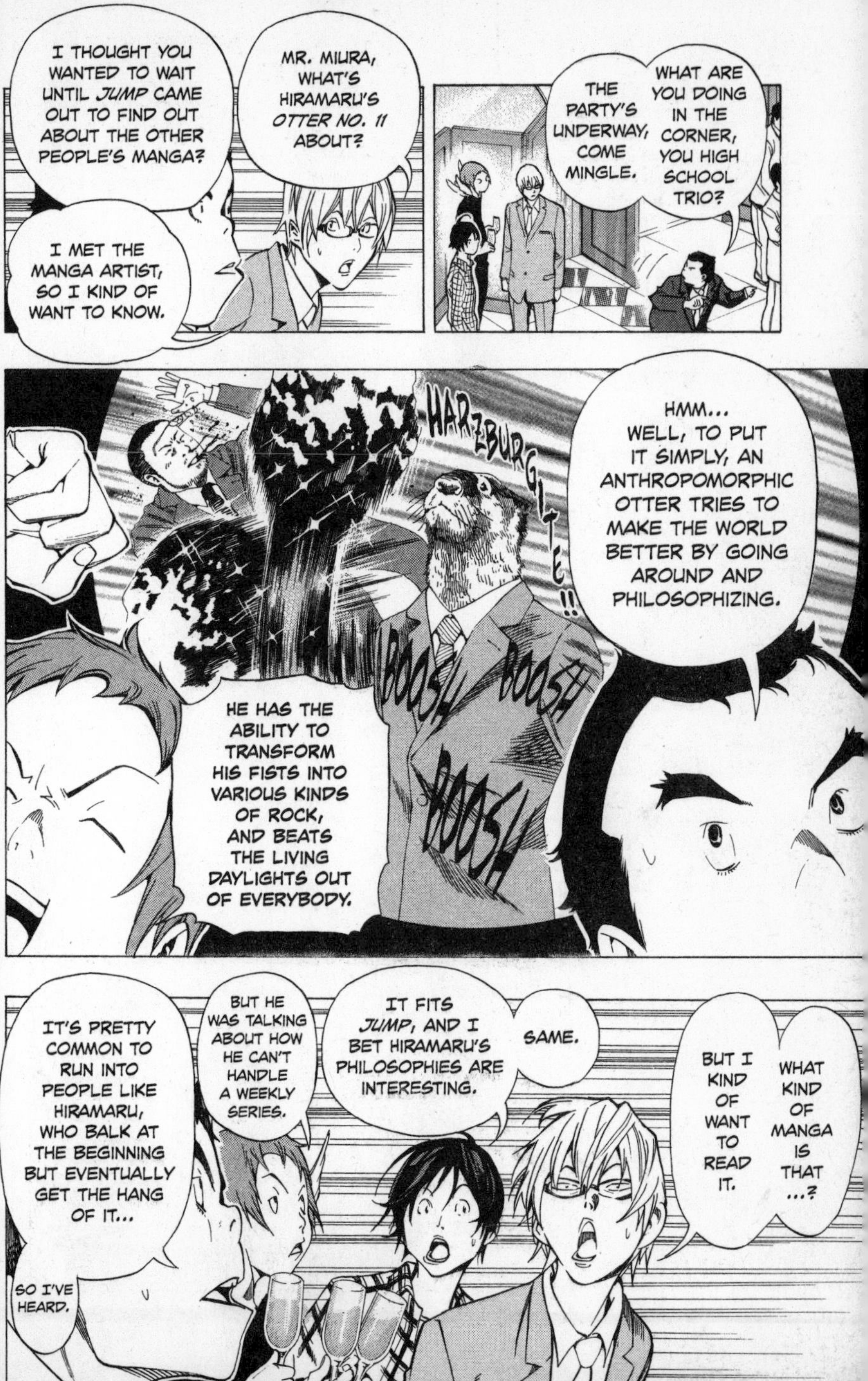
WHAT ARE YOU DOING IN THE CORNER, YOU HIGH SCHOOL TRIO?
THE PARTY'S UNDERWAY, COME MINGLE.
MR. MIURA, WHAT'S HIRAMARU'S OTTER NO. 11 ABOUT?
I THOUGHT YOU WANTED TO WAIT UNTIL JUMP CAME OUT TO FIND OUT ABOUT THE OTHER PEOPLE'S MANGA?
I MET THE MANGA ARTIST, SO I KIND OF WANT TO KNOW.
HMM... WELL, TO PUT IT SIMPLY, AN ANTHROPOMORPHIC OTTER TRIES TO MAKE THE WORLD BETTER BY GOING AROUND AND PHILOSOPHIZING.
HARZBURGITE!!
BOOSH
BOOSH
BOOSH
HE HAS THE ABILITY TO TRANSFORM HIS FISTS INTO VARIOUS KINDS OF ROCK, AND BEATS THE LIVING DAYLIGHTS OUT OF EVERYBODY.
WHAT KIND OF MANGA IS THAT ...?
BUT I KIND OF WANT TO READ IT.
SAME.
IT FITS JUMP, AND I BET HIRAMARU'S PHILOSOPHIES ARE INTERESTING.
BUT HE WAS TALKING ABOUT HOW HE CAN'T HANDLE A WEEKLY SERIES.
IT'S PRETTY COMMON TO RUN INTO PEOPLE LIKE HIRAMARU, WHO BALK AT THE BEGINNING BUT EVENTUALLY GET THE HANG OF IT...
SO I'VE HEARD.

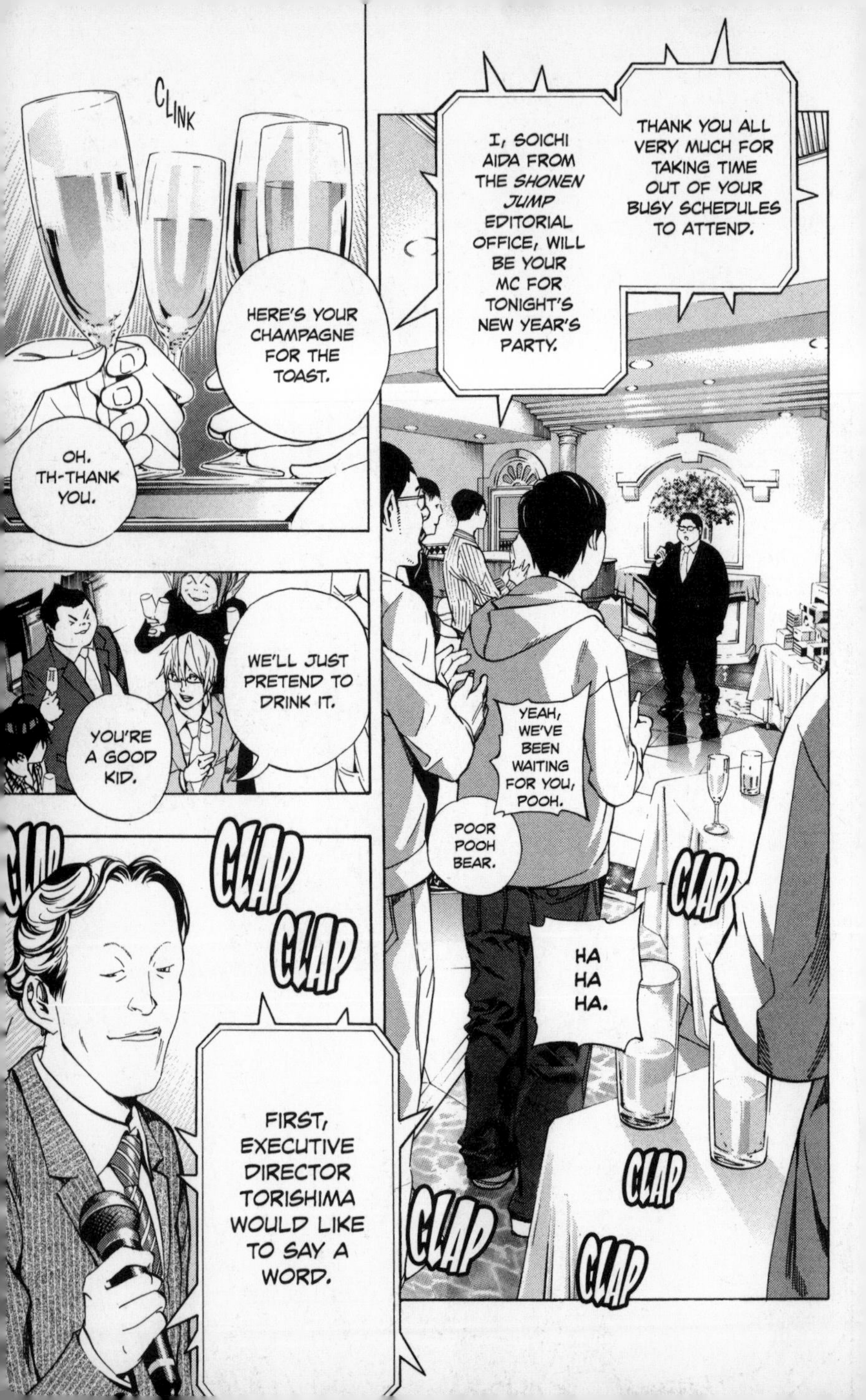
THANK YOU ALL VERY MUCH FOR TAKING TIME OUT OF YOUR BUSY SCHEDULES TO ATTEND.
I, SOICHI AIDA FROM THE *SHONEN JUMP* EDITORIAL OFFICE, WILL BE YOUR MC FOR TONIGHT'S NEW YEAR'S PARTY.
YEAH, WE'VE BEEN WAITING FOR YOU, POOH.
POOR POOH BEAR.
CLAP
HA HA HA.
CLAP
CLAP
CLAP
CLINK
HERE'S YOUR CHAMPAGNE FOR THE TOAST.
OH. TH-THANK YOU.
WE'LL JUST PRETEND TO DRINK IT.
YOU'RE A GOOD KID.
CLAP
CLAP
FIRST, EXECUTIVE DIRECTOR TORISHIMA WOULD LIKE TO SAY A WORD.

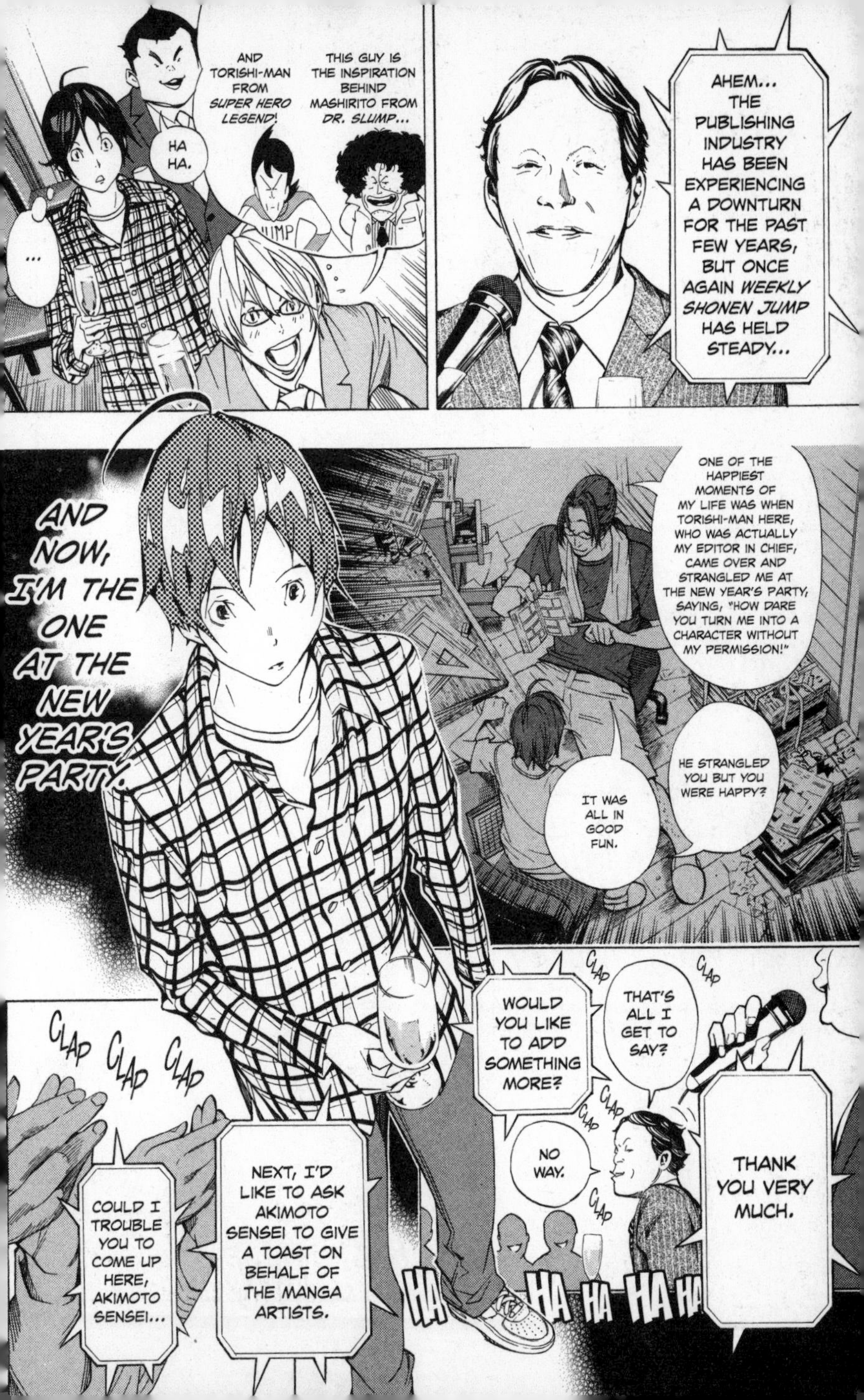
AHEM... THE PUBLISHING INDUSTRY HAS BEEN EXPERIENCING A DOWNTURN FOR THE PAST FEW YEARS, BUT ONCE AGAIN WEEKLY SHONEN JUMP HAS HELD STEADY...
THIS GUY IS THE INSPIRATION BEHIND MASHIRITO FROM DR. SLUMP...
AND TORISHI-MAN FROM SUPER HERO LEGEND!
HA HA.
...
ONE OF THE HAPPIEST MOMENTS OF MY LIFE WAS WHEN TORISHI-MAN HERE, WHO WAS ACTUALLY MY EDITOR IN CHIEF, CAME OVER AND STRANGLED ME AT THE NEW YEAR'S PARTY, SAYING, "HOW DARE YOU TURN ME INTO A CHARACTER WITHOUT MY PERMISSION!"
HE STRANGLED YOU BUT YOU WERE HAPPY?
IT WAS ALL IN GOOD FUN.
AND NOW, I'M THE ONE AT THE NEW YEAR'S PARTY.
THANK YOU VERY MUCH.
CLAP
CLAP
THAT'S ALL I GET TO SAY?
WOULD YOU LIKE TO ADD SOMETHING MORE?
CLAP
CLAP
NO WAY.
CLAP
HA HA HA HA HA
NEXT, I'D LIKE TO ASK AKIMOTO SENSEI TO GIVE A TOAST ON BEHALF OF THE MANGA ARTISTS.
COULD I TROUBLE YOU TO COME UP HERE, AKIMOTO SENSEI...
CLAP CLAP CLAP

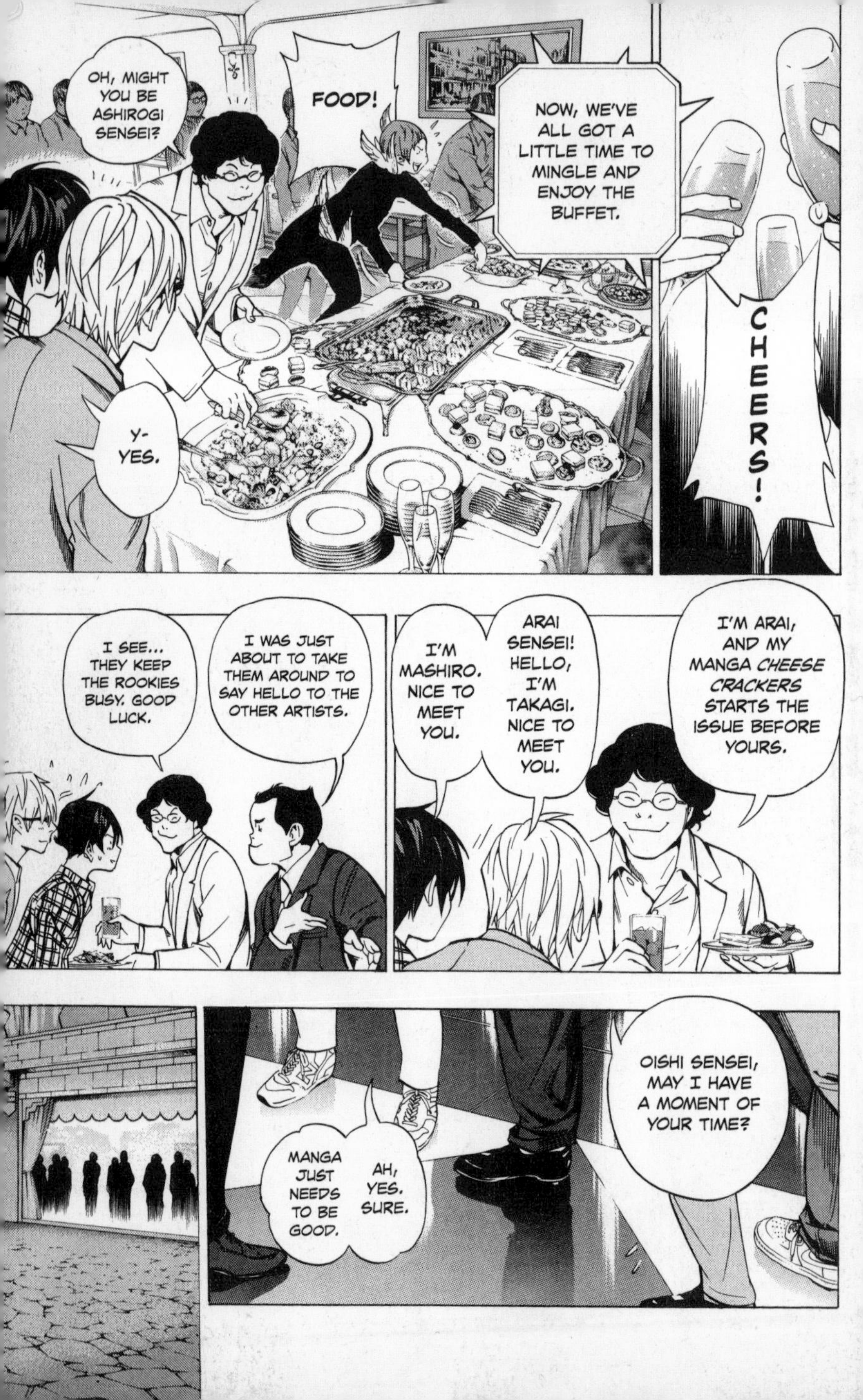
CHEERS!
NOW, WE'VE ALL GOT A LITTLE TIME TO MINGLE AND ENJOY THE BUFFET.
FOOD!
OH, MIGHT YOU BE ASHIROGI SENSEI?
Y- YES.
I'M ARAI, AND MY MANGA *CHEESE CRACKERS* STARTS THE ISSUE BEFORE YOURS.
ARAI SENSEI! HELLO, I'M TAKAGI. NICE TO MEET YOU.
I'M MASHIRO. NICE TO MEET YOU.
I WAS JUST ABOUT TO TAKE THEM AROUND TO SAY HELLO TO THE OTHER ARTISTS.
I SEE... THEY KEEP THE ROOKIES BUSY. GOOD LUCK.
OISHI SENSEI, MAY I HAVE A MOMENT OF YOUR TIME?
AH, YES. SURE.
MANGA JUST NEEDS TO BE GOOD.

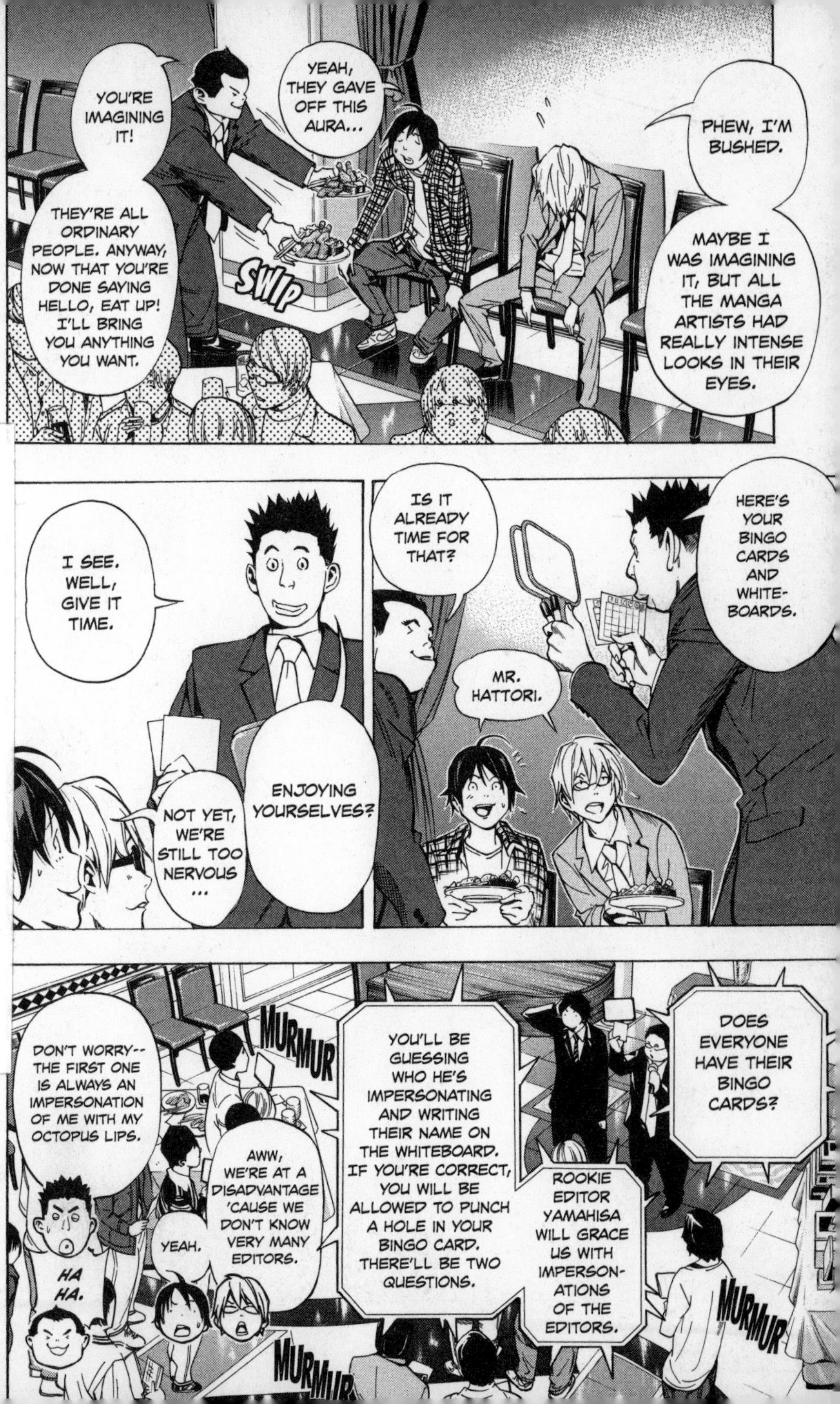
PHEW, I'M BUSHED.
MAYBE I WAS IMAGINING IT, BUT ALL THE MANGA ARTISTS HAD REALLY INTENSE LOOKS IN THEIR EYES.
YEAH, THEY GAVE OFF THIS AURA...
YOU'RE IMAGINING IT!
THEY'RE ALL ORDINARY PEOPLE. ANYWAY, NOW THAT YOU'RE DONE SAYING HELLO, EAT UP! I'LL BRING YOU ANYTHING YOU WANT.
SWIP
HERE'S YOUR BINGO CARDS AND WHITE-BOARDS.
IS IT ALREADY TIME FOR THAT?
MR. HATTORI.
ENJOYING YOURSELVES?
NOT YET, WE'RE STILL TOO NERVOUS...
I SEE. WELL, GIVE IT TIME.
DOES EVERYONE HAVE THEIR BINGO CARDS?
ROOKIE EDITOR YAMAHISA WILL GRACE US WITH IMPERSON-ATIONS OF THE EDITORS.
MURMUR
YOU'LL BE GUESSING WHO HE'S IMPERSONATING AND WRITING THEIR NAME ON THE WHITEBOARD. IF YOU'RE CORRECT, YOU WILL BE ALLOWED TO PUNCH A HOLE IN YOUR BINGO CARD. THERE'LL BE TWO QUESTIONS.
MURMUR
DON'T WORRY-- THE FIRST ONE IS ALWAYS AN IMPERSONATION OF ME WITH MY OCTOPUS LIPS.
AWW, WE'RE AT A DISADVANTAGE 'CAUSE WE DON'T KNOW VERY MANY EDITORS.
YEAH.
HA HA.
MURMUR

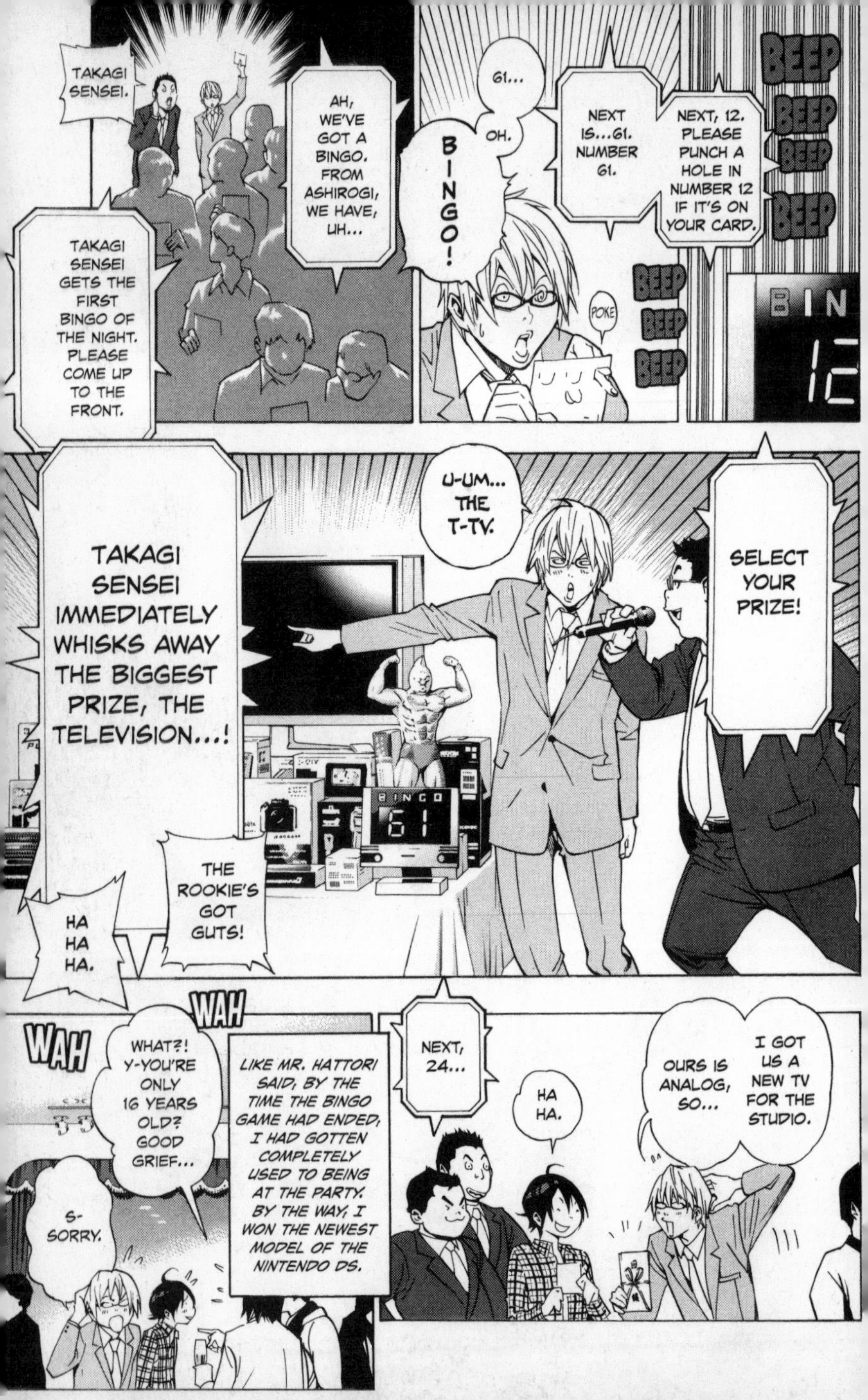
BEEP
BEEP
BEEP
BEEP
NEXT, 12. PLEASE PUNCH A HOLE IN NUMBER 12 IF IT'S ON YOUR CARD.
NEXT IS...61. NUMBER 61.
61...
OH.
BINGO!
BEEP
BEEP
BEEP
POKE
BIN
12
AH, WE'VE GOT A BINGO. FROM ASHIROGI, WE HAVE, UH...
TAKAGI SENSEI.
TAKAGI SENSEI GETS THE FIRST BINGO OF THE NIGHT. PLEASE COME UP TO THE FRONT.
SELECT YOUR PRIZE!
U-UM... THE T-TV.
TAKAGI SENSEI IMMEDIATELY WHISKS AWAY THE BIGGEST PRIZE, THE TELEVISION...!
BINGO
61
THE ROOKIE'S GOT GUTS!
HA HA HA.
I GOT US A NEW TV FOR THE STUDIO.
OURS IS ANALOG, SO...
HA HA.
NEXT, 24...
LIKE MR. HATTORI SAID, BY THE TIME THE BINGO GAME HAD ENDED, I HAD GOTTEN COMPLETELY USED TO BEING AT THE PARTY. BY THE WAY, I WON THE NEWEST MODEL OF THE NINTENDO DS.
WAH
WAH
WHAT?! Y-YOU'RE ONLY 16 YEARS OLD? GOOD GRIEF...
S-SORRY.

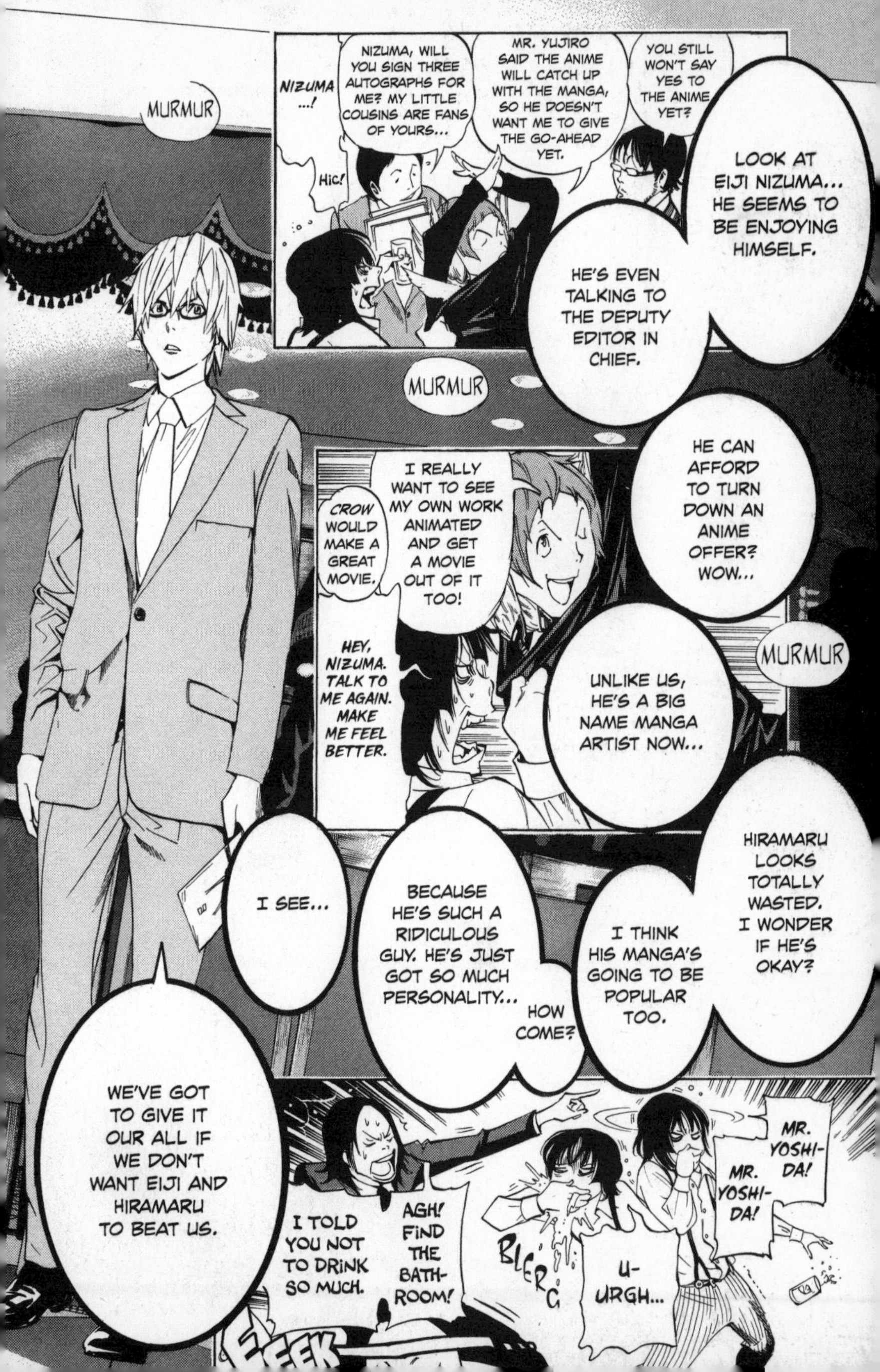
YOU STILL WON'T SAY YES TO THE ANIME YET?
MR. YUJIRO SAID THE ANIME WILL CATCH UP WITH THE MANGA, SO HE DOESN'T WANT ME TO GIVE THE GO-AHEAD YET.
NIZUMA, WILL YOU SIGN THREE AUTOGRAPHS FOR ME? MY LITTLE COUSINS ARE FANS OF YOURS...
NIZUMA ...!
Hic!
MURMUR
LOOK AT EIJI NIZUMA... HE SEEMS TO BE ENJOYING HIMSELF.
HE'S EVEN TALKING TO THE DEPUTY EDITOR IN CHIEF.
MURMUR
HE CAN AFFORD TO TURN DOWN AN ANIME OFFER? WOW...
I REALLY WANT TO SEE MY OWN WORK ANIMATED AND GET A MOVIE OUT OF IT TOO!
CROW WOULD MAKE A GREAT MOVIE.
HEY, NIZUMA. TALK TO ME AGAIN. MAKE ME FEEL BETTER.
MURMUR
UNLIKE US, HE'S A BIG NAME MANGA ARTIST NOW...
HIRAMARU LOOKS TOTALLY WASTED. I WONDER IF HE'S OKAY?
I THINK HIS MANGA'S GOING TO BE POPULAR TOO.
HOW COME?
BECAUSE HE'S SUCH A RIDICULOUS GUY. HE'S JUST GOT SO MUCH PERSONALITY...
I SEE...
WE'VE GOT TO GIVE IT OUR ALL IF WE DON'T WANT EIJI AND HIRAMARU TO BEAT US.
MR. YOSHIDA!
MR. YOSHIDA!
U-URGH...
BLERG
AGH! FIND THE BATHROOM!
I TOLD YOU NOT TO DRINK SO MUCH.
EEEK

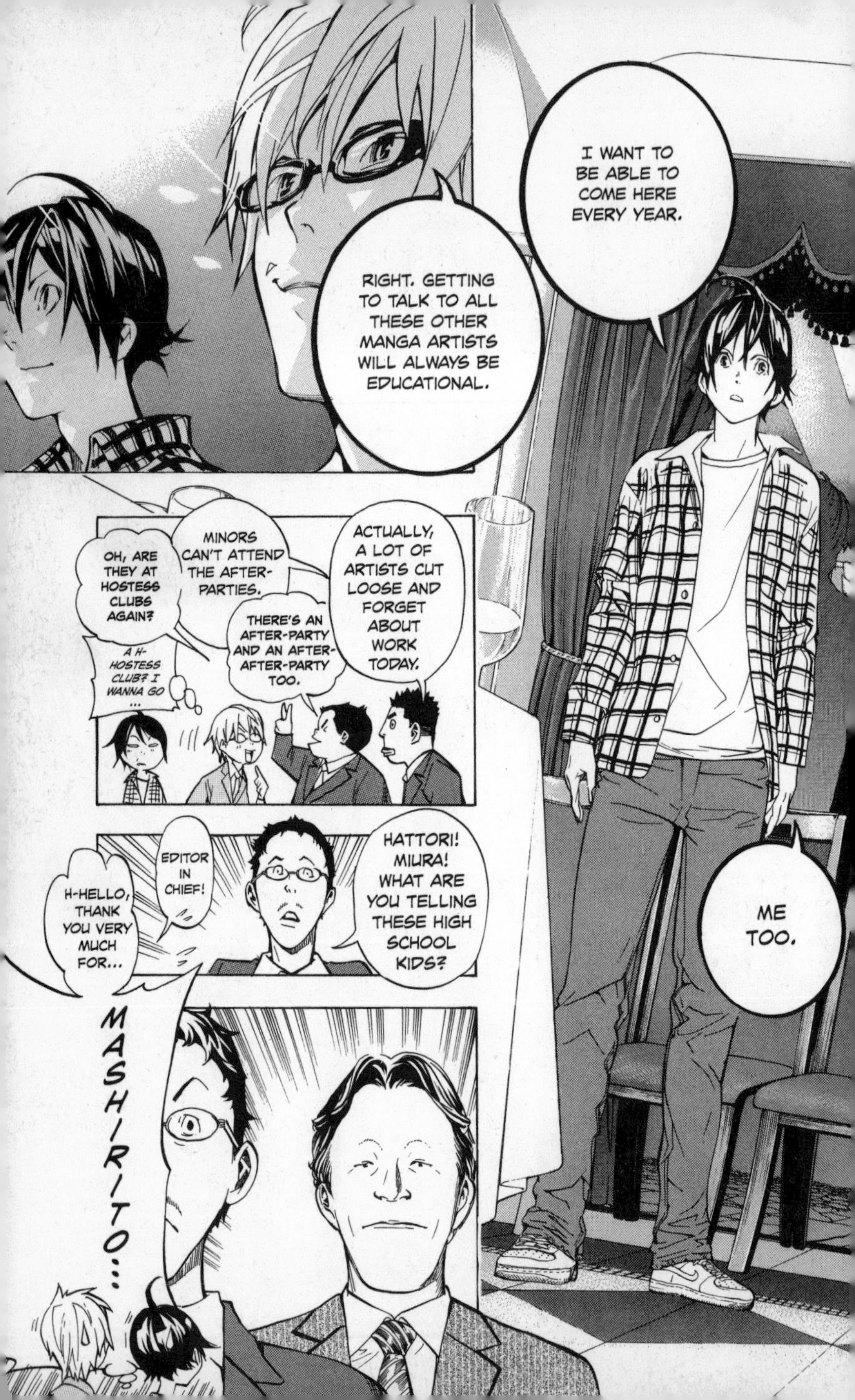

I WANT TO BE ABLE TO COME HERE EVERY YEAR.
ME TOO.
RIGHT. GETTING TO TALK TO ALL THESE OTHER MANGA ARTISTS WILL ALWAYS BE EDUCATIONAL.
ACTUALLY, A LOT OF ARTISTS CUT LOOSE AND FORGET ABOUT WORK TODAY.
THERE'S AN AFTER-PARTY AND AN AFTER-AFTER-PARTY TOO.
MINORS CAN'T ATTEND THE AFTER-PARTIES.
OH, ARE THEY AT HOSTESS CLUBS AGAIN?
A H-HOSTESS CLUB? I WANNA GO ...
HATTORI! MIURA! WHAT ARE YOU TELLING THESE HIGH SCHOOL KIDS?
EDITOR IN CHIEF!
H-HELLO, THANK YOU VERY MUCH FOR...
MASHIRITO...

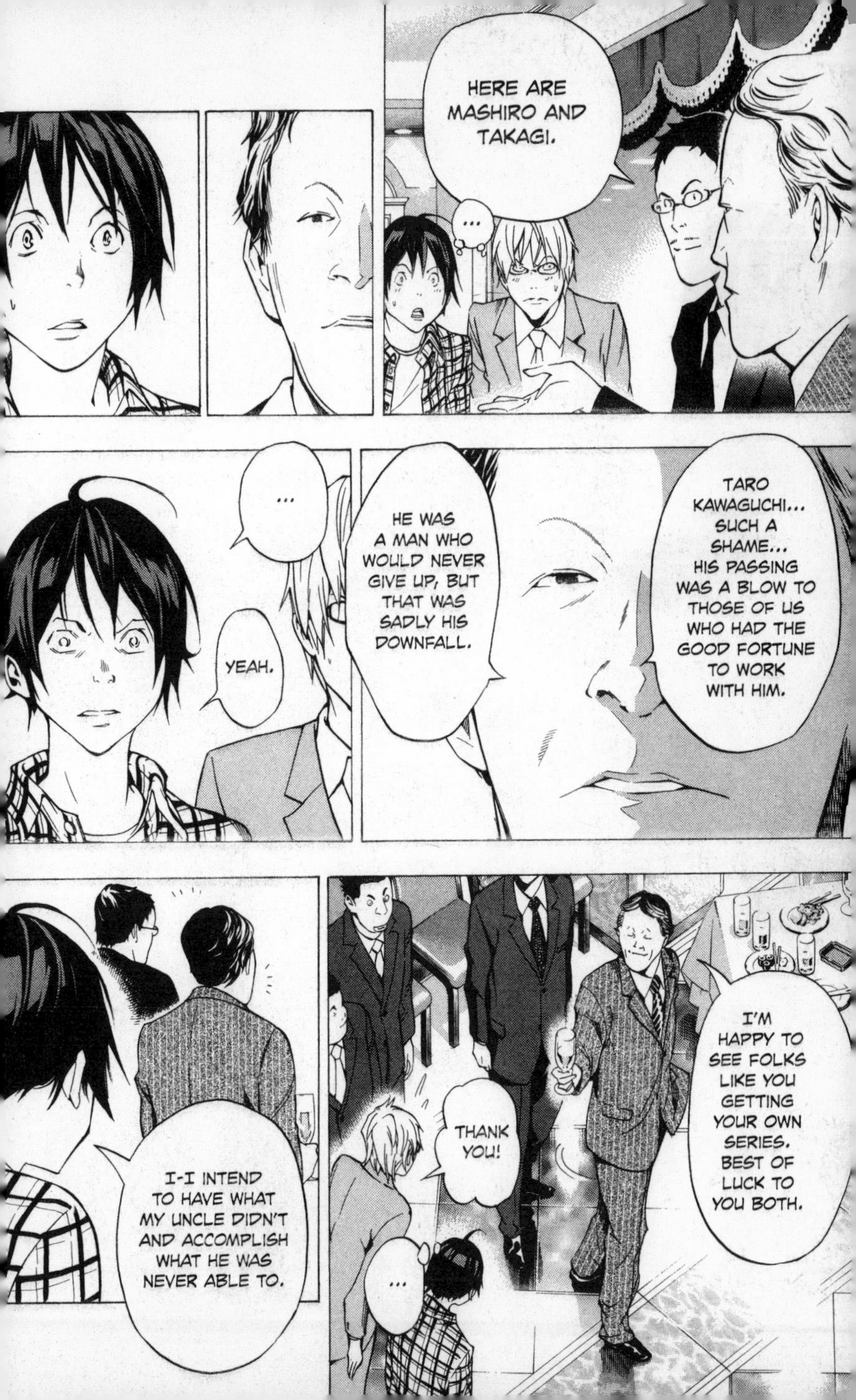
HERE ARE MASHIRO AND TAKAGI.
...
TARO KAWAGUCHI... SUCH A SHAME... HIS PASSING WAS A BLOW TO THOSE OF US WHO HAD THE GOOD FORTUNE TO WORK WITH HIM.
HE WAS A MAN WHO WOULD NEVER GIVE UP, BUT THAT WAS SADLY HIS DOWNFALL.
...
YEAH.
I'M HAPPY TO SEE FOLKS LIKE YOU GETTING YOUR OWN SERIES. BEST OF LUCK TO YOU BOTH.
THANK YOU!
...
I-I INTEND TO HAVE WHAT MY UNCLE DIDN'T AND ACCOMPLISH WHAT HE WAS NEVER ABLE TO.

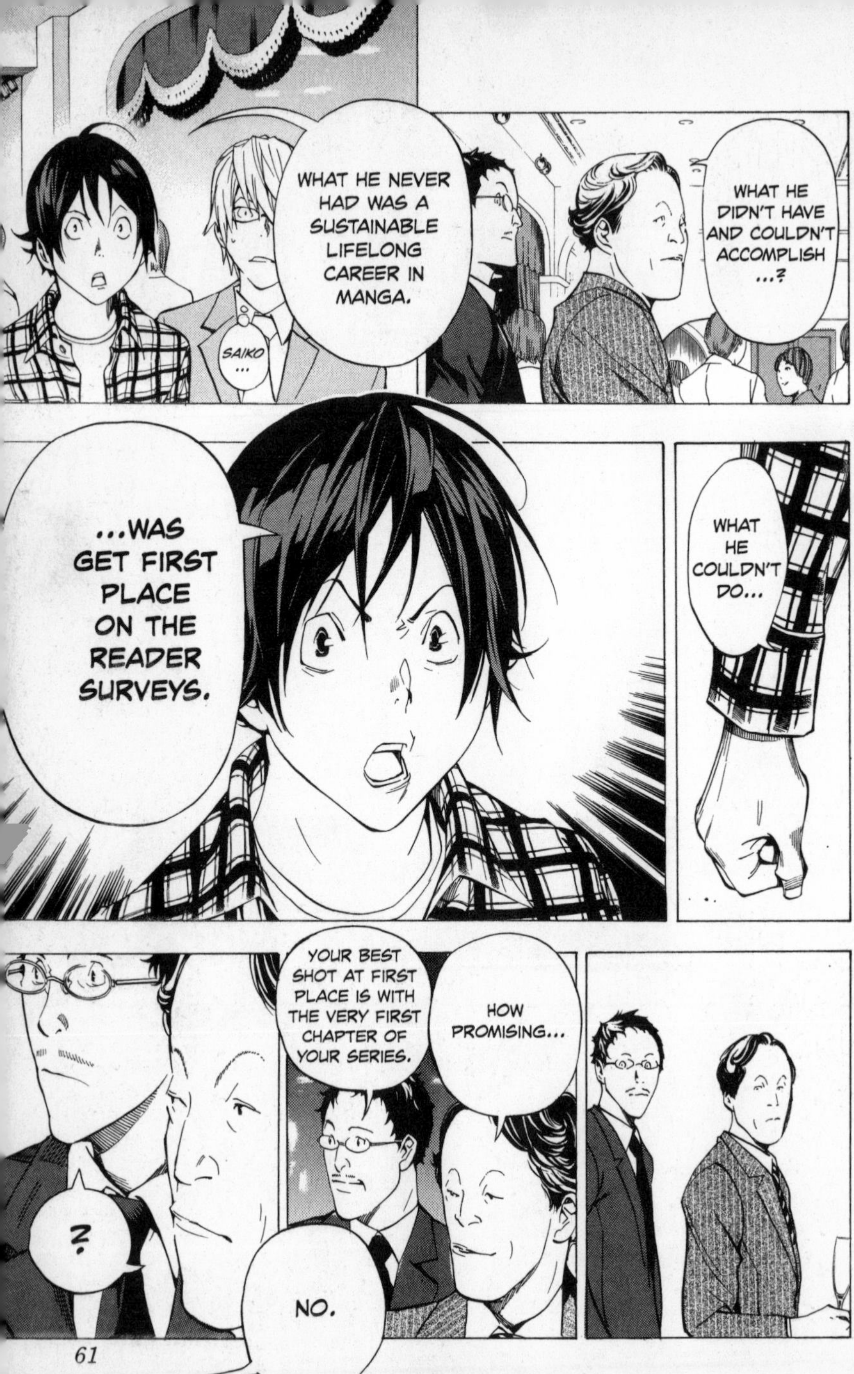
WHAT HE DIDN'T HAVE AND COULDN'T ACCOMPLISH ...?
WHAT HE NEVER HAD WAS A SUSTAINABLE LIFELONG CAREER IN MANGA.
SAIKO ...
WHAT HE COULDN'T DO...
...WAS GET FIRST PLACE ON THE READER SURVEYS.
HOW PROMISING...
YOUR BEST SHOT AT FIRST PLACE IS WITH THE VERY FIRST CHAPTER OF YOUR SERIES.
?
NO.

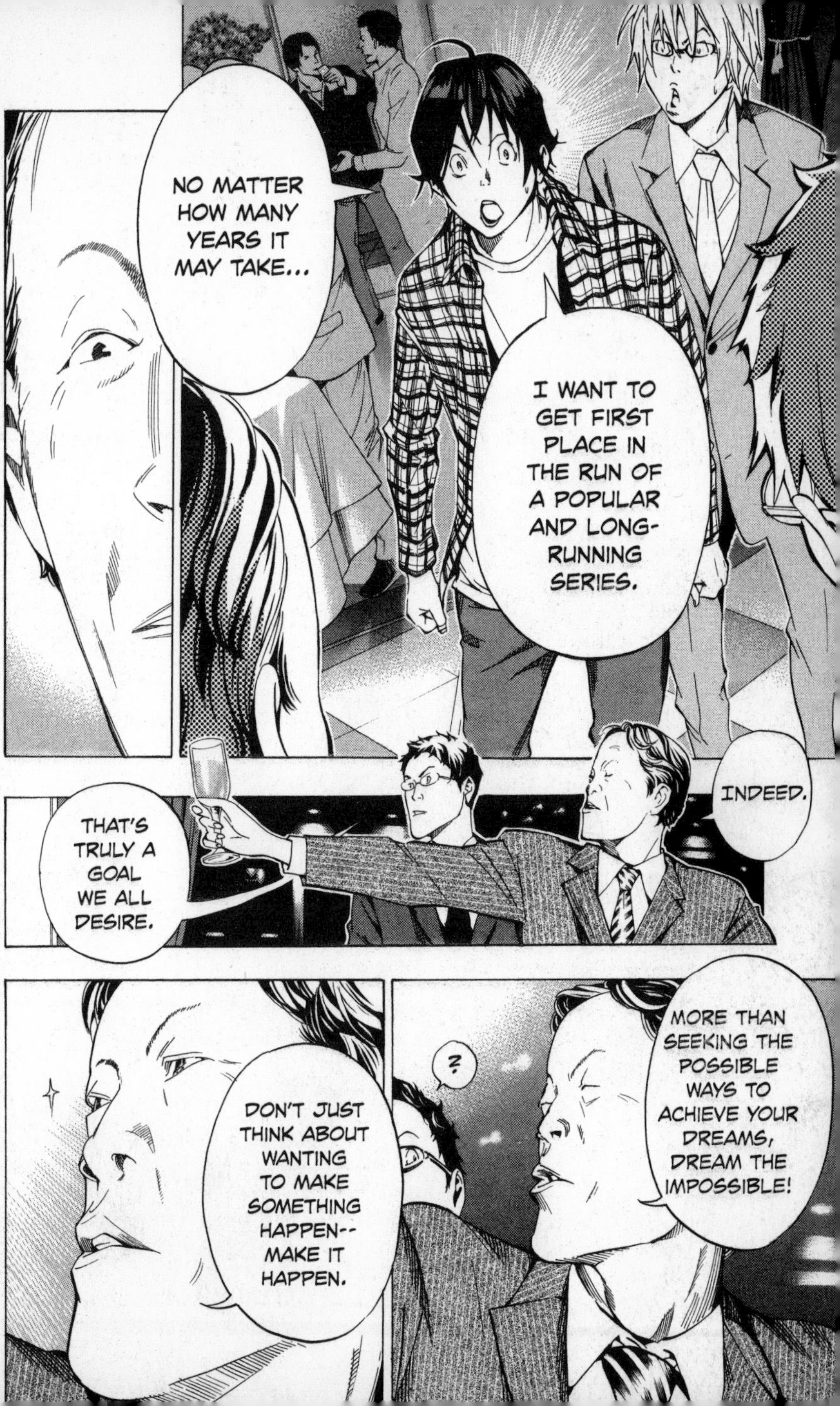
NO MATTER HOW MANY YEARS IT MAY TAKE...
I WANT TO GET FIRST PLACE IN THE RUN OF A POPULAR AND LONG-RUNNING SERIES.
INDEED.
THAT'S TRULY A GOAL WE ALL DESIRE.
MORE THAN SEEKING THE POSSIBLE WAYS TO ACHIEVE YOUR DREAMS, DREAM THE IMPOSSIBLE!
?
DON'T JUST THINK ABOUT WANTING TO MAKE SOMETHING HAPPEN-- MAKE IT HAPPEN.

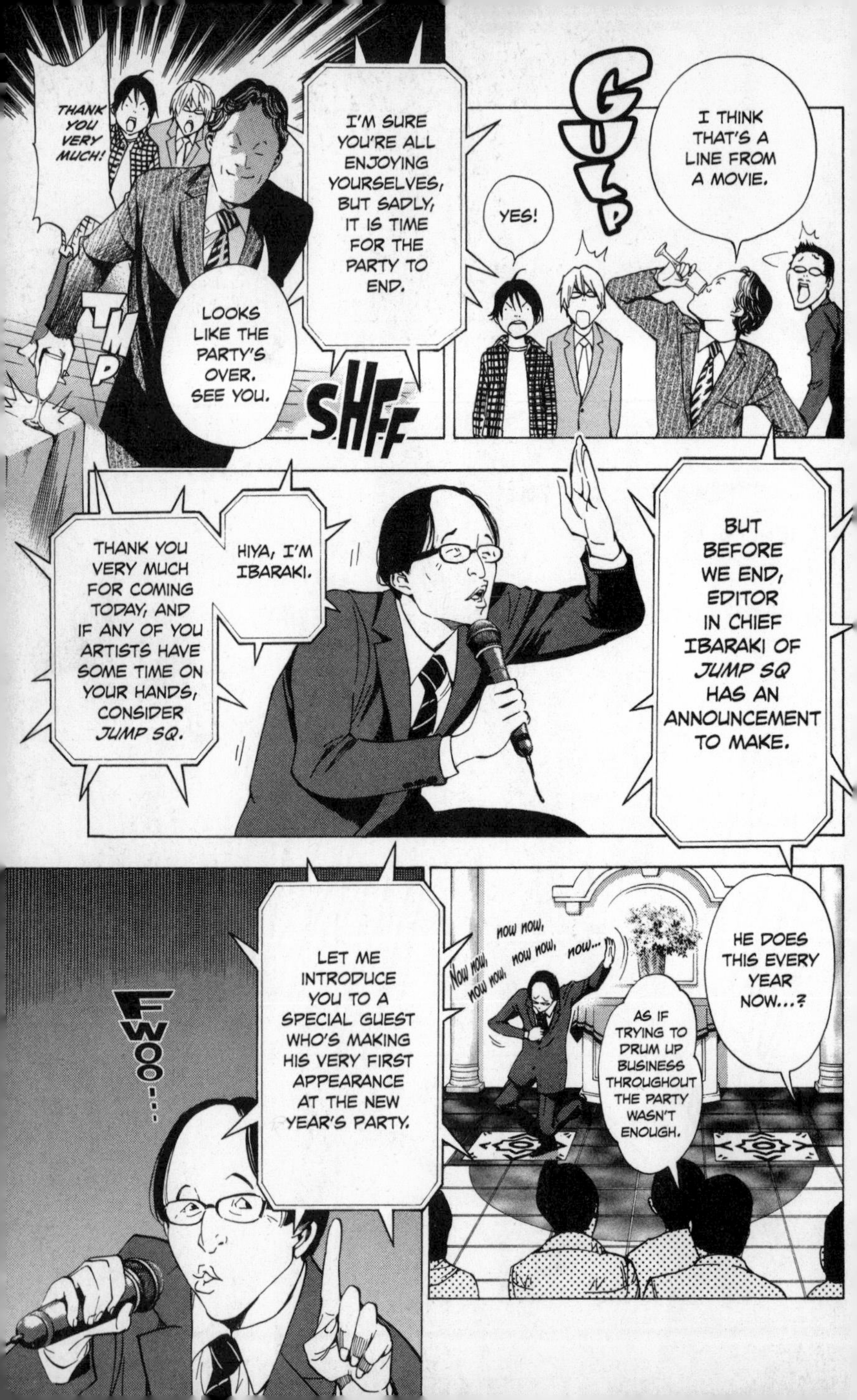
I THINK THAT'S A LINE FROM A MOVIE.
GULP
YES!
I'M SURE YOU'RE ALL ENJOYING YOURSELVES, BUT SADLY, IT IS TIME FOR THE PARTY TO END.
THANK YOU VERY MUCH!
LOOKS LIKE THE PARTY'S OVER. SEE YOU.
SHFF
TMP
BUT BEFORE WE END, EDITOR IN CHIEF IBARAKI OF *JUMP SQ* HAS AN ANNOUNCEMENT TO MAKE.
HIYA, I'M IBARAKI.
THANK YOU VERY MUCH FOR COMING TODAY, AND IF ANY OF YOU ARTISTS HAVE SOME TIME ON YOUR HANDS, CONSIDER *JUMP SQ*.
HE DOES THIS EVERY YEAR NOW...?
AS IF TRYING TO DRUM UP BUSINESS THROUGHOUT THE PARTY WASN'T ENOUGH.
now now, now now, now now, now...
Now now, now now,
LET ME INTRODUCE YOU TO A SPECIAL GUEST WHO'S MAKING HIS VERY FIRST APPEARANCE AT THE NEW YEAR'S PARTY.
FWOO...

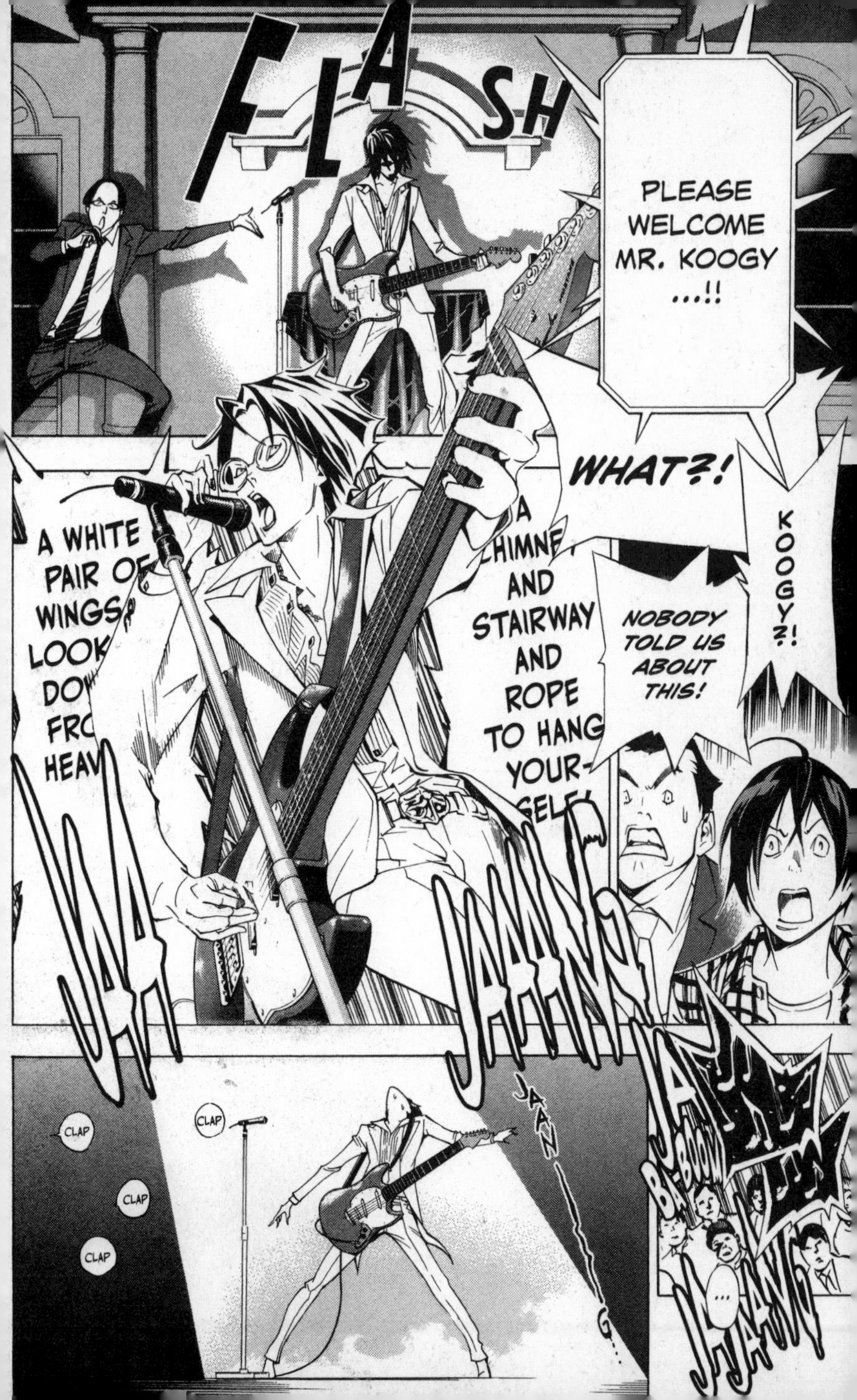
FLASH
PLEASE WELCOME MR. KOOGY ...!!
KOOGY?!
WHAT?!
NOBODY TOLD US ABOUT THIS!
A HIMNE AND STAIRWAY AND ROPE TO HANG YOUR-SELF
A WHITE PAIR OF WINGS LOOK DOW FRO HEAV
JAAANG
BA-BOOM
JAAN...G...
CLAP
CLAP
CLAP
CLAP
...

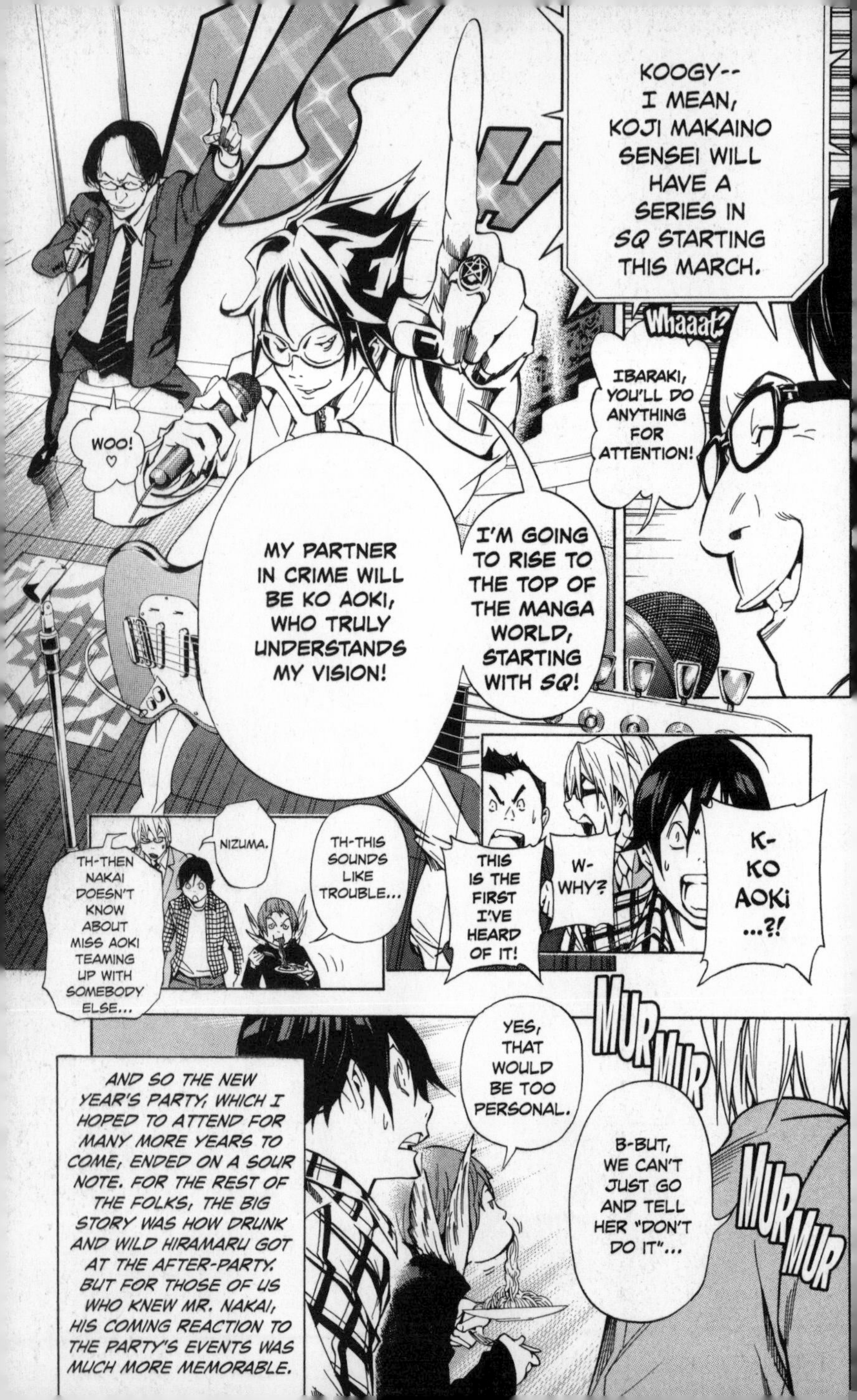
KOOGY-- I MEAN, KOJI MAKAINO SENSEI WILL HAVE A SERIES IN SQ STARTING THIS MARCH.
Whaaat?
IBARAKI, YOU'LL DO ANYTHING FOR ATTENTION!
I'M GOING TO RISE TO THE TOP OF THE MANGA WORLD, STARTING WITH SQ!
MY PARTNER IN CRIME WILL BE KO AOKI, WHO TRULY UNDERSTANDS MY VISION!
WOO! ♥
K-KO AOKI...?!
W-WHY?
THIS IS THE FIRST I'VE HEARD OF IT!
TH-THIS SOUNDS LIKE TROUBLE...
NIZUMA.
TH-THEN NAKAI DOESN'T KNOW ABOUT MISS AOKI TEAMING UP WITH SOMEBODY ELSE...
MURMUR
MURMUR
B-BUT, WE CAN'T JUST GO AND TELL HER "DON'T DO IT"...
YES, THAT WOULD BE TOO PERSONAL.
AND SO THE NEW YEAR'S PARTY, WHICH I HOPED TO ATTEND FOR MANY MORE YEARS TO COME, ENDED ON A SOUR NOTE. FOR THE REST OF THE FOLKS, THE BIG STORY WAS HOW DRUNK AND WILD HIRAMARU GOT AT THE AFTER-PARTY. BUT FOR THOSE OF US WHO KNEW MR. NAKAI, HIS COMING REACTION TO THE PARTY'S EVENTS WAS MUCH MORE MEMORABLE.

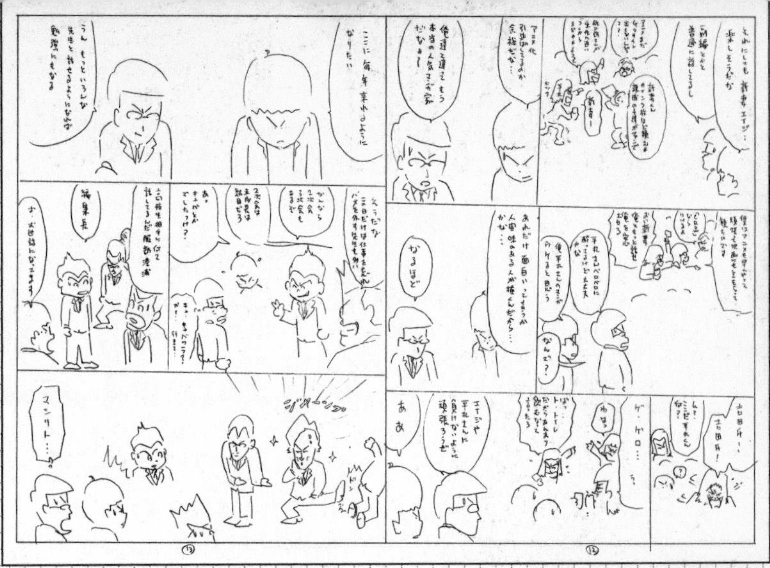

OHBA'S STORYBOARD

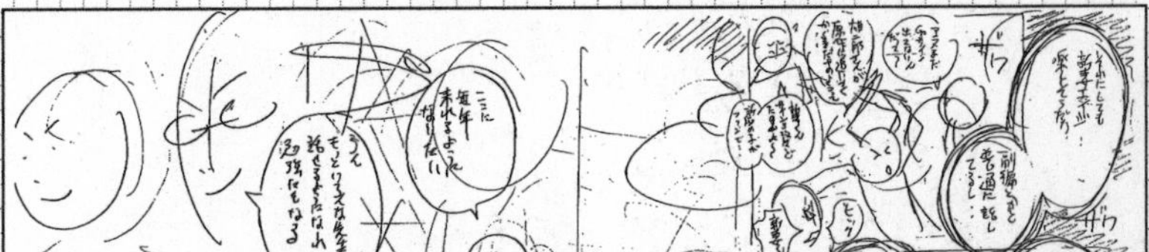

OBATA'S STORYBOARD

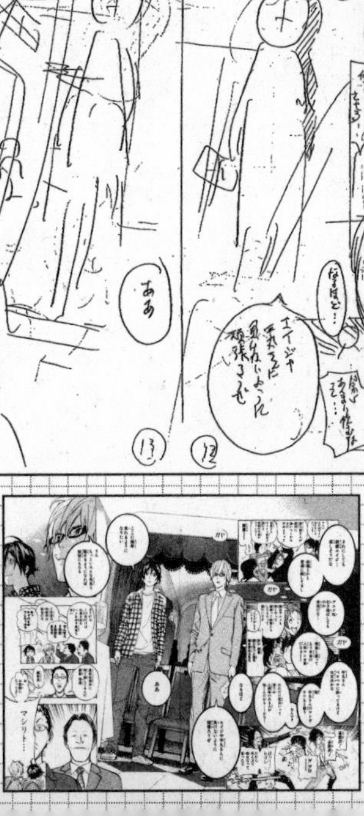

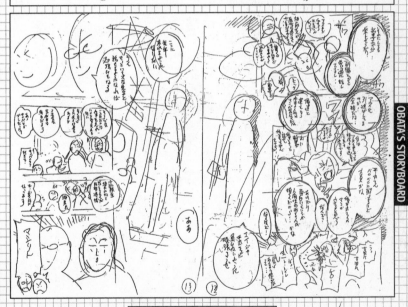

COMPLETE!

※CREATOR STORYBOARDS AND FINISHED PAGES IN JAPANESE

BAKUMAN。 vol.5

"Until the Final Draft Is Complete"

Chapter 37, pp. 58-59

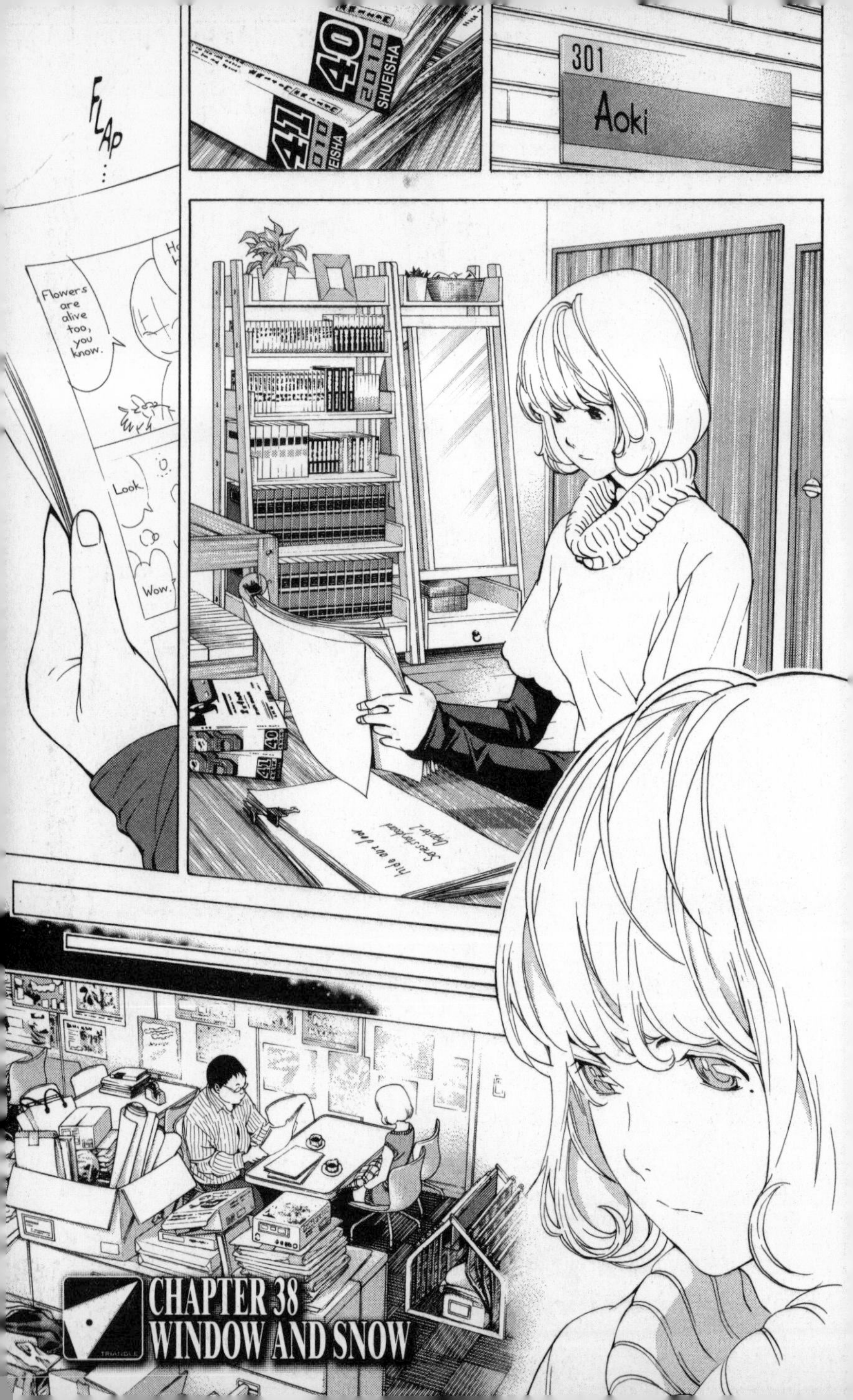
301
Aoki
40
2010
SHUEISHA
41
2010
SHUEISHA
FLAP...
Flowers are alive too, you know.
Look.
Wow.

CHAPTER 38
WINDOW AND SNOW

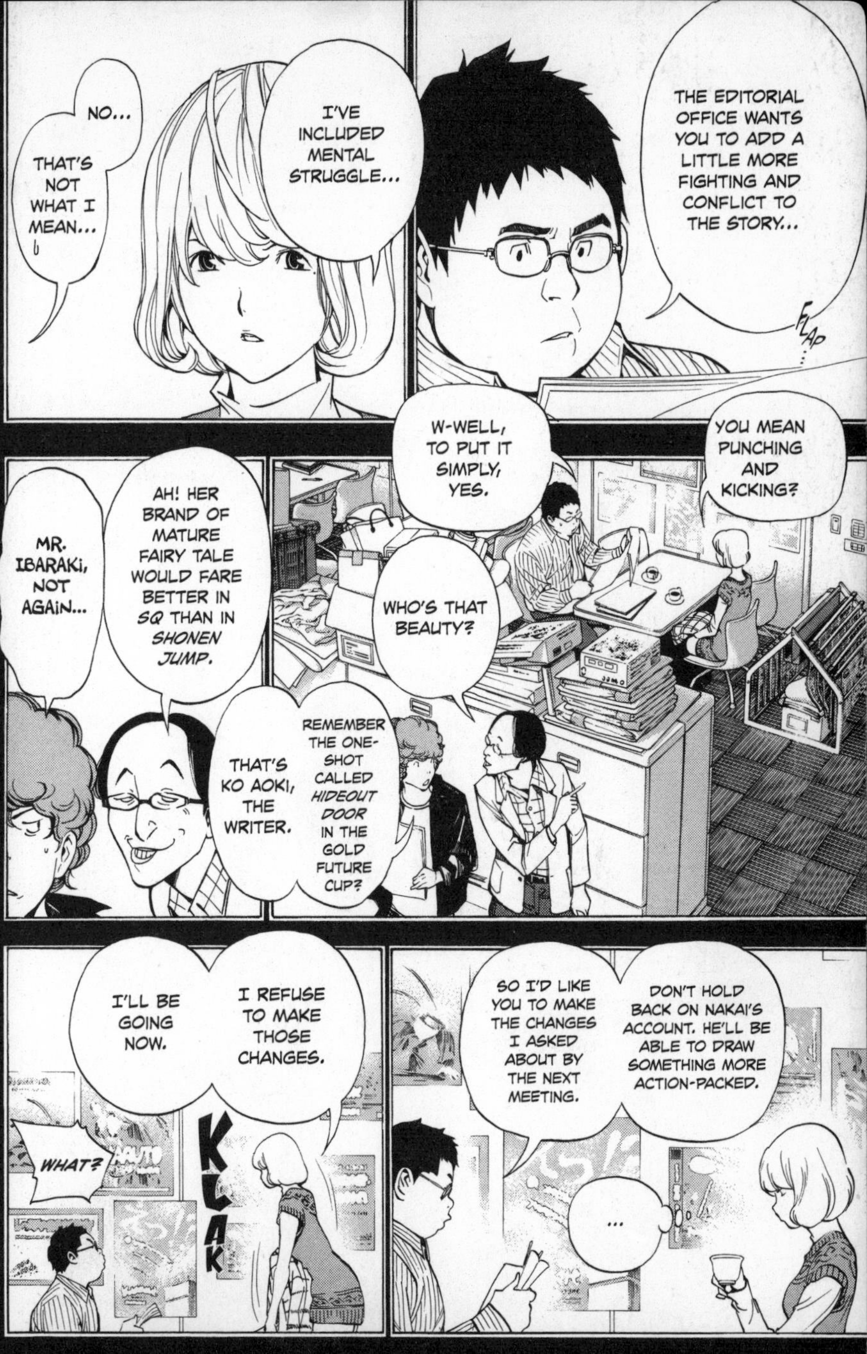
THE EDITORIAL OFFICE WANTS YOU TO ADD A LITTLE MORE FIGHTING AND CONFLICT TO THE STORY...
FLAP...
I'VE INCLUDED MENTAL STRUGGLE...
NO...
THAT'S NOT WHAT I MEAN...
YOU MEAN PUNCHING AND KICKING?
W-WELL, TO PUT IT SIMPLY, YES.
WHO'S THAT BEAUTY?
REMEMBER THE ONE-SHOT CALLED *HIDEOUT DOOR* IN THE GOLD FUTURE CUP?
THAT'S KO AOKI, THE WRITER.
AH! HER BRAND OF MATURE FAIRY TALE WOULD FARE BETTER IN *SQ* THAN IN *SHONEN JUMP*.
MR. IBARAKI, NOT AGAIN...
DON'T HOLD BACK ON NAKAI'S ACCOUNT. HE'LL BE ABLE TO DRAW SOMETHING MORE ACTION-PACKED.
SO I'D LIKE YOU TO MAKE THE CHANGES I ASKED ABOUT BY THE NEXT MEETING.
...
I REFUSE TO MAKE THOSE CHANGES.
I'LL BE GOING NOW.
KLAK
WHAT?

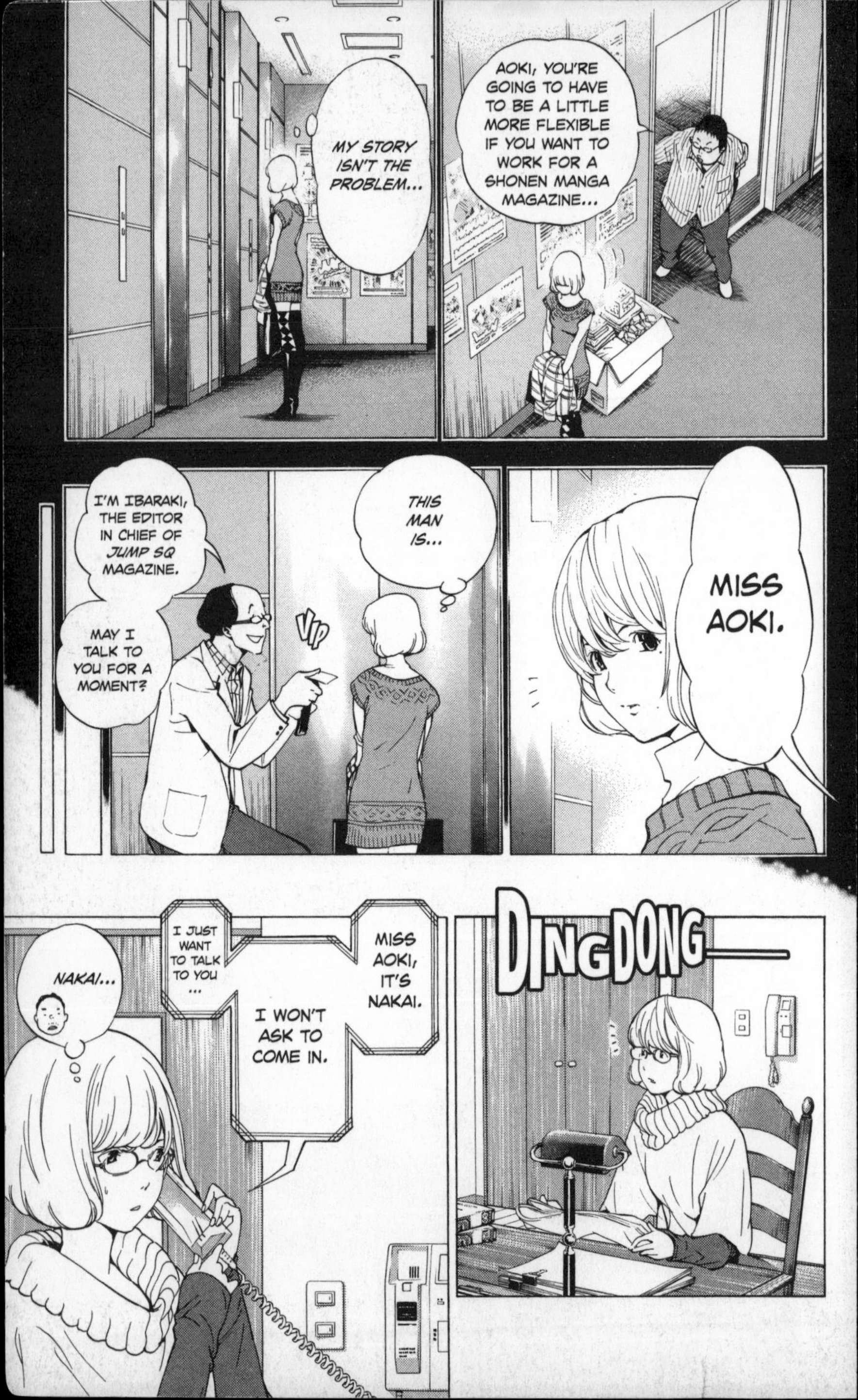
AOKI, YOU'RE GOING TO HAVE TO BE A LITTLE MORE FLEXIBLE IF YOU WANT TO WORK FOR A SHONEN MANGA MAGAZINE...
MY STORY ISN'T THE PROBLEM...
MISS AOKI.
THIS MAN IS...
I'M IBARAKI, THE EDITOR IN CHIEF OF JUMP SQ MAGAZINE.
VIP
MAY I TALK TO YOU FOR A MOMENT?
DINGDONG
MISS AOKI, IT'S NAKAI.
I JUST WANT TO TALK TO YOU ...
I WON'T ASK TO COME IN.
NAKAI...

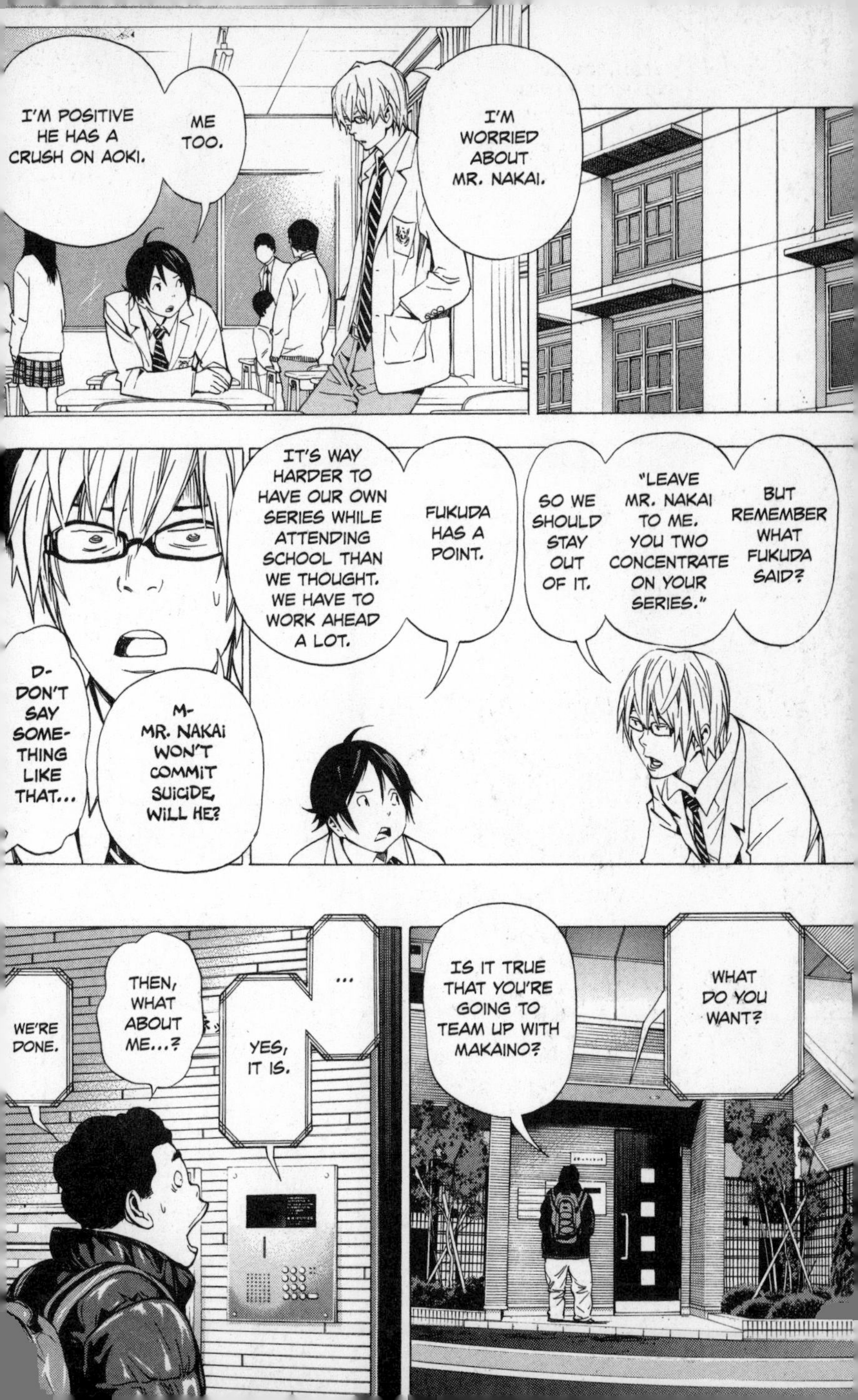
I'M WORRIED ABOUT MR. NAKAI.
ME TOO.
I'M POSITIVE HE HAS A CRUSH ON AOKI.
BUT REMEMBER WHAT FUKUDA SAID?
"LEAVE MR. NAKAI TO ME. YOU TWO CONCENTRATE ON YOUR SERIES."
SO WE SHOULD STAY OUT OF IT.
FUKUDA HAS A POINT.
IT'S WAY HARDER TO HAVE OUR OWN SERIES WHILE ATTENDING SCHOOL THAN WE THOUGHT. WE HAVE TO WORK AHEAD A LOT.
M- MR. NAKAI WON'T COMMIT SUICIDE, WILL HE?
D- DON'T SAY SOME-THING LIKE THAT...
WHAT DO YOU WANT?
IS IT TRUE THAT YOU'RE GOING TO TEAM UP WITH MAKAINO?
...
YES, IT IS.
THEN, WHAT ABOUT ME...?
WE'RE DONE.

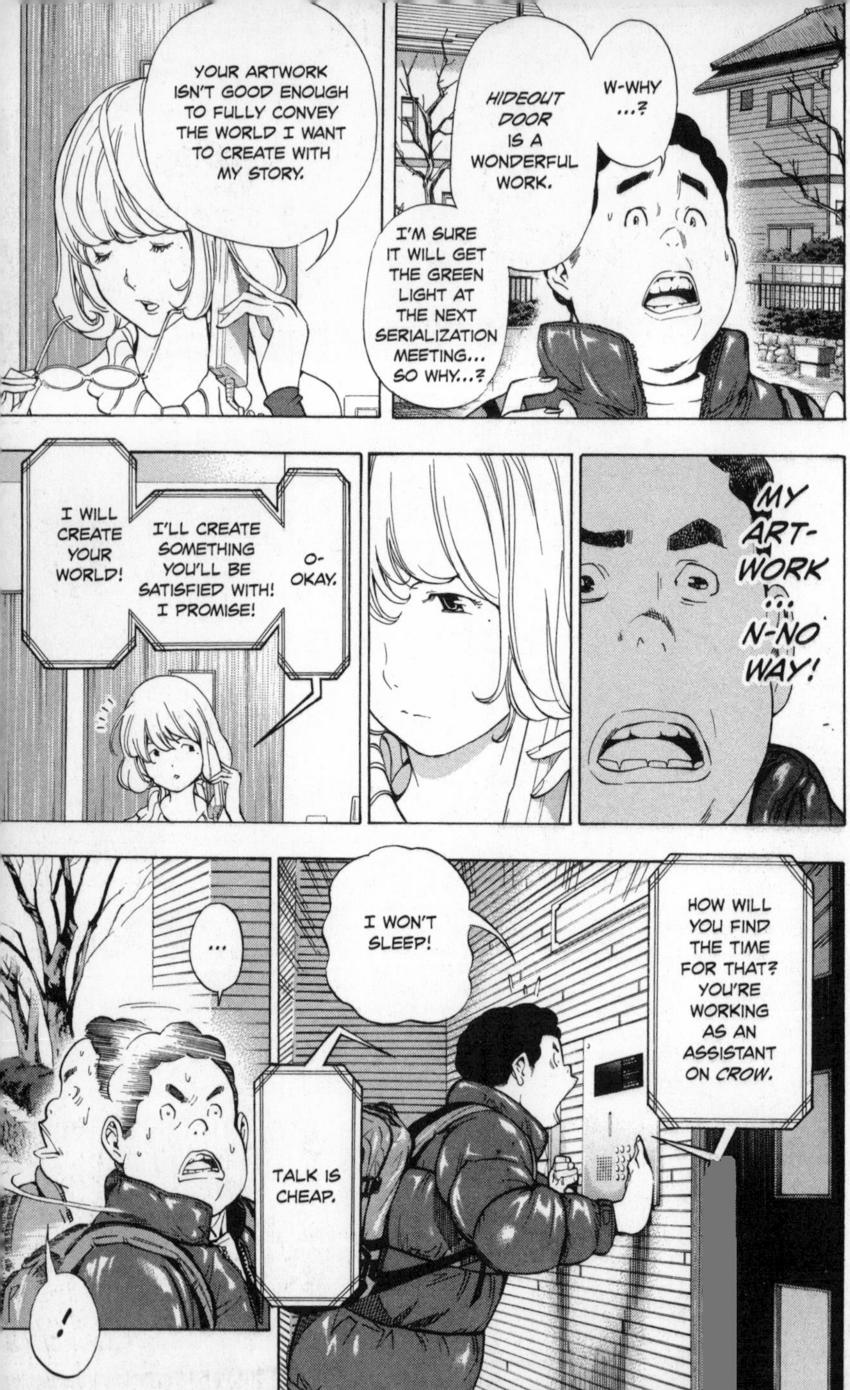
W-WHY ...?
HIDEOUT DOOR IS A WONDERFUL WORK.
I'M SURE IT WILL GET THE GREEN LIGHT AT THE NEXT SERIALIZATION MEETING... SO WHY...?
YOUR ARTWORK ISN'T GOOD ENOUGH TO FULLY CONVEY THE WORLD I WANT TO CREATE WITH MY STORY.
MY ART-WORK... N-NO WAY!
I WILL CREATE YOUR WORLD!
I'LL CREATE SOMETHING YOU'LL BE SATISFIED WITH! I PROMISE!
O-OKAY.
HOW WILL YOU FIND THE TIME FOR THAT? YOU'RE WORKING AS AN ASSISTANT ON *CROW*.
I WON'T SLEEP!
TALK IS CHEAP.
...
!

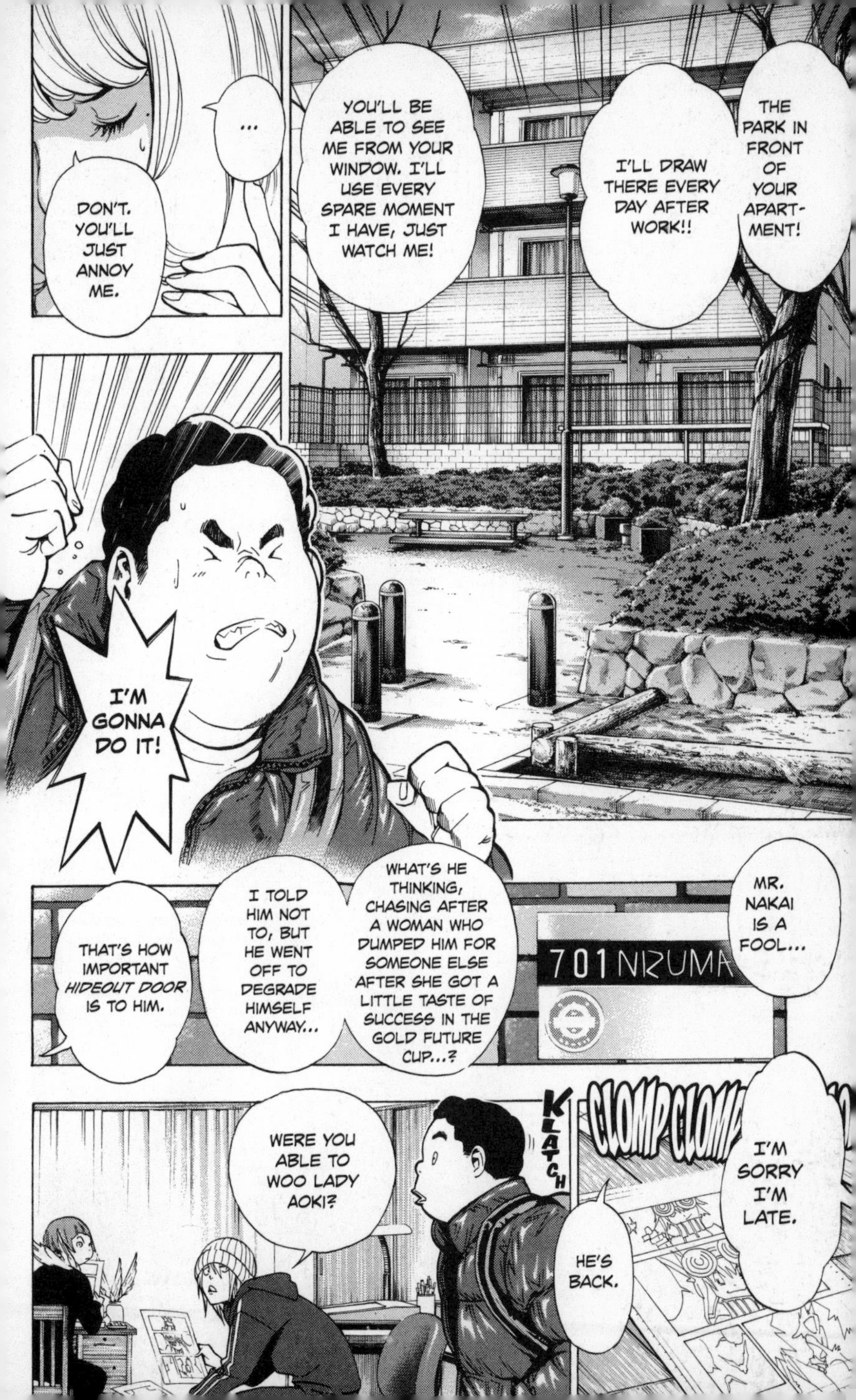
THE PARK IN FRONT OF YOUR APARTMENT!
I'LL DRAW THERE EVERY DAY AFTER WORK!!
YOU'LL BE ABLE TO SEE ME FROM YOUR WINDOW. I'LL USE EVERY SPARE MOMENT I HAVE, JUST WATCH ME!
...
DON'T. YOU'LL JUST ANNOY ME.
I'M GONNA DO IT!
MR. NAKAI IS A FOOL...
701 NIZUMA
WHAT'S HE THINKING, CHASING AFTER A WOMAN WHO DUMPED HIM FOR SOMEONE ELSE AFTER SHE GOT A LITTLE TASTE OF SUCCESS IN THE GOLD FUTURE CUP...?
I TOLD HIM NOT TO, BUT HE WENT OFF TO DEGRADE HIMSELF ANYWAY...
THAT'S HOW IMPORTANT *HIDEOUT DOOR* IS TO HIM.
CLOMP CLOMP
I'M SORRY I'M LATE.
KLATCH
HE'S BACK.
WERE YOU ABLE TO WOO LADY AOKI?

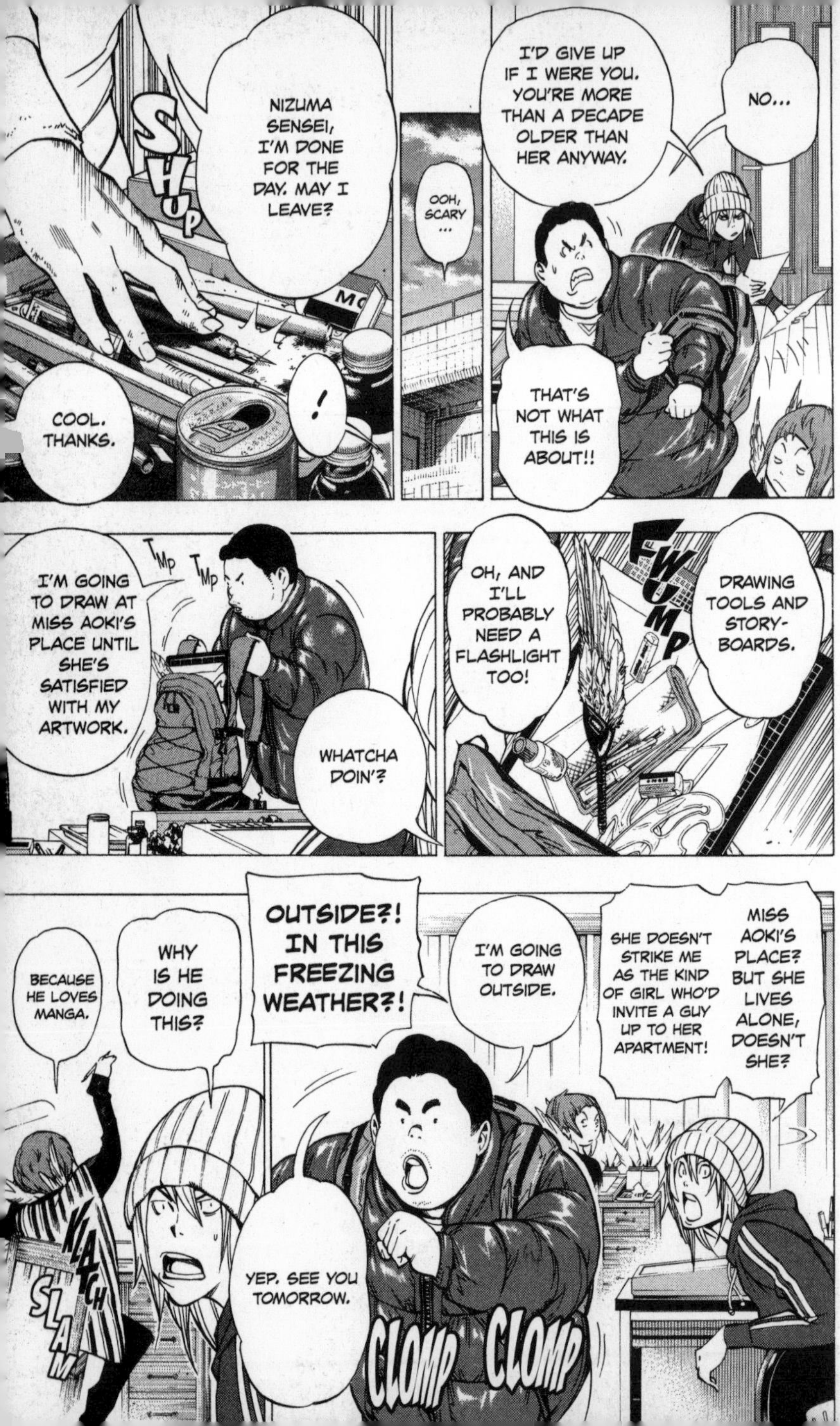
NO...
I'D GIVE UP IF I WERE YOU. YOU'RE MORE THAN A DECADE OLDER THAN HER ANYWAY.
THAT'S NOT WHAT THIS IS ABOUT!!
OOH, SCARY ...
SHUP
NIZUMA SENSEI, I'M DONE FOR THE DAY. MAY I LEAVE?
!
COOL. THANKS.
DRAWING TOOLS AND STORY-BOARDS.
FWUMP
OH, AND I'LL PROBABLY NEED A FLASHLIGHT TOO!
TMP TMP
WHATCHA DOIN'?
I'M GOING TO DRAW AT MISS AOKI'S PLACE UNTIL SHE'S SATISFIED WITH MY ARTWORK.
MISS AOKI'S PLACE? BUT SHE LIVES ALONE, DOESN'T SHE?
SHE DOESN'T STRIKE ME AS THE KIND OF GIRL WHO'D INVITE A GUY UP TO HER APARTMENT!
I'M GOING TO DRAW OUTSIDE.
OUTSIDE?! IN THIS FREEZING WEATHER?!
WHY IS HE DOING THIS?
BECAUSE HE LOVES MANGA.
YEP. SEE YOU TOMORROW.
CLOMP CLOMP
KLACH
SLAM

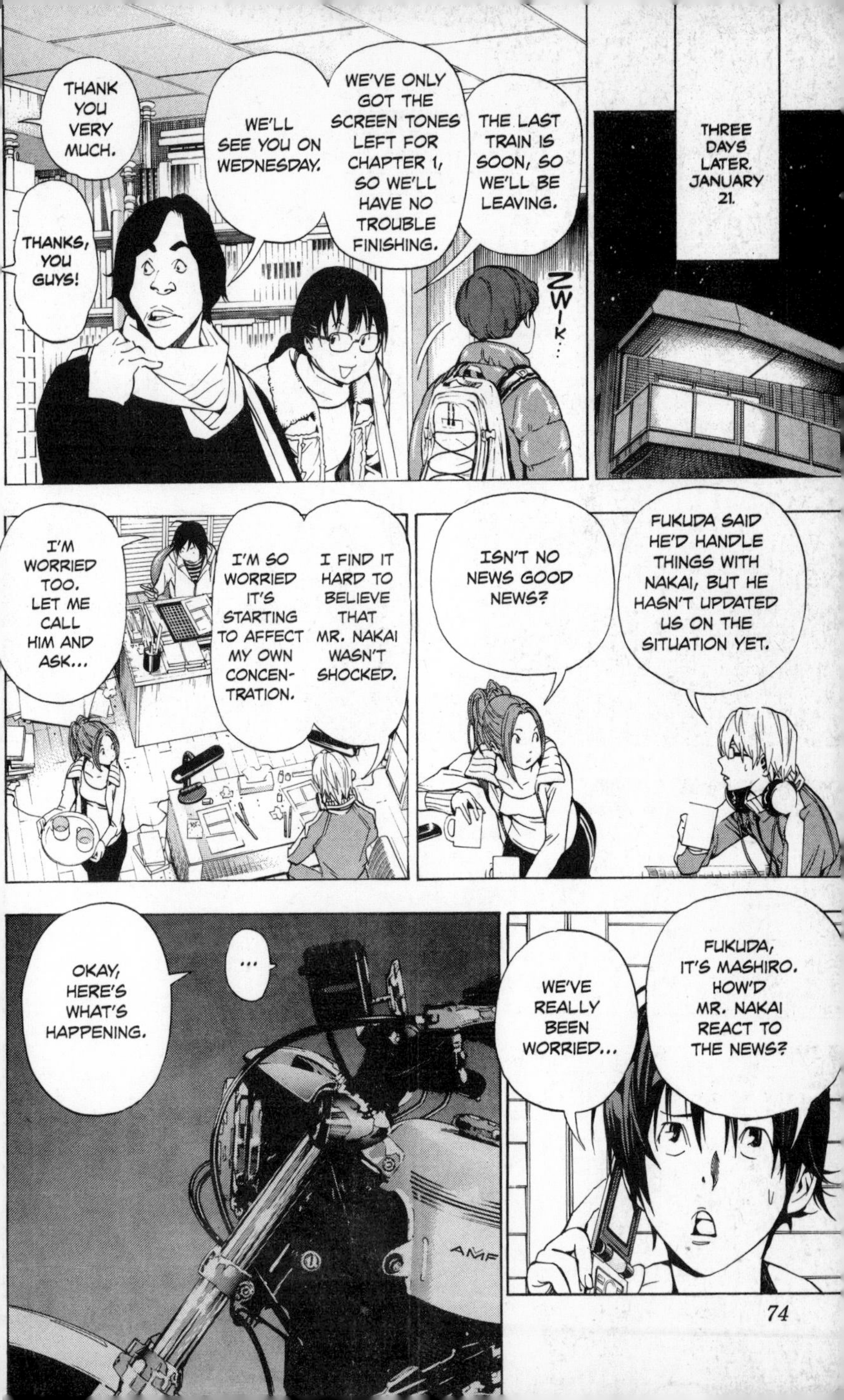
THREE DAYS LATER. JANUARY 21.
THE LAST TRAIN IS SOON, SO WE'LL BE LEAVING.
ZWIK...
WE'VE ONLY GOT THE SCREEN TONES LEFT FOR CHAPTER 1, SO WE'LL HAVE NO TROUBLE FINISHING.
WE'LL SEE YOU ON WEDNESDAY.
THANK YOU VERY MUCH.
THANKS, YOU GUYS!
FUKUDA SAID HE'D HANDLE THINGS WITH NAKAI, BUT HE HASN'T UPDATED US ON THE SITUATION YET.
ISN'T NO NEWS GOOD NEWS?
I FIND IT HARD TO BELIEVE THAT MR. NAKAI WASN'T SHOCKED.
I'M SO WORRIED IT'S STARTING TO AFFECT MY OWN CONCEN-TRATION.
I'M WORRIED TOO. LET ME CALL HIM AND ASK...
FUKUDA, IT'S MASHIRO. HOW'D MR. NAKAI REACT TO THE NEWS?
WE'VE REALLY BEEN WORRIED...
...
OKAY, HERE'S WHAT'S HAPPENING.
AMF

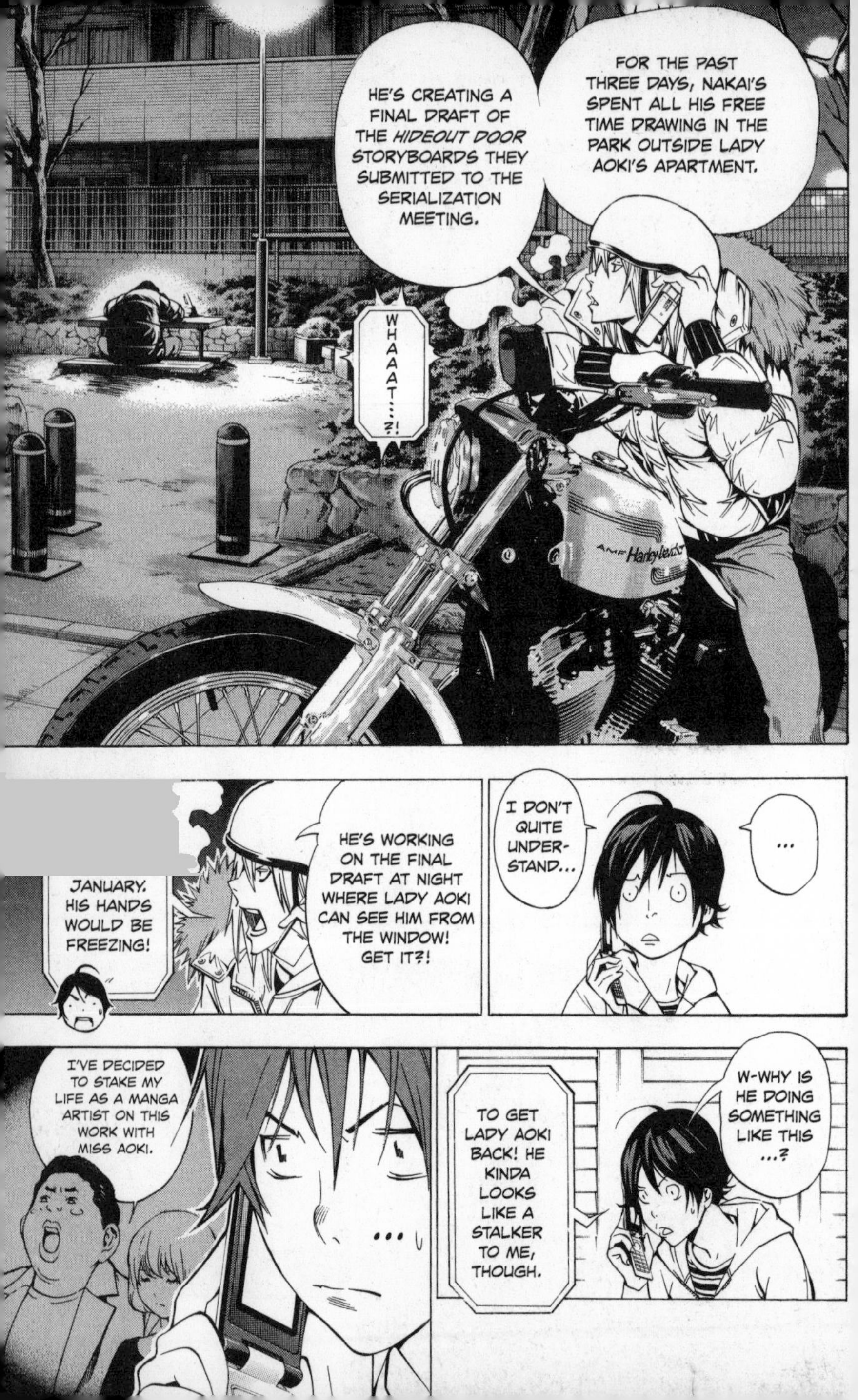
FOR THE PAST THREE DAYS, NAKAI'S SPENT ALL HIS FREE TIME DRAWING IN THE PARK OUTSIDE LADY AOKI'S APARTMENT.
HE'S CREATING A FINAL DRAFT OF THE *HIDEOUT DOOR* STORYBOARDS THEY SUBMITTED TO THE SERIALIZATION MEETING.
WHAAAT...?!
AMF Harley-Davidson
...
I DON'T QUITE UNDER-STAND...
HE'S WORKING ON THE FINAL DRAFT AT NIGHT WHERE LADY AOKI CAN SEE HIM FROM THE WINDOW! GET IT?!
JANUARY. HIS HANDS WOULD BE FREEZING!
W-WHY IS HE DOING SOMETHING LIKE THIS ...?
TO GET LADY AOKI BACK! HE KINDA LOOKS LIKE A STALKER TO ME, THOUGH.
I'VE DECIDED TO STAKE MY LIFE AS A MANGA ARTIST ON THIS WORK WITH MISS AOKI.
...

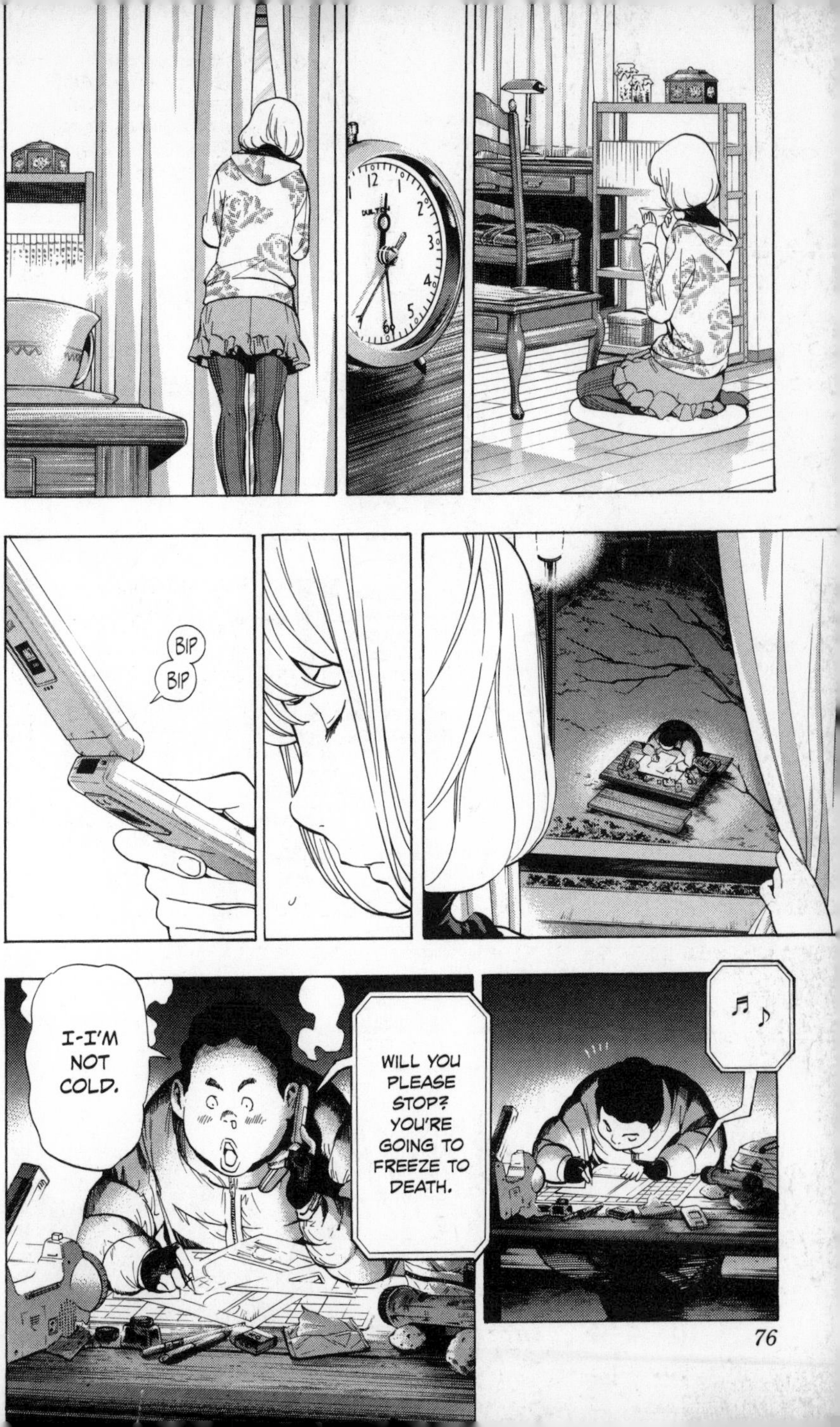
BIP BIP
♬ ♪
WILL YOU PLEASE STOP? YOU'RE GOING TO FREEZE TO DEATH.
I-I'M NOT COLD.

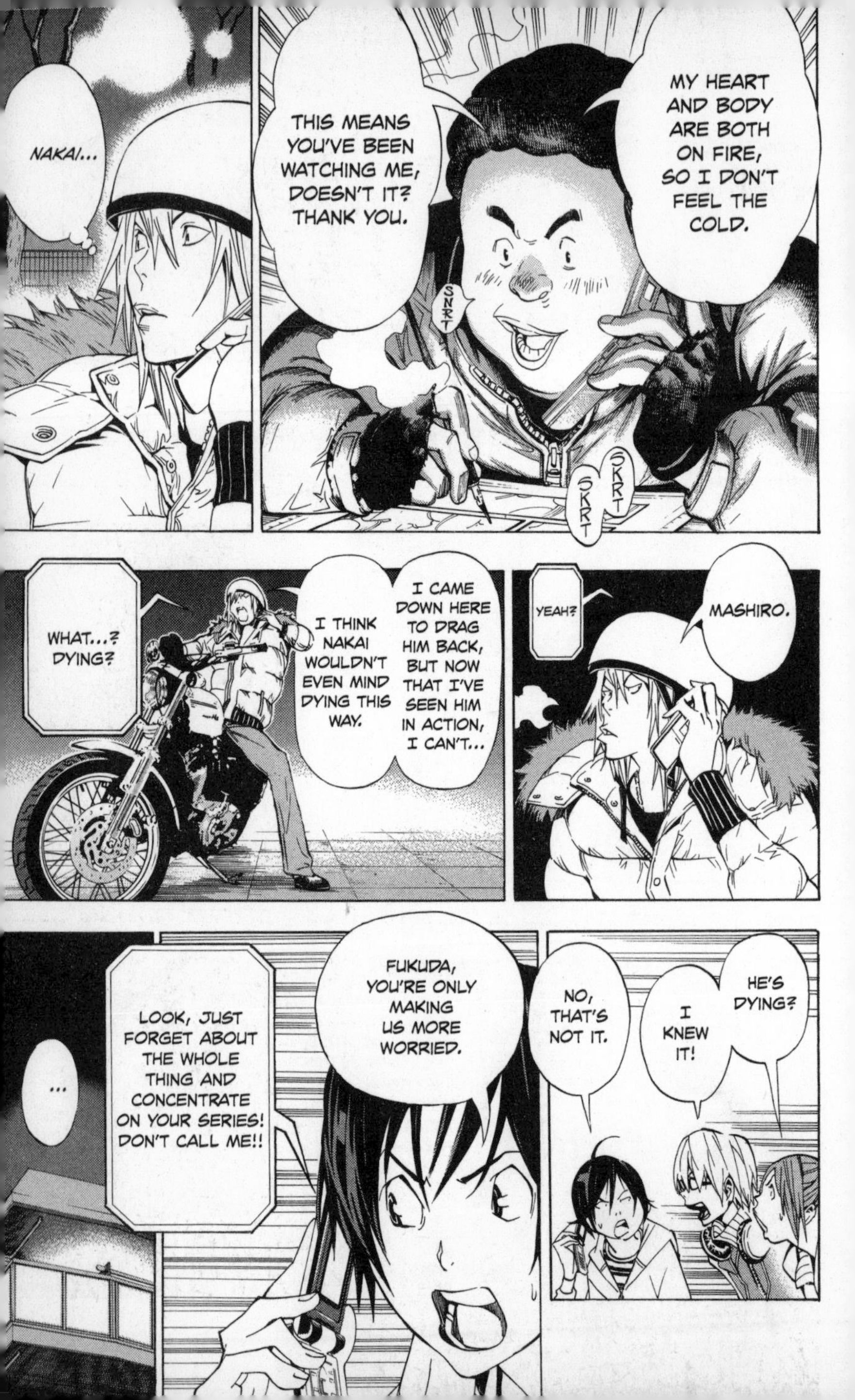
MY HEART AND BODY ARE BOTH ON FIRE, SO I DON'T FEEL THE COLD.
THIS MEANS YOU'VE BEEN WATCHING ME, DOESN'T IT? THANK YOU.
SNRT
SKRT
SKRT
NAKAI...
MASHIRO.
YEAH?
I CAME DOWN HERE TO DRAG HIM BACK, BUT NOW THAT I'VE SEEN HIM IN ACTION, I CAN'T...
I THINK NAKAI WOULDN'T EVEN MIND DYING THIS WAY.
WHAT...? DYING?
HE'S DYING?
I KNEW IT!
NO, THAT'S NOT IT.
FUKUDA, YOU'RE ONLY MAKING US MORE WORRIED.
LOOK, JUST FORGET ABOUT THE WHOLE THING AND CONCENTRATE ON YOUR SERIES! DON'T CALL ME!!
...

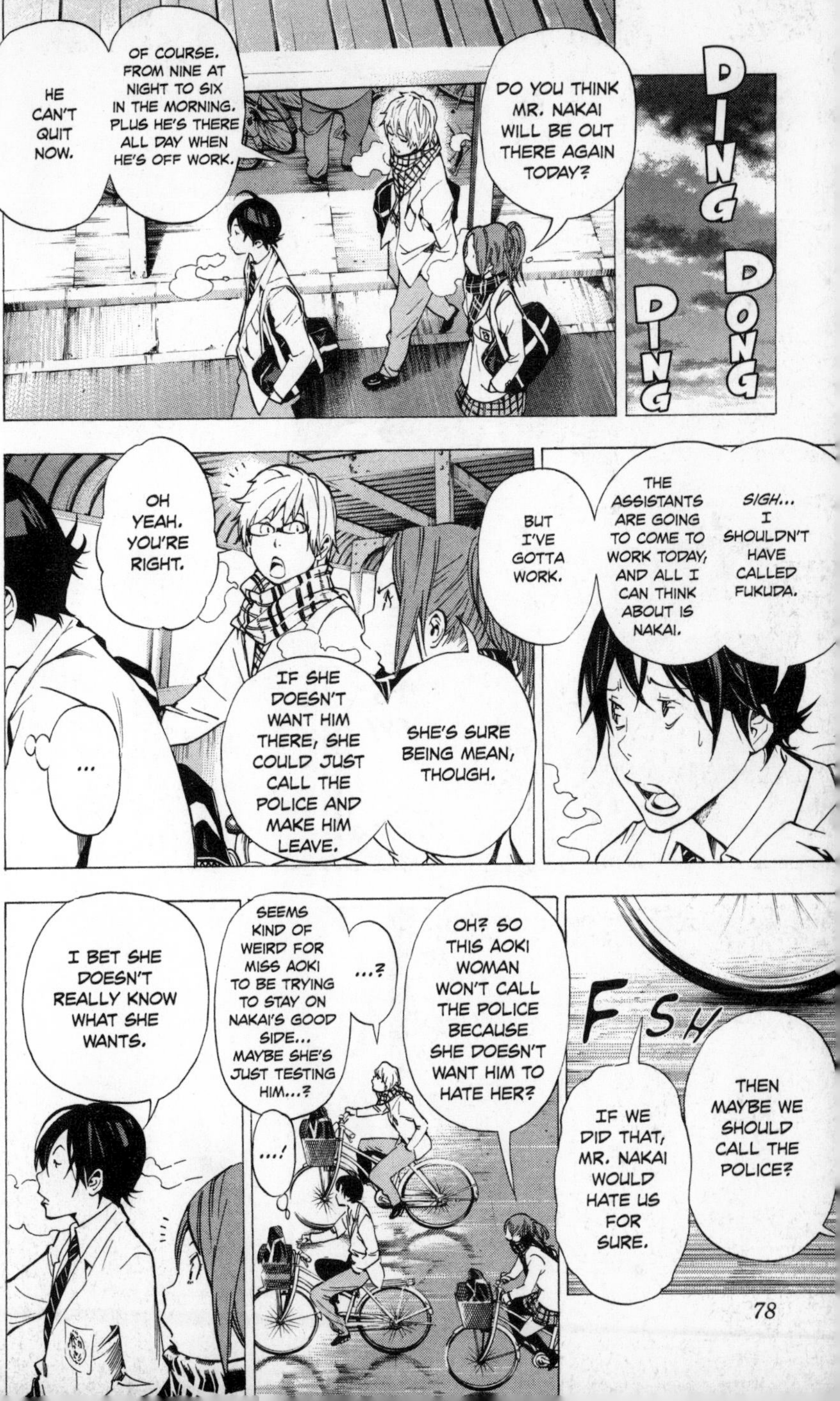
DING DONG
DING DONG
DO YOU THINK MR. NAKAI WILL BE OUT THERE AGAIN TODAY?
OF COURSE. FROM NINE AT NIGHT TO SIX IN THE MORNING. PLUS HE'S THERE ALL DAY WHEN HE'S OFF WORK.
HE CAN'T QUIT NOW.
SIGH... I SHOULDN'T HAVE CALLED FUKUDA.
THE ASSISTANTS ARE GOING TO COME TO WORK TODAY, AND ALL I CAN THINK ABOUT IS NAKAI.
BUT I'VE GOTTA WORK.
OH YEAH. YOU'RE RIGHT.
SHE'S SURE BEING MEAN, THOUGH.
IF SHE DOESN'T WANT HIM THERE, SHE COULD JUST CALL THE POLICE AND MAKE HIM LEAVE.
...
THEN MAYBE WE SHOULD CALL THE POLICE?
FSH
IF WE DID THAT, MR. NAKAI WOULD HATE US FOR SURE.
OH? SO THIS AOKI WOMAN WON'T CALL THE POLICE BECAUSE SHE DOESN'T WANT HIM TO HATE HER?
...?
SEEMS KIND OF WEIRD FOR MISS AOKI TO BE TRYING TO STAY ON NAKAI'S GOOD SIDE... MAYBE SHE'S JUST TESTING HIM...?
...!
I BET SHE DOESN'T REALLY KNOW WHAT SHE WANTS.

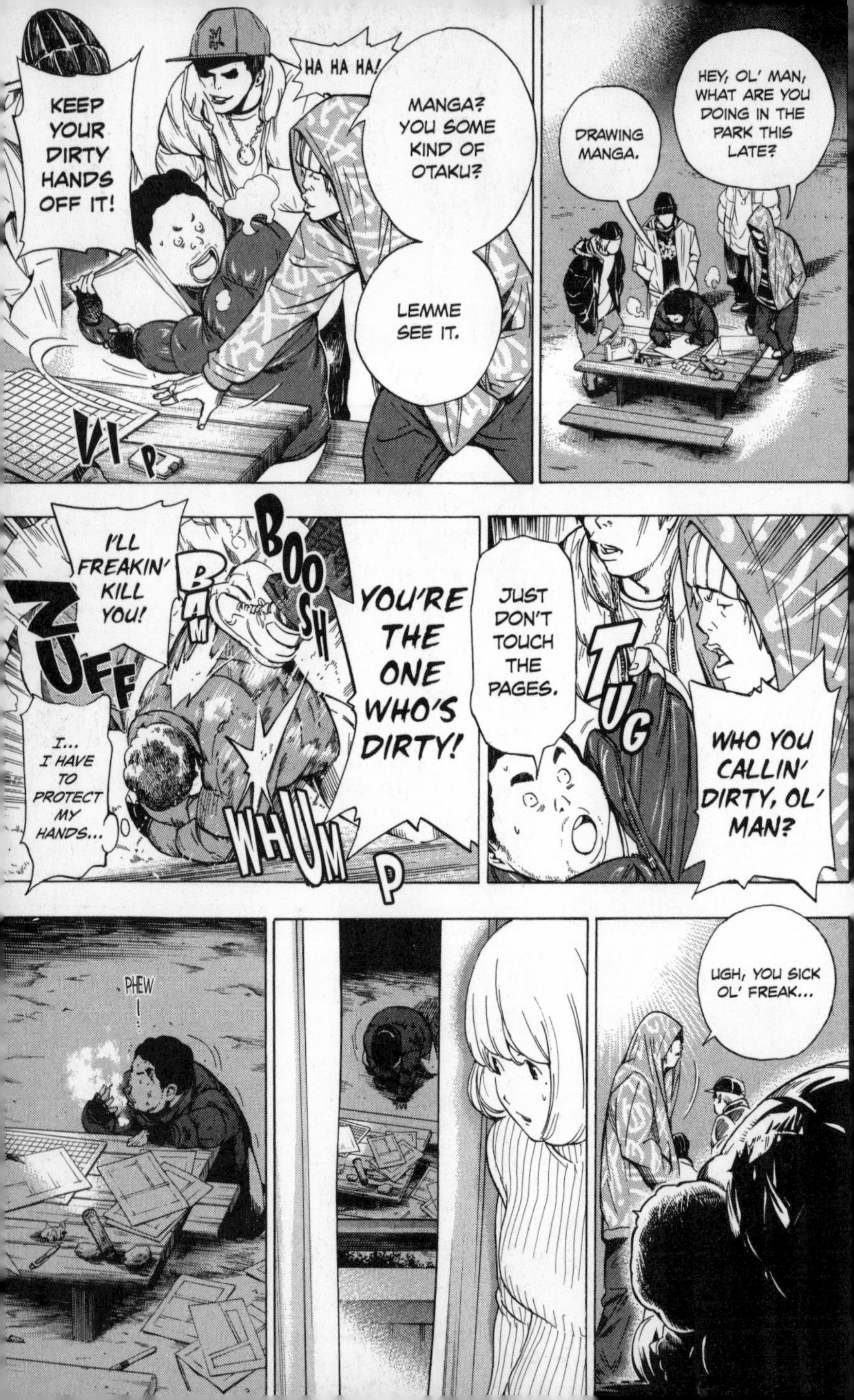

HEY, OL' MAN, WHAT ARE YOU DOING IN THE PARK THIS LATE?
DRAWING MANGA.
HA HA HA!
MANGA? YOU SOME KIND OF OTAKU?
LEMME SEE IT.
VIP
KEEP YOUR DIRTY HANDS OFF IT!
WHO YOU CALLIN' DIRTY, OL' MAN?
TUG
JUST DON'T TOUCH THE PAGES.
YOU'RE THE ONE WHO'S DIRTY!
BOOSH
BAM
I'LL FREAKIN' KILL YOU!
ZUFF
WHUMP
I... I HAVE TO PROTECT MY HANDS...
UGH, YOU SICK OL' FREAK...
PHEW
!

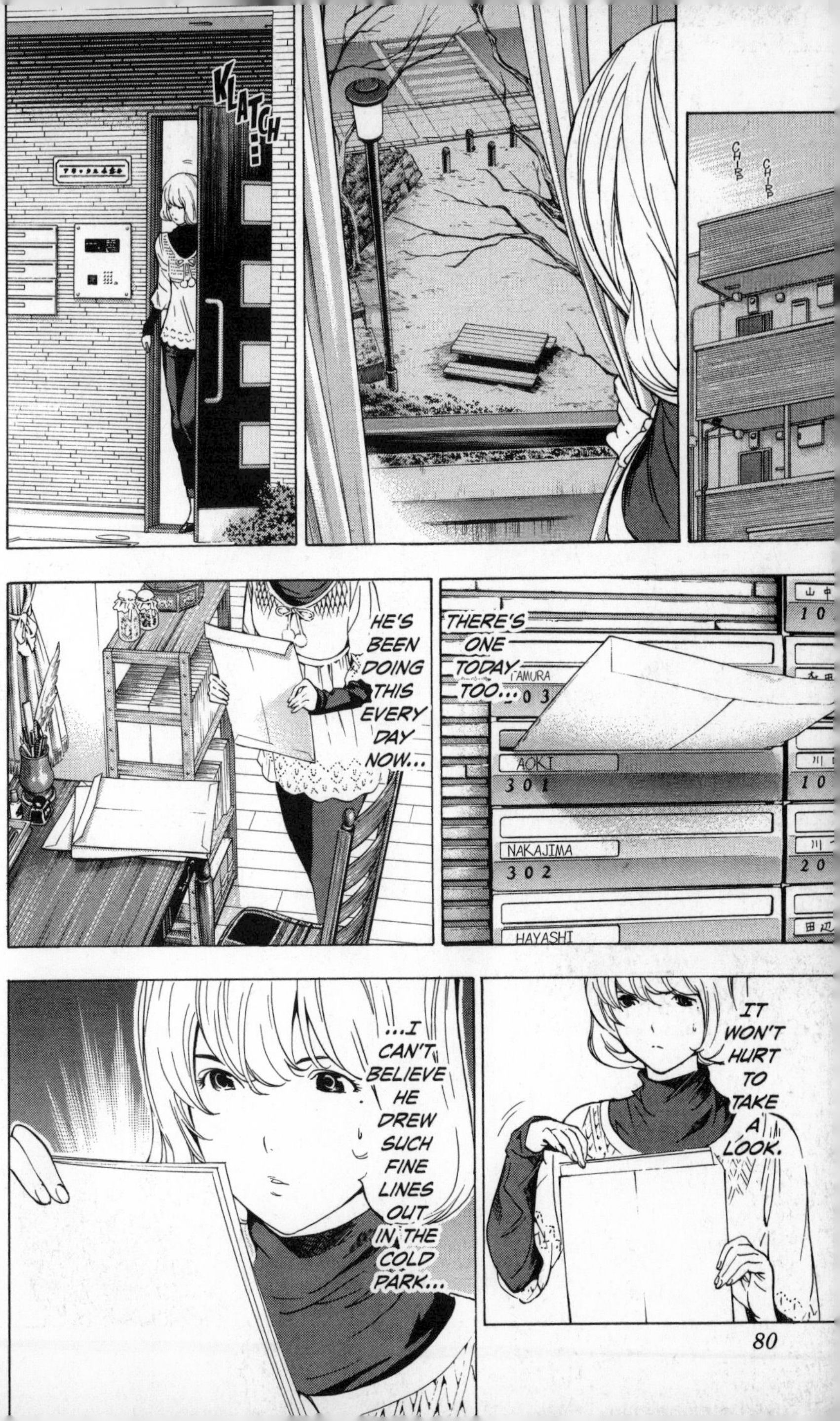
CHIRP
CHIRP
KLATCH
THERE'S ONE TODAY TOO...
AOKI
301
NAKAJIMA
302
HAYASHI
HE'S BEEN DOING THIS EVERY DAY NOW...
IT WON'T HURT TO TAKE A LOOK.
...I CAN'T BELIEVE HE DREW SUCH FINE LINES OUT IN THE COLD PARK...

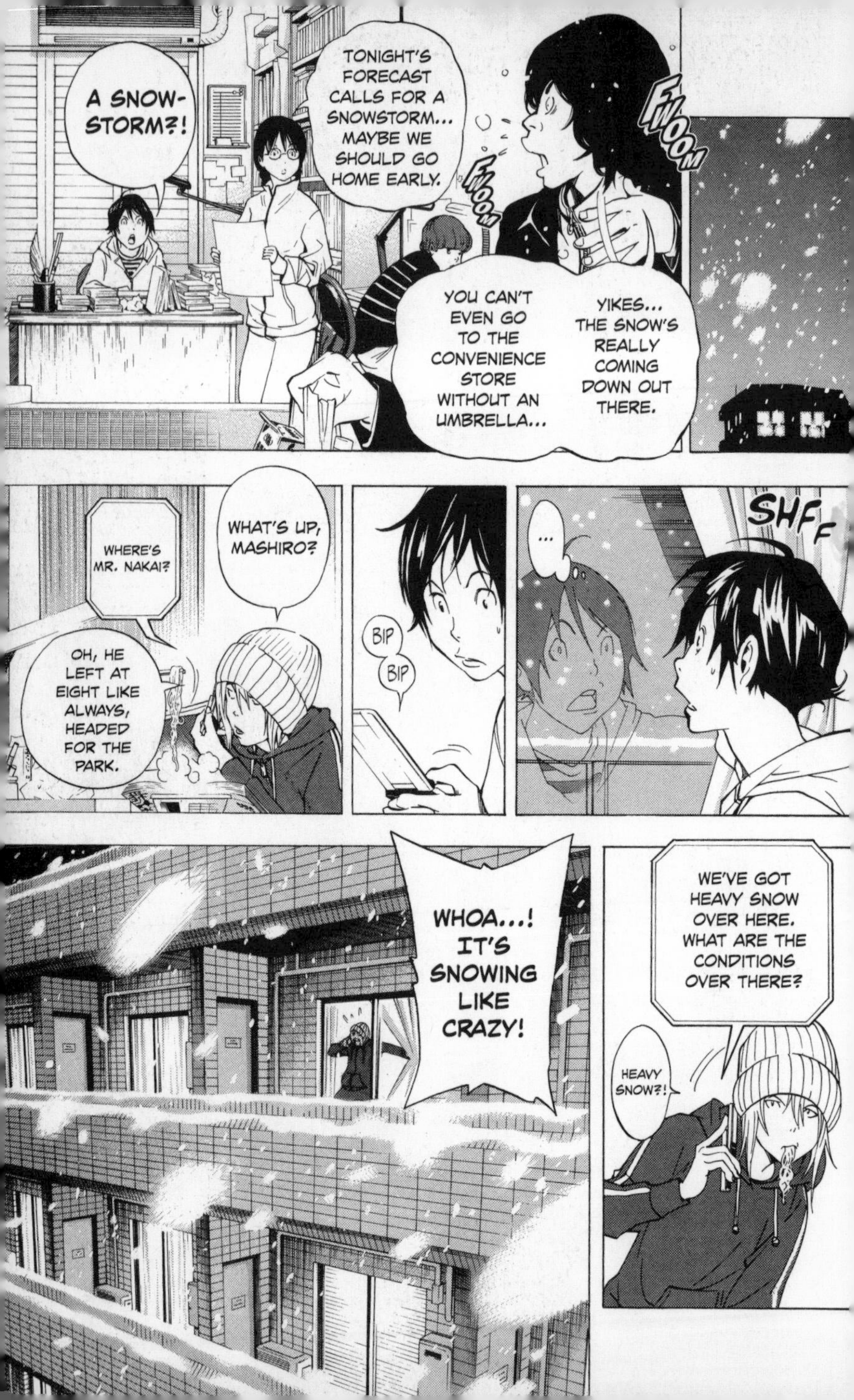
FWOOM
FWOOM
TONIGHT'S FORECAST CALLS FOR A SNOWSTORM... MAYBE WE SHOULD GO HOME EARLY.
A SNOW-STORM?!
YIKES... THE SNOW'S REALLY COMING DOWN OUT THERE.
YOU CAN'T EVEN GO TO THE CONVENIENCE STORE WITHOUT AN UMBRELLA...
SHFF
...
BIP
BIP
WHAT'S UP, MASHIRO?
WHERE'S MR. NAKAI?
OH, HE LEFT AT EIGHT LIKE ALWAYS, HEADED FOR THE PARK.
WE'VE GOT HEAVY SNOW OVER HERE. WHAT ARE THE CONDITIONS OVER THERE?
HEAVY SNOW?!
WHOA...! IT'S SNOWING LIKE CRAZY!

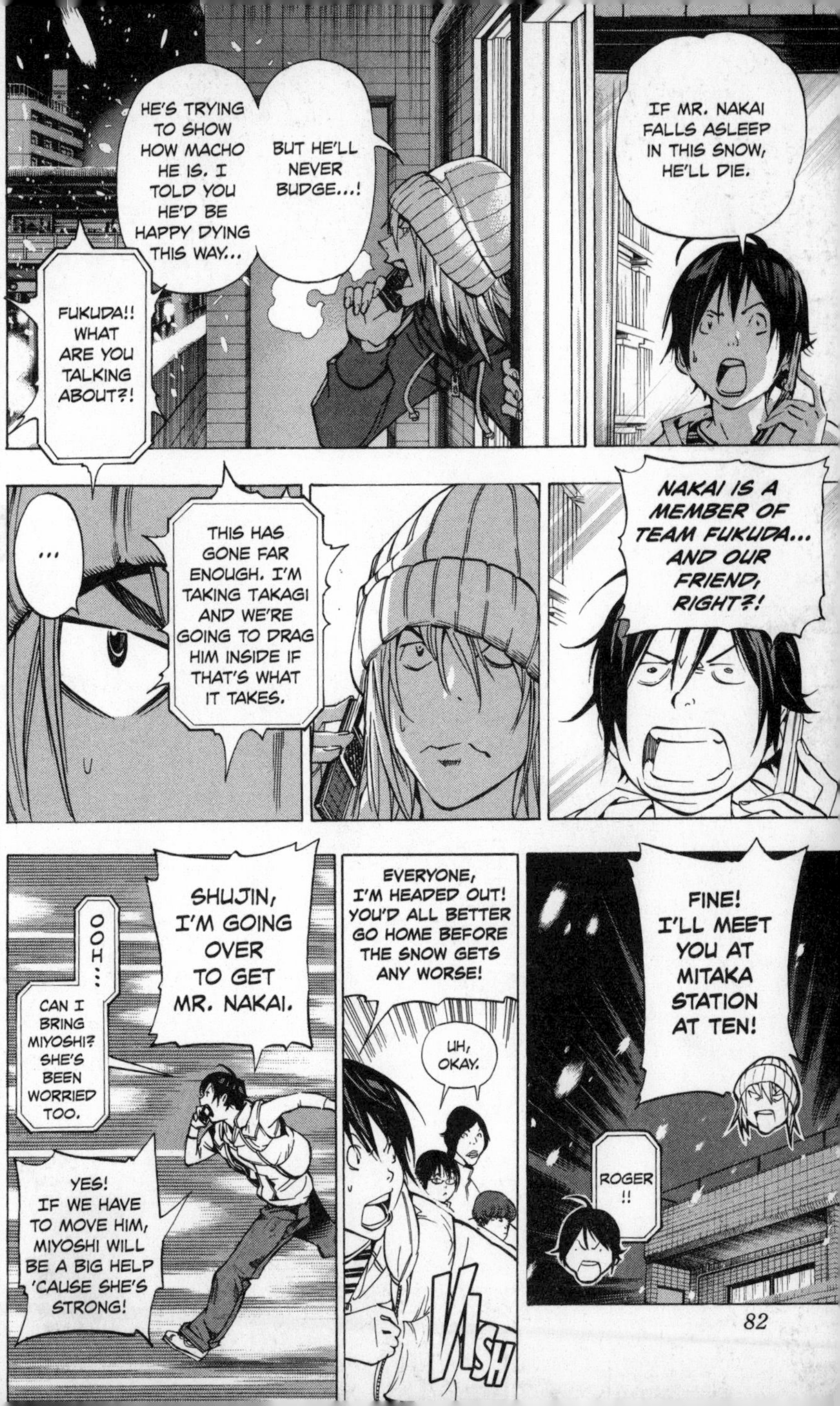
IF MR. NAKAI FALLS ASLEEP IN THIS SNOW, HE'LL DIE.
BUT HE'LL NEVER BUDGE...!
HE'S TRYING TO SHOW HOW MACHO HE IS. I TOLD YOU HE'D BE HAPPY DYING THIS WAY...
FUKUDA!! WHAT ARE YOU TALKING ABOUT?!
NAKAI IS A MEMBER OF TEAM FUKUDA... AND OUR FRIEND, RIGHT?!
THIS HAS GONE FAR ENOUGH. I'M TAKING TAKAGI AND WE'RE GOING TO DRAG HIM INSIDE IF THAT'S WHAT IT TAKES.
...
FINE! I'LL MEET YOU AT MITAKA STATION AT TEN!
ROGER!!
EVERYONE, I'M HEADED OUT! YOU'D ALL BETTER GO HOME BEFORE THE SNOW GETS ANY WORSE!
UH, OKAY.
VISH
SHUJIN, I'M GOING OVER TO GET MR. NAKAI.
OOH...
CAN I BRING MIYOSHI? SHE'S BEEN WORRIED TOO.
YES! IF WE HAVE TO MOVE HIM, MIYOSHI WILL BE A BIG HELP 'CAUSE SHE'S STRONG!

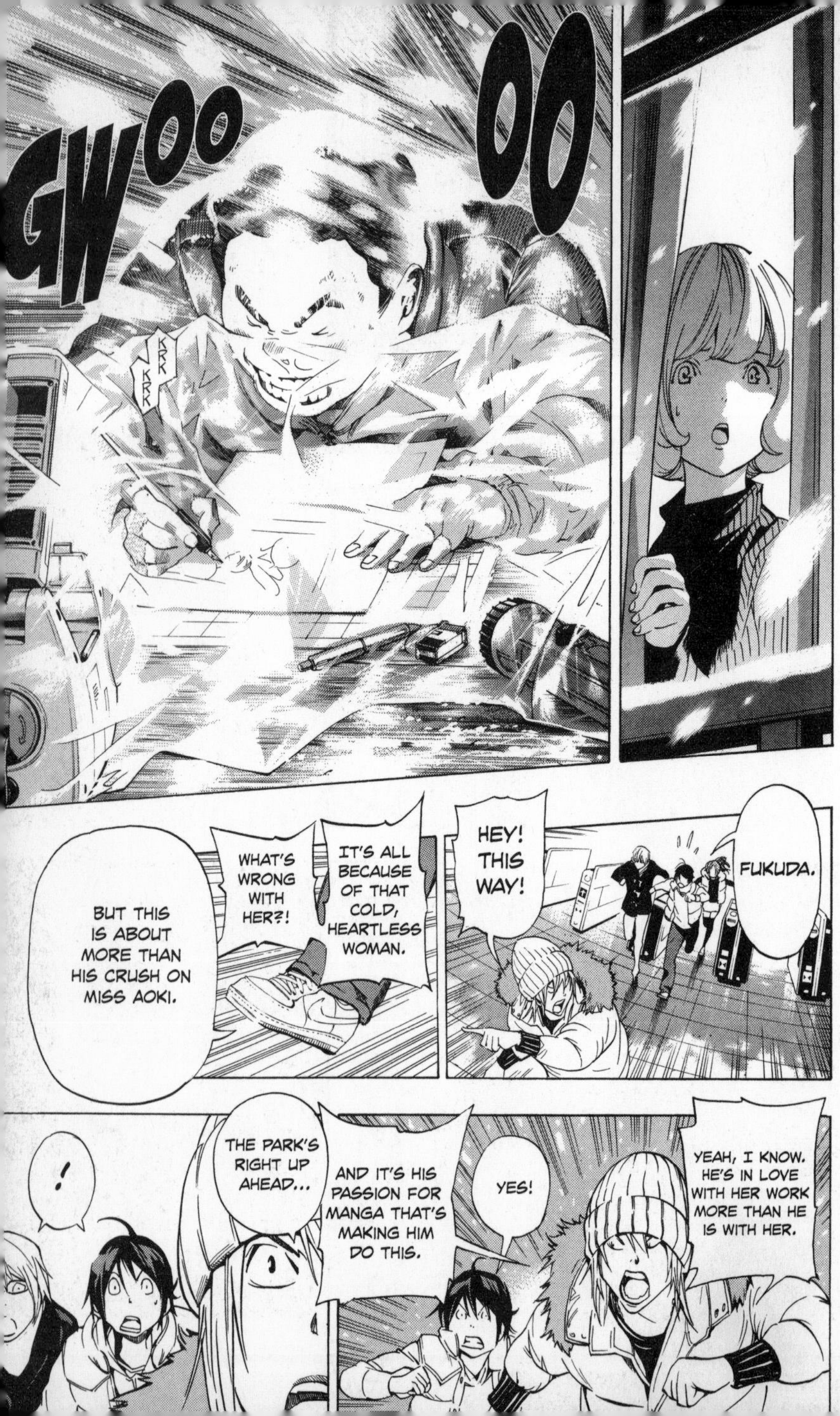
GWOOOO
KRK KRK
FUKUDA.
HEY! THIS WAY!
IT'S ALL BECAUSE OF THAT COLD, HEARTLESS WOMAN.
WHAT'S WRONG WITH HER?!
BUT THIS IS ABOUT MORE THAN HIS CRUSH ON MISS AOKI.
YEAH, I KNOW. HE'S IN LOVE WITH HER WORK MORE THAN HE IS WITH HER.
YES!
AND IT'S HIS PASSION FOR MANGA THAT'S MAKING HIM DO THIS.
THE PARK'S RIGHT UP AHEAD...
!

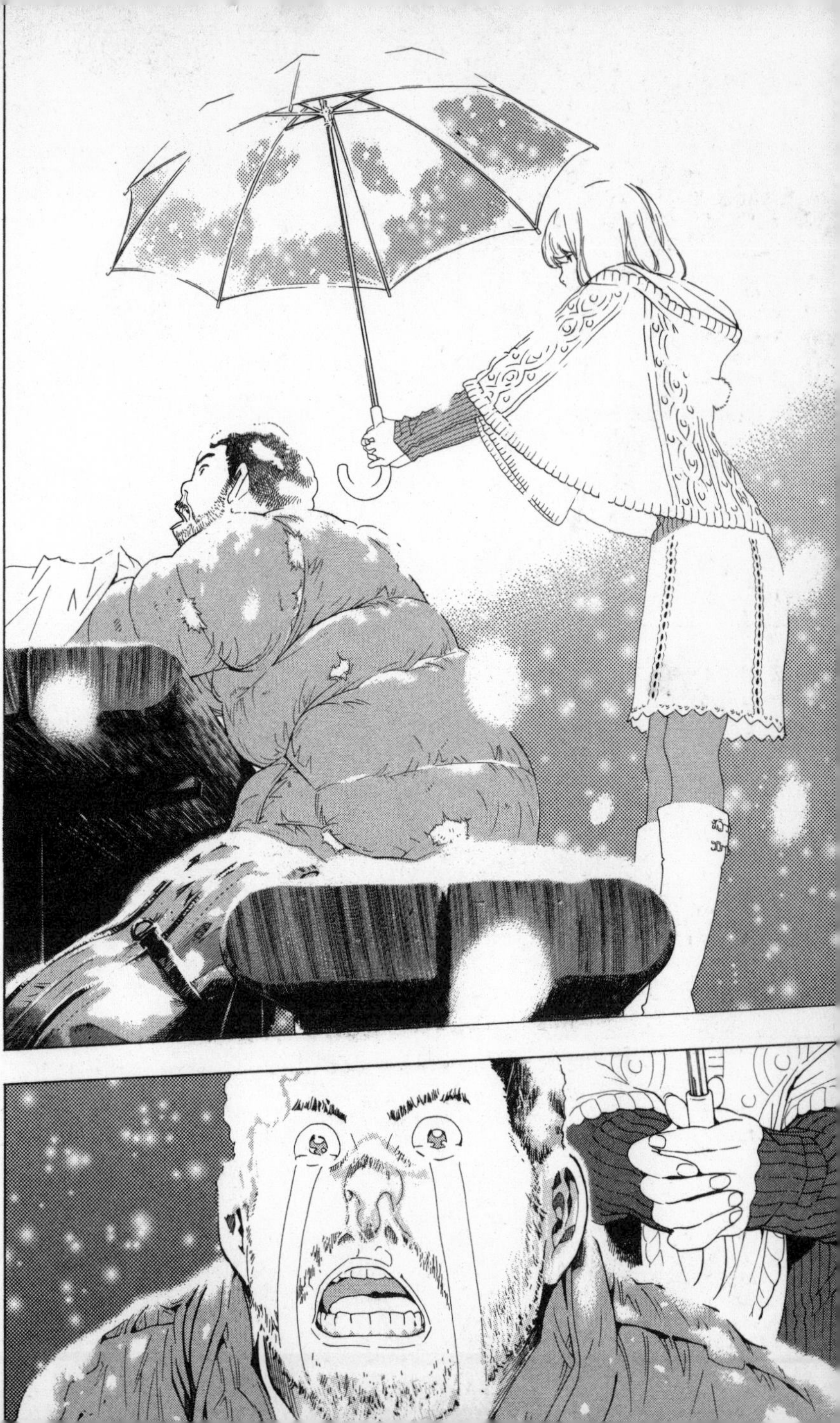

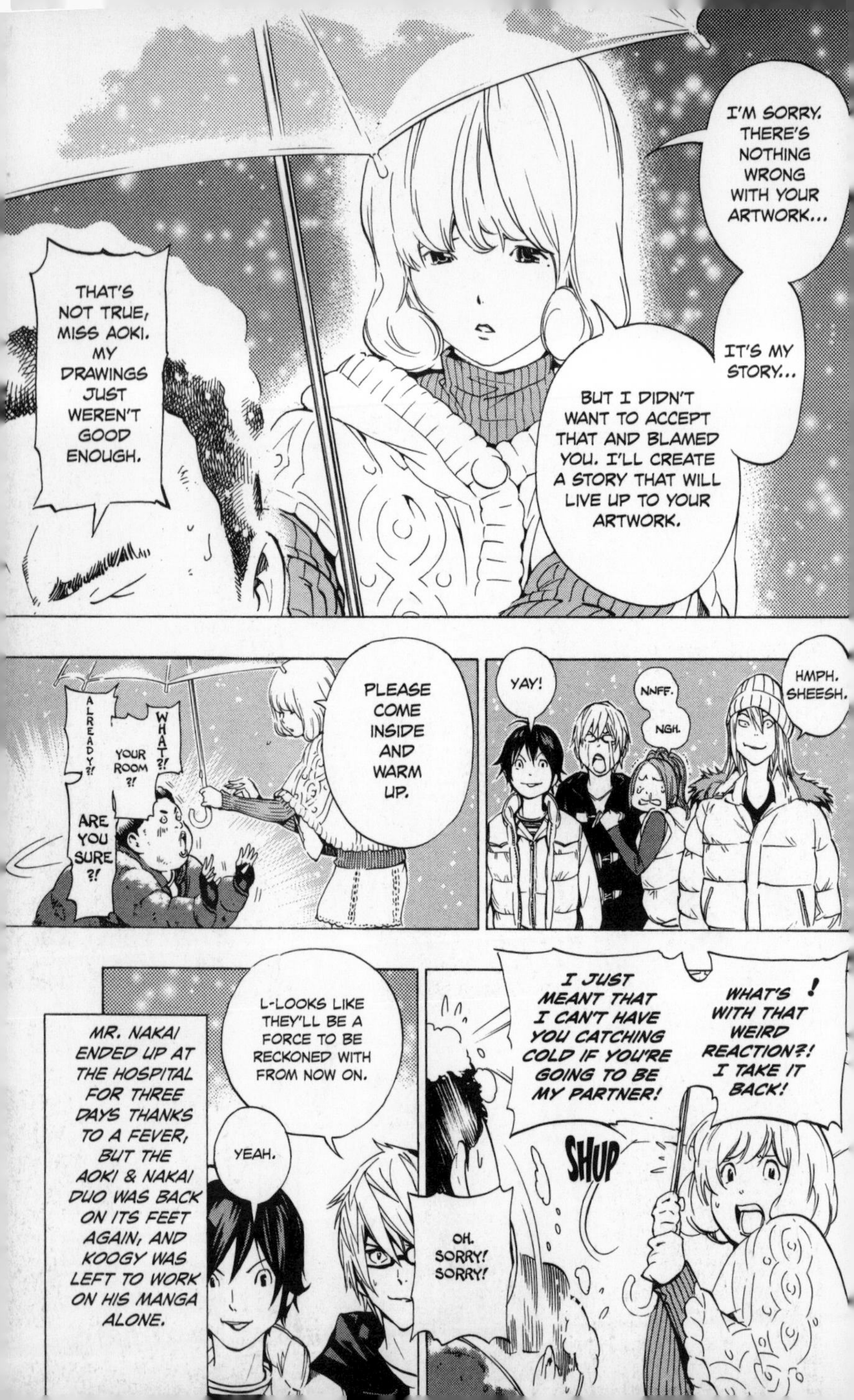
I'M SORRY. THERE'S NOTHING WRONG WITH YOUR ARTWORK...
IT'S MY STORY...
BUT I DIDN'T WANT TO ACCEPT THAT AND BLAMED YOU. I'LL CREATE A STORY THAT WILL LIVE UP TO YOUR ARTWORK.
THAT'S NOT TRUE, MISS AOKI. MY DRAWINGS JUST WEREN'T GOOD ENOUGH.
HMPH. SHEESH.
NNFF.
NGH.
YAY!
PLEASE COME INSIDE AND WARM UP.
WHAT?!
YOUR ROOM?!
ALREADY?!
ARE YOU SURE?!
WHAT'S WITH THAT WEIRD REACTION?! I TAKE IT BACK!
I JUST MEANT THAT I CAN'T HAVE YOU CATCHING COLD IF YOU'RE GOING TO BE MY PARTNER!
SHUP
OH. SORRY! SORRY!
L-LOOKS LIKE THEY'LL BE A FORCE TO BE RECKONED WITH FROM NOW ON.
YEAH.
MR. NAKAI ENDED UP AT THE HOSPITAL FOR THREE DAYS THANKS TO A FEVER, BUT THE AOKI & NAKAI DUO WAS BACK ON ITS FEET AGAIN, AND KOOGY WAS LEFT TO WORK ON HIS MANGA ALONE.

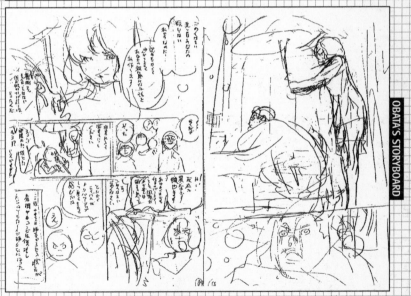

OHBA'S STORYBOARD

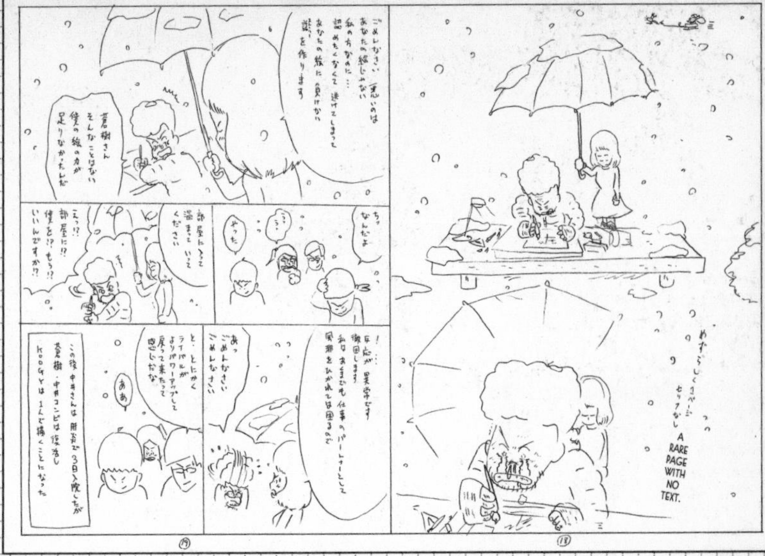

めずらしくこのページセリフなし
A RARE PAGE WITH NO TEXT.
ごめんなさい 悪いのは あなたの絵じゃない 私の方なの… 認めたくなくて 逃げてしまって あなたの絵に負けない話を作ります
蒼樹さん そんなことはない 僕の絵の力が足りなかったんだ
ちっ なんだよ
う…
やった
部屋に入って 温まって いってください
えっ!? 部屋に!? 僕を!? もう!? いいんですか!?
!… 反応が異常です 撤回します 私はあくまでも仕事のパートナーとして 風邪をひかれては困るので
あっ ごめんなさい ごめんなさい
と、とにかく ライバルが よりパワーアップして 戻って来たって 感じだな
ああ
この後中井さんは 肺炎で3日入院したが 蒼樹・中井コンビは 復活し K.O.O.Kとは1人で描くことになった

OBATA'S STORYBOARD

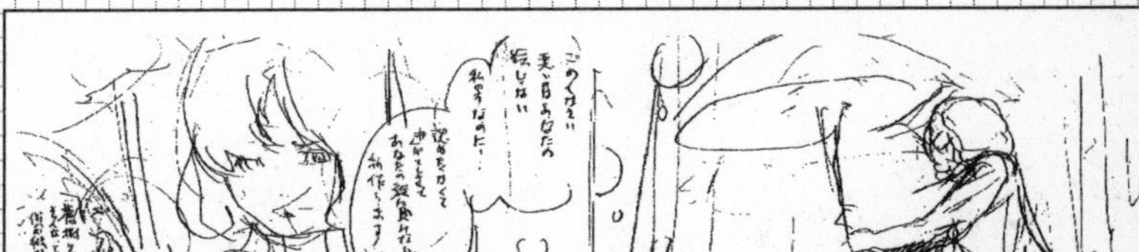

COMPLETE!

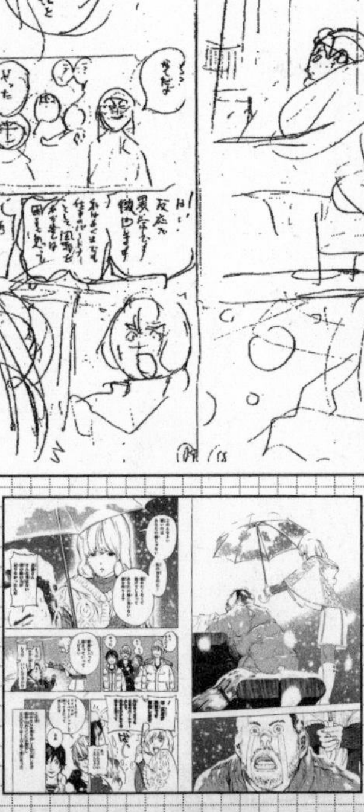

※CREATOR STORYBOARDS AND FINISHED PAGES IN JAPANESE

BAKUMAN。 vol.5

"Until the Final Draft Is Complete"

Chapter 38, pp. 84-85

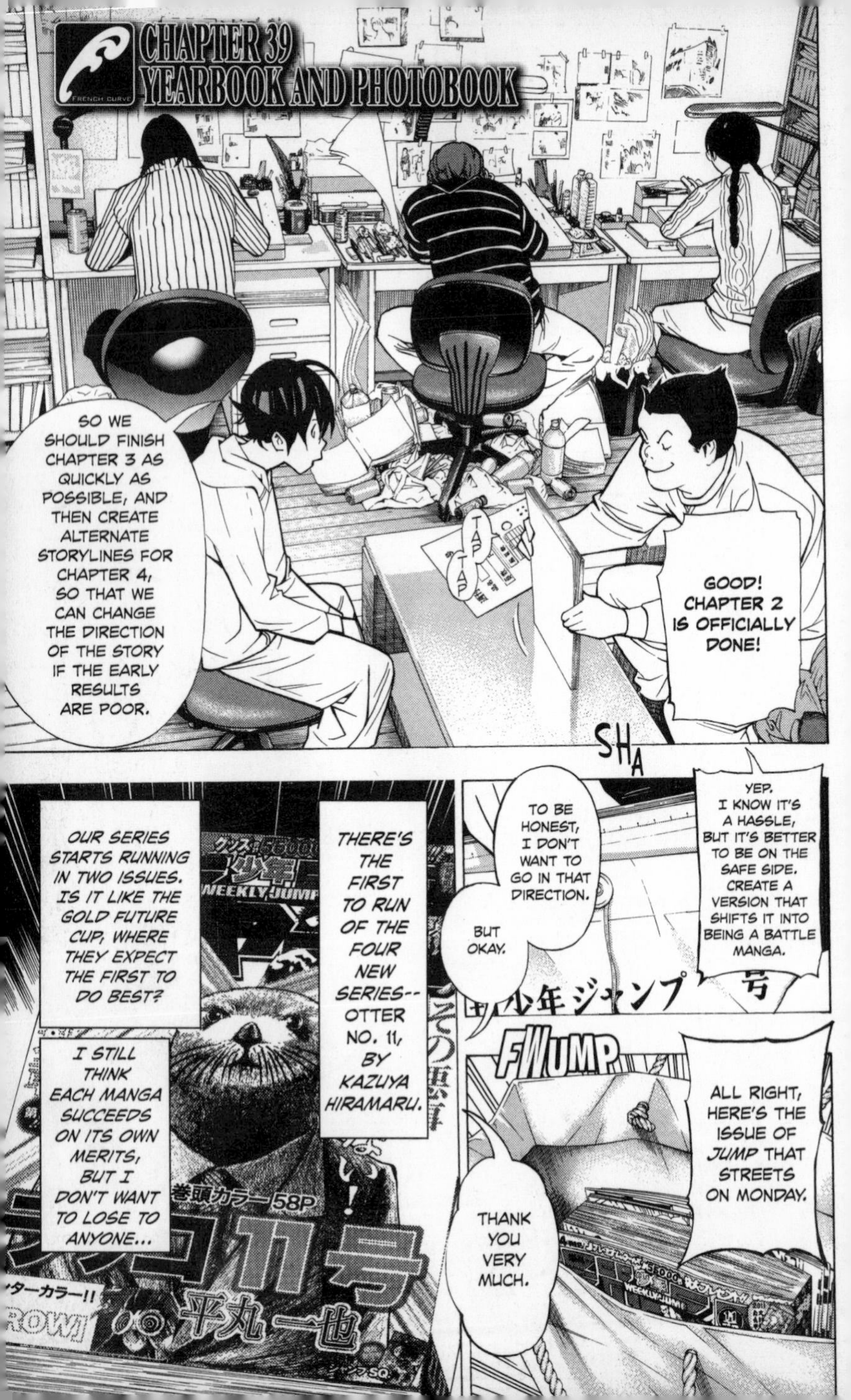

CHAPTER 39
YEARBOOK AND PHOTOBOOK
FRENCH CURVE
TAP TAP
GOOD! CHAPTER 2 IS OFFICIALLY DONE!
SO WE SHOULD FINISH CHAPTER 3 AS QUICKLY AS POSSIBLE, AND THEN CREATE ALTERNATE STORYLINES FOR CHAPTER 4, SO THAT WE CAN CHANGE THE DIRECTION OF THE STORY IF THE EARLY RESULTS ARE POOR.
SHA
YEP. I KNOW IT'S A HASSLE, BUT IT'S BETTER TO BE ON THE SAFE SIDE. CREATE A VERSION THAT SHIFTS IT INTO BEING A BATTLE MANGA.
TO BE HONEST, I DON'T WANT TO GO IN THAT DIRECTION.
BUT OKAY.
少年ジャンプ 号
FWUMP
ALL RIGHT, HERE'S THE ISSUE OF *JUMP* THAT STREETS ON MONDAY.
THANK YOU VERY MUCH.
THERE'S THE FIRST TO RUN OF THE FOUR NEW SERIES-- OTTER NO. 11, BY KAZUYA HIRAMARU.
OUR SERIES STARTS RUNNING IN TWO ISSUES. IS IT LIKE THE GOLD FUTURE CUP, WHERE THEY EXPECT THE FIRST TO DO BEST?
I STILL THINK EACH MANGA SUCCEEDS ON ITS OWN MERITS, BUT I DON'T WANT TO LOSE TO ANYONE...
WEEKLY JUMP
巻頭カラー 58P
11号
平丸一也

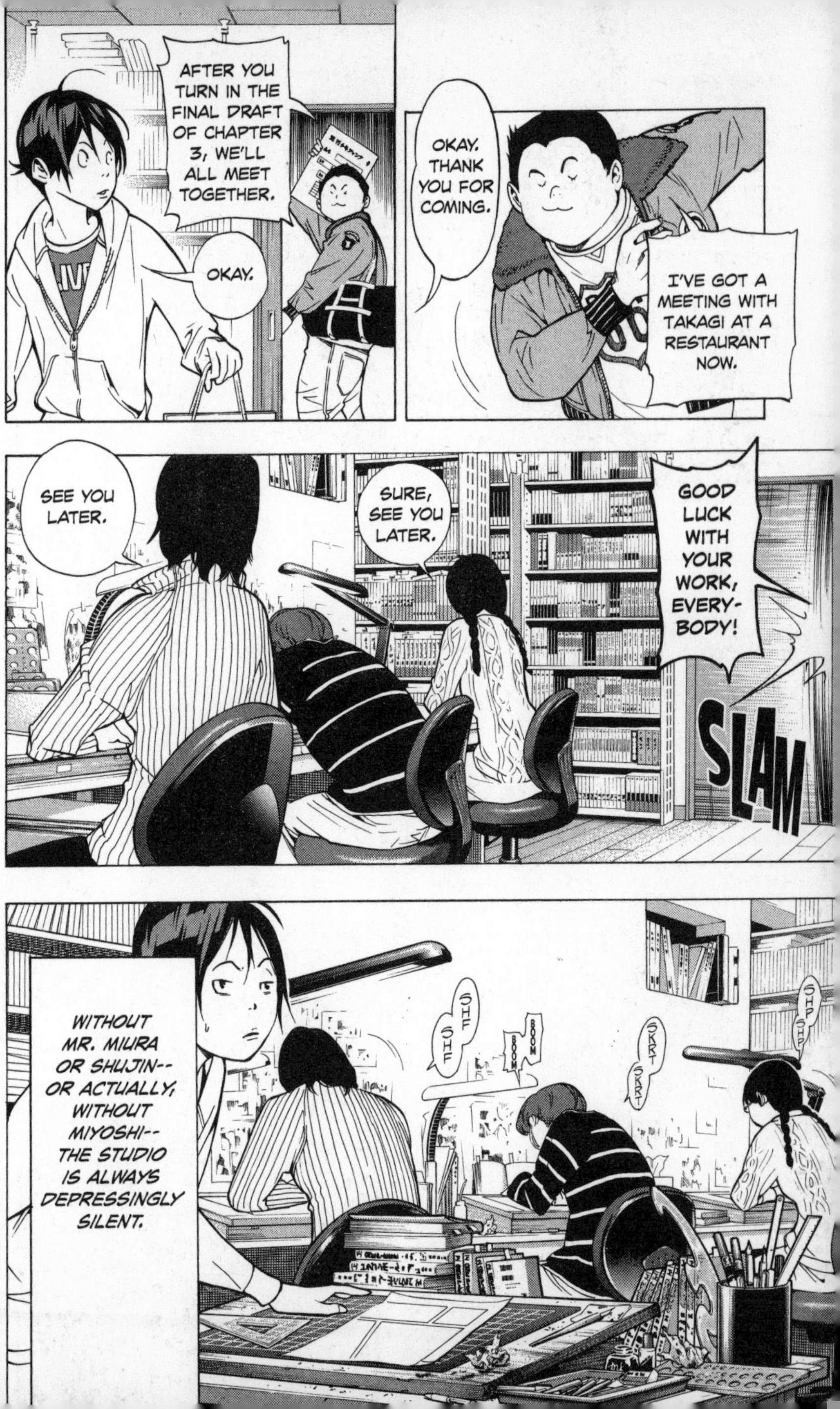
OKAY. THANK YOU FOR COMING.
I'VE GOT A MEETING WITH TAKAGI AT A RESTAURANT NOW.
AFTER YOU TURN IN THE FINAL DRAFT OF CHAPTER 3, WE'LL ALL MEET TOGETHER.
OKAY.
GOOD LUCK WITH YOUR WORK, EVERY-BODY!
SLAM
SURE, SEE YOU LATER.
SEE YOU LATER.
SHP SHP
SKRT SKRT
BOOM BOOM
SHF SHF
WITHOUT MR. MIURA OR SHUJIN-- OR ACTUALLY, WITHOUT MIYOSHI-- THE STUDIO IS ALWAYS DEPRESSINGLY SILENT.

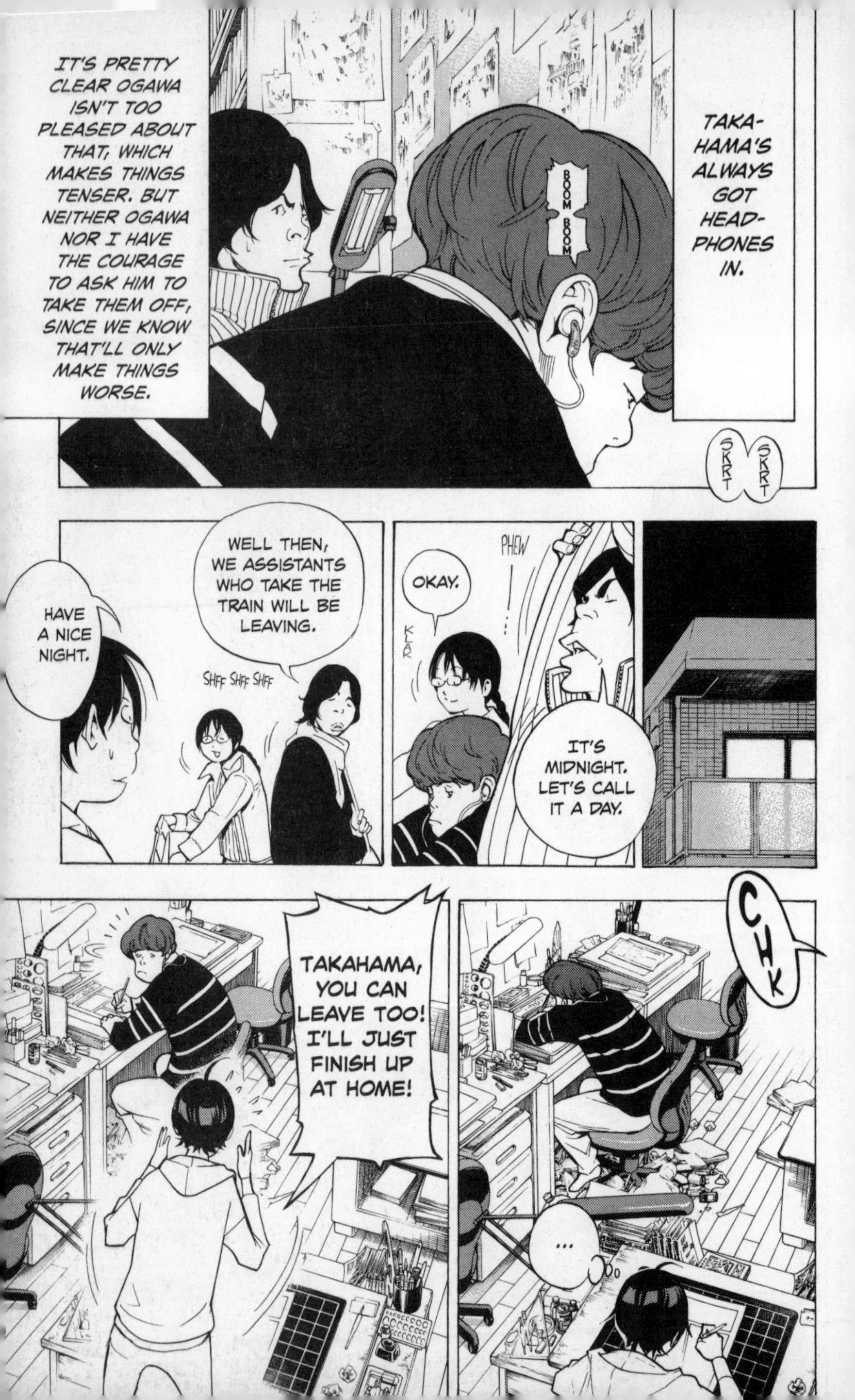
TAKAHAMA'S ALWAYS GOT HEADPHONES IN.
BOOM BOOM
IT'S PRETTY CLEAR OGAWA ISN'T TOO PLEASED ABOUT THAT, WHICH MAKES THINGS TENSER. BUT NEITHER OGAWA NOR I HAVE THE COURAGE TO ASK HIM TO TAKE THEM OFF, SINCE WE KNOW THAT'LL ONLY MAKE THINGS WORSE.
SKRT SKRT
PHEW
IT'S MIDNIGHT. LET'S CALL IT A DAY.
OKAY.
KLAR
WELL THEN, WE ASSISTANTS WHO TAKE THE TRAIN WILL BE LEAVING.
SHFF SHFF SHFF
HAVE A NICE NIGHT.
CHK
...
TAKAHAMA, YOU CAN LEAVE TOO! I'LL JUST FINISH UP AT HOME!

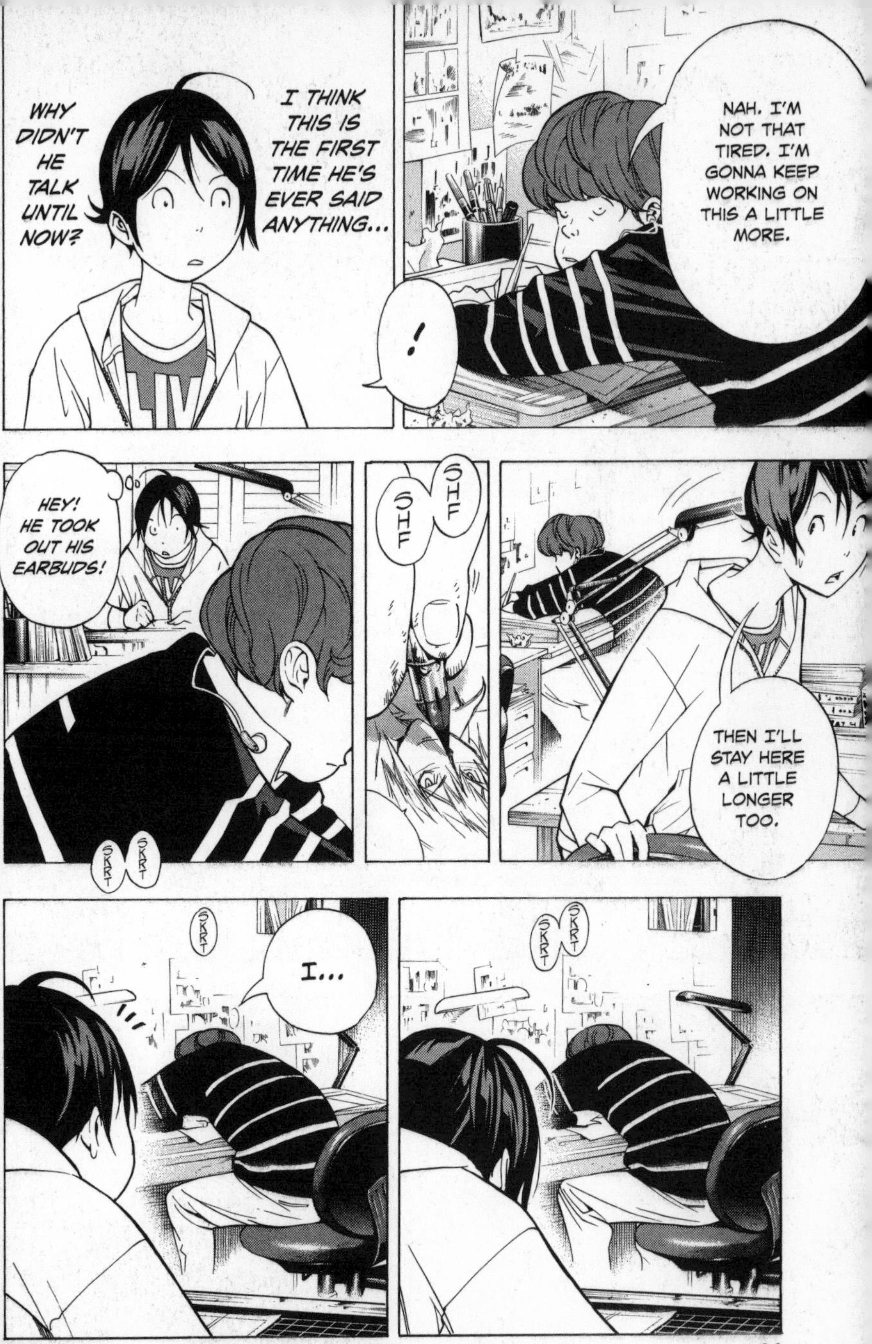
NAH. I'M NOT THAT TIRED. I'M GONNA KEEP WORKING ON THIS A LITTLE MORE.
!
I THINK THIS IS THE FIRST TIME HE'S EVER SAID ANYTHING...
WHY DIDN'T HE TALK UNTIL NOW?
THEN I'LL STAY HERE A LITTLE LONGER TOO.
SHF
SHF
HEY! HE TOOK OUT HIS EARBUDS!
SKRT
SKRT
SKRT
SKRT
SKRT
I...

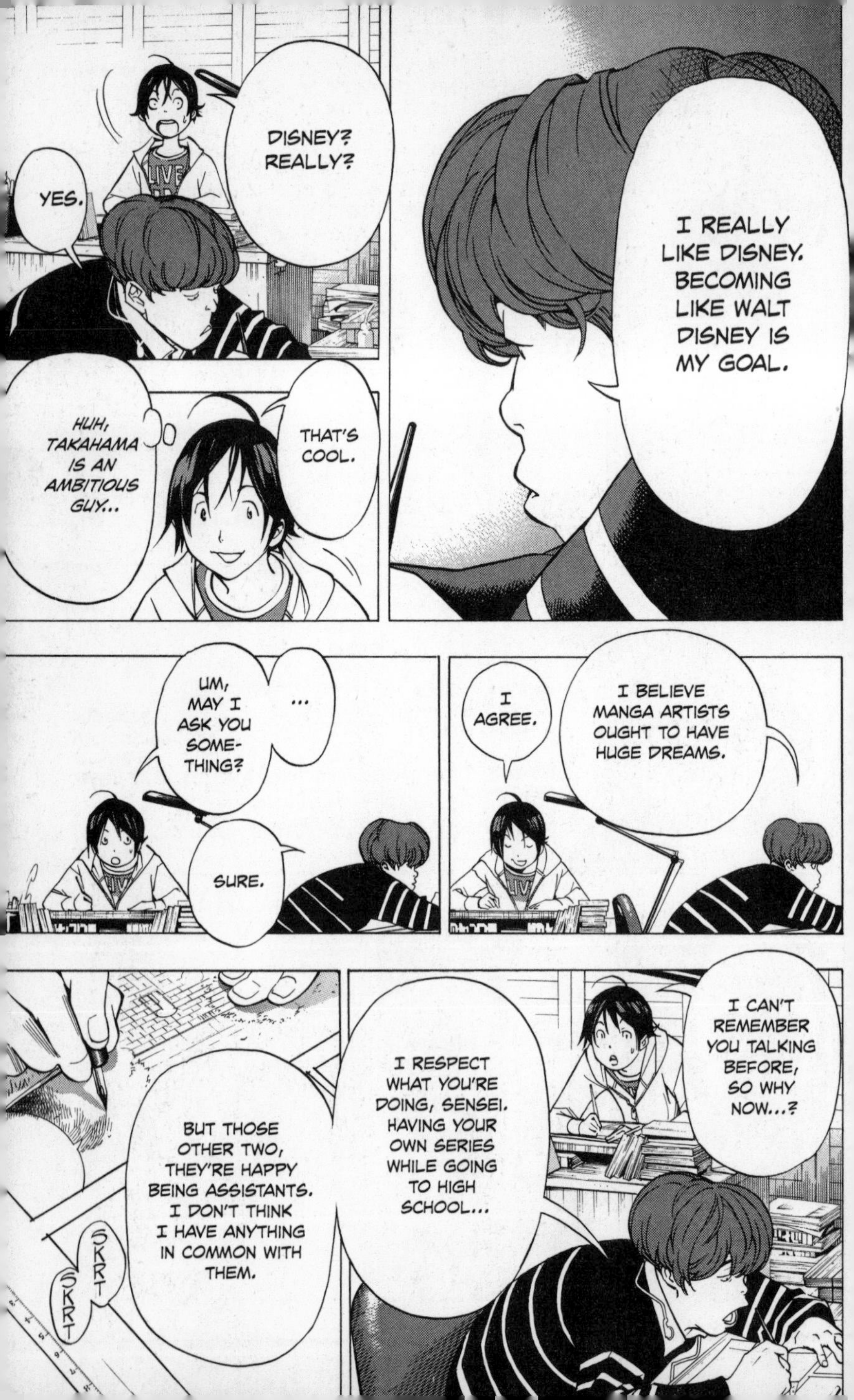
I REALLY LIKE DISNEY. BECOMING LIKE WALT DISNEY IS MY GOAL.
DISNEY? REALLY?
YES.
THAT'S COOL.
HUH, TAKAHAMA IS AN AMBITIOUS GUY...
I BELIEVE MANGA ARTISTS OUGHT TO HAVE HUGE DREAMS.
I AGREE.
...
UM, MAY I ASK YOU SOME-THING?
SURE.
I CAN'T REMEMBER YOU TALKING BEFORE, SO WHY NOW...?
I RESPECT WHAT YOU'RE DOING, SENSEI. HAVING YOUR OWN SERIES WHILE GOING TO HIGH SCHOOL...
BUT THOSE OTHER TWO, THEY'RE HAPPY BEING ASSISTANTS. I DON'T THINK I HAVE ANYTHING IN COMMON WITH THEM.
SKRT
SKRT

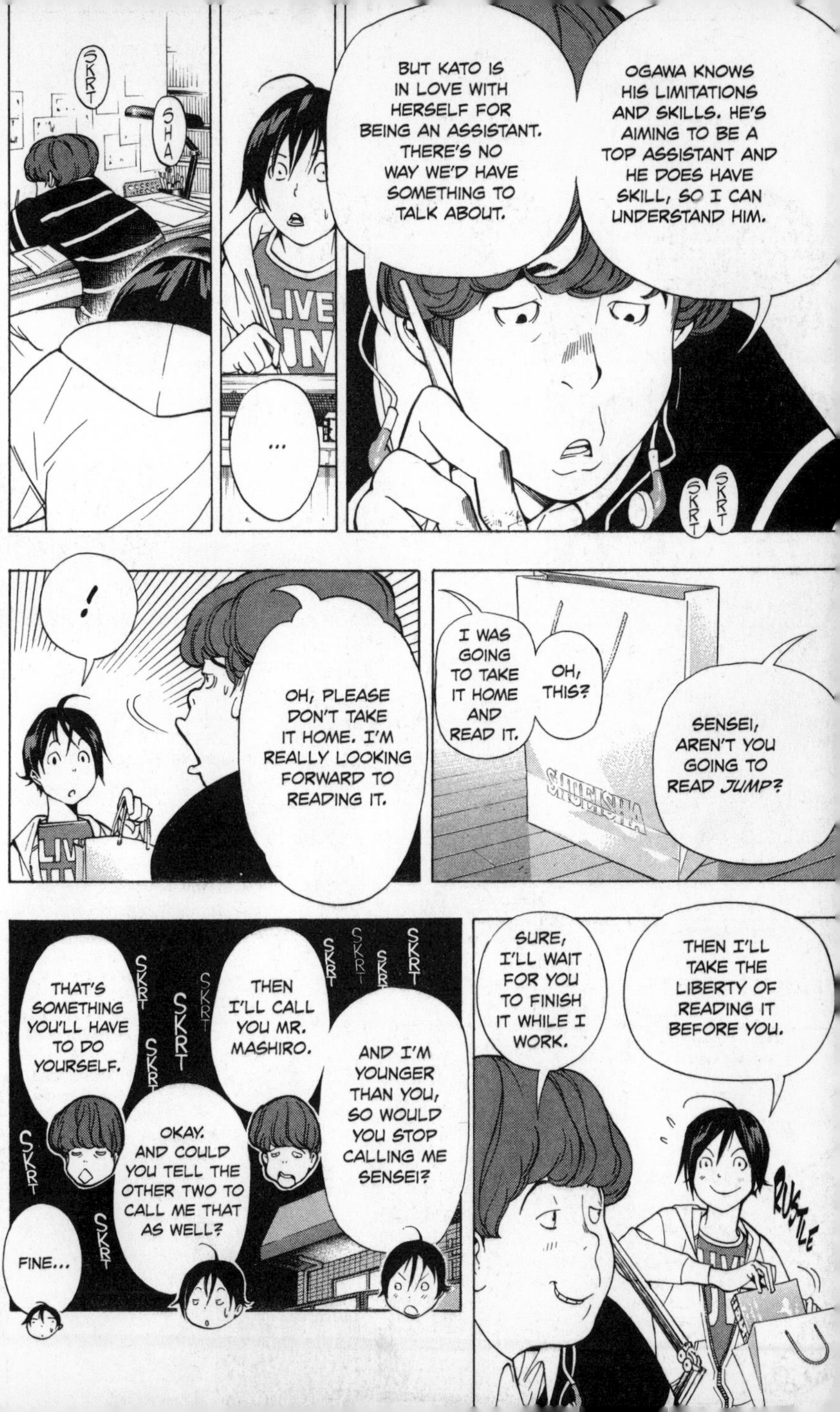
OGAWA KNOWS HIS LIMITATIONS AND SKILLS. HE'S AIMING TO BE A TOP ASSISTANT AND HE DOES HAVE SKILL, SO I CAN UNDERSTAND HIM.
BUT KATO IS IN LOVE WITH HERSELF FOR BEING AN ASSISTANT. THERE'S NO WAY WE'D HAVE SOMETHING TO TALK ABOUT.
SKRT
SKRT
...
SKRT
SHA
SENSEI, AREN'T YOU GOING TO READ *JUMP*?
OH, THIS?
I WAS GOING TO TAKE IT HOME AND READ IT.
SHUEISHA
OH, PLEASE DON'T TAKE IT HOME. I'M REALLY LOOKING FORWARD TO READING IT.
!
THEN I'LL TAKE THE LIBERTY OF READING IT BEFORE YOU.
SURE, I'LL WAIT FOR YOU TO FINISH IT WHILE I WORK.
RUSTLE
SKRT
SKRT
SKRT
AND I'M YOUNGER THAN YOU, SO WOULD YOU STOP CALLING ME SENSEI?
THEN I'LL CALL YOU MR. MASHIRO.
SKRT
SKRT
SKRT
OKAY. AND COULD YOU TELL THE OTHER TWO TO CALL ME THAT AS WELL?
THAT'S SOMETHING YOU'LL HAVE TO DO YOURSELF.
SKRT
SKRT
SKRT
FINE...

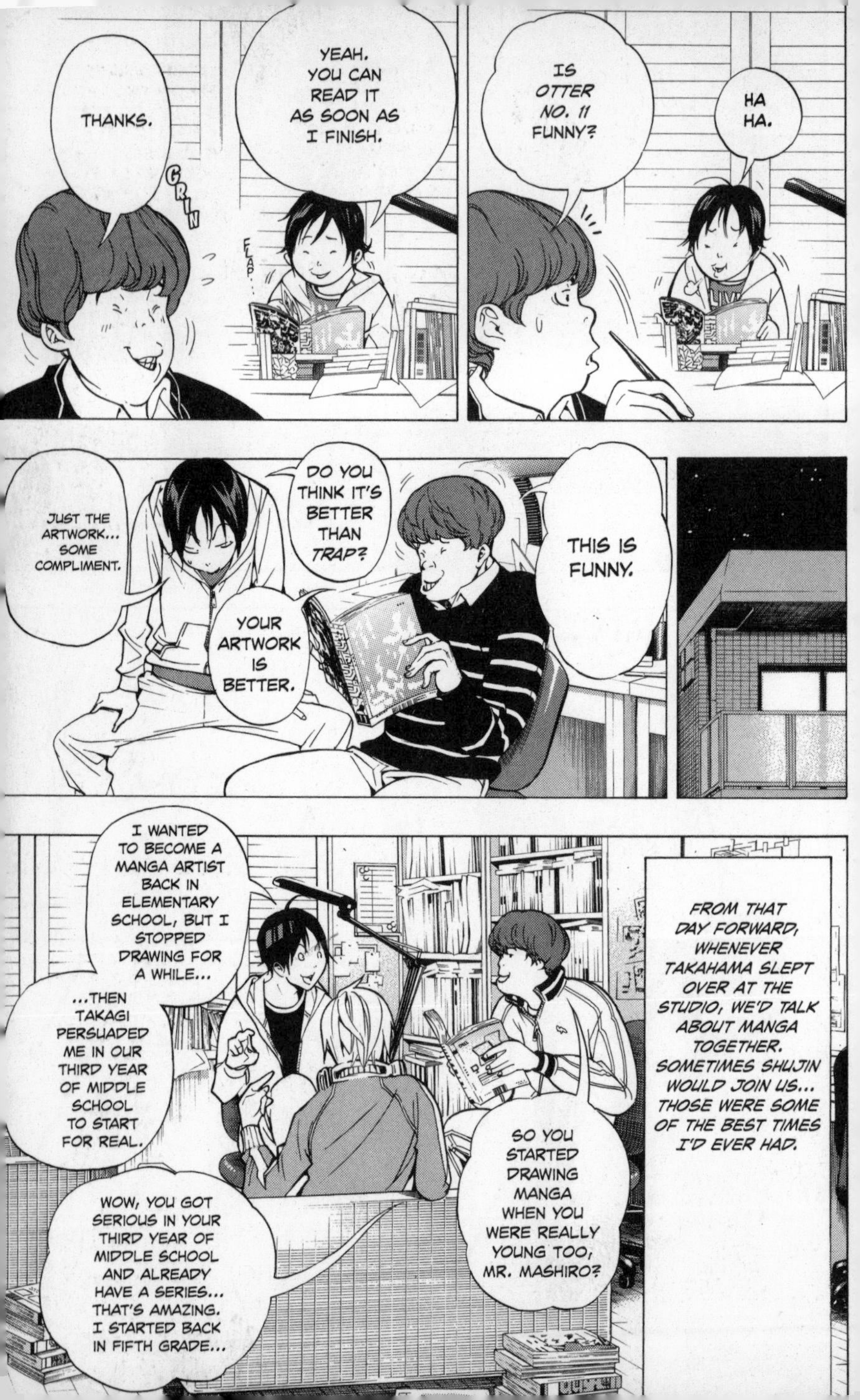
HA HA.
IS *OTTER NO. 11* FUNNY?
YEAH. YOU CAN READ IT AS SOON AS I FINISH.
THANKS.
GRIN
FLAP...
THIS IS FUNNY.
DO YOU THINK IT'S BETTER THAN *TRAP*?
YOUR ARTWORK IS BETTER.
JUST THE ARTWORK... SOME COMPLIMENT.
FROM THAT DAY FORWARD, WHENEVER TAKAHAMA SLEPT OVER AT THE STUDIO, WE'D TALK ABOUT MANGA TOGETHER. SOMETIMES SHUJIN WOULD JOIN US... THOSE WERE SOME OF THE BEST TIMES I'D EVER HAD.
I WANTED TO BECOME A MANGA ARTIST BACK IN ELEMENTARY SCHOOL, BUT I STOPPED DRAWING FOR A WHILE...
...THEN TAKAGI PERSUADED ME IN OUR THIRD YEAR OF MIDDLE SCHOOL TO START FOR REAL.
SO YOU STARTED DRAWING MANGA WHEN YOU WERE REALLY YOUNG TOO, MR. MASHIRO?
WOW, YOU GOT SERIOUS IN YOUR THIRD YEAR OF MIDDLE SCHOOL AND ALREADY HAVE A SERIES... THAT'S AMAZING. I STARTED BACK IN FIFTH GRADE...

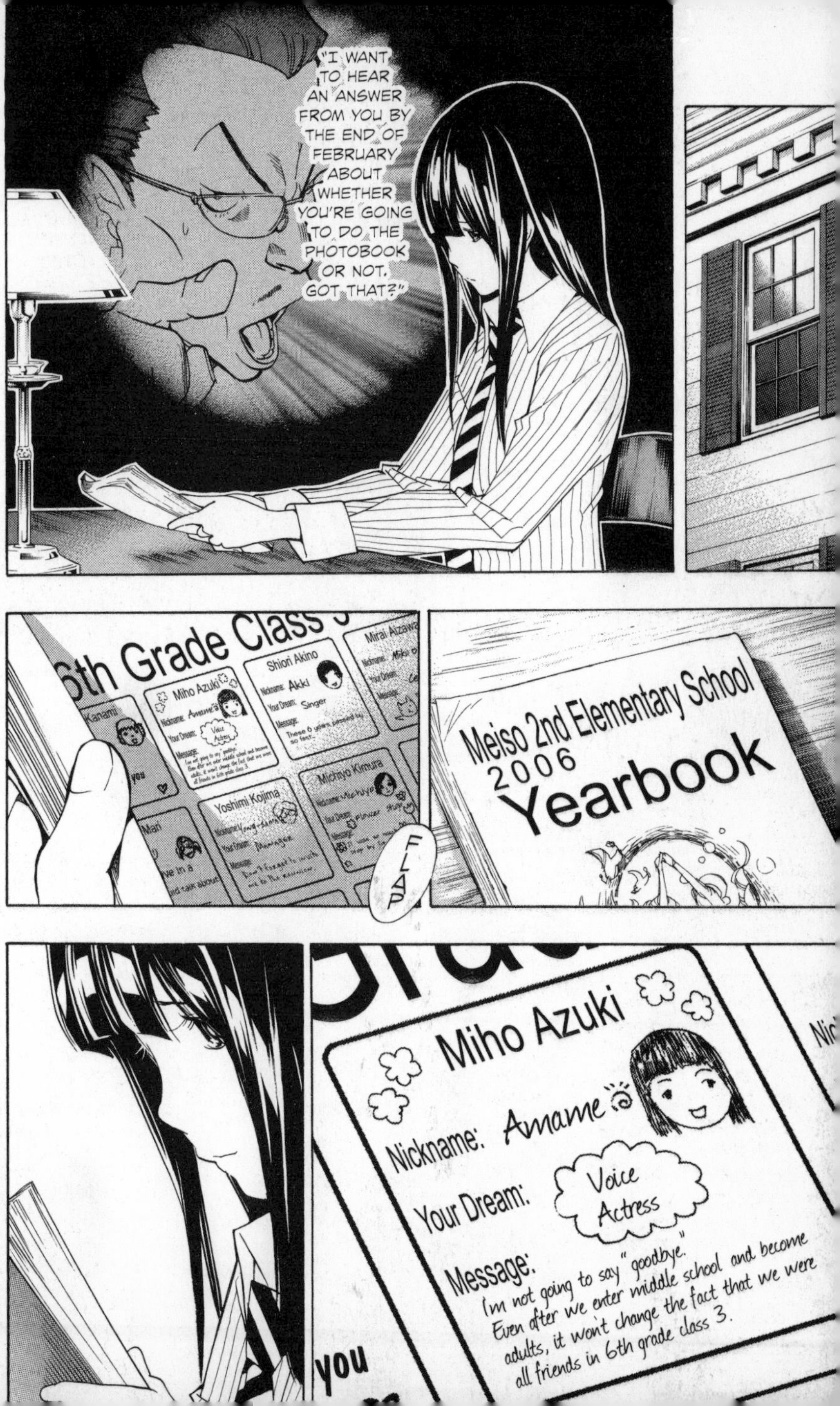
"I WANT TO HEAR AN ANSWER FROM YOU BY THE END OF FEBRUARY ABOUT WHETHER YOU'RE GOING TO DO THE PHOTOBOOK OR NOT. GOT THAT?"
Meiso 2nd Elementary School
2006
Yearbook
6th Grade Class
Mirai Aizawa
Shiori Akino
Nickname: Akki
Your Dream: Singer
Message: These 6 years passed by so fast...
Miho Azuki
Kanami
Michiyo Kimura
Yoshimi Kojima
Mari
FLAP
Miho Azuki
Nickname: Amame
Your Dream: Voice Actress
Message: I'm not going to say "goodbye." Even after we enter middle school and become adults, it won't change the fact that we were all friends in 6th grade class 3.
you
Nic

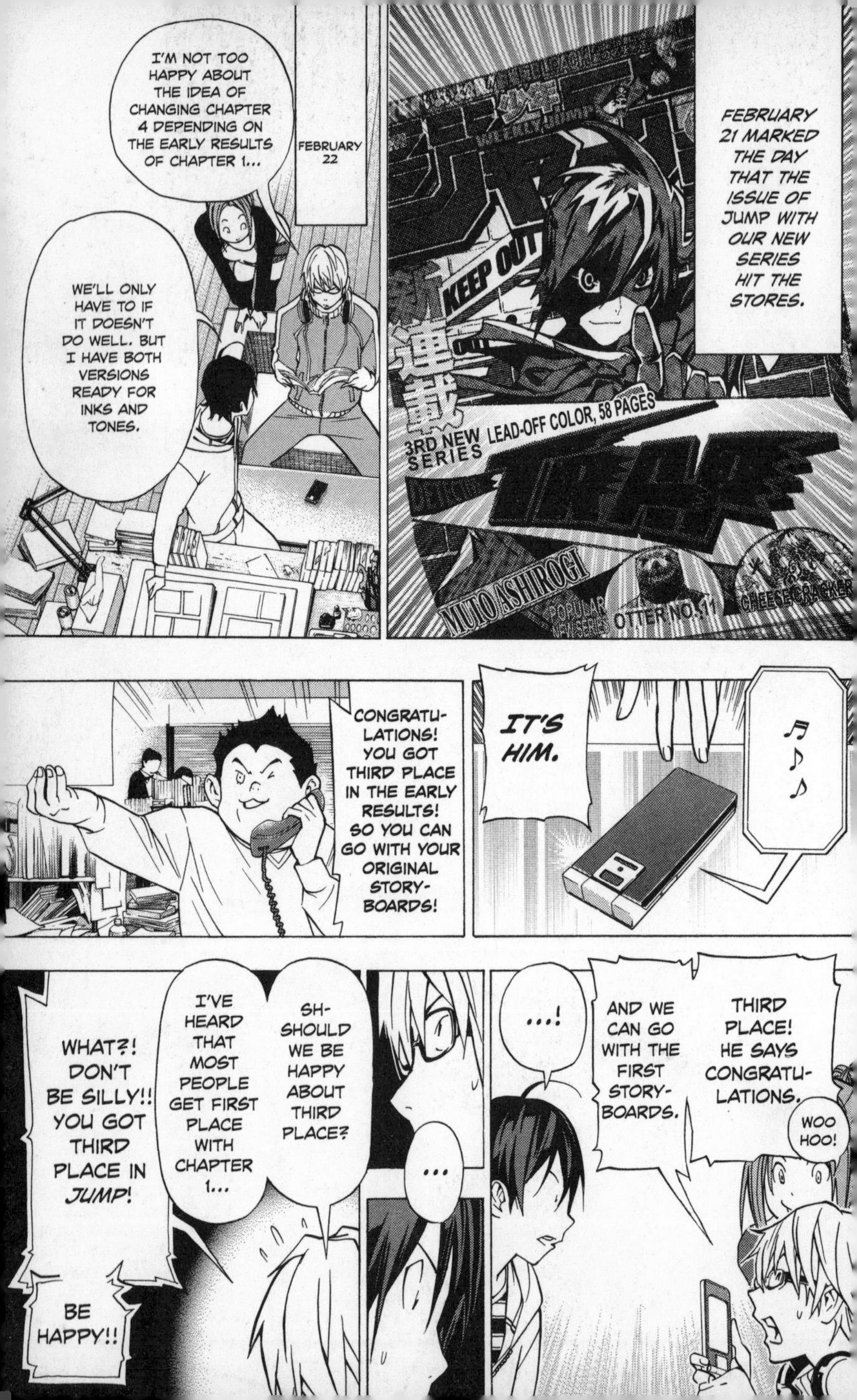
FEBRUARY 21 MARKED THE DAY THAT THE ISSUE OF JUMP WITH OUR NEW SERIES HIT THE STORES.
KEEP OUT
3RD NEW SERIES
LEAD-OFF COLOR, 58 PAGES
MUTO ASHIROGI
POPULAR NEW SERIES
OTTER NO. 11
CHEESE CRACKER
FEBRUARY 22
I'M NOT TOO HAPPY ABOUT THE IDEA OF CHANGING CHAPTER 4 DEPENDING ON THE EARLY RESULTS OF CHAPTER 1...
WE'LL ONLY HAVE TO IF IT DOESN'T DO WELL. BUT I HAVE BOTH VERSIONS READY FOR INKS AND TONES.
♬ ♪ ♪
IT'S HIM.
CONGRATULATIONS! YOU GOT THIRD PLACE IN THE EARLY RESULTS! SO YOU CAN GO WITH YOUR ORIGINAL STORYBOARDS!
THIRD PLACE! HE SAYS CONGRATULATIONS.
WOO HOO!
AND WE CAN GO WITH THE FIRST STORYBOARDS.
...!
...
SH-SHOULD WE BE HAPPY ABOUT THIRD PLACE?
I'VE HEARD THAT MOST PEOPLE GET FIRST PLACE WITH CHAPTER 1...
WHAT?! DON'T BE SILLY!! YOU GOT THIRD PLACE IN *JUMP*!
BE HAPPY!!

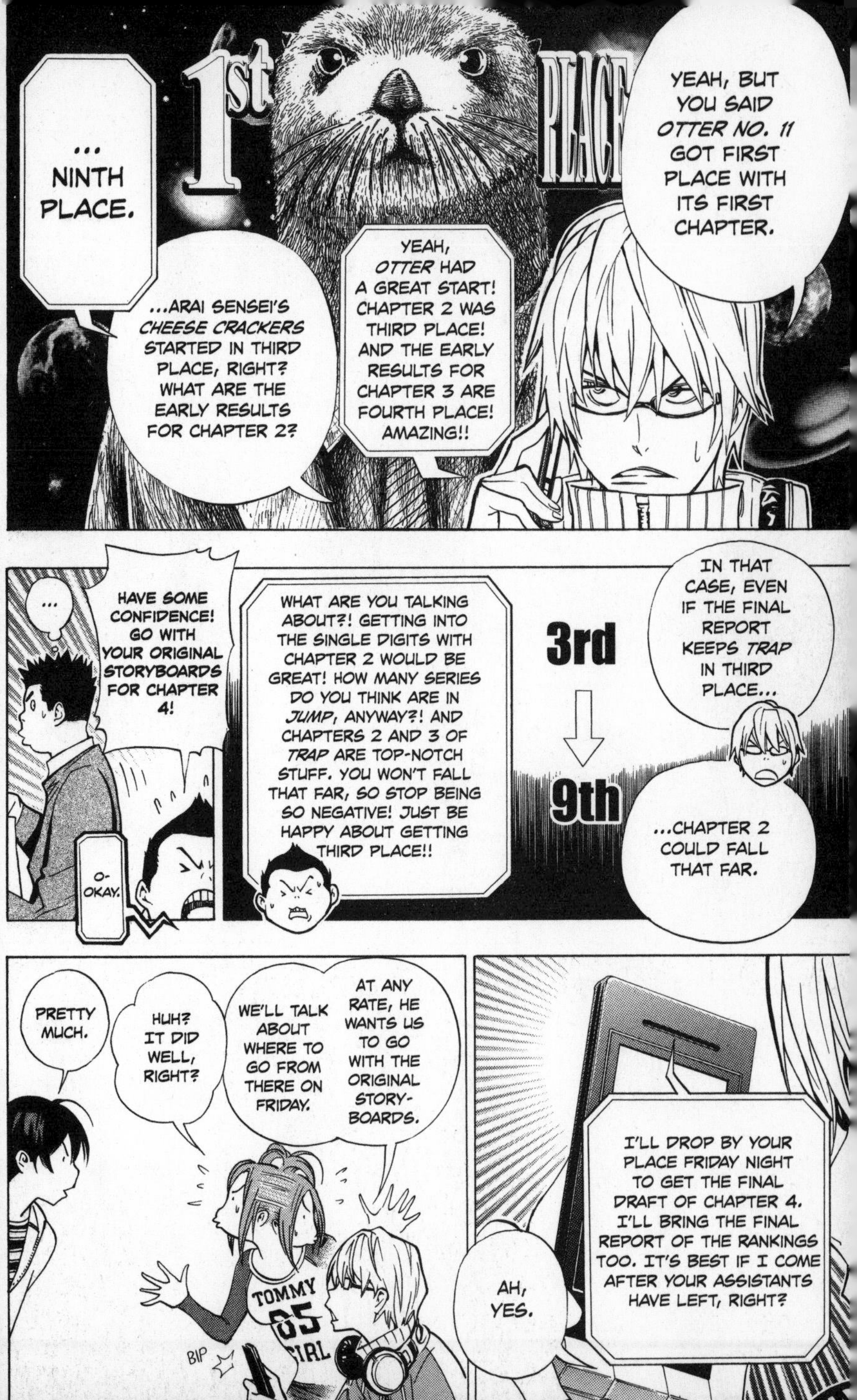
YEAH, BUT YOU SAID *OTTER NO. 11* GOT FIRST PLACE WITH ITS FIRST CHAPTER.
1st PLACE
YEAH, *OTTER* HAD A GREAT START! CHAPTER 2 WAS THIRD PLACE! AND THE EARLY RESULTS FOR CHAPTER 3 ARE FOURTH PLACE! AMAZING!!
...ARAI SENSEI'S *CHEESE CRACKERS* STARTED IN THIRD PLACE, RIGHT? WHAT ARE THE EARLY RESULTS FOR CHAPTER 2?
... NINTH PLACE.
IN THAT CASE, EVEN IF THE FINAL REPORT KEEPS *TRAP* IN THIRD PLACE...
3rd
9th
...CHAPTER 2 COULD FALL THAT FAR.
WHAT ARE YOU TALKING ABOUT?! GETTING INTO THE SINGLE DIGITS WITH CHAPTER 2 WOULD BE GREAT! HOW MANY SERIES DO YOU THINK ARE IN *JUMP*, ANYWAY?! AND CHAPTERS 2 AND 3 OF *TRAP* ARE TOP-NOTCH STUFF. YOU WON'T FALL THAT FAR, SO STOP BEING SO NEGATIVE! JUST BE HAPPY ABOUT GETTING THIRD PLACE!!
HAVE SOME CONFIDENCE! GO WITH YOUR ORIGINAL STORYBOARDS FOR CHAPTER 4!
...
O-OKAY.
I'LL DROP BY YOUR PLACE FRIDAY NIGHT TO GET THE FINAL DRAFT OF CHAPTER 4. I'LL BRING THE FINAL REPORT OF THE RANKINGS TOO. IT'S BEST IF I COME AFTER YOUR ASSISTANTS HAVE LEFT, RIGHT?
AH, YES.
AT ANY RATE, HE WANTS US TO GO WITH THE ORIGINAL STORY-BOARDS.
WE'LL TALK ABOUT WHERE TO GO FROM THERE ON FRIDAY.
HUH? IT DID WELL, RIGHT?
PRETTY MUCH.
TOMMY 85 GIRL
BIP

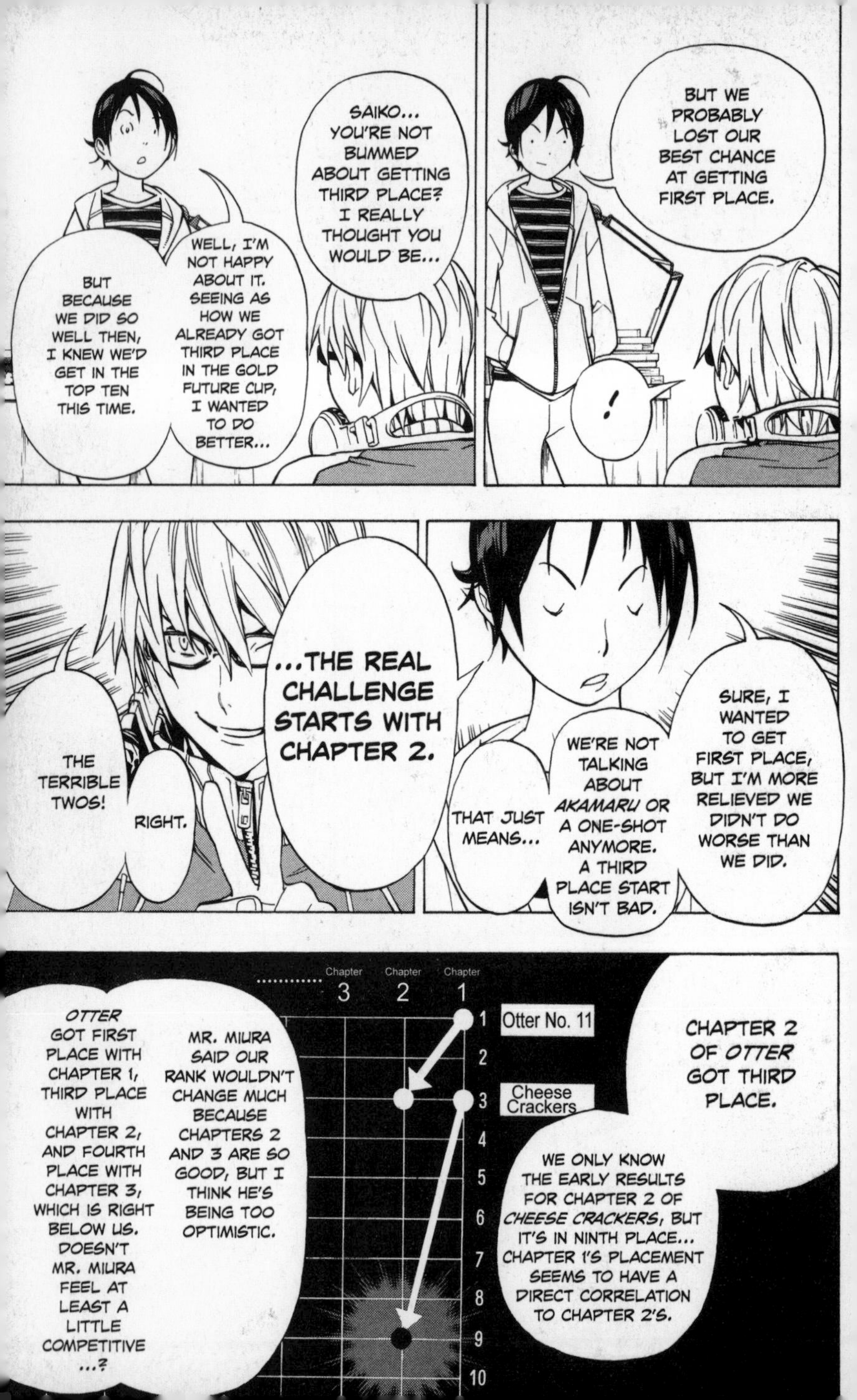
BUT WE PROBABLY LOST OUR BEST CHANCE AT GETTING FIRST PLACE.
!
SAIKO... YOU'RE NOT BUMMED ABOUT GETTING THIRD PLACE? I REALLY THOUGHT YOU WOULD BE...
WELL, I'M NOT HAPPY ABOUT IT. SEEING AS HOW WE ALREADY GOT THIRD PLACE IN THE GOLD FUTURE CUP, I WANTED TO DO BETTER...
BUT BECAUSE WE DID SO WELL THEN, I KNEW WE'D GET IN THE TOP TEN THIS TIME.
SURE, I WANTED TO GET FIRST PLACE, BUT I'M MORE RELIEVED WE DIDN'T DO WORSE THAN WE DID.
WE'RE NOT TALKING ABOUT *AKAMARU* OR A ONE-SHOT ANYMORE. A THIRD PLACE START ISN'T BAD.
THAT JUST MEANS...
...THE REAL CHALLENGE STARTS WITH CHAPTER 2.
RIGHT.
THE TERRIBLE TWOS!
CHAPTER 2 OF *OTTER* GOT THIRD PLACE.
Chapter 3
Chapter 2
Chapter 1
1
2
3
4
5
6
7
8
9
10
Otter No. 11
Cheese Crackers
WE ONLY KNOW THE EARLY RESULTS FOR CHAPTER 2 OF *CHEESE CRACKERS*, BUT IT'S IN NINTH PLACE... CHAPTER 1'S PLACEMENT SEEMS TO HAVE A DIRECT CORRELATION TO CHAPTER 2'S.
MR. MIURA SAID OUR RANK WOULDN'T CHANGE MUCH BECAUSE CHAPTERS 2 AND 3 ARE SO GOOD, BUT I THINK HE'S BEING TOO OPTIMISTIC.
OTTER GOT FIRST PLACE WITH CHAPTER 1, THIRD PLACE WITH CHAPTER 2, AND FOURTH PLACE WITH CHAPTER 3, WHICH IS RIGHT BELOW US. DOESN'T MR. MIURA FEEL AT LEAST A LITTLE COMPETITIVE ...?

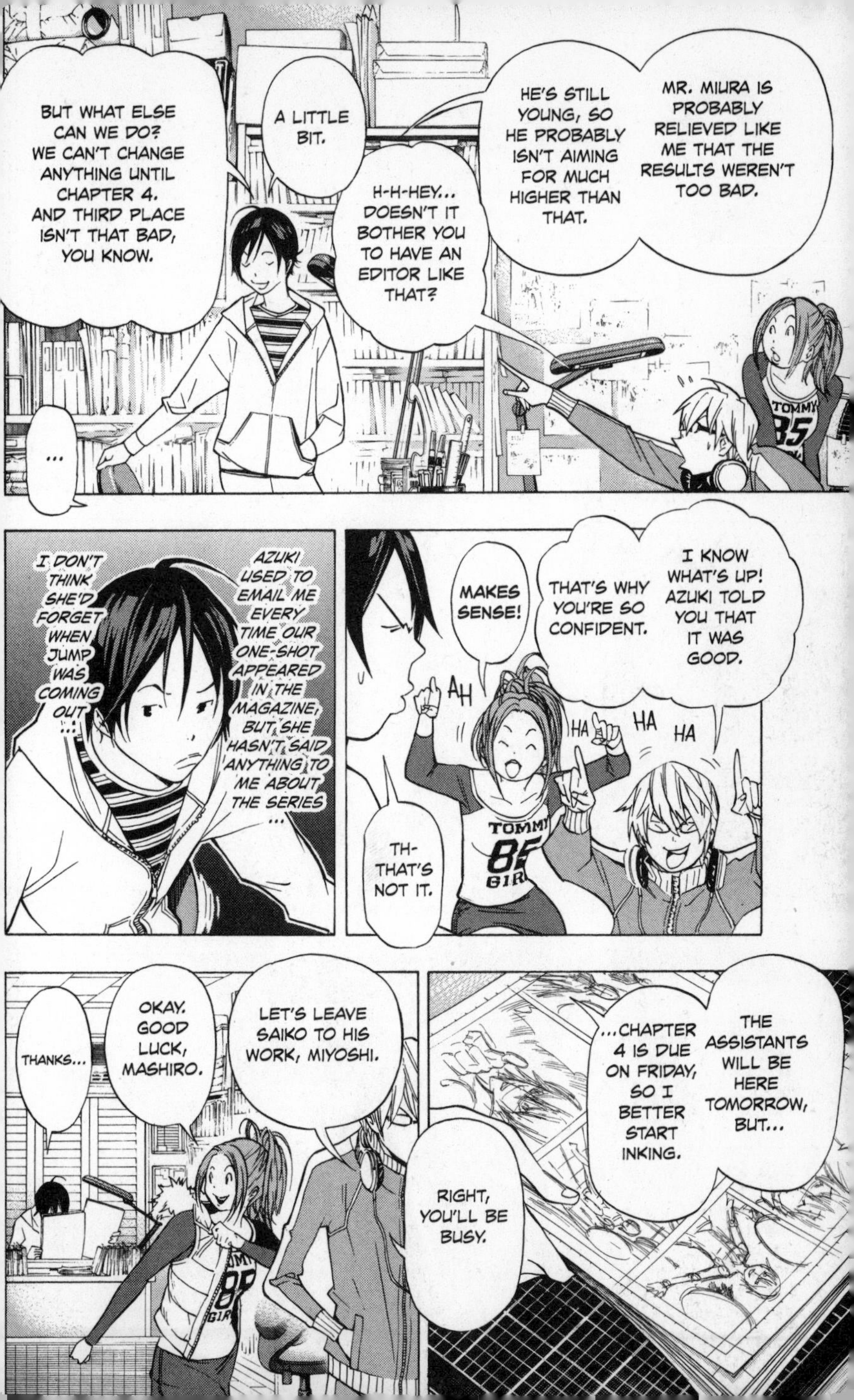
MR. MIURA IS PROBABLY RELIEVED LIKE ME THAT THE RESULTS WEREN'T TOO BAD.
HE'S STILL YOUNG, SO HE PROBABLY ISN'T AIMING FOR MUCH HIGHER THAN THAT.
H-H-HEY... DOESN'T IT BOTHER YOU TO HAVE AN EDITOR LIKE THAT?
A LITTLE BIT.
BUT WHAT ELSE CAN WE DO? WE CAN'T CHANGE ANYTHING UNTIL CHAPTER 4. AND THIRD PLACE ISN'T THAT BAD, YOU KNOW.
...
I KNOW WHAT'S UP! AZUKI TOLD YOU THAT IT WAS GOOD.
THAT'S WHY YOU'RE SO CONFIDENT.
MAKES SENSE!
AH
HA HA HA
TH- THAT'S NOT IT.
AZUKI USED TO EMAIL ME EVERY TIME OUR ONE-SHOT APPEARED IN THE MAGAZINE, BUT SHE HASN'T SAID ANYTHING TO ME ABOUT THE SERIES...
I DON'T THINK SHE'D FORGET WHEN JUMP WAS COMING OUT...
THE ASSISTANTS WILL BE HERE TOMORROW, BUT...
...CHAPTER 4 IS DUE ON FRIDAY, SO I BETTER START INKING.
RIGHT, YOU'LL BE BUSY.
LET'S LEAVE SAIKO TO HIS WORK, MIYOSHI.
OKAY. GOOD LUCK, MASHIRO.
THANKS...

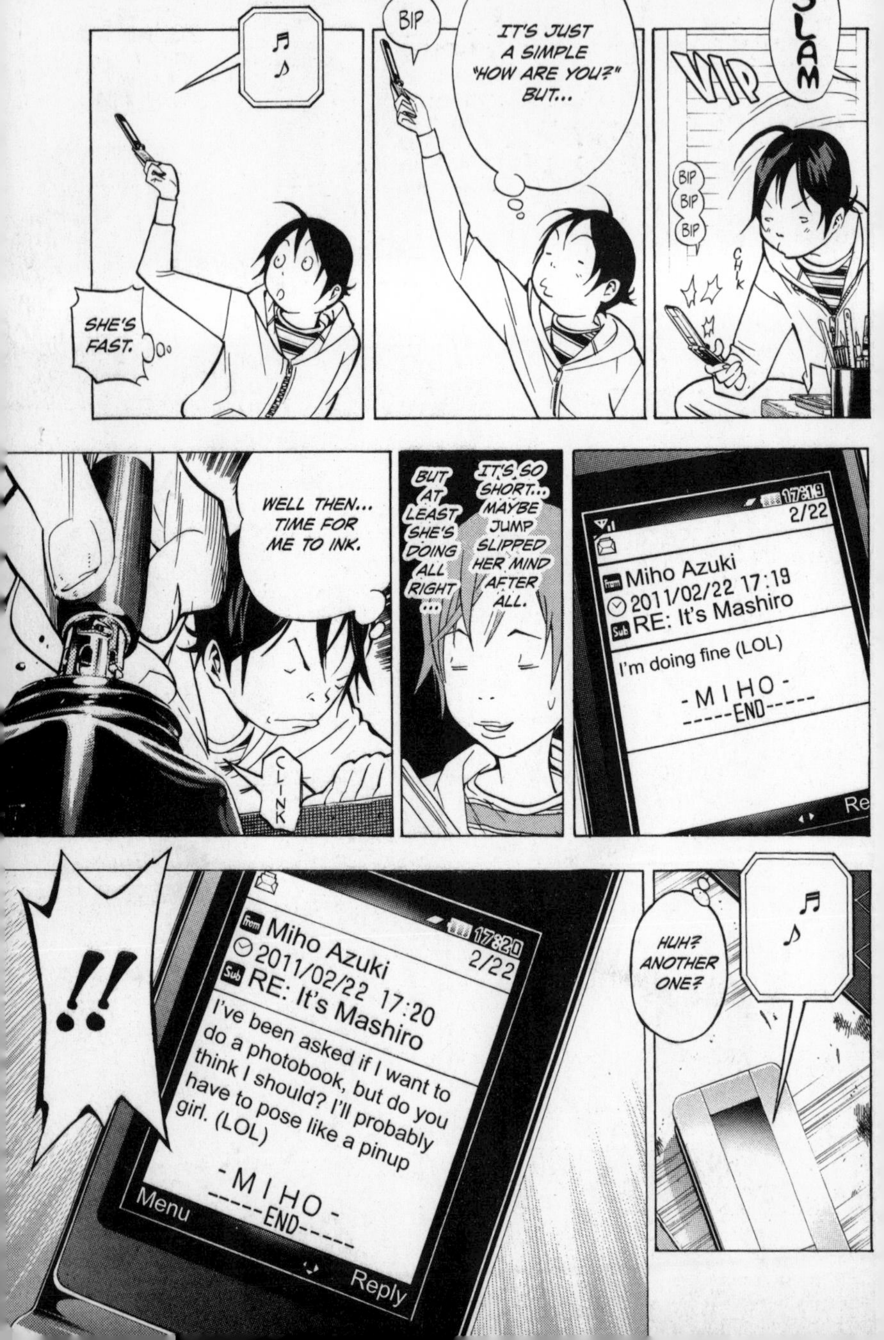
SLAM
VIP
BIP
BIP
BIP
CHIK
BIP
IT'S JUST A SIMPLE "HOW ARE YOU?" BUT...
♬ ♪
SHE'S FAST.
17:19
2/22
Miho Azuki
2011/02/22 17:19
RE: It's Mashiro
I'm doing fine (LOL)
-MIHO-
-----END-----
Re
IT'S SO SHORT... MAYBE JUMP SLIPPED HER MIND AFTER ALL.
BUT AT LEAST SHE'S DOING ALL RIGHT...
WELL THEN... TIME FOR ME TO INK.
CLINK
♬ ♪
HUH? ANOTHER ONE?
17:20
2/22
Miho Azuki
2011/02/22 17:20
RE: It's Mashiro
I've been asked if I want to do a photobook, but do you think I should? I'll probably have to pose like a pinup girl. (LOL)
-MIHO-
-----END-----
Menu
Reply
!!

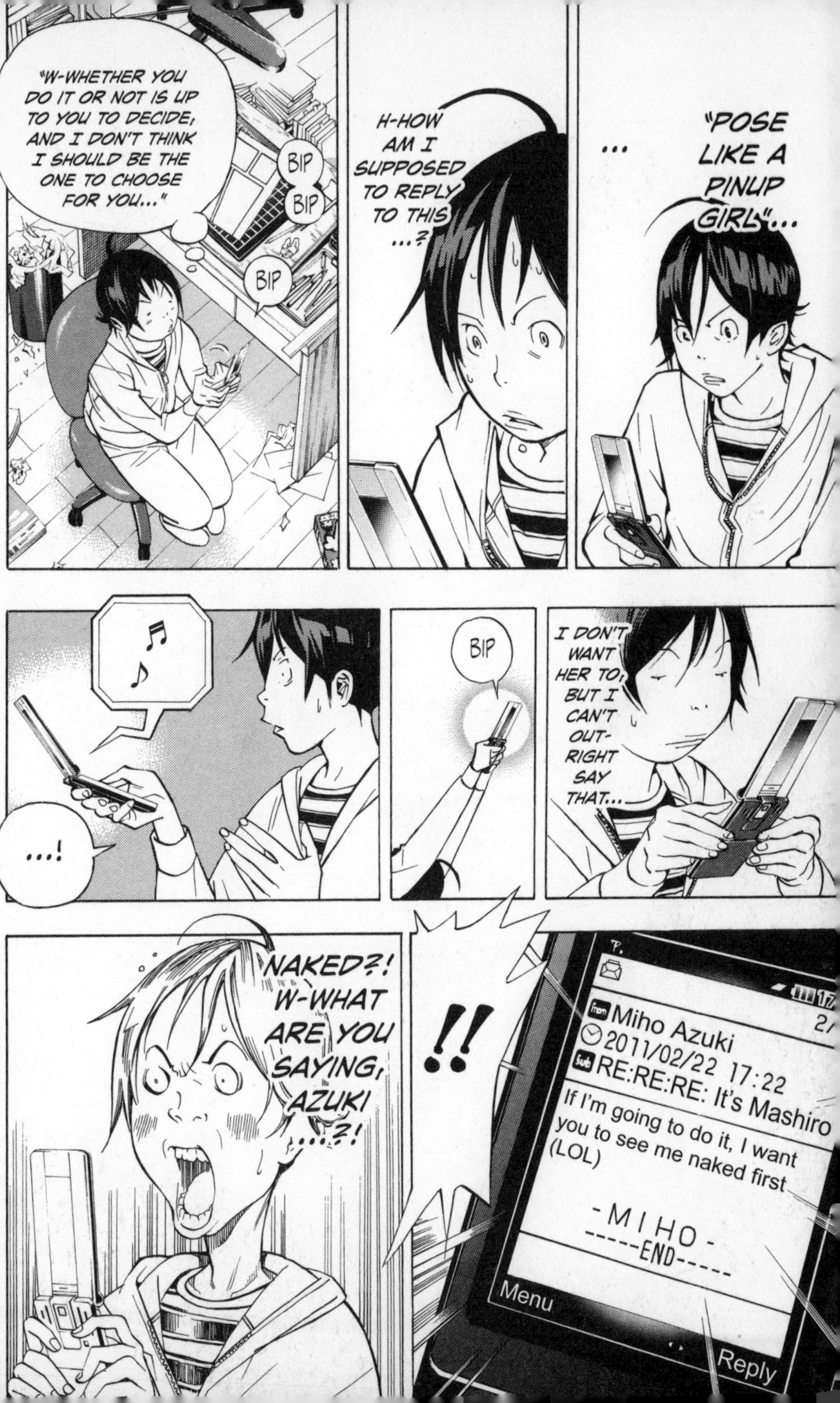
"POSE LIKE A PINUP GIRL"...
...
H-HOW AM I SUPPOSED TO REPLY TO THIS ...?
"W-WHETHER YOU DO IT OR NOT IS UP TO YOU TO DECIDE, AND I DON'T THINK I SHOULD BE THE ONE TO CHOOSE FOR YOU..."
BIP
BIP
BIP
I DON'T WANT HER TO, BUT I CAN'T OUT-RIGHT SAY THAT...
BIP
♬ ♪
...!
!!
Miho Azuki
2011/02/22 17:22
RE:RE:RE: It's Mashiro
If I'm going to do it, I want you to see me naked first (LOL)
-MIHO-
-----END-----
Menu
Reply
NAKED?! W-WHAT ARE YOU SAYING, AZUKI...?!

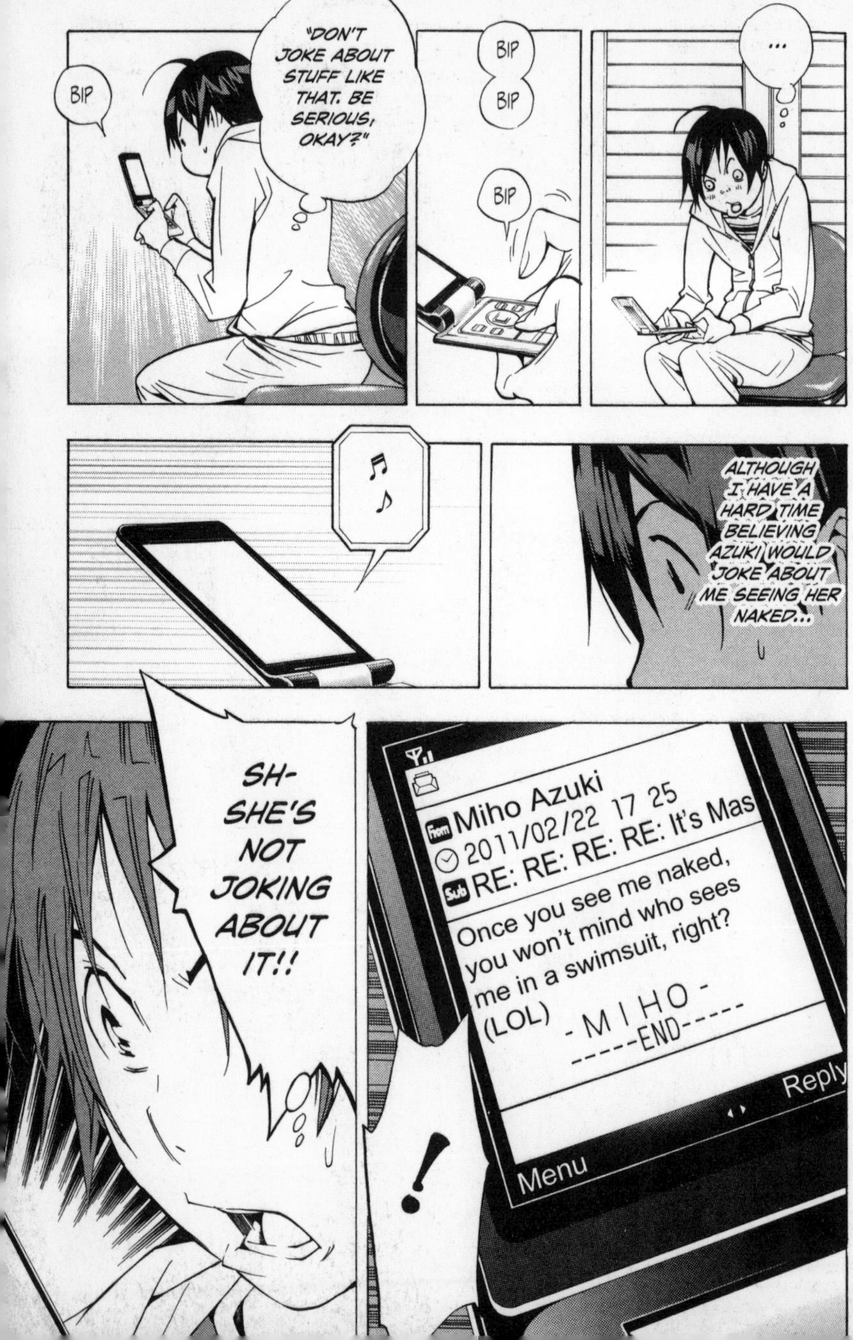
...
BIP
BIP
BIP
"DON'T JOKE ABOUT STUFF LIKE THAT. BE SERIOUS, OKAY?"
BIP
ALTHOUGH I HAVE A HARD TIME BELIEVING AZUKI WOULD JOKE ABOUT ME SEEING HER NAKED...
♪ ♪
From Miho Azuki
2011/02/22 17 25
Sub RE: RE: RE: RE: It's Mas
Once you see me naked, you won't mind who sees me in a swimsuit, right? (LOL)
- M I H O -
-----END-----
Menu
Reply
!
SH-SHE'S NOT JOKING ABOUT IT!!

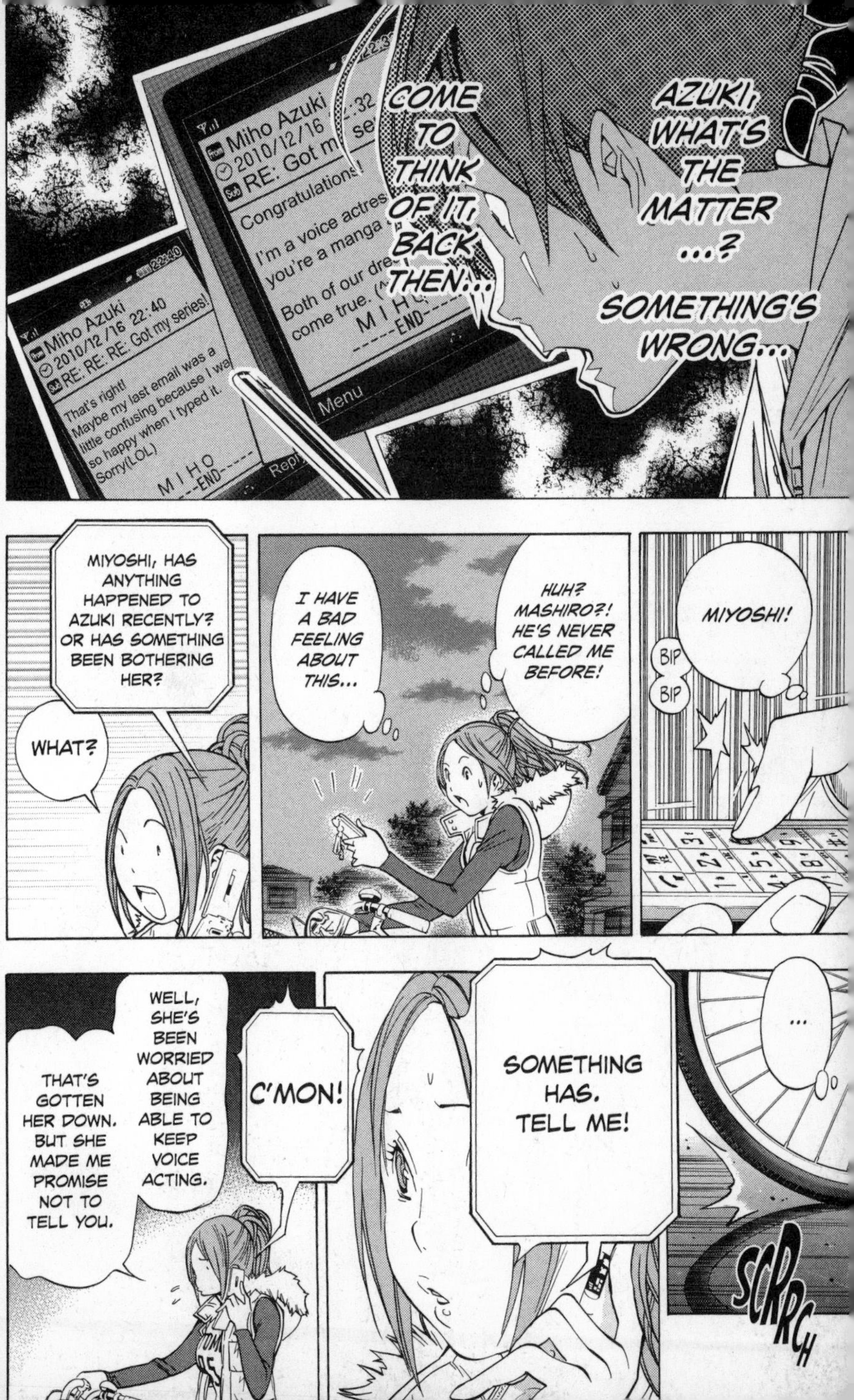
AZUKI, WHAT'S THE MATTER ...? SOMETHING'S WRONG...
COME TO THINK OF IT, BACK THEN...
Miho Azuki
2010/12/16
RE: Got m
Congratulations!
I'm a voice actres
you're a manga
Both of our dre
come true.
MIHO
END
Menu
Miho Azuki
2010/12/16 22:40
RE: RE: RE: Got my series!
That's right!
Maybe my last email was a little confusing because I wa so happy when I typed it.
Sorry(LOL)
MIHO
END
Reply
MIYOSHI!
BIP
BIP
HUH? MASHIRO?! HE'S NEVER CALLED ME BEFORE!
I HAVE A BAD FEELING ABOUT THIS...
MIYOSHI, HAS ANYTHING HAPPENED TO AZUKI RECENTLY? OR HAS SOMETHING BEEN BOTHERING HER?
WHAT?
...
SCRRCH
SOMETHING HAS. TELL ME!
C'MON!
WELL, SHE'S BEEN WORRIED ABOUT BEING ABLE TO KEEP VOICE ACTING.
THAT'S GOTTEN HER DOWN. BUT SHE MADE ME PROMISE NOT TO TELL YOU.

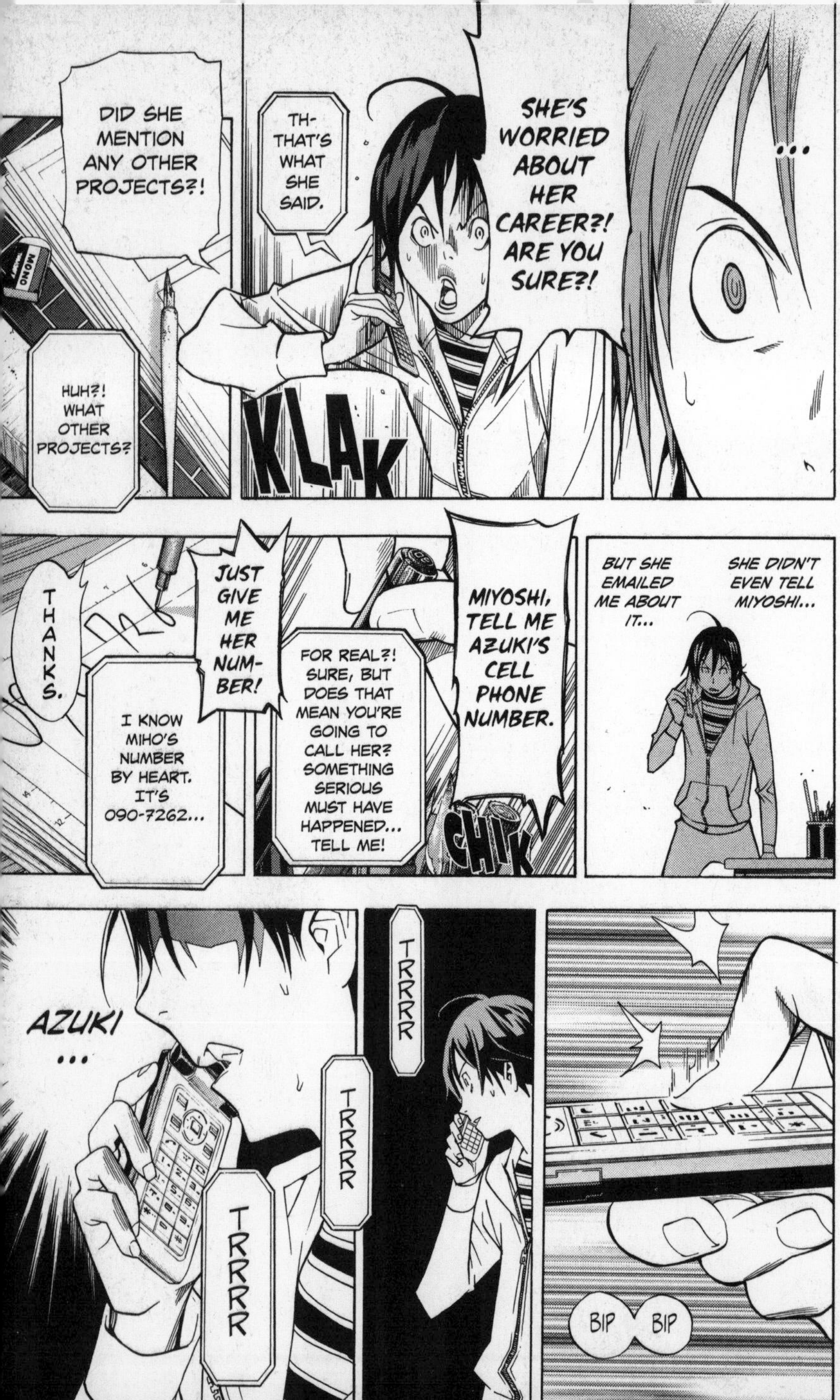
...
SHE'S WORRIED ABOUT HER CAREER?! ARE YOU SURE?!
TH- THAT'S WHAT SHE SAID.
KLAK
DID SHE MENTION ANY OTHER PROJECTS?!
HUH?! WHAT OTHER PROJECTS?
SHE DIDN'T EVEN TELL MIYOSHI...
BUT SHE EMAILED ME ABOUT IT...
MIYOSHI, TELL ME AZUKI'S CELL PHONE NUMBER.
FOR REAL?! SURE, BUT DOES THAT MEAN YOU'RE GOING TO CALL HER? SOMETHING SERIOUS MUST HAVE HAPPENED... TELL ME!
CHIK
JUST GIVE ME HER NUMBER!
I KNOW MIHO'S NUMBER BY HEART. IT'S 090-7262...
THANKS.
BIP
BIP
TRRRR
TRRRR
TRRRR
AZUKI...

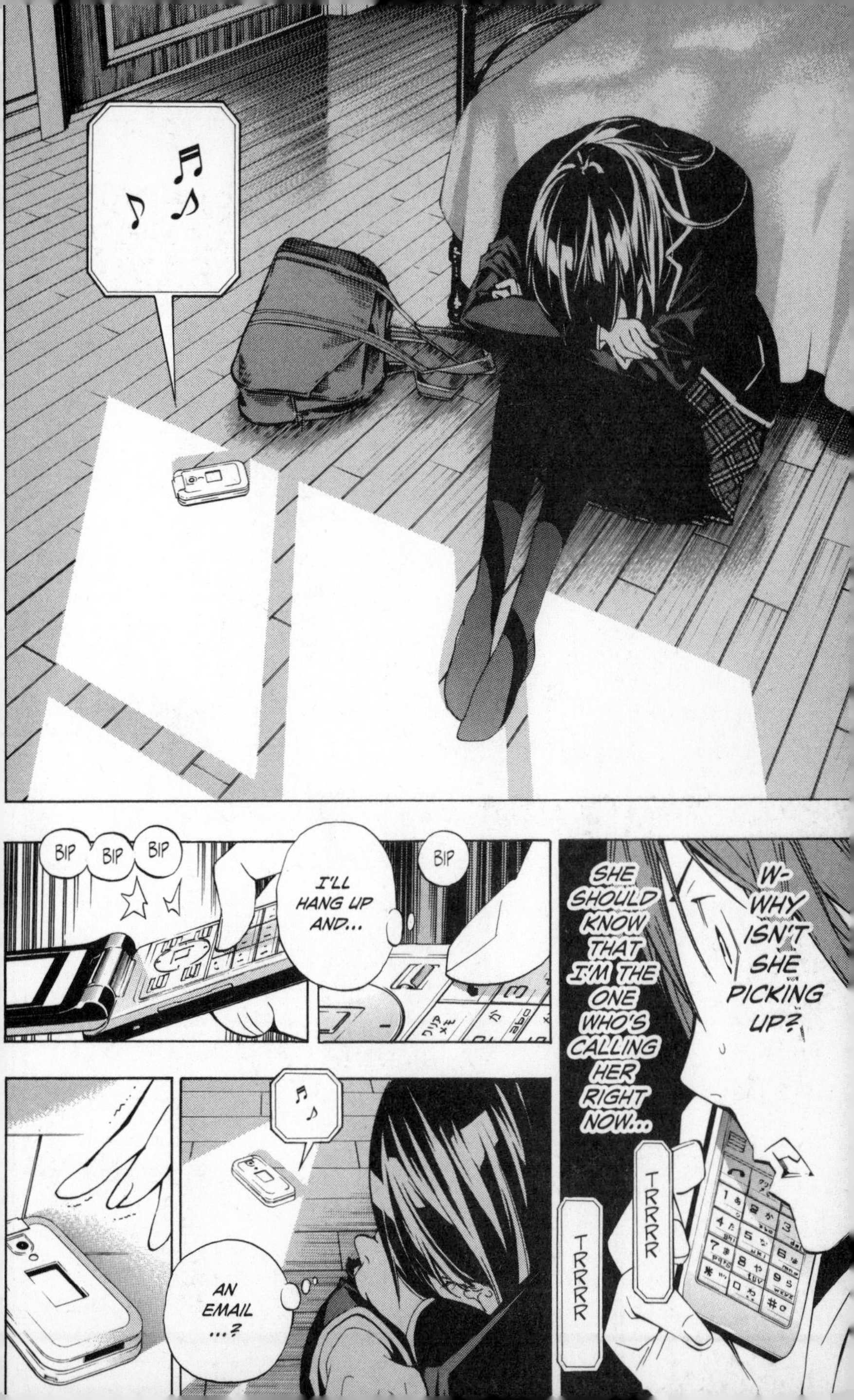
W-WHY ISN'T SHE PICKING UP?
SHE SHOULD KNOW THAT I'M THE ONE WHO'S CALLING HER RIGHT NOW...
TRRRR
TRRRR
BIP
I'LL HANG UP AND...
BIP
BIP
BIP
AN EMAIL ...?

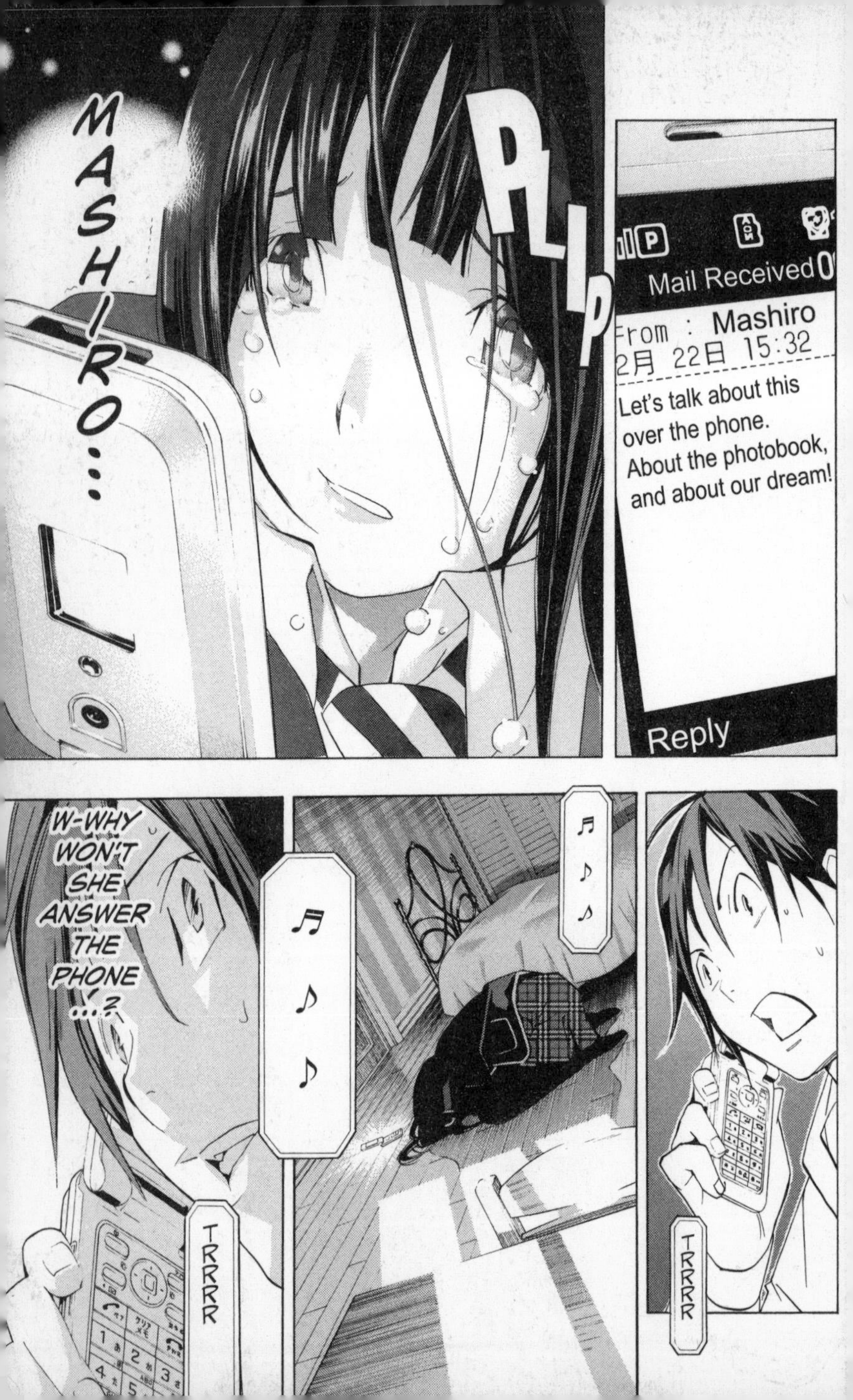
Mail Received
From : Mashiro
2月 22日 15:32
Let's talk about this over the phone. About the photobook, and about our dream!
Reply
RIP
MASHIRO...
TRRRR
♬ ♪ ♪
♬ ♪ ♪
W-WHY WON'T SHE ANSWER THE PHONE ...?
TRRRR

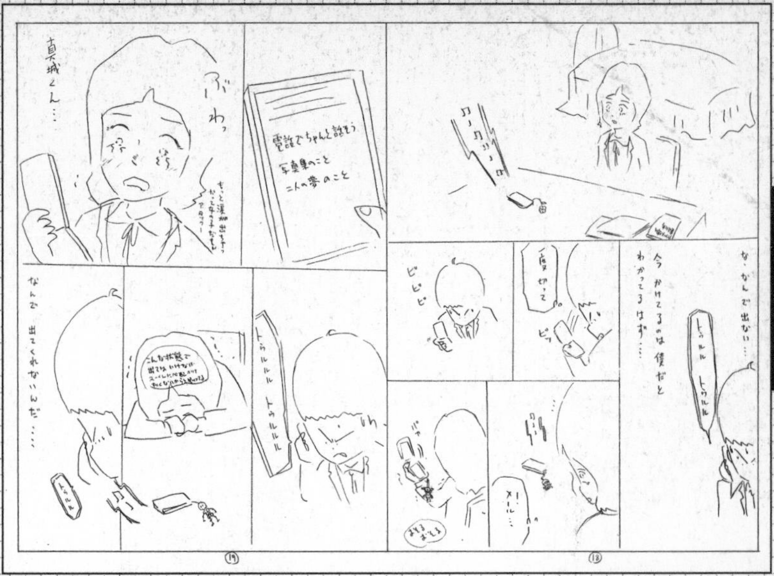

な、なんで出ない…
トゥルル
トゥルル
今かけてるのは僕だとわかってるはず…
一度切って
ピッ
ピピピ
メール…
電話でちゃんと話そう
写真集のこと
二人の夢のこと
真城くん…
ぶわっ
トゥルルル
トゥルルル
なんで出てくれないんだ…

OHBA'S STORYBOARD

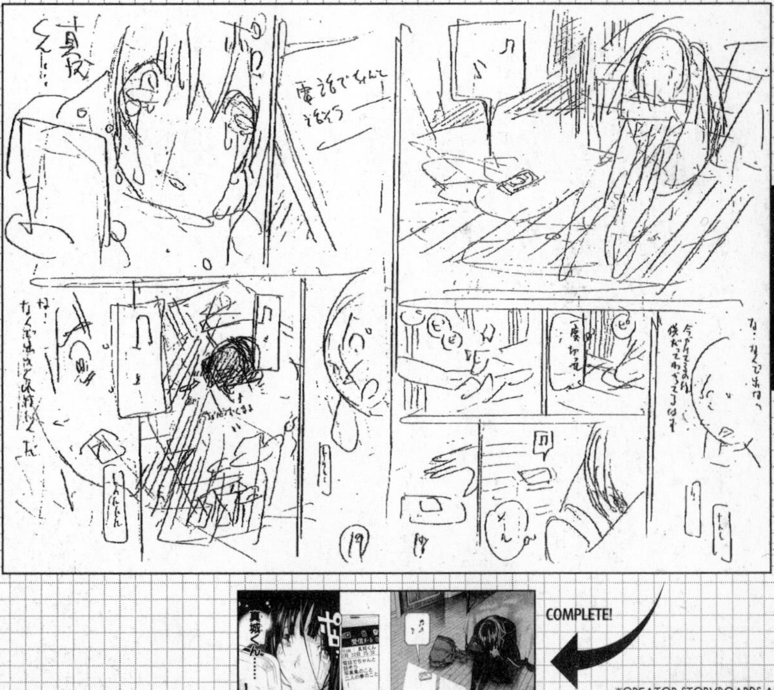

一度切って
メール
電話でちゃんと話そう
真城くん…

OBATA'S STORYBOARD

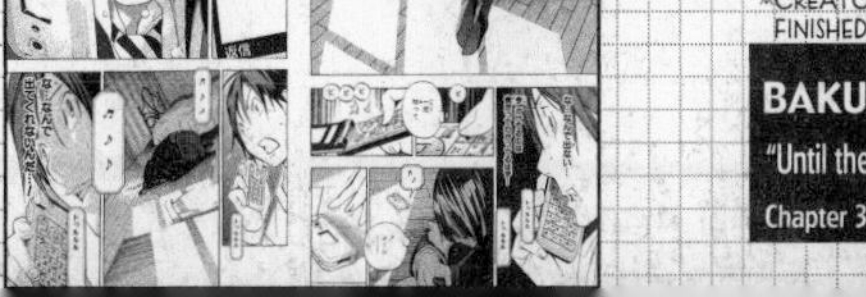

COMPLETE!

*CREATOR STORYBOARDS AND FINISHED PAGES IN JAPANESE

BAKUMAN。 vol. 5

"Until the Final Draft Is Complete"

Chapter 39, pp. 104-105

CHAPTER 40
BEACH AND UPS-AND-DOWNS

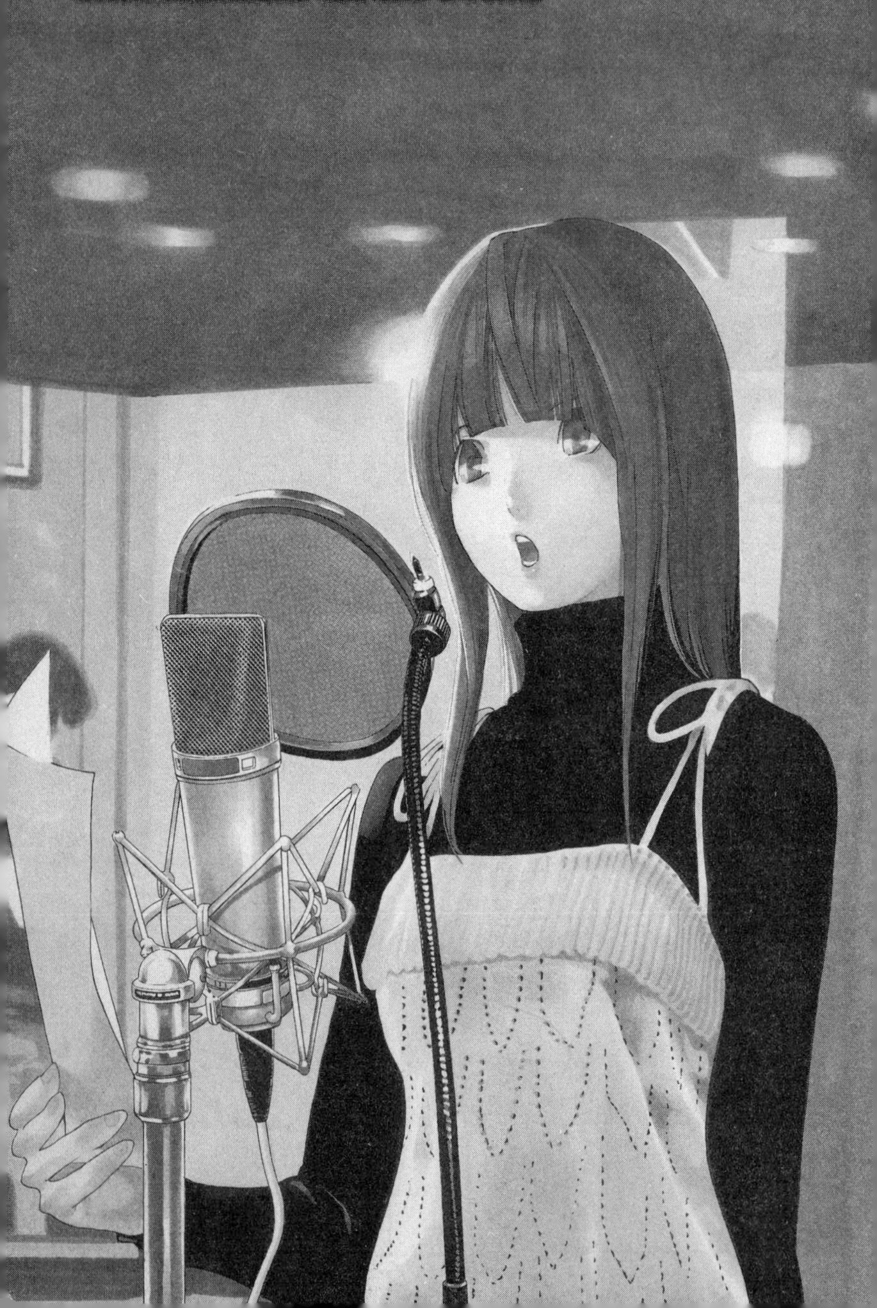

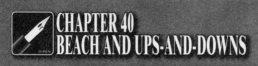

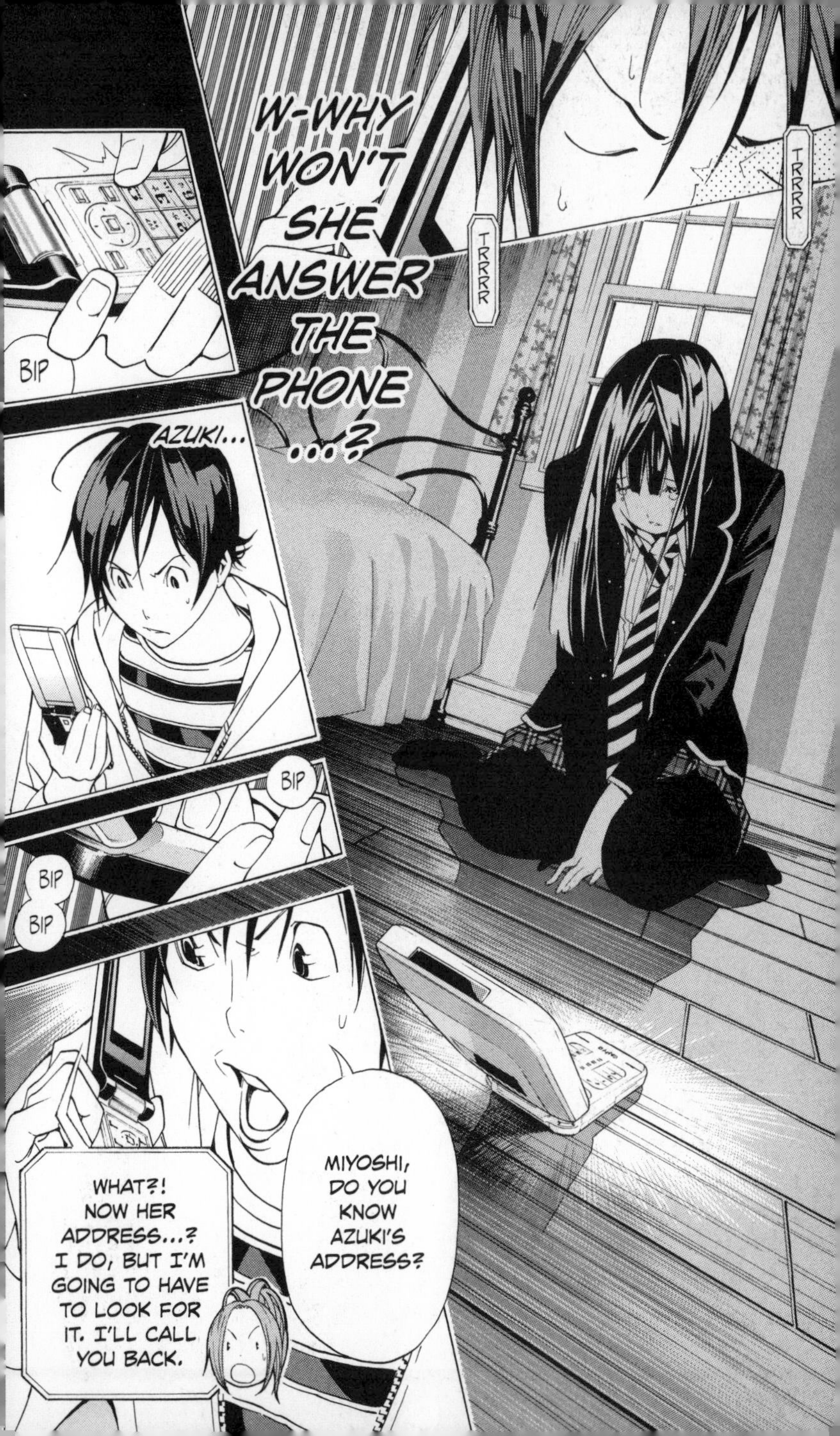
TRRRR
TRRRR
W-WHY WON'T SHE ANSWER THE PHONE...?
BIP
AZUKI...
BIP
BIP
BIP
MIYOSHI, DO YOU KNOW AZUKI'S ADDRESS?
WHAT?! NOW HER ADDRESS...? I DO, BUT I'M GOING TO HAVE TO LOOK FOR IT. I'LL CALL YOU BACK.

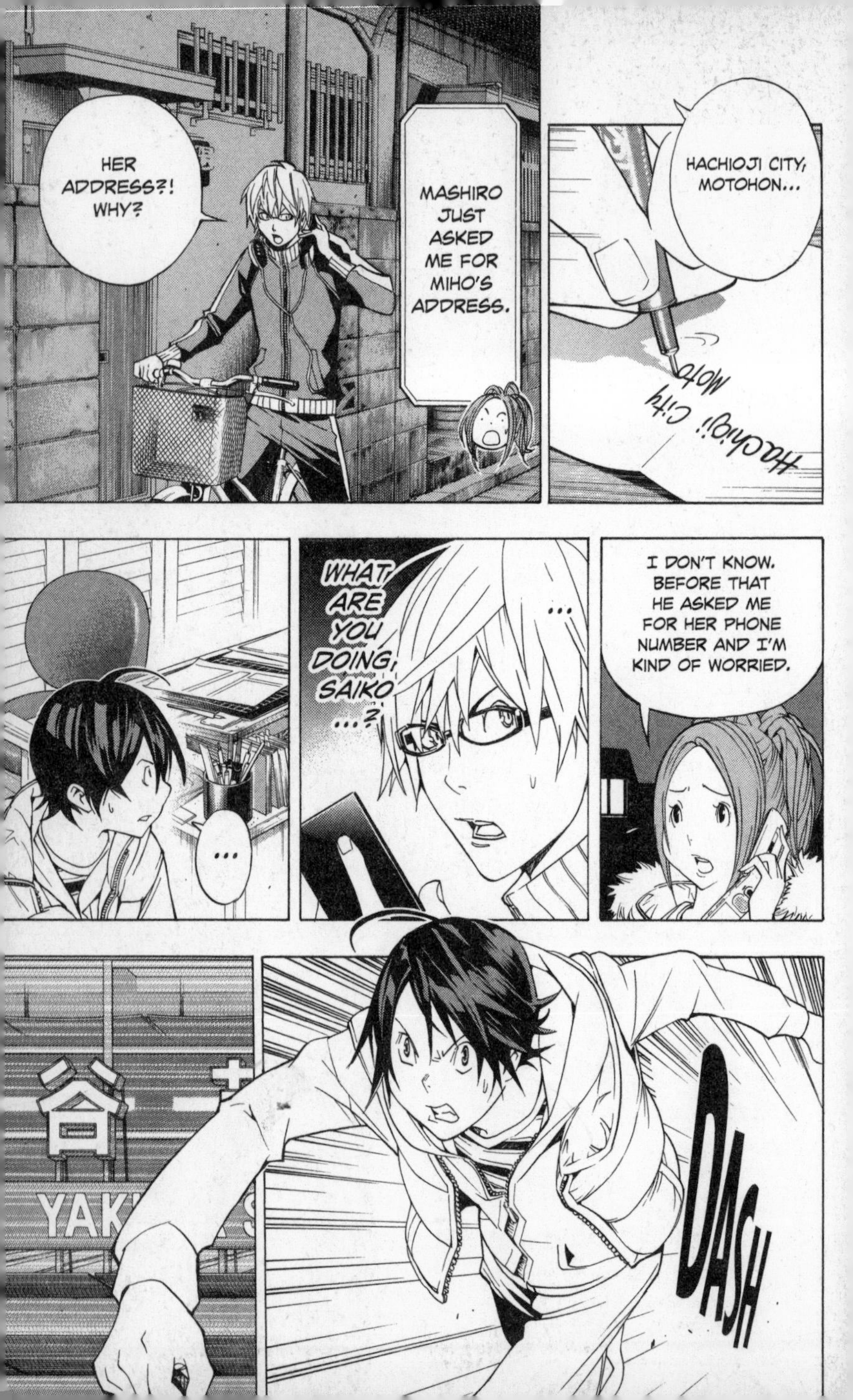
HACHIOJI CITY, MOTOHON...
Hachioji City Moto
MASHIRO JUST ASKED ME FOR MIHO'S ADDRESS.
HER ADDRESS?! WHY?
I DON'T KNOW. BEFORE THAT HE ASKED ME FOR HER PHONE NUMBER AND I'M KIND OF WORRIED.
...
WHAT ARE YOU DOING, SAIKO...?
...
DASH
YAK

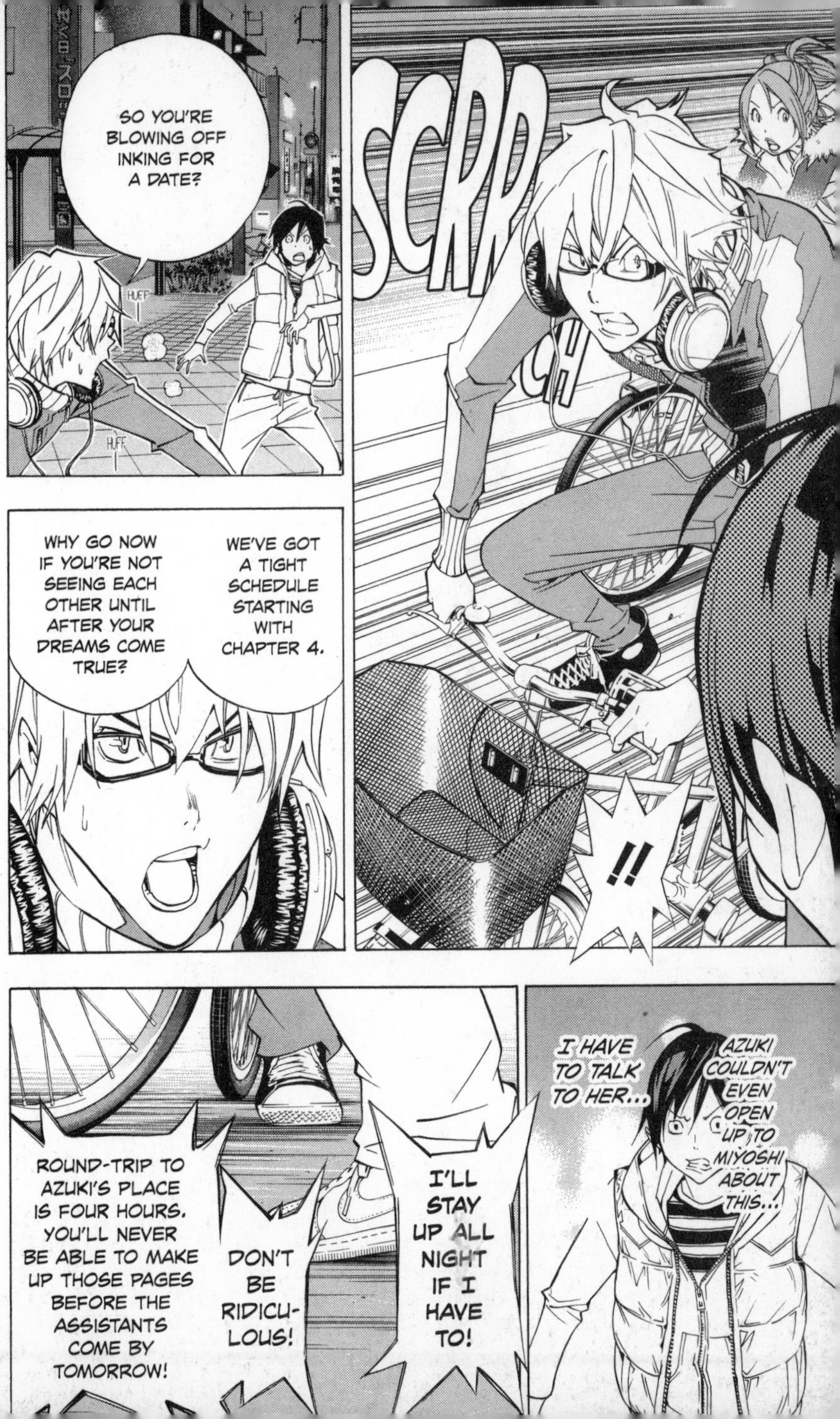
SCRR
CH
!!
SO YOU'RE BLOWING OFF INKING FOR A DATE?
HUFF
HUFF
WE'VE GOT A TIGHT SCHEDULE STARTING WITH CHAPTER 4.
WHY GO NOW IF YOU'RE NOT SEEING EACH OTHER UNTIL AFTER YOUR DREAMS COME TRUE?
AZUKI COULDN'T EVEN OPEN UP TO MIYOSHI ABOUT THIS...
I HAVE TO TALK TO HER...
I'LL STAY UP ALL NIGHT IF I HAVE TO!
DON'T BE RIDICU-LOUS!
ROUND-TRIP TO AZUKI'S PLACE IS FOUR HOURS. YOU'LL NEVER BE ABLE TO MAKE UP THOSE PAGES BEFORE THE ASSISTANTS COME BY TOMORROW!

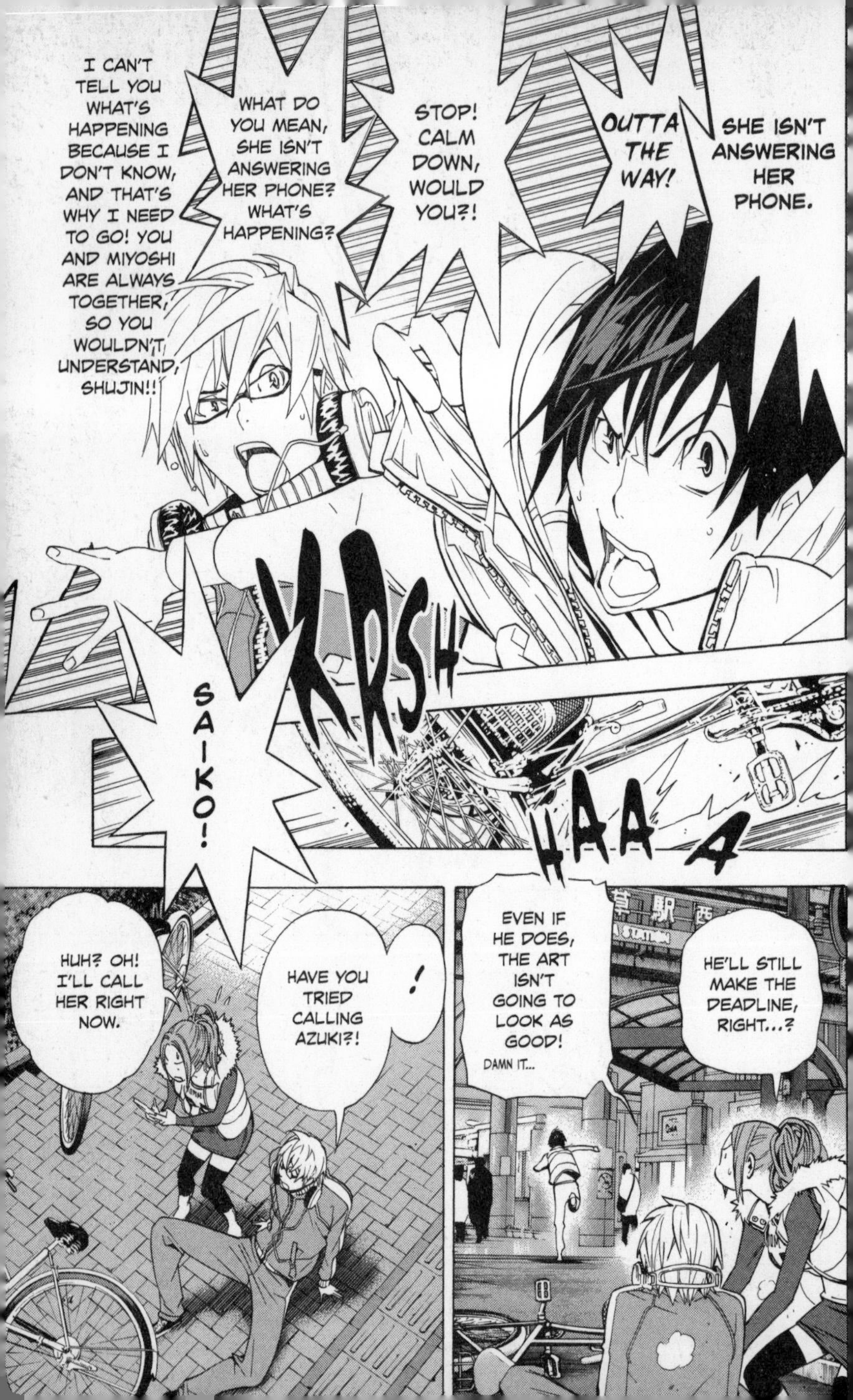
SHE ISN'T ANSWERING HER PHONE.
OUTTA THE WAY!
STOP! CALM DOWN, WOULD YOU?!
WHAT DO YOU MEAN, SHE ISN'T ANSWERING HER PHONE? WHAT'S HAPPENING?
I CAN'T TELL YOU WHAT'S HAPPENING BECAUSE I DON'T KNOW, AND THAT'S WHY I NEED TO GO! YOU AND MIYOSHI ARE ALWAYS TOGETHER, SO YOU WOULDN'T UNDERSTAND, SHUJIN!!
KRSH
HAAA
SAIKO!
HE'LL STILL MAKE THE DEADLINE, RIGHT...?
EVEN IF HE DOES, THE ART ISN'T GOING TO LOOK AS GOOD!
DAMN IT...
!
HAVE YOU TRIED CALLING AZUKI?!
HUH? OH! I'LL CALL HER RIGHT NOW.

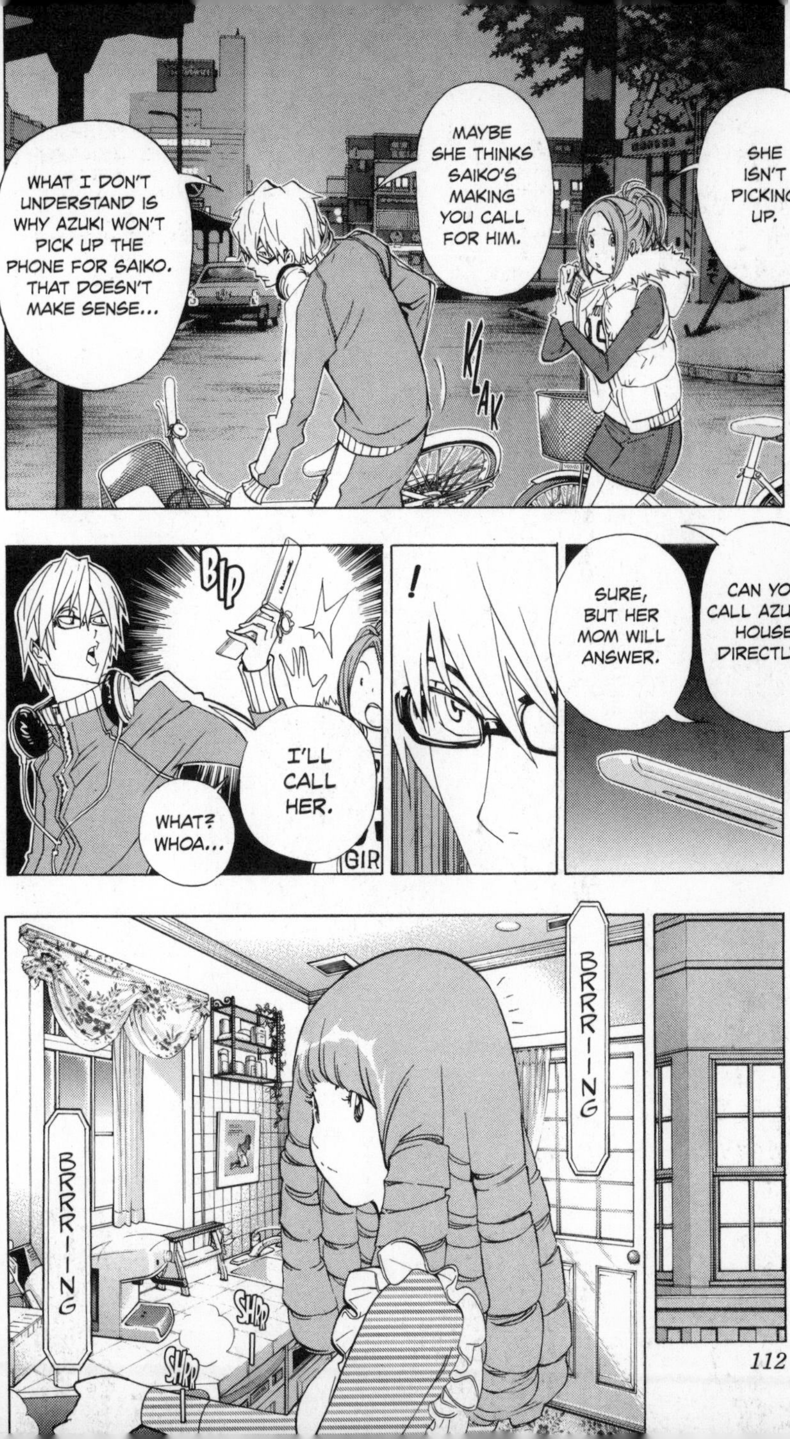
SHE ISN'T PICKING UP.
MAYBE SHE THINKS SAIKO'S MAKING YOU CALL FOR HIM.
WHAT I DON'T UNDERSTAND IS WHY AZUKI WON'T PICK UP THE PHONE FOR SAIKO. THAT DOESN'T MAKE SENSE...
KLAK
CAN YOU CALL AZUKI'S HOUSE DIRECTLY?
SURE, BUT HER MOM WILL ANSWER.
!
BIP
I'LL CALL HER.
WHAT? WHOA...
BRRRING
BRRRING
SHRR
SHRR

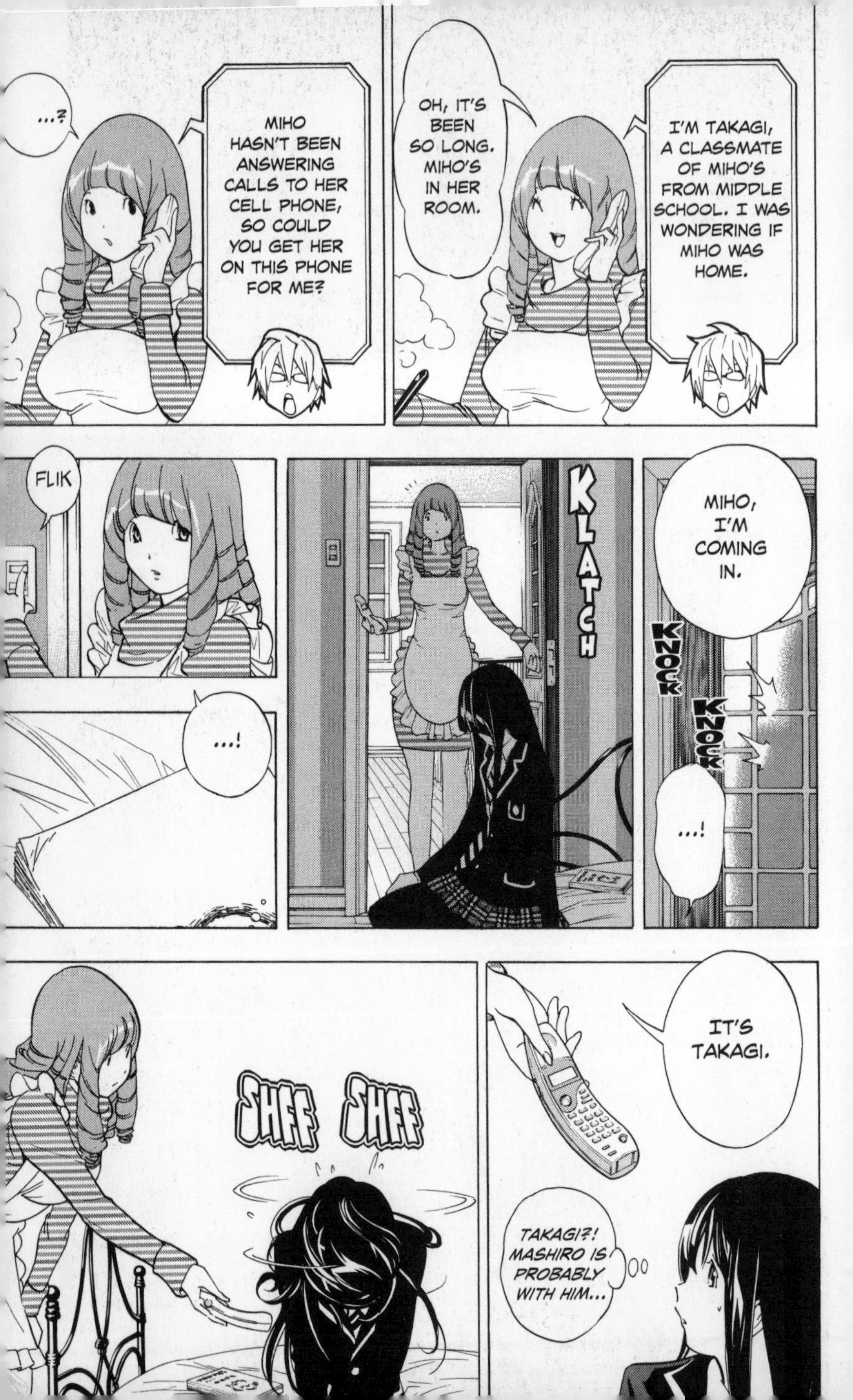
I'M TAKAGI, A CLASSMATE OF MIHO'S FROM MIDDLE SCHOOL. I WAS WONDERING IF MIHO WAS HOME.
OH, IT'S BEEN SO LONG. MIHO'S IN HER ROOM.
MIHO HASN'T BEEN ANSWERING CALLS TO HER CELL PHONE, SO COULD YOU GET HER ON THIS PHONE FOR ME?
...?
MIHO, I'M COMING IN.
KNOCK
KNOCK
...!
KLATCH
FLIK
...!
IT'S TAKAGI.
TAKAGI?! MASHIRO IS PROBABLY WITH HIM...
SHFF SHFF

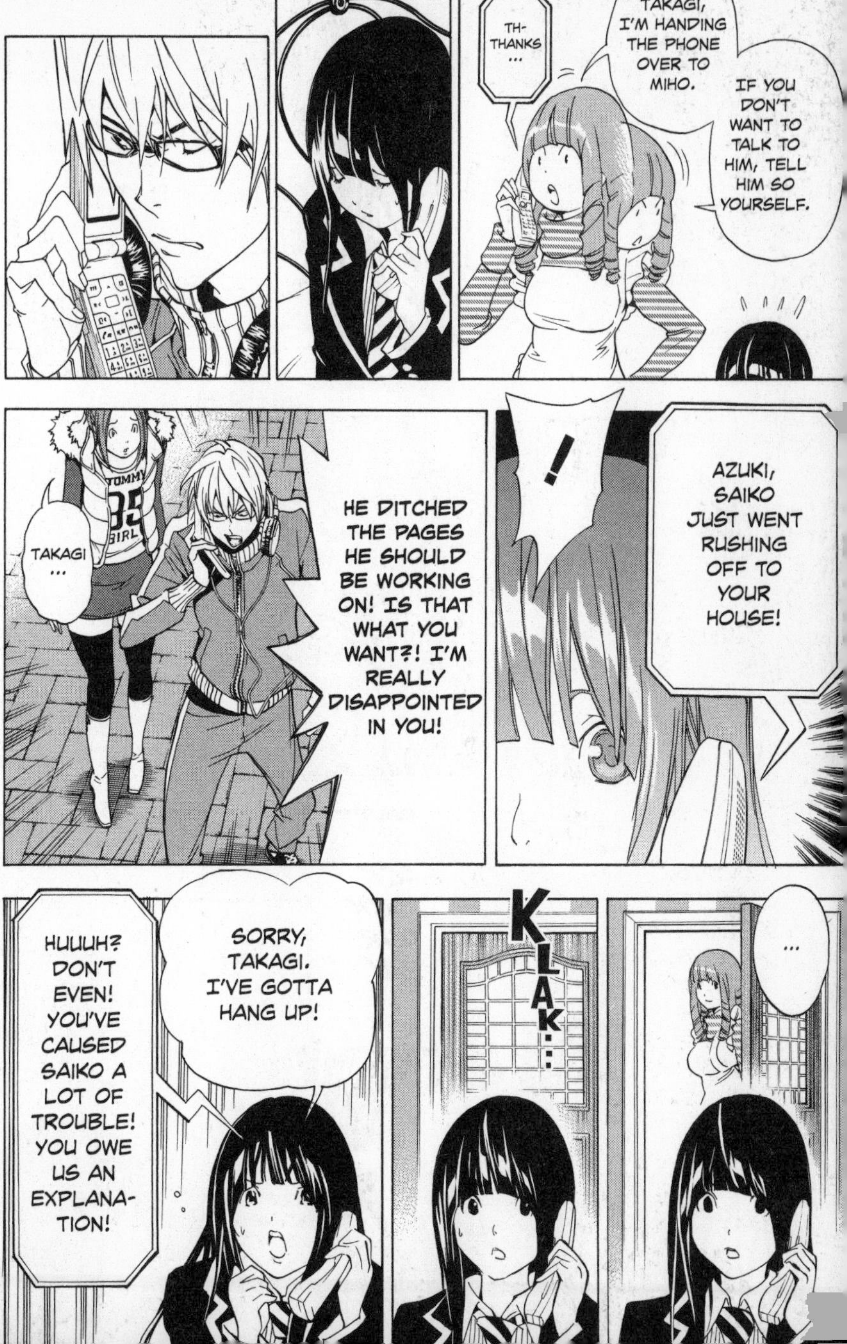
TAKAGI, I'M HANDING THE PHONE OVER TO MIHO.
IF YOU DON'T WANT TO TALK TO HIM, TELL HIM SO YOURSELF.
TH-THANKS ...
!
AZUKI, SAIKO JUST WENT RUSHING OFF TO YOUR HOUSE!
HE DITCHED THE PAGES HE SHOULD BE WORKING ON! IS THAT WHAT YOU WANT?! I'M REALLY DISAPPOINTED IN YOU!
TAKAGI ...
...
KLAK...
SORRY, TAKAGI. I'VE GOTTA HANG UP!
HUUUH? DON'T EVEN! YOU'VE CAUSED SAIKO A LOT OF TROUBLE! YOU OWE US AN EXPLANATION!

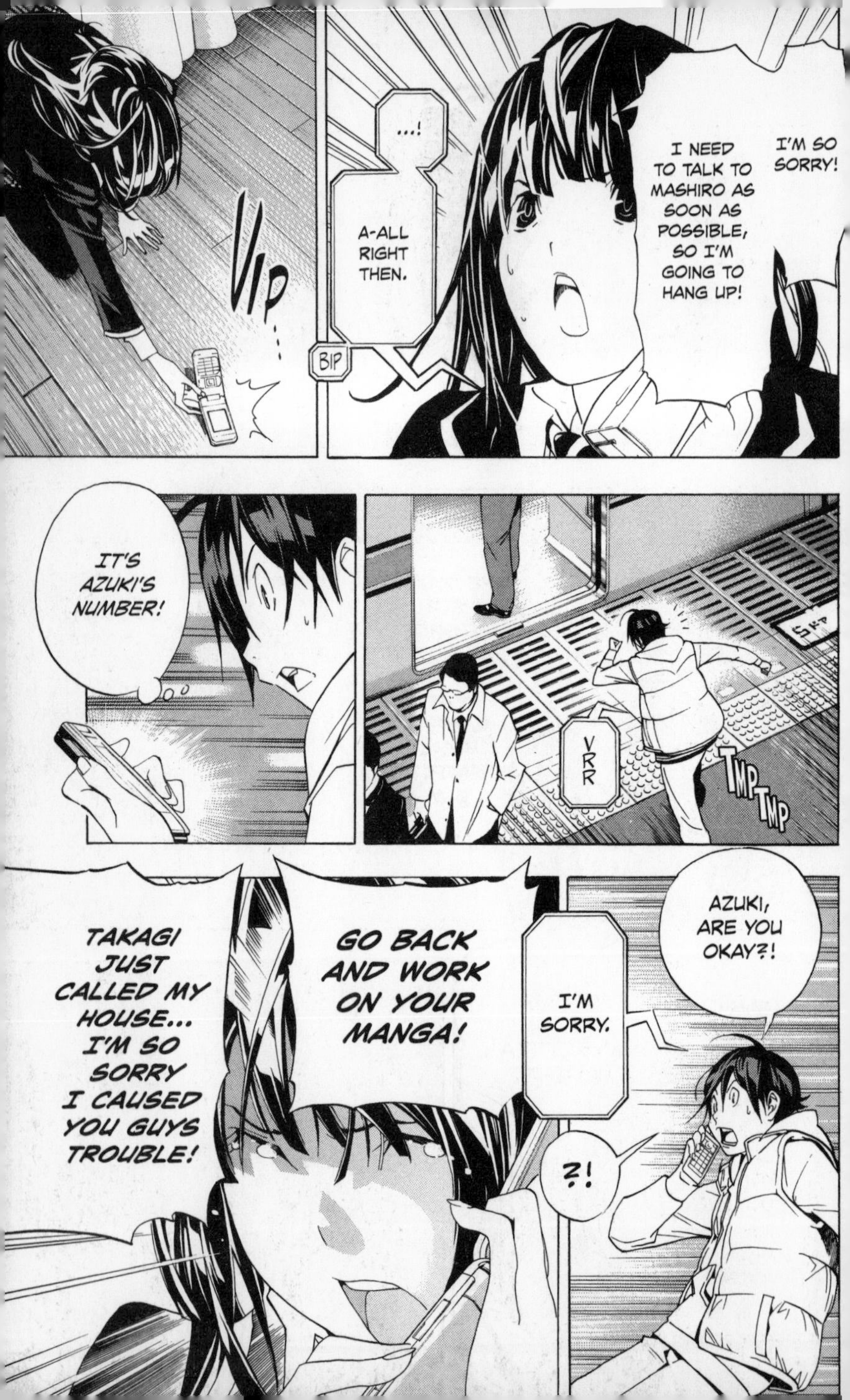
I'M SO SORRY!
I NEED TO TALK TO MASHIRO AS SOON AS POSSIBLE, SO I'M GOING TO HANG UP!
...!
A-ALL RIGHT THEN.
BIP
VRR
TMP TMP
IT'S AZUKI'S NUMBER!
AZUKI, ARE YOU OKAY?!
I'M SORRY.
?!
GO BACK AND WORK ON YOUR MANGA!
TAKAGI JUST CALLED MY HOUSE... I'M SO SORRY I CAUSED YOU GUYS TROUBLE!

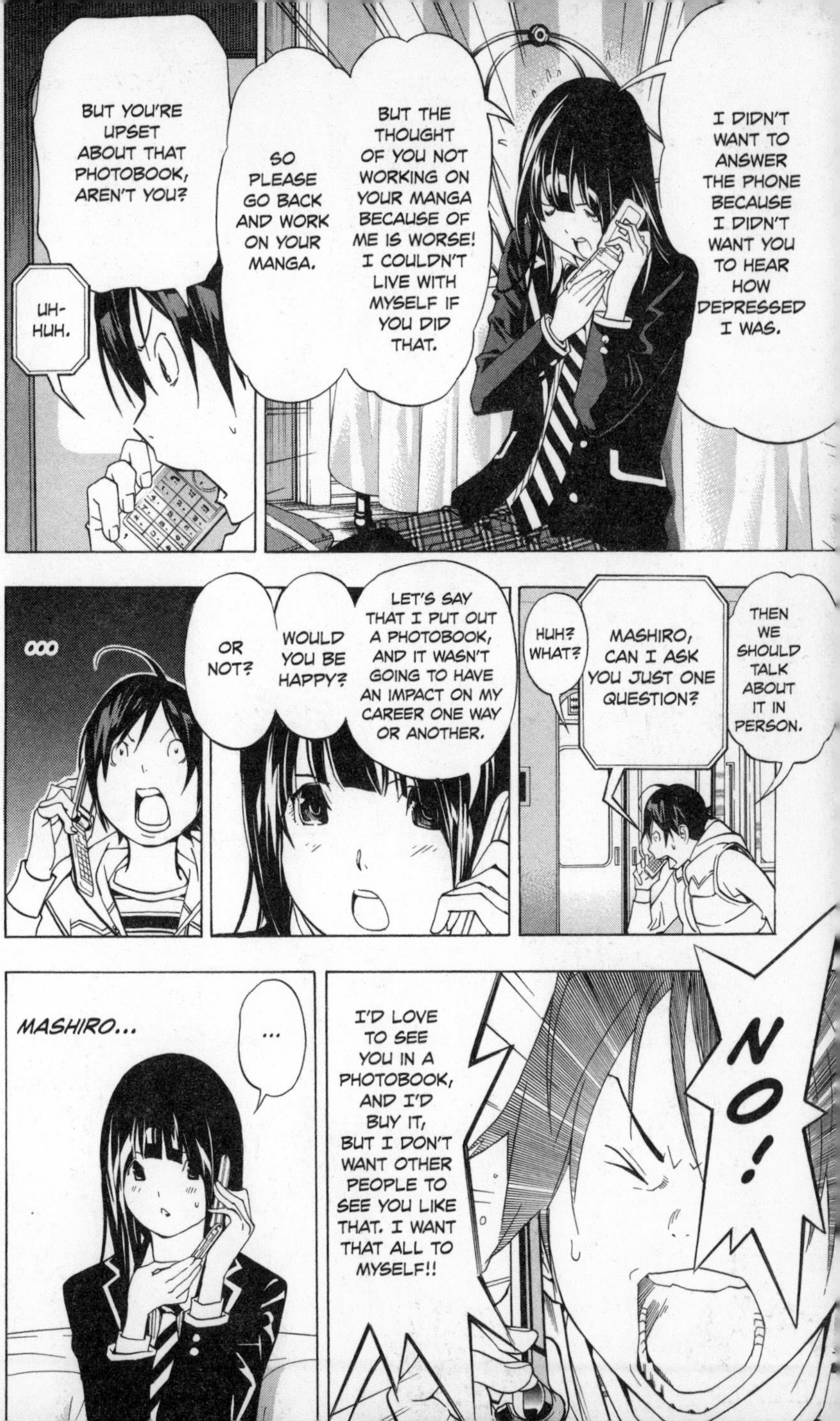
I DIDN'T WANT TO ANSWER THE PHONE BECAUSE I DIDN'T WANT YOU TO HEAR HOW DEPRESSED I WAS.
BUT THE THOUGHT OF YOU NOT WORKING ON YOUR MANGA BECAUSE OF ME IS WORSE! I COULDN'T LIVE WITH MYSELF IF YOU DID THAT.
SO PLEASE GO BACK AND WORK ON YOUR MANGA.
BUT YOU'RE UPSET ABOUT THAT PHOTOBOOK, AREN'T YOU?
UH-HUH.
THEN WE SHOULD TALK ABOUT IT IN PERSON.
MASHIRO, CAN I ASK YOU JUST ONE QUESTION?
HUH? WHAT?
LET'S SAY THAT I PUT OUT A PHOTOBOOK, AND IT WASN'T GOING TO HAVE AN IMPACT ON MY CAREER ONE WAY OR ANOTHER.
WOULD YOU BE HAPPY?
OR NOT?
ooo
NO!
I'D LOVE TO SEE YOU IN A PHOTOBOOK, AND I'D BUY IT, BUT I DON'T WANT OTHER PEOPLE TO SEE YOU LIKE THAT. I WANT THAT ALL TO MYSELF!!
...
MASHIRO...

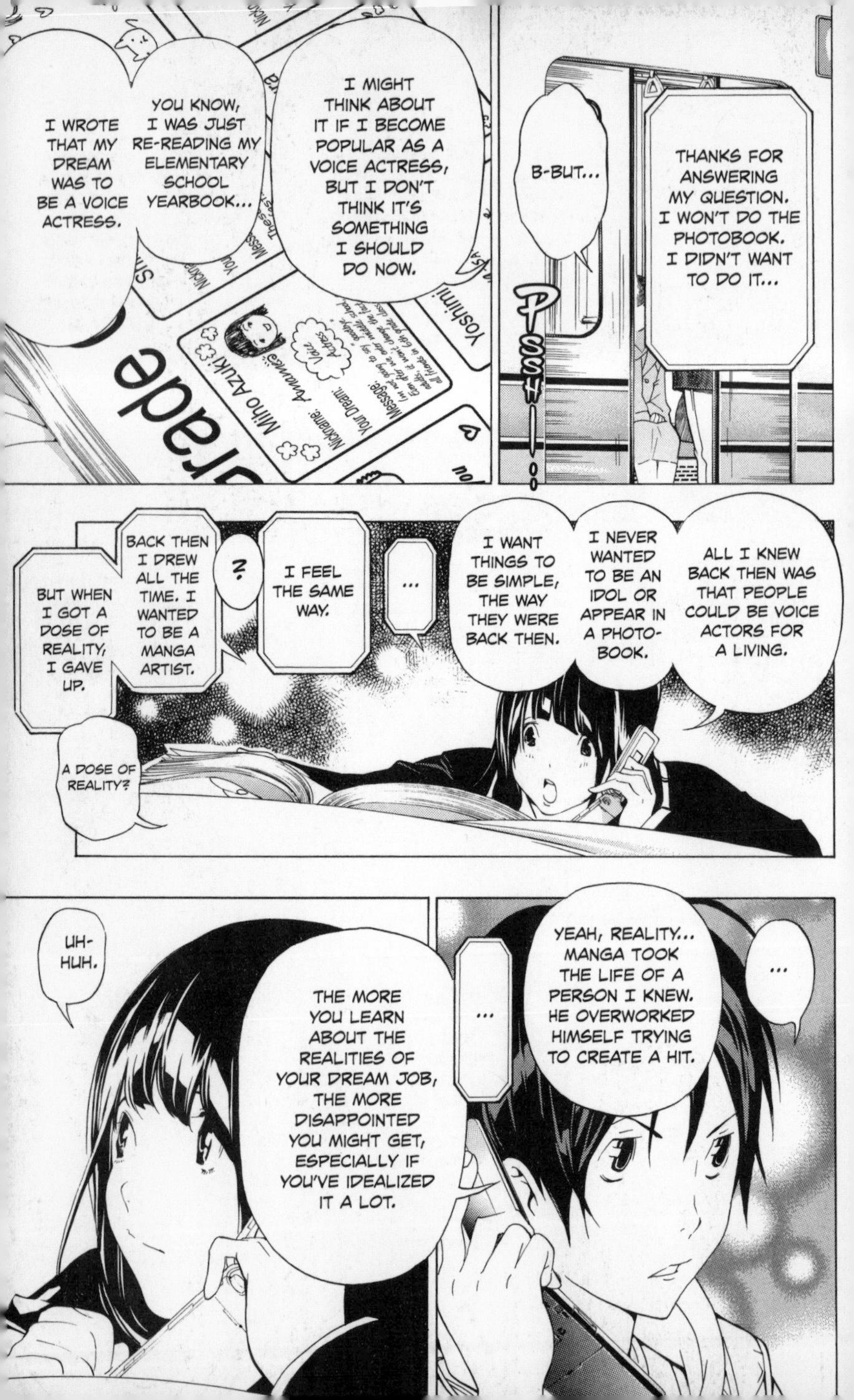
THANKS FOR ANSWERING MY QUESTION. I WON'T DO THE PHOTOBOOK. I DIDN'T WANT TO DO IT...
B-BUT...
PSSHH...
I MIGHT THINK ABOUT IT IF I BECOME POPULAR AS A VOICE ACTRESS, BUT I DON'T THINK IT'S SOMETHING I SHOULD DO NOW.
YOU KNOW, I WAS JUST RE-READING MY ELEMENTARY SCHOOL YEARBOOK...
I WROTE THAT MY DREAM WAS TO BE A VOICE ACTRESS.
ALL I KNEW BACK THEN WAS THAT PEOPLE COULD BE VOICE ACTORS FOR A LIVING.
I NEVER WANTED TO BE AN IDOL OR APPEAR IN A PHOTO-BOOK.
I WANT THINGS TO BE SIMPLE, THE WAY THEY WERE BACK THEN.
...
I FEEL THE SAME WAY.
?
BACK THEN I DREW ALL THE TIME. I WANTED TO BE A MANGA ARTIST.
BUT WHEN I GOT A DOSE OF REALITY, I GAVE UP.
A DOSE OF REALITY?
...
YEAH, REALITY... MANGA TOOK THE LIFE OF A PERSON I KNEW. HE OVERWORKED HIMSELF TRYING TO CREATE A HIT.
...
THE MORE YOU LEARN ABOUT THE REALITIES OF YOUR DREAM JOB, THE MORE DISAPPOINTED YOU MIGHT GET, ESPECIALLY IF YOU'VE IDEALIZED IT A LOT.
UH-HUH.

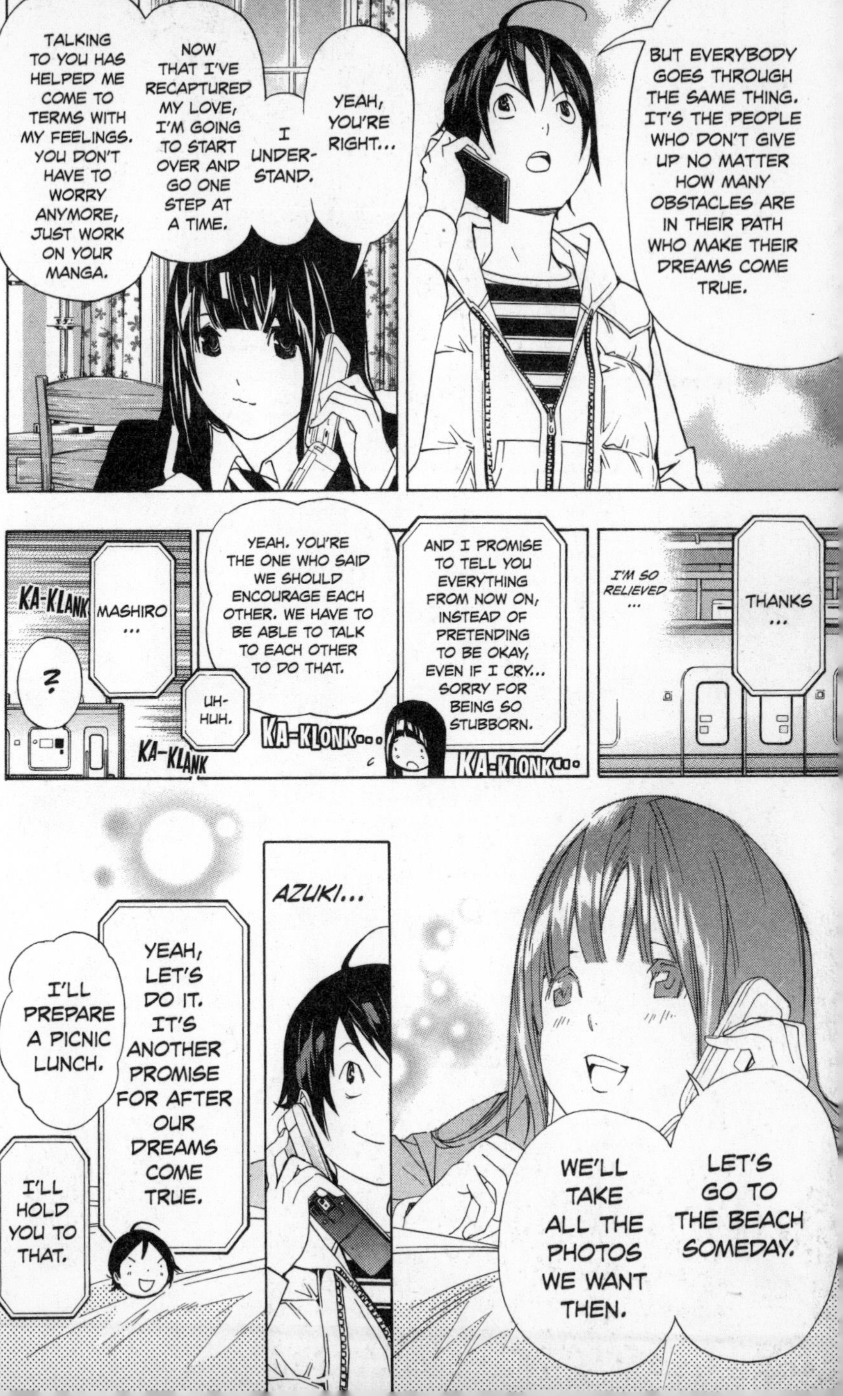
BUT EVERYBODY GOES THROUGH THE SAME THING. IT'S THE PEOPLE WHO DON'T GIVE UP NO MATTER HOW MANY OBSTACLES ARE IN THEIR PATH WHO MAKE THEIR DREAMS COME TRUE.
YEAH, YOU'RE RIGHT...
I UNDER-STAND.
NOW THAT I'VE RECAPTURED MY LOVE, I'M GOING TO START OVER AND GO ONE STEP AT A TIME.
TALKING TO YOU HAS HELPED ME COME TO TERMS WITH MY FEELINGS. YOU DON'T HAVE TO WORRY ANYMORE, JUST WORK ON YOUR MANGA.
THANKS...
I'M SO RELIEVED...
AND I PROMISE TO TELL YOU EVERYTHING FROM NOW ON, INSTEAD OF PRETENDING TO BE OKAY, EVEN IF I CRY... SORRY FOR BEING SO STUBBORN.
KA-KLONK...
YEAH. YOU'RE THE ONE WHO SAID WE SHOULD ENCOURAGE EACH OTHER. WE HAVE TO BE ABLE TO TALK TO EACH OTHER TO DO THAT.
UH-HUH.
KA-KLONK...
MASHIRO...
KA-KLANK
?
KA-KLANK
LET'S GO TO THE BEACH SOMEDAY.
WE'LL TAKE ALL THE PHOTOS WE WANT THEN.
AZUKI...
YEAH, LET'S DO IT. IT'S ANOTHER PROMISE FOR AFTER OUR DREAMS COME TRUE.
I'LL PREPARE A PICNIC LUNCH.
I'LL HOLD YOU TO THAT.

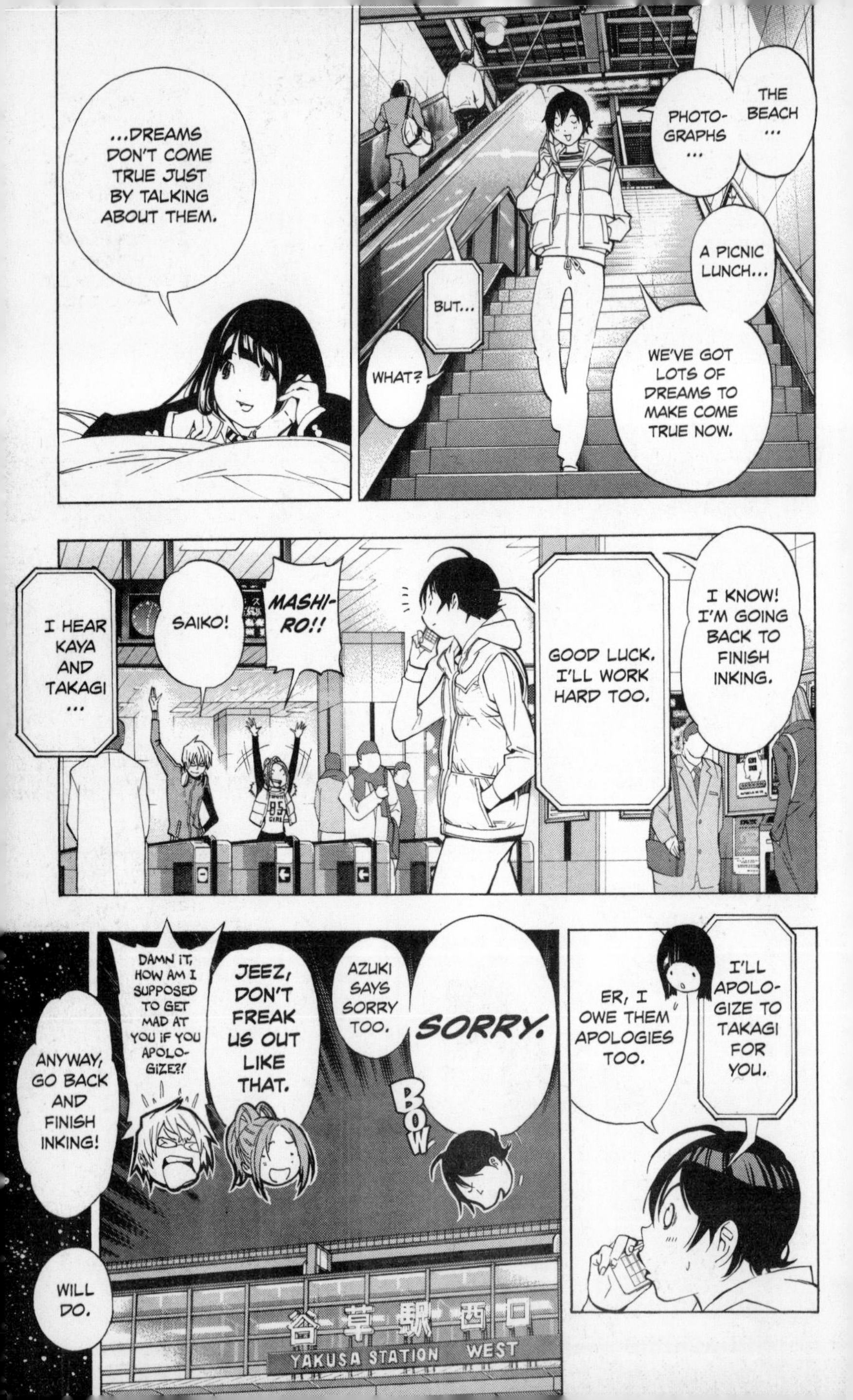
THE BEACH...
PHOTO-GRAPHS...
A PICNIC LUNCH...
WE'VE GOT LOTS OF DREAMS TO MAKE COME TRUE NOW.
BUT...
WHAT?
...DREAMS DON'T COME TRUE JUST BY TALKING ABOUT THEM.
I KNOW! I'M GOING BACK TO FINISH INKING.
GOOD LUCK. I'LL WORK HARD TOO.
MASHI-RO!!
SAIKO!
I HEAR KAYA AND TAKAGI...
I'LL APOLO-GIZE TO TAKAGI FOR YOU.
ER, I OWE THEM APOLOGIES TOO.
SORRY.
BOW
AZUKI SAYS SORRY TOO.
JEEZ, DON'T FREAK US OUT LIKE THAT.
DAMN IT, HOW AM I SUPPOSED TO GET MAD AT YOU IF YOU APOLO-GIZE?!
ANYWAY, GO BACK AND FINISH INKING!
WILL DO.
谷草駅西口
YAKUSA STATION WEST

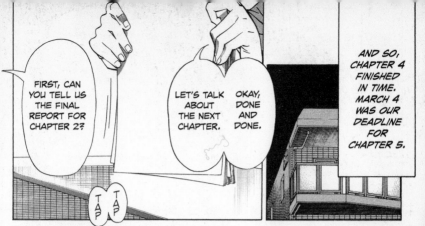

AND SO, CHAPTER 4 FINISHED IN TIME. MARCH 4 WAS OUR DEADLINE FOR CHAPTER 5.

FIRST, CAN YOU TELL US THE FINAL REPORT FOR CHAPTER 2?

LET'S TALK ABOUT THE NEXT CHAPTER.

OKAY, DONE AND DONE.

TAP TAP

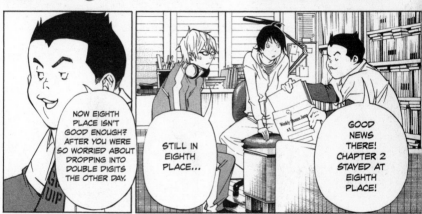

NOW EIGHTH PLACE ISN'T GOOD ENOUGH? AFTER YOU WERE SO WORRIED ABOUT DROPPING INTO DOUBLE DIGITS THE OTHER DAY.

STILL IN EIGHTH PLACE...

GOOD NEWS THERE! CHAPTER 2 STAYED AT EIGHTH PLACE!

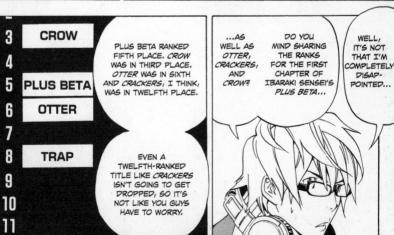

-	
3	CROW
4	
5	PLUS BETA
6	OTTER
7	
8	TRAP
9	
10	
11	
12	CRACKERS
13	

PLUS BETA RANKED FIFTH PLACE. CROW WAS IN THIRD PLACE. OTTER WAS IN SIXTH AND CRACKERS, I THINK, WAS IN TWELFTH PLACE.

...AS WELL AS OTTER, CRACKERS, AND CROW?

DO YOU MIND SHARING THE RANKS FOR THE FIRST CHAPTER OF IBARAKI SENSEI'S PLUS BETA...

WELL, IT'S NOT THAT I'M COMPLETELY DISAP-POINTED...

EVEN A TWELFTH-RANKED TITLE LIKE CRACKERS ISN'T GOING TO GET DROPPED, SO IT'S NOT LIKE YOU GUYS HAVE TO WORRY.

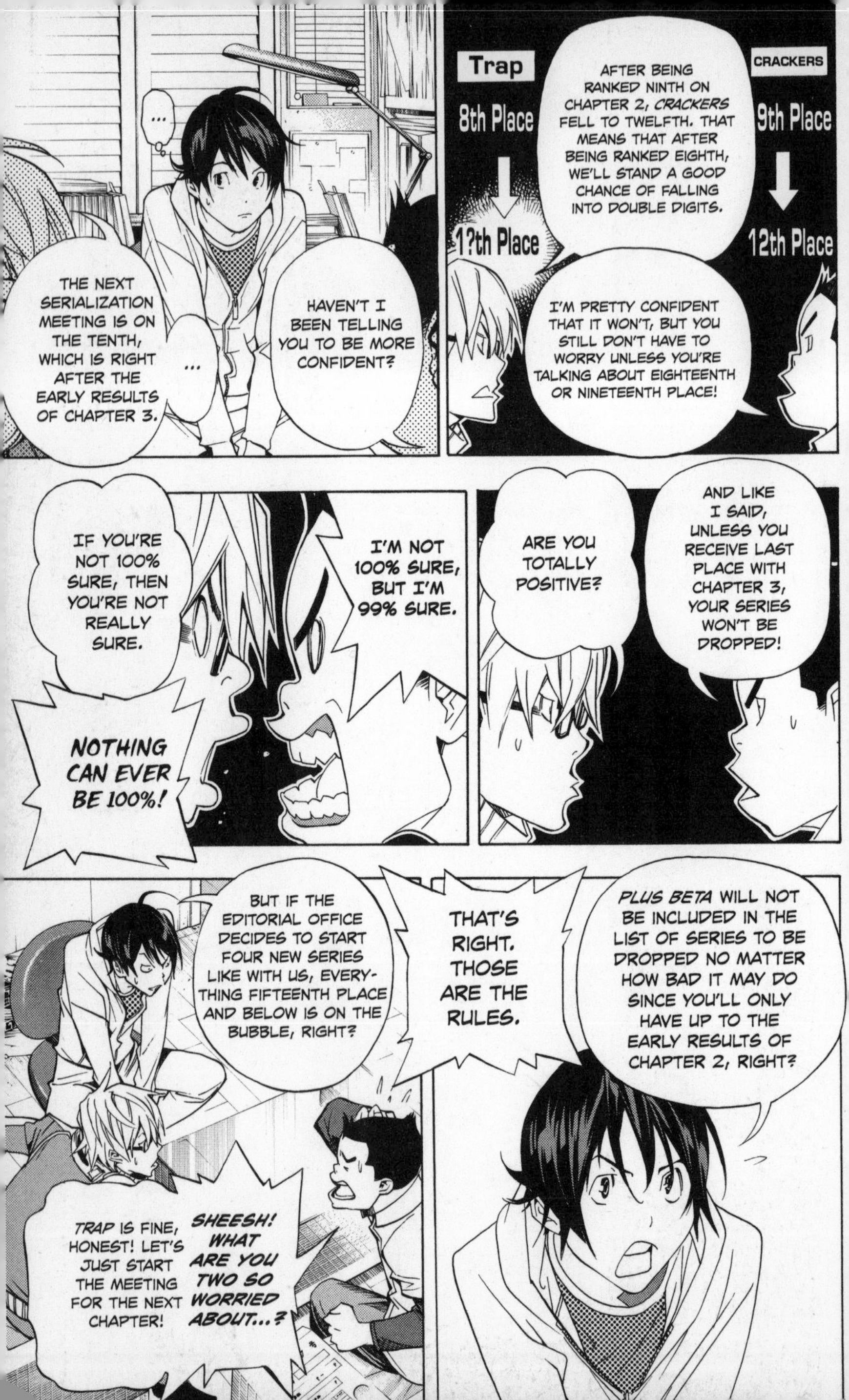
Trap
8th Place
1?th Place
CRACKERS
9th Place
12th Place
AFTER BEING RANKED NINTH ON CHAPTER 2, *CRACKERS* FELL TO TWELFTH. THAT MEANS THAT AFTER BEING RANKED EIGHTH, WE'LL STAND A GOOD CHANCE OF FALLING INTO DOUBLE DIGITS.
I'M PRETTY CONFIDENT THAT IT WON'T, BUT YOU STILL DON'T HAVE TO WORRY UNLESS YOU'RE TALKING ABOUT EIGHTEENTH OR NINETEENTH PLACE!
...
HAVEN'T I BEEN TELLING YOU TO BE MORE CONFIDENT?
...
THE NEXT SERIALIZATION MEETING IS ON THE TENTH, WHICH IS RIGHT AFTER THE EARLY RESULTS OF CHAPTER 3.
AND LIKE I SAID, UNLESS YOU RECEIVE LAST PLACE WITH CHAPTER 3, YOUR SERIES WON'T BE DROPPED!
ARE YOU TOTALLY POSITIVE?
I'M NOT 100% SURE, BUT I'M 99% SURE.
IF YOU'RE NOT 100% SURE, THEN YOU'RE NOT REALLY SURE.
NOTHING CAN EVER BE 100%!
PLUS BETA WILL NOT BE INCLUDED IN THE LIST OF SERIES TO BE DROPPED NO MATTER HOW BAD IT MAY DO SINCE YOU'LL ONLY HAVE UP TO THE EARLY RESULTS OF CHAPTER 2, RIGHT?
THAT'S RIGHT. THOSE ARE THE RULES.
BUT IF THE EDITORIAL OFFICE DECIDES TO START FOUR NEW SERIES LIKE WITH US, EVERY-THING FIFTEENTH PLACE AND BELOW IS ON THE BUBBLE, RIGHT?
SHEESH! WHAT ARE YOU TWO SO WORRIED ABOUT...?
TRAP IS FINE, HONEST! LET'S JUST START THE MEETING FOR THE NEXT CHAPTER!

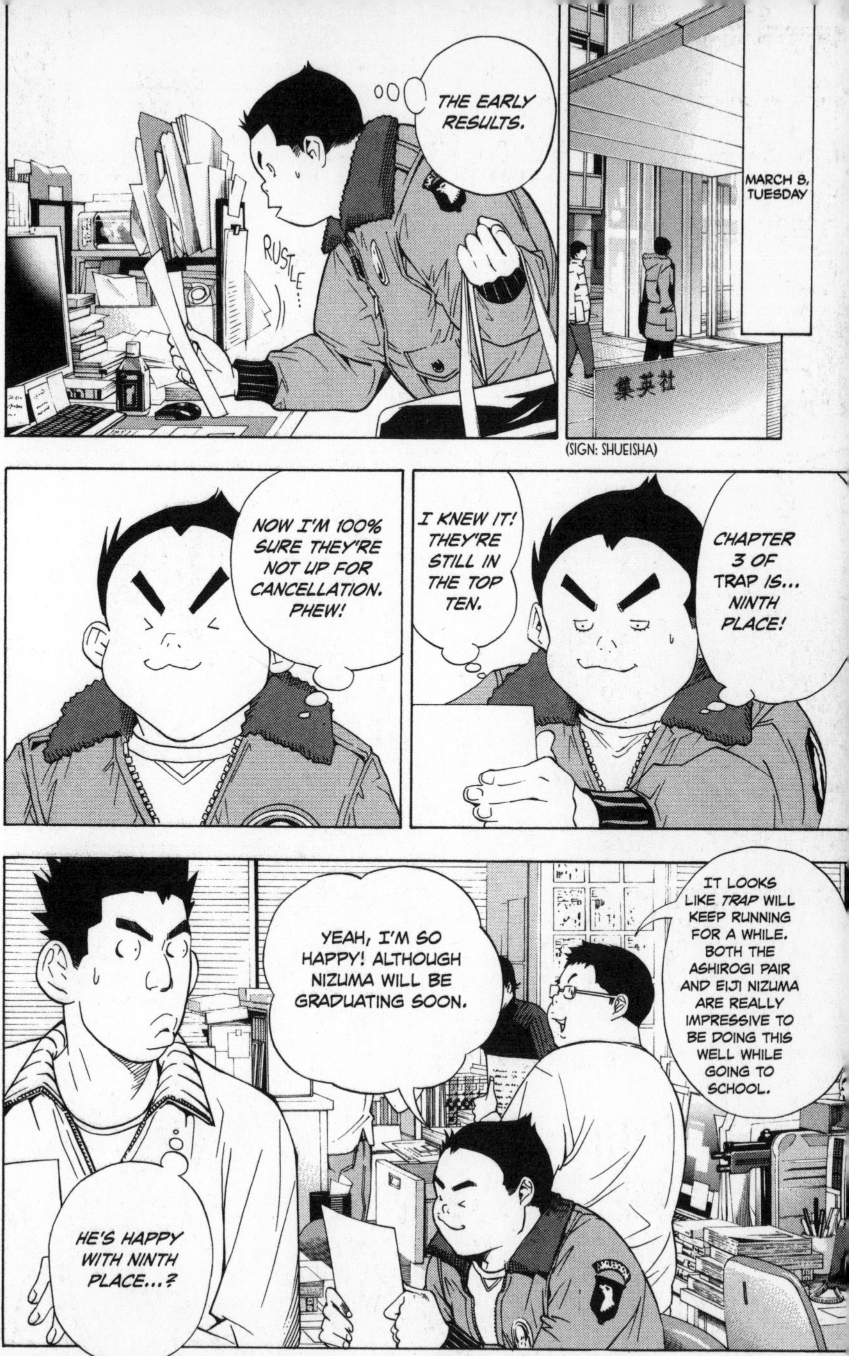
MARCH 8, TUESDAY
集英社
(SIGN: SHUEISHA)
THE EARLY RESULTS.
RUSTLE...
CHAPTER 3 OF TRAP IS... NINTH PLACE!
I KNEW IT! THEY'RE STILL IN THE TOP TEN.
NOW I'M 100% SURE THEY'RE NOT UP FOR CANCELLATION. PHEW!
IT LOOKS LIKE *TRAP* WILL KEEP RUNNING FOR A WHILE. BOTH THE ASHIROGI PAIR AND EIJI NIZUMA ARE REALLY IMPRESSIVE TO BE DOING THIS WELL WHILE GOING TO SCHOOL.
YEAH, I'M SO HAPPY! ALTHOUGH NIZUMA WILL BE GRADUATING SOON.
HE'S HAPPY WITH NINTH PLACE...?

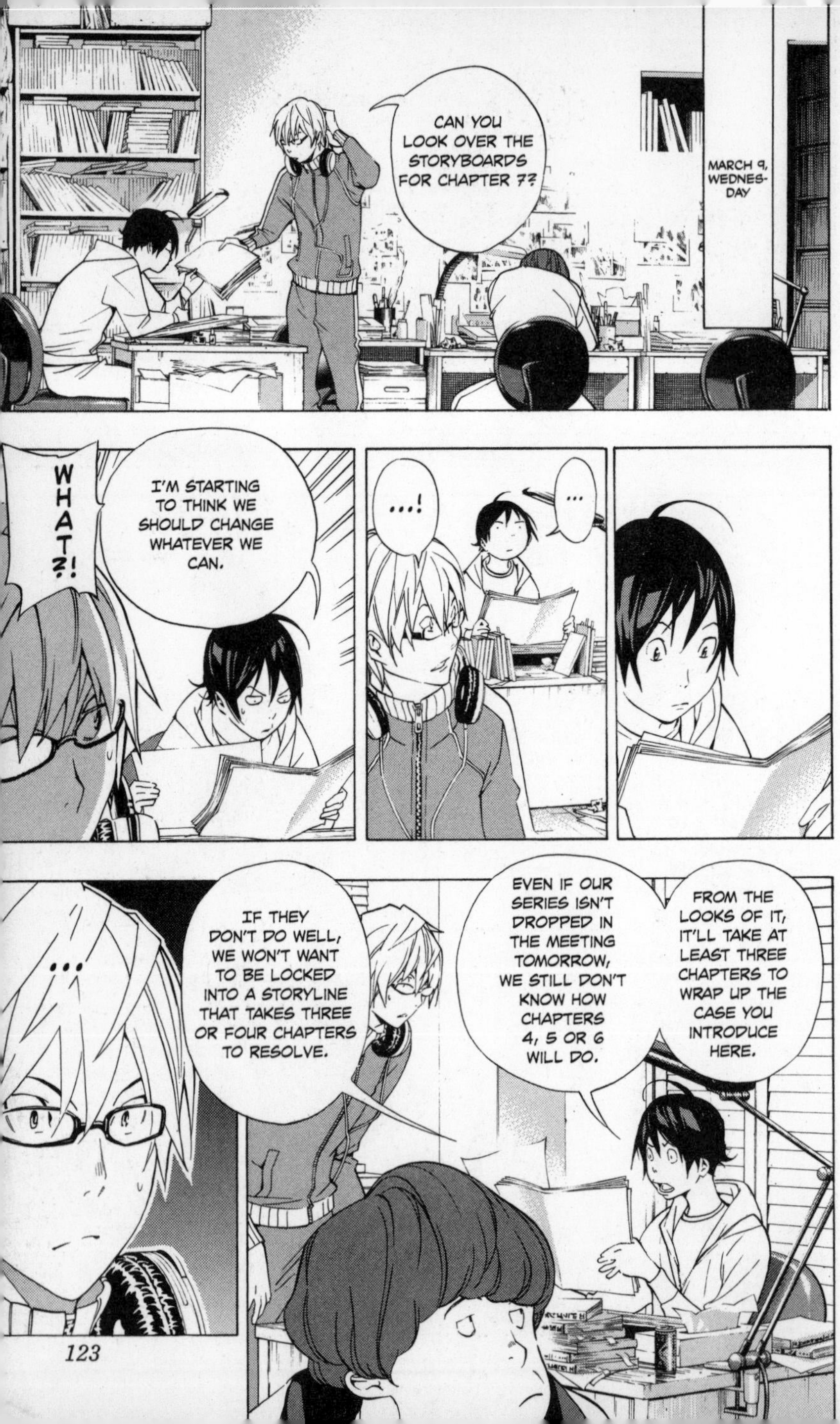
MARCH 9, WEDNESDAY
CAN YOU LOOK OVER THE STORYBOARDS FOR CHAPTER 7?
...
...!
I'M STARTING TO THINK WE SHOULD CHANGE WHATEVER WE CAN.
WHAT?!
FROM THE LOOKS OF IT, IT'LL TAKE AT LEAST THREE CHAPTERS TO WRAP UP THE CASE YOU INTRODUCE HERE.
EVEN IF OUR SERIES ISN'T DROPPED IN THE MEETING TOMORROW, WE STILL DON'T KNOW HOW CHAPTERS 4, 5 OR 6 WILL DO.
IF THEY DON'T DO WELL, WE WON'T WANT TO BE LOCKED INTO A STORYLINE THAT TAKES THREE OR FOUR CHAPTERS TO RESOLVE.
...

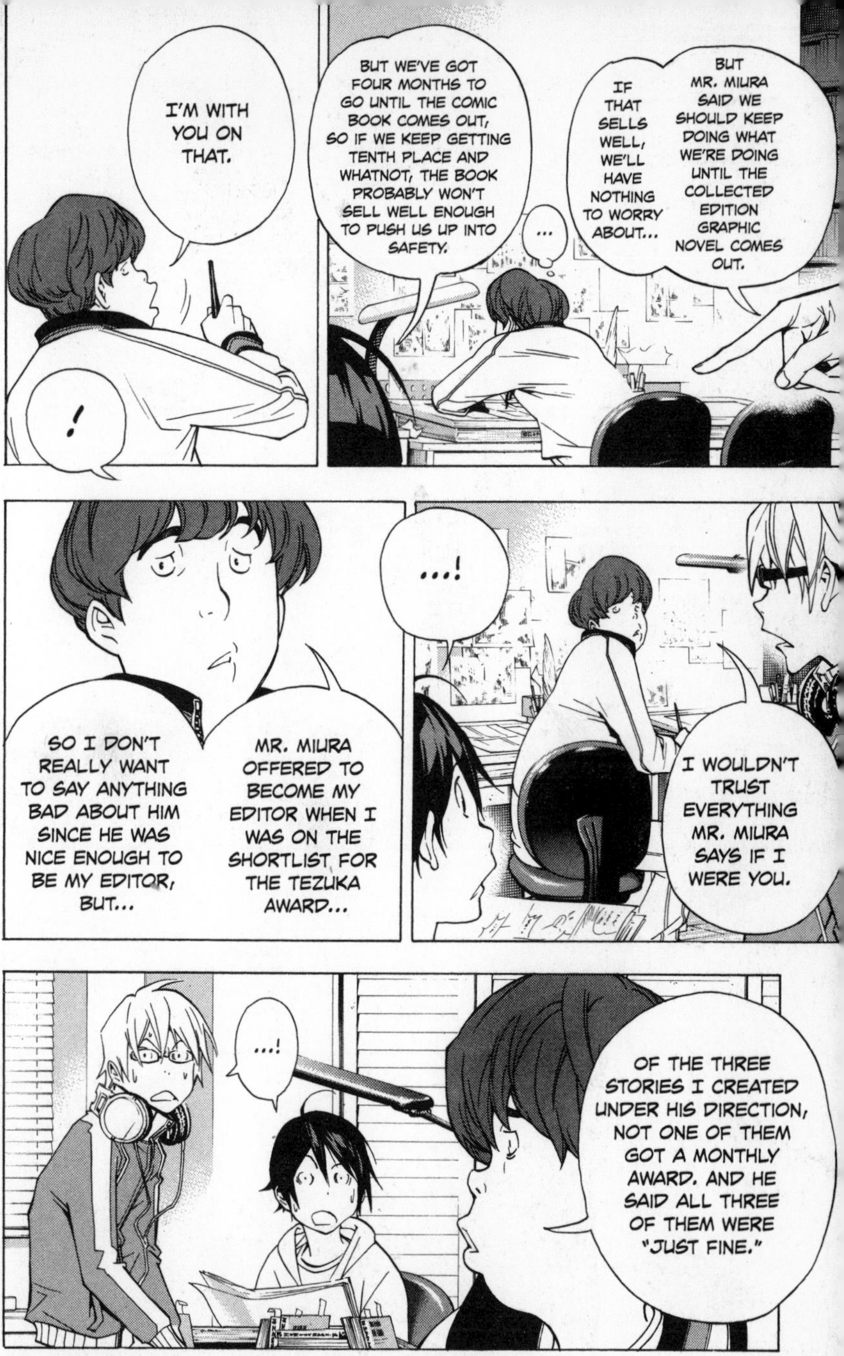
BUT MR. MIURA SAID WE SHOULD KEEP DOING WHAT WE'RE DOING UNTIL THE COLLECTED EDITION GRAPHIC NOVEL COMES OUT.
IF THAT SELLS WELL, WE'LL HAVE NOTHING TO WORRY ABOUT...
...
BUT WE'VE GOT FOUR MONTHS TO GO UNTIL THE COMIC BOOK COMES OUT, SO IF WE KEEP GETTING TENTH PLACE AND WHATNOT, THE BOOK PROBABLY WON'T SELL WELL ENOUGH TO PUSH US UP INTO SAFETY.
I'M WITH YOU ON THAT.
!
I WOULDN'T TRUST EVERYTHING MR. MIURA SAYS IF I WERE YOU.
...!
MR. MIURA OFFERED TO BECOME MY EDITOR WHEN I WAS ON THE SHORTLIST FOR THE TEZUKA AWARD...
SO I DON'T REALLY WANT TO SAY ANYTHING BAD ABOUT HIM SINCE HE WAS NICE ENOUGH TO BE MY EDITOR, BUT...
OF THE THREE STORIES I CREATED UNDER HIS DIRECTION, NOT ONE OF THEM GOT A MONTHLY AWARD. AND HE SAID ALL THREE OF THEM WERE "JUST FINE."
...!

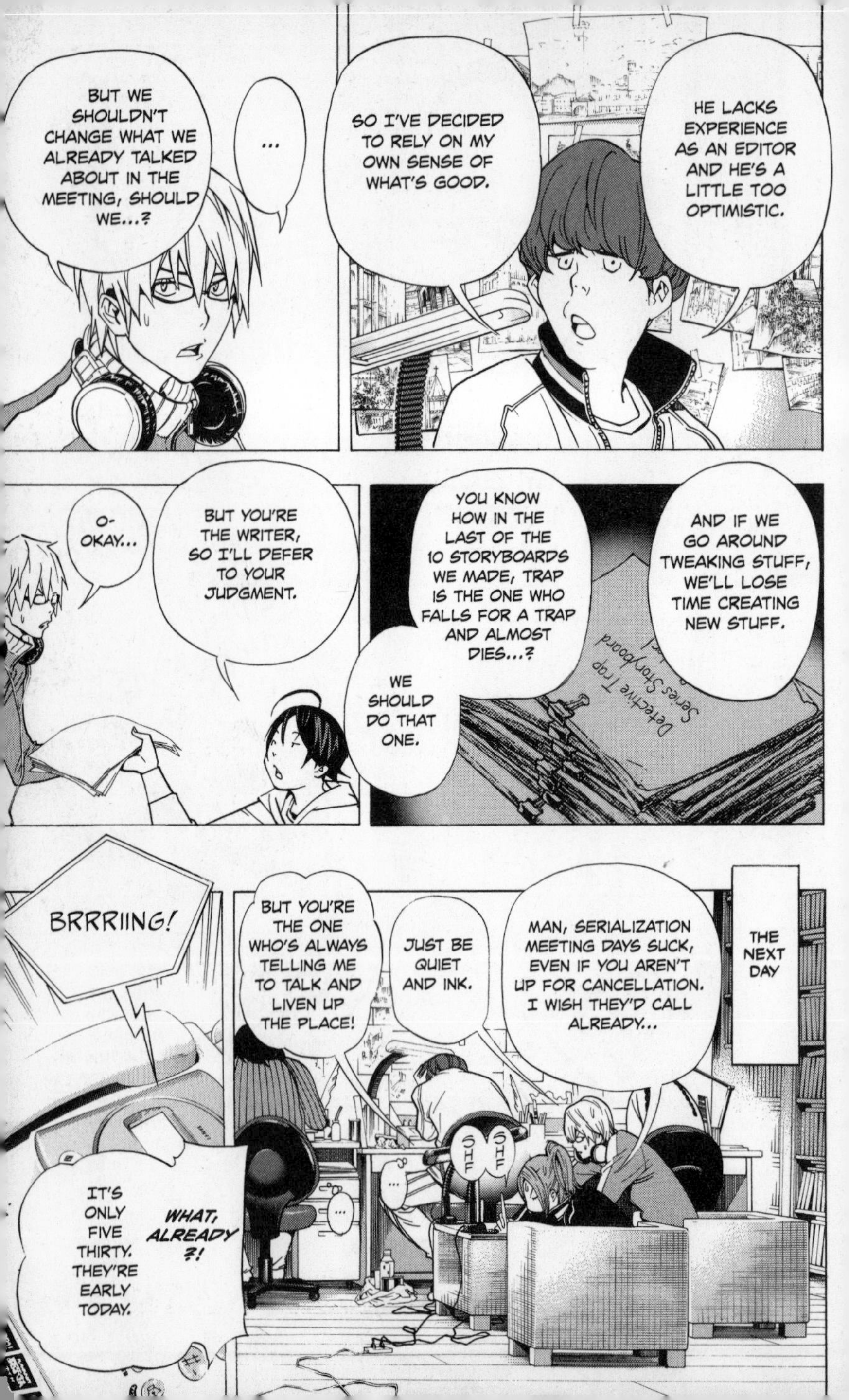
HE LACKS EXPERIENCE AS AN EDITOR AND HE'S A LITTLE TOO OPTIMISTIC.
SO I'VE DECIDED TO RELY ON MY OWN SENSE OF WHAT'S GOOD.
...
BUT WE SHOULDN'T CHANGE WHAT WE ALREADY TALKED ABOUT IN THE MEETING, SHOULD WE...?
AND IF WE GO AROUND TWEAKING STUFF, WE'LL LOSE TIME CREATING NEW STUFF.
YOU KNOW HOW IN THE LAST OF THE 10 STORYBOARDS WE MADE, TRAP IS THE ONE WHO FALLS FOR A TRAP AND ALMOST DIES...?
Detective Trap Series Storyboard
WE SHOULD DO THAT ONE.
BUT YOU'RE THE WRITER, SO I'LL DEFER TO YOUR JUDGMENT.
O-OKAY...
THE NEXT DAY
MAN, SERIALIZATION MEETING DAYS SUCK, EVEN IF YOU AREN'T UP FOR CANCELLATION. I WISH THEY'D CALL ALREADY...
JUST BE QUIET AND INK.
BUT YOU'RE THE ONE WHO'S ALWAYS TELLING ME TO TALK AND LIVEN UP THE PLACE!
SHF
SHF
...
...
BRRRIING!
WHAT, ALREADY?!
IT'S ONLY FIVE THIRTY. THEY'RE EARLY TODAY.

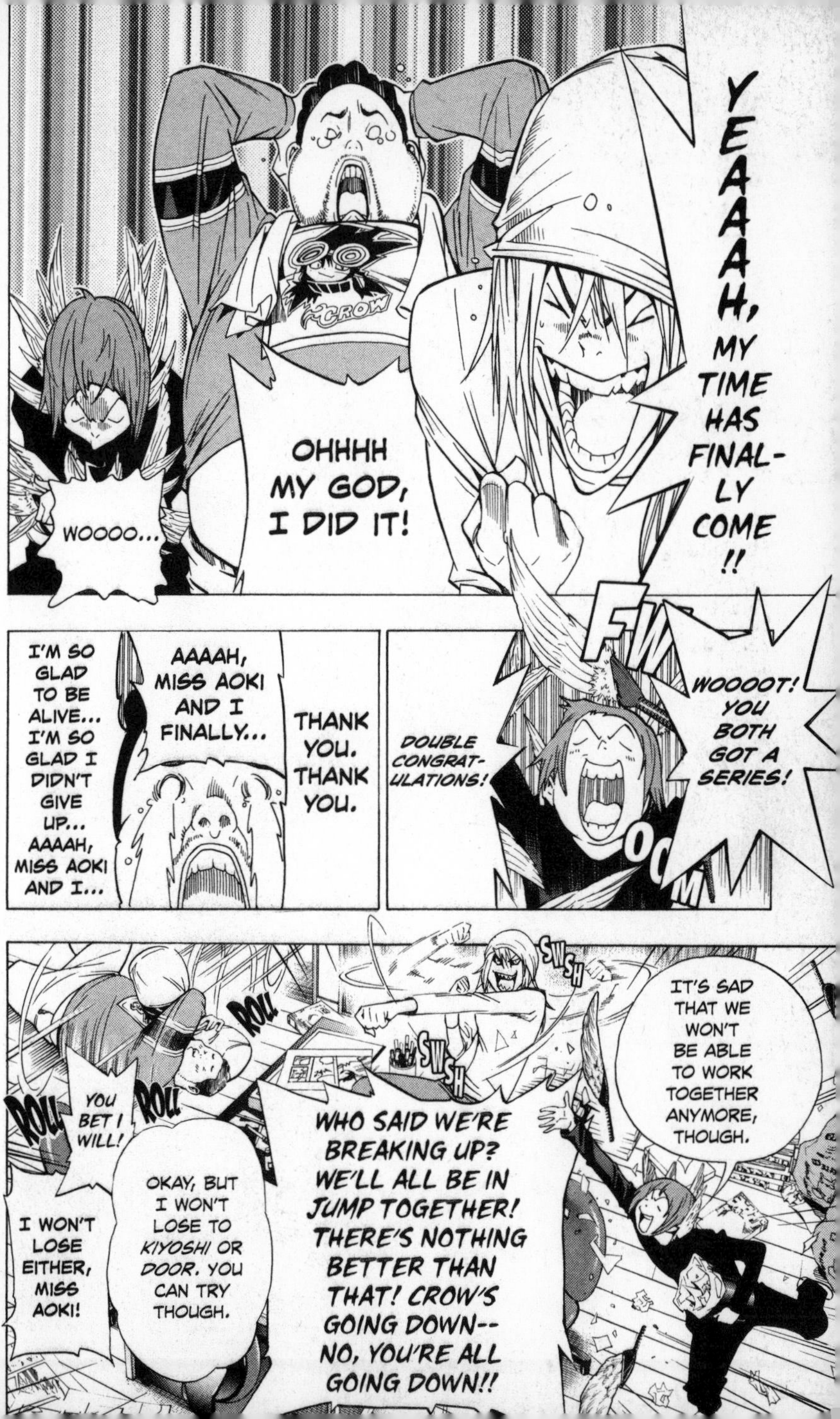
YEAAAAH, MY TIME HAS FINAL-LY COME!!
OHHHH MY GOD, I DID IT!
WOOOO...
WOOOOT! YOU BOTH GOT A SERIES!
DOUBLE CONGRAT-ULATIONS!
THANK YOU. THANK YOU.
AAAAH, MISS AOKI AND I FINALLY...
I'M SO GLAD TO BE ALIVE... I'M SO GLAD I DIDN'T GIVE UP... AAAAH, MISS AOKI AND I...
SWSH
IT'S SAD THAT WE WON'T BE ABLE TO WORK TOGETHER ANYMORE, THOUGH.
SWSH
WHO SAID WE'RE BREAKING UP? WE'LL ALL BE IN JUMP TOGETHER! THERE'S NOTHING BETTER THAN THAT! CROW'S GOING DOWN-- NO, YOU'RE ALL GOING DOWN!!
ROLL
OKAY, BUT I WON'T LOSE TO KIYOSHI OR DOOR. YOU CAN TRY THOUGH.
ROLL
YOU BET I WILL!
ROLL
I WON'T LOSE EITHER, MISS AOKI!

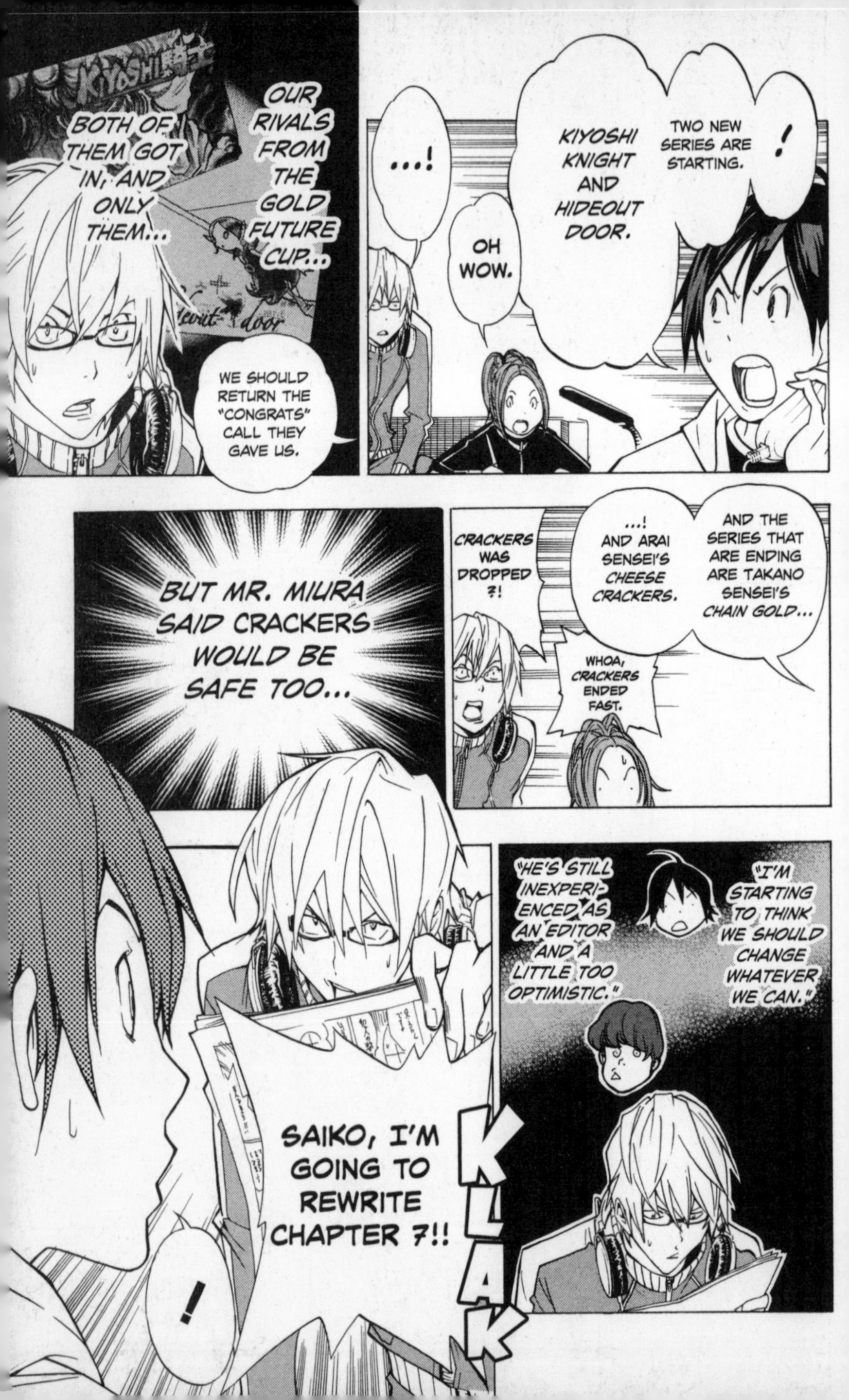
!
TWO NEW SERIES ARE STARTING.
KIYOSHI KNIGHT AND HIDEOUT DOOR.
...!
OH WOW.
OUR RIVALS FROM THE GOLD FUTURE CUP...
BOTH OF THEM GOT IN, AND ONLY THEM...
WE SHOULD RETURN THE "CONGRATS" CALL THEY GAVE US.
AND THE SERIES THAT ARE ENDING ARE TAKANO SENSEI'S CHAIN GOLD...
...! AND ARAI SENSEI'S CHEESE CRACKERS.
CRACKERS WAS DROPPED ?!
WHOA, CRACKERS ENDED FAST.
BUT MR. MIURA SAID CRACKERS WOULD BE SAFE TOO...
"I'M STARTING TO THINK WE SHOULD CHANGE WHATEVER WE CAN."
"HE'S STILL INEXPERIENCED AS AN EDITOR AND A LITTLE TOO OPTIMISTIC."
KLAK
SAIKO, I'M GOING TO REWRITE CHAPTER 7!!
!

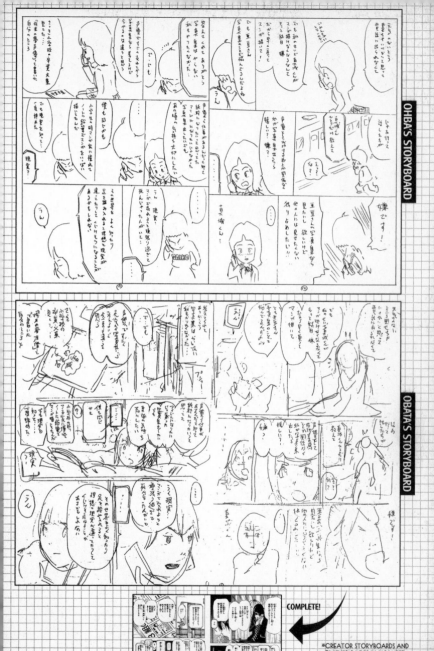

OHBA'S STORYBOARD

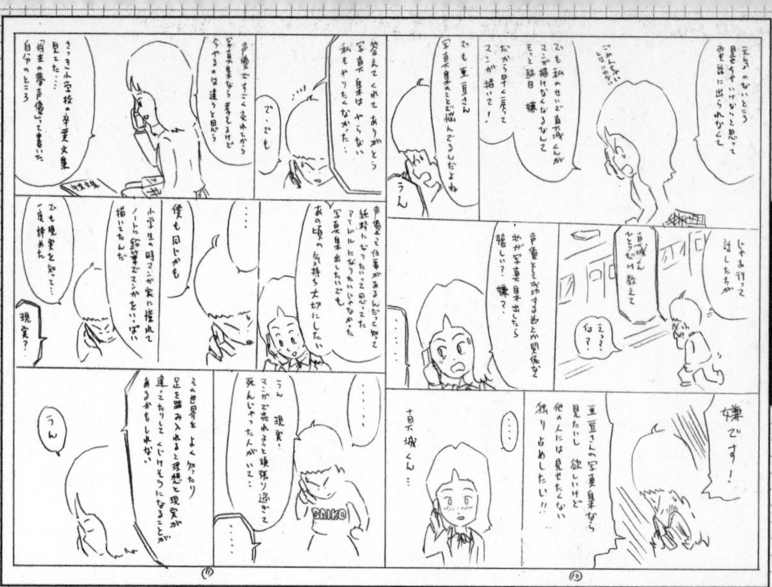
ごめんなさい
元気のないところ見せちゃいけないと思って電話に出られなくて
でも私のせいで真城くんがマンガ描けなくなるなんてもっと駄目 嫌
だから早く戻ってマンガ描いて!
でも亜豆さん写真集のことで悩んでるんだよね
うん
じゃあ行って話したら
真城くんひとつだけ教えて
えっ? 何?
声優として成功する為とか関係なく私が写真集出したら嬉しい? 嫌?
……
嫌です!
亜豆さんの写真集なら見たいし欲しいけど他の人には見せたくない 独り占めしたい!!
……
真城くん…
答えてくれてありがとう 写真集はやらない 私もやりたくなかった…
で・でも
声優ですごく売れてから写真集なら考えるけど今やるのは違うと思う
さっき小学校の卒業文集見てた… 『将来の夢声優』って書いた自分のところ
声優って仕事があるんだって知って純粋になりたいと思った アイドルになりたいんじゃなかった 写真集出したいんでもない あの頃の気持ち大切にしたい
……
僕も同じかも
小学生の時マンガ家に憧れてノートに鉛筆でマンガをいっぱい描いてたんだ
でも現実を知って… 一度諦めた
現実?
……
うん 現実! マンガで売れようと頑張り過ぎて死んじゃった人がいて…
……
その世界をよく知ったり足を踏み入れると理想と現実が違ったりしてくじけそうになることがあるかもしれない
うん

OBATA'S STORYBOARD

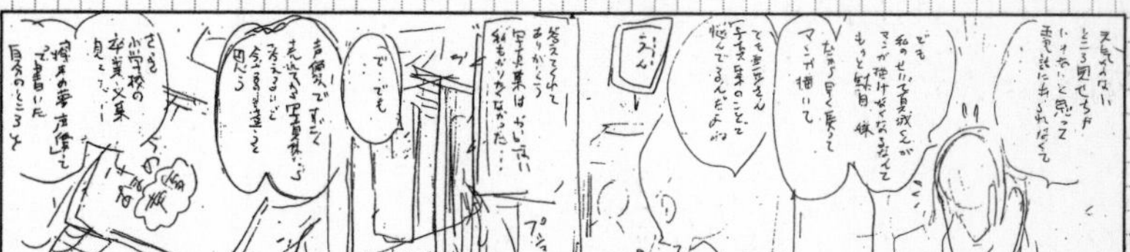

COMPLETE!

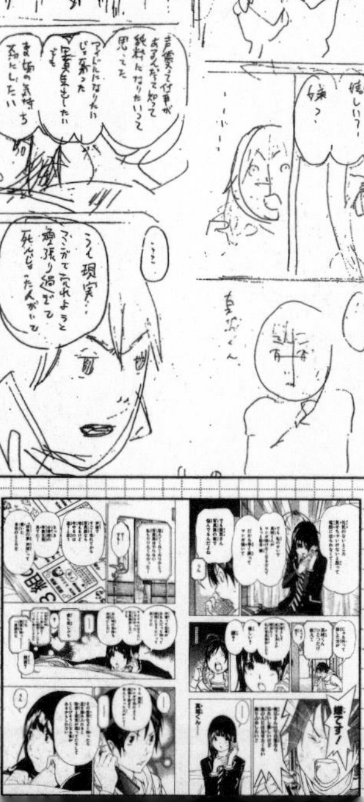

※CREATOR STORYBOARDS AND FINISHED PAGES IN JAPANESE

BAKUMAN。 vol. 5

"Until the Final Draft Is Complete"

Chapter 40, pp. 116-117

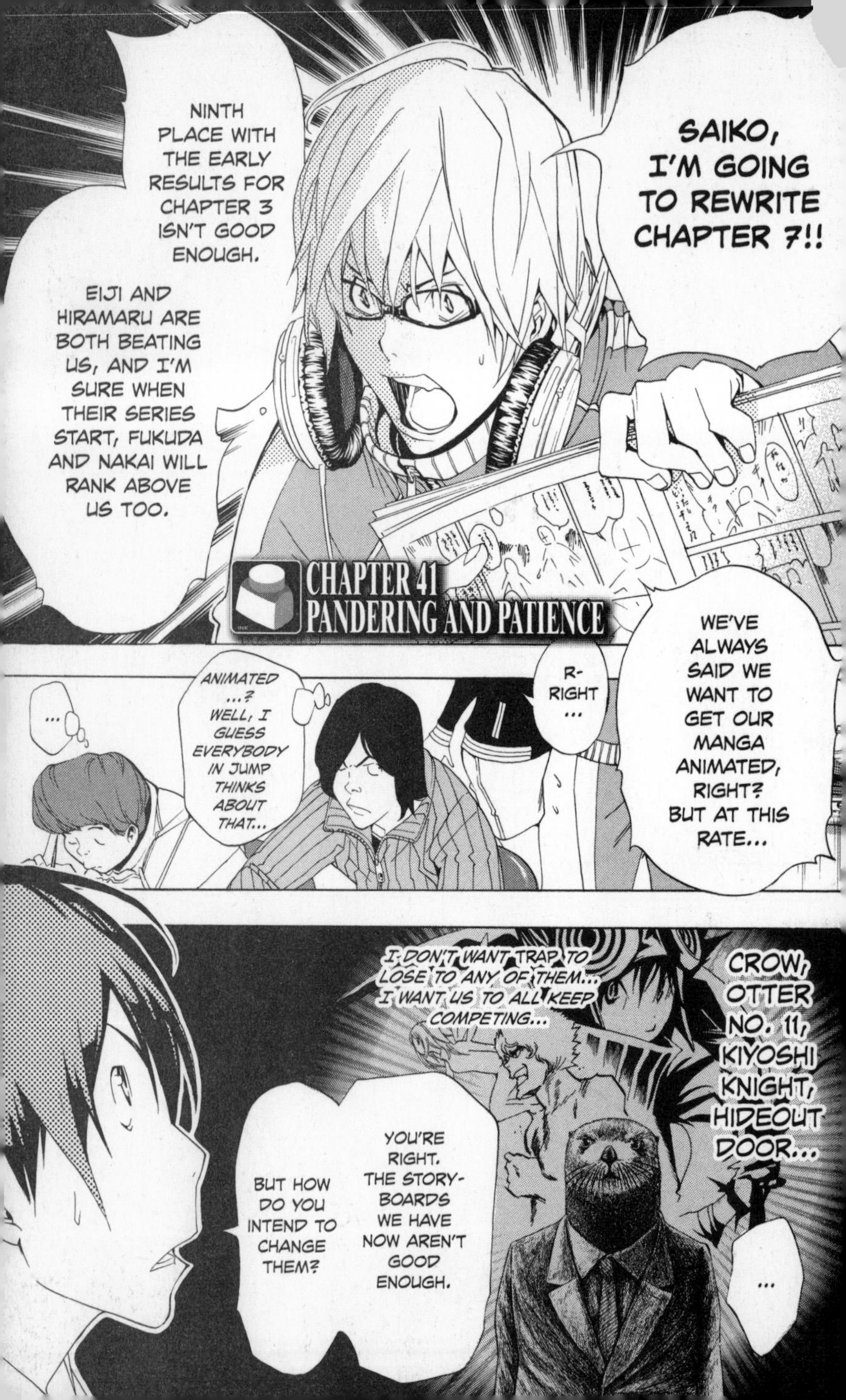
SAIKO, I'M GOING TO REWRITE CHAPTER 7!!
NINTH PLACE WITH THE EARLY RESULTS FOR CHAPTER 3 ISN'T GOOD ENOUGH.
EIJI AND HIRAMARU ARE BOTH BEATING US, AND I'M SURE WHEN THEIR SERIES START, FUKUDA AND NAKAI WILL RANK ABOVE US TOO.
CHAPTER 41
PANDERING AND PATIENCE
WE'VE ALWAYS SAID WE WANT TO GET OUR MANGA ANIMATED, RIGHT? BUT AT THIS RATE...
R-RIGHT...
ANIMATED...? WELL, I GUESS EVERYBODY IN JUMP THINKS ABOUT THAT...
...
CROW, OTTER NO. 11, KIYOSHI KNIGHT, HIDEOUT DOOR...
I DON'T WANT TRAP TO LOSE TO ANY OF THEM... I WANT US TO ALL KEEP COMPETING...
...
YOU'RE RIGHT. THE STORYBOARDS WE HAVE NOW AREN'T GOOD ENOUGH.
BUT HOW DO YOU INTEND TO CHANGE THEM?

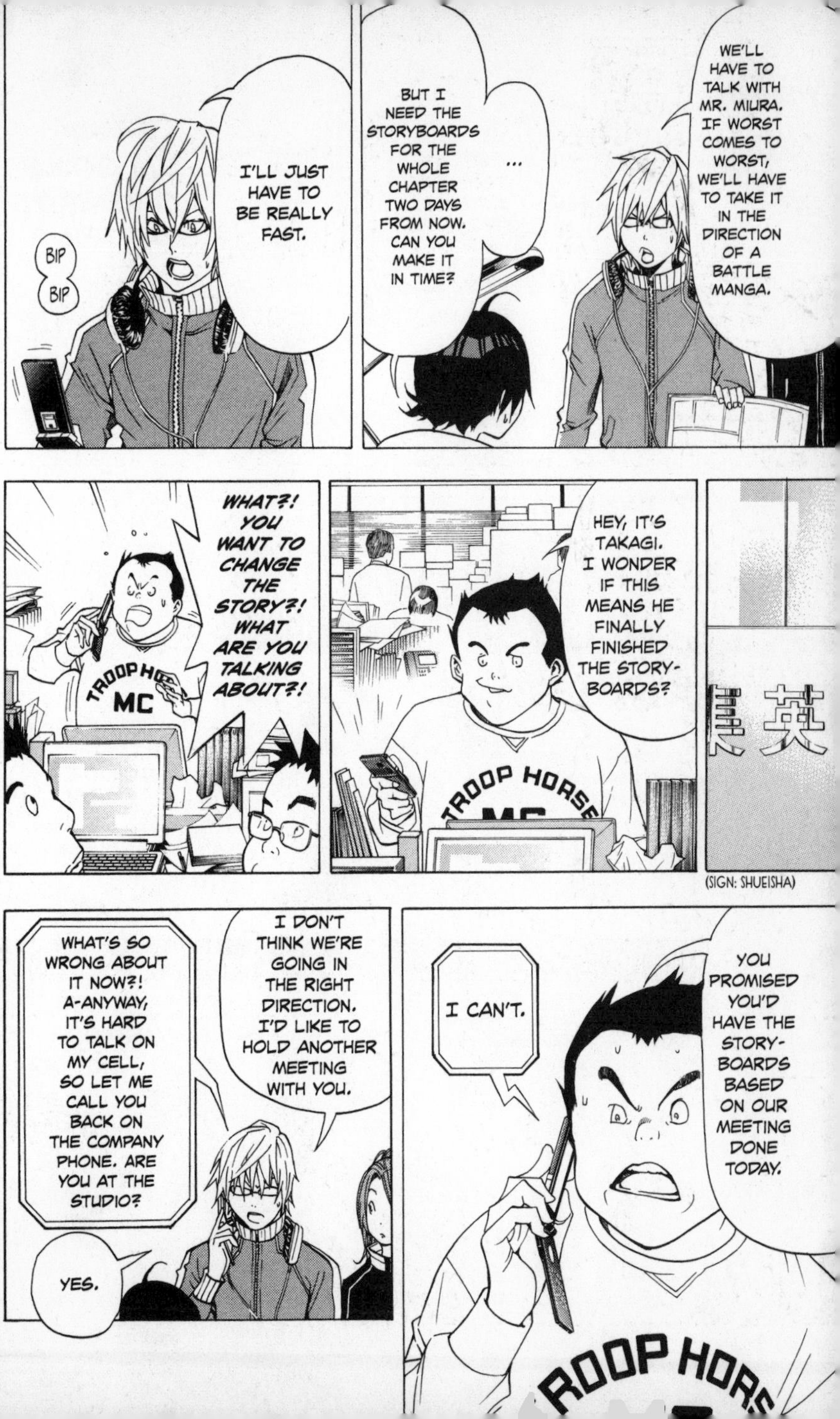
WE'LL HAVE TO TALK WITH MR. MIURA. IF WORST COMES TO WORST, WE'LL HAVE TO TAKE IT IN THE DIRECTION OF A BATTLE MANGA.
...
BUT I NEED THE STORYBOARDS FOR THE WHOLE CHAPTER TWO DAYS FROM NOW. CAN YOU MAKE IT IN TIME?
I'LL JUST HAVE TO BE REALLY FAST.
BIP
BIP
(SIGN: SHUEISHA)
HEY, IT'S TAKAGI. I WONDER IF THIS MEANS HE FINALLY FINISHED THE STORY-BOARDS?
TROOP HORSE MC
WHAT?! YOU WANT TO CHANGE THE STORY?! WHAT ARE YOU TALKING ABOUT?!
YOU PROMISED YOU'D HAVE THE STORY-BOARDS BASED ON OUR MEETING DONE TODAY.
I CAN'T.
I DON'T THINK WE'RE GOING IN THE RIGHT DIRECTION. I'D LIKE TO HOLD ANOTHER MEETING WITH YOU.
WHAT'S SO WRONG ABOUT IT NOW?! A-ANYWAY, IT'S HARD TO TALK ON MY CELL, SO LET ME CALL YOU BACK ON THE COMPANY PHONE. ARE YOU AT THE STUDIO?
YES.

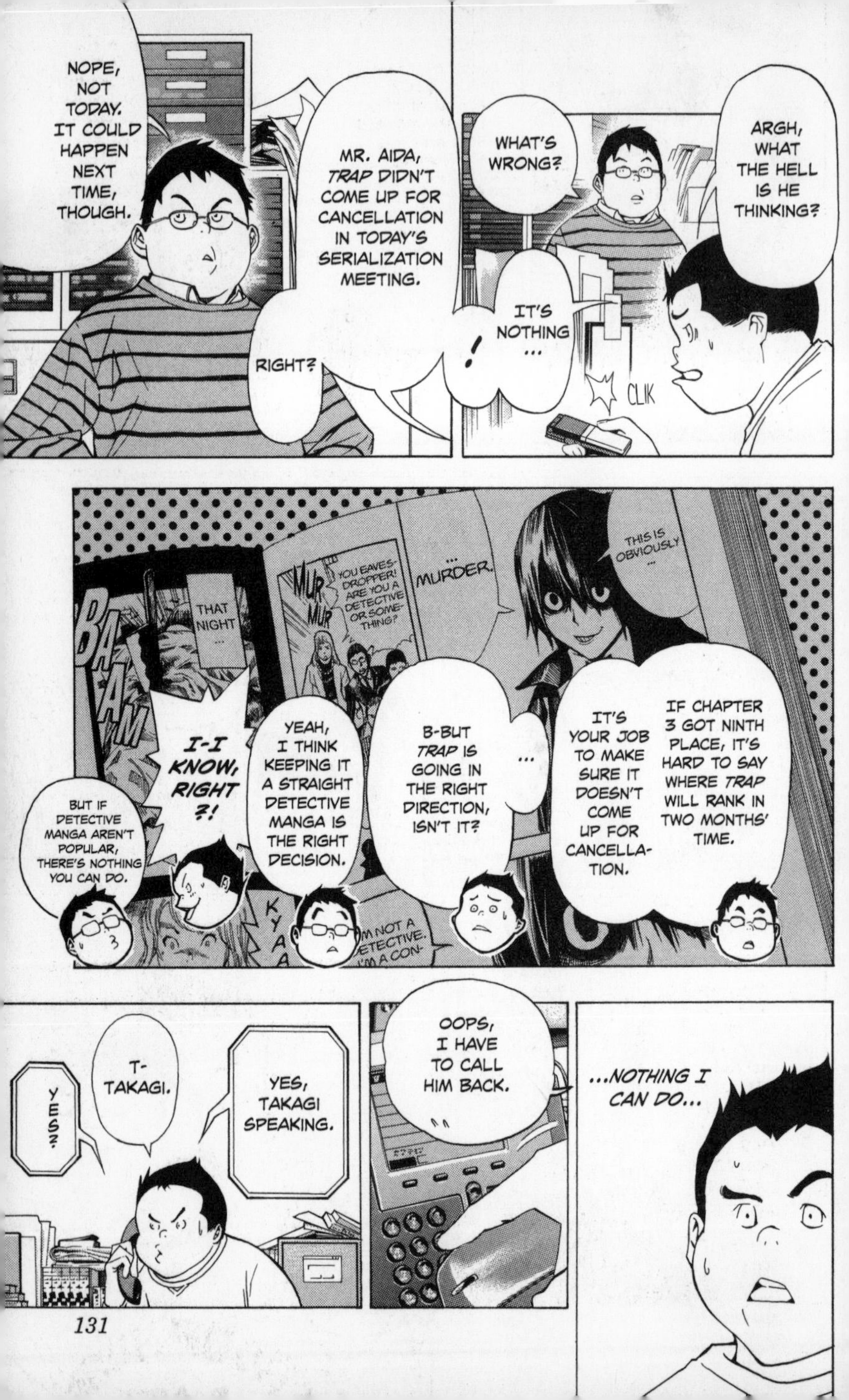
ARGH, WHAT THE HELL IS HE THINKING?
WHAT'S WRONG?
IT'S NOTHING ...
!
CLIK
MR. AIDA, *TRAP* DIDN'T COME UP FOR CANCELLATION IN TODAY'S SERIALIZATION MEETING.
RIGHT?
NOPE, NOT TODAY. IT COULD HAPPEN NEXT TIME, THOUGH.
THIS IS OBVIOUSLY ...
... MURDER.
YOU EAVES-DROPPER! ARE YOU A DETECTIVE OR SOME-THING?
MUR MUR
THAT NIGHT ...
BAAM
IF CHAPTER 3 GOT NINTH PLACE, IT'S HARD TO SAY WHERE *TRAP* WILL RANK IN TWO MONTHS' TIME.
IT'S YOUR JOB TO MAKE SURE IT DOESN'T COME UP FOR CANCELLA-TION.
...
B-BUT *TRAP* IS GOING IN THE RIGHT DIRECTION, ISN'T IT?
YEAH, I THINK KEEPING IT A STRAIGHT DETECTIVE MANGA IS THE RIGHT DECISION.
I'M NOT A DETECTIVE. I'M A CON-
KYAA
I-I KNOW, RIGHT?!
BUT IF DETECTIVE MANGA AREN'T POPULAR, THERE'S NOTHING YOU CAN DO.
...NOTHING I CAN DO...
OOPS, I HAVE TO CALL HIM BACK.
YES, TAKAGI SPEAKING.
T-TAKAGI.
YES?

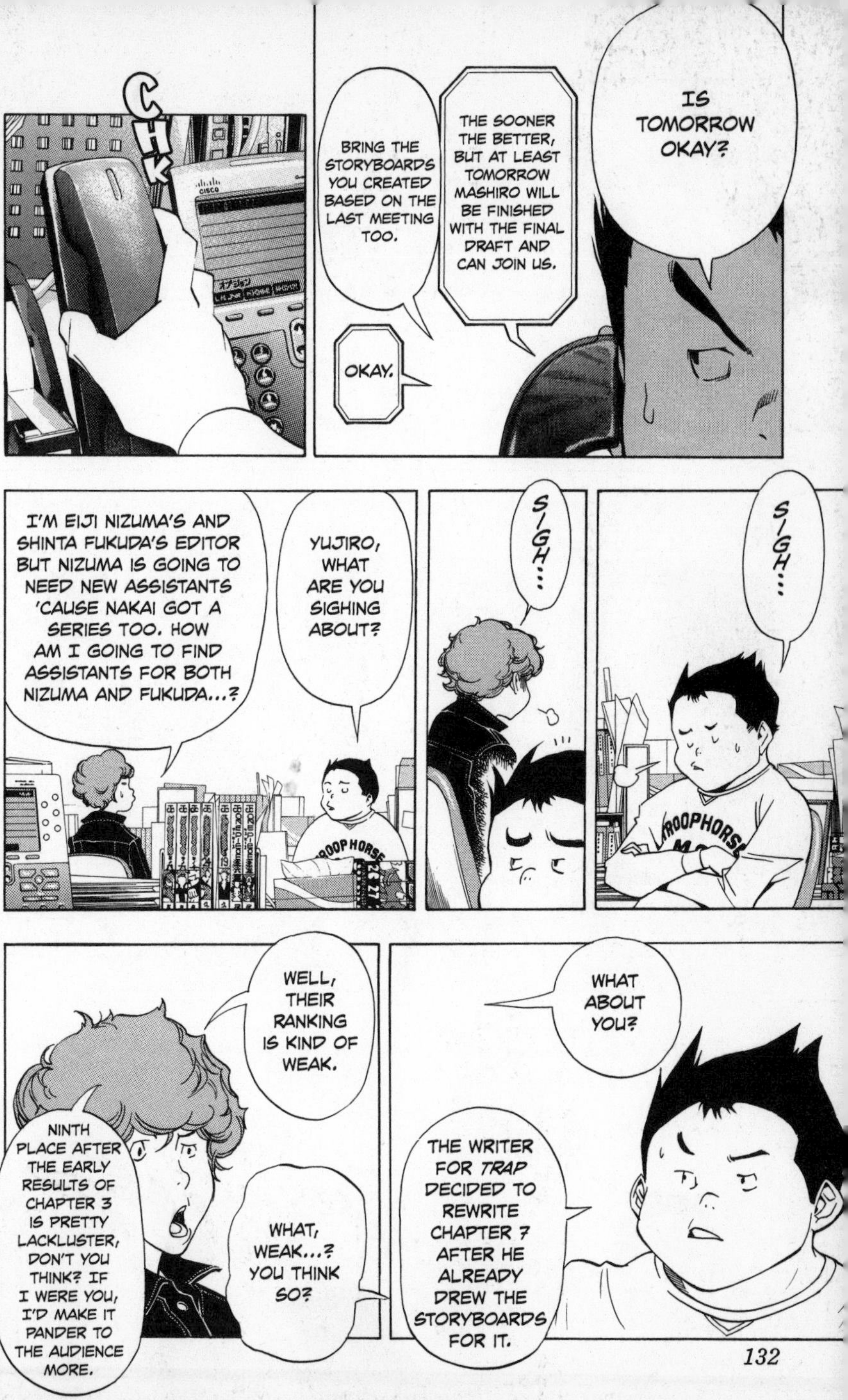
IS TOMORROW OKAY?
THE SOONER THE BETTER, BUT AT LEAST TOMORROW MASHIRO WILL BE FINISHED WITH THE FINAL DRAFT AND CAN JOIN US.
BRING THE STORYBOARDS YOU CREATED BASED ON THE LAST MEETING TOO.
OKAY.
CHK
SIGH...
SIGH...
YUJIRO, WHAT ARE YOU SIGHING ABOUT?
I'M EIJI NIZUMA'S AND SHINTA FUKUDA'S EDITOR BUT NIZUMA IS GOING TO NEED NEW ASSISTANTS 'CAUSE NAKAI GOT A SERIES TOO. HOW AM I GOING TO FIND ASSISTANTS FOR BOTH NIZUMA AND FUKUDA...?
WHAT ABOUT YOU?
THE WRITER FOR *TRAP* DECIDED TO REWRITE CHAPTER 7 AFTER HE ALREADY DREW THE STORYBOARDS FOR IT.
WELL, THEIR RANKING IS KIND OF WEAK.
WHAT, WEAK...? YOU THINK SO?
NINTH PLACE AFTER THE EARLY RESULTS OF CHAPTER 3 IS PRETTY LACKLUSTER, DON'T YOU THINK? IF I WERE YOU, I'D MAKE IT PANDER TO THE AUDIENCE MORE.

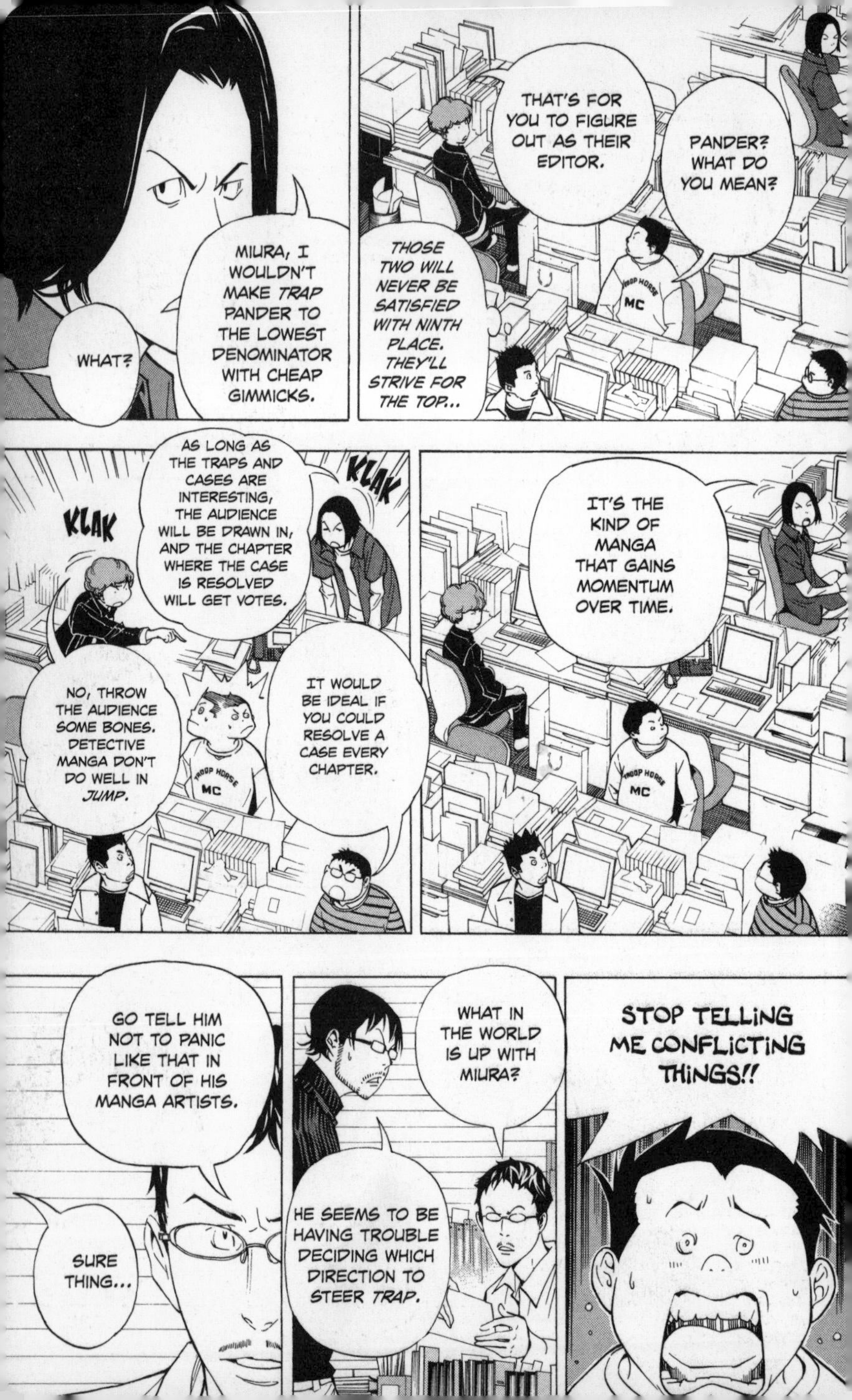
PANDER? WHAT DO YOU MEAN?
THAT'S FOR YOU TO FIGURE OUT AS THEIR EDITOR.
THOSE TWO WILL NEVER BE SATISFIED WITH NINTH PLACE. THEY'LL STRIVE FOR THE TOP...
MIURA, I WOULDN'T MAKE *TRAP* PANDER TO THE LOWEST DENOMINATOR WITH CHEAP GIMMICKS.
WHAT?
IT'S THE KIND OF MANGA THAT GAINS MOMENTUM OVER TIME.
KLAK
AS LONG AS THE TRAPS AND CASES ARE INTERESTING, THE AUDIENCE WILL BE DRAWN IN, AND THE CHAPTER WHERE THE CASE IS RESOLVED WILL GET VOTES.
KLAK
IT WOULD BE IDEAL IF YOU COULD RESOLVE A CASE EVERY CHAPTER.
NO, THROW THE AUDIENCE SOME BONES. DETECTIVE MANGA DON'T DO WELL IN *JUMP*.
STOP TELLING ME CONFLICTING THINGS!!
WHAT IN THE WORLD IS UP WITH MIURA?
HE SEEMS TO BE HAVING TROUBLE DECIDING WHICH DIRECTION TO STEER *TRAP*.
GO TELL HIM NOT TO PANIC LIKE THAT IN FRONT OF HIS MANGA ARTISTS.
SURE THING...

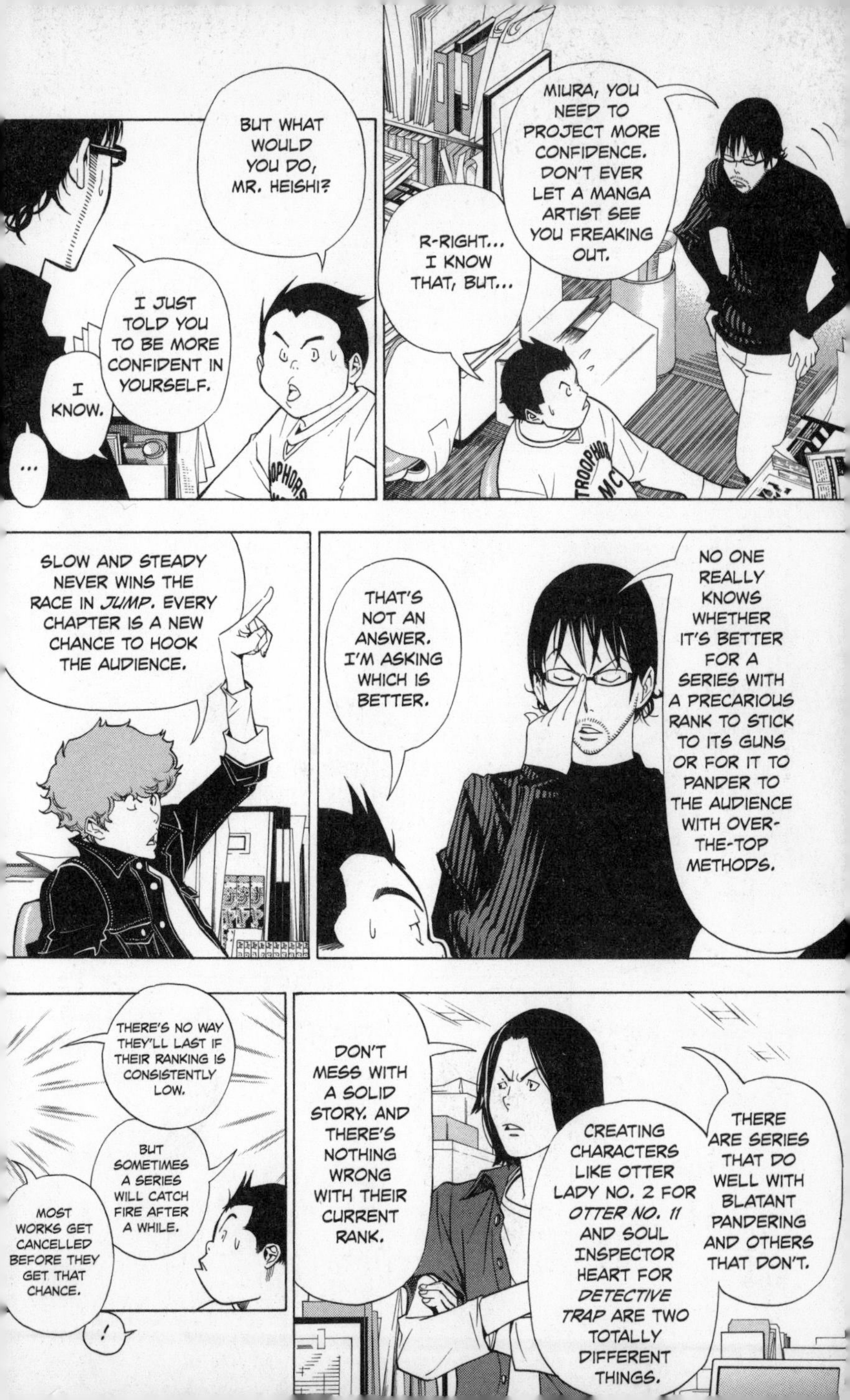
MIURA, YOU NEED TO PROJECT MORE CONFIDENCE. DON'T EVER LET A MANGA ARTIST SEE YOU FREAKING OUT.
R-RIGHT... I KNOW THAT, BUT...
BUT WHAT WOULD YOU DO, MR. HEISHI?
I JUST TOLD YOU TO BE MORE CONFIDENT IN YOURSELF.
I KNOW.
...
NO ONE REALLY KNOWS WHETHER IT'S BETTER FOR A SERIES WITH A PRECARIOUS RANK TO STICK TO ITS GUNS OR FOR IT TO PANDER TO THE AUDIENCE WITH OVER-THE-TOP METHODS.
THAT'S NOT AN ANSWER. I'M ASKING WHICH IS BETTER.
SLOW AND STEADY NEVER WINS THE RACE IN *JUMP*. EVERY CHAPTER IS A NEW CHANCE TO HOOK THE AUDIENCE.
THERE ARE SERIES THAT DO WELL WITH BLATANT PANDERING AND OTHERS THAT DON'T.
CREATING CHARACTERS LIKE OTTER LADY NO. 2 FOR *OTTER NO. 11* AND SOUL INSPECTOR HEART FOR *DETECTIVE TRAP* ARE TWO TOTALLY DIFFERENT THINGS.
DON'T MESS WITH A SOLID STORY. AND THERE'S NOTHING WRONG WITH THEIR CURRENT RANK.
THERE'S NO WAY THEY'LL LAST IF THEIR RANKING IS CONSISTENTLY LOW.
BUT SOMETIMES A SERIES WILL CATCH FIRE AFTER A WHILE.
MOST WORKS GET CANCELLED BEFORE THEY GET THAT CHANCE.
!

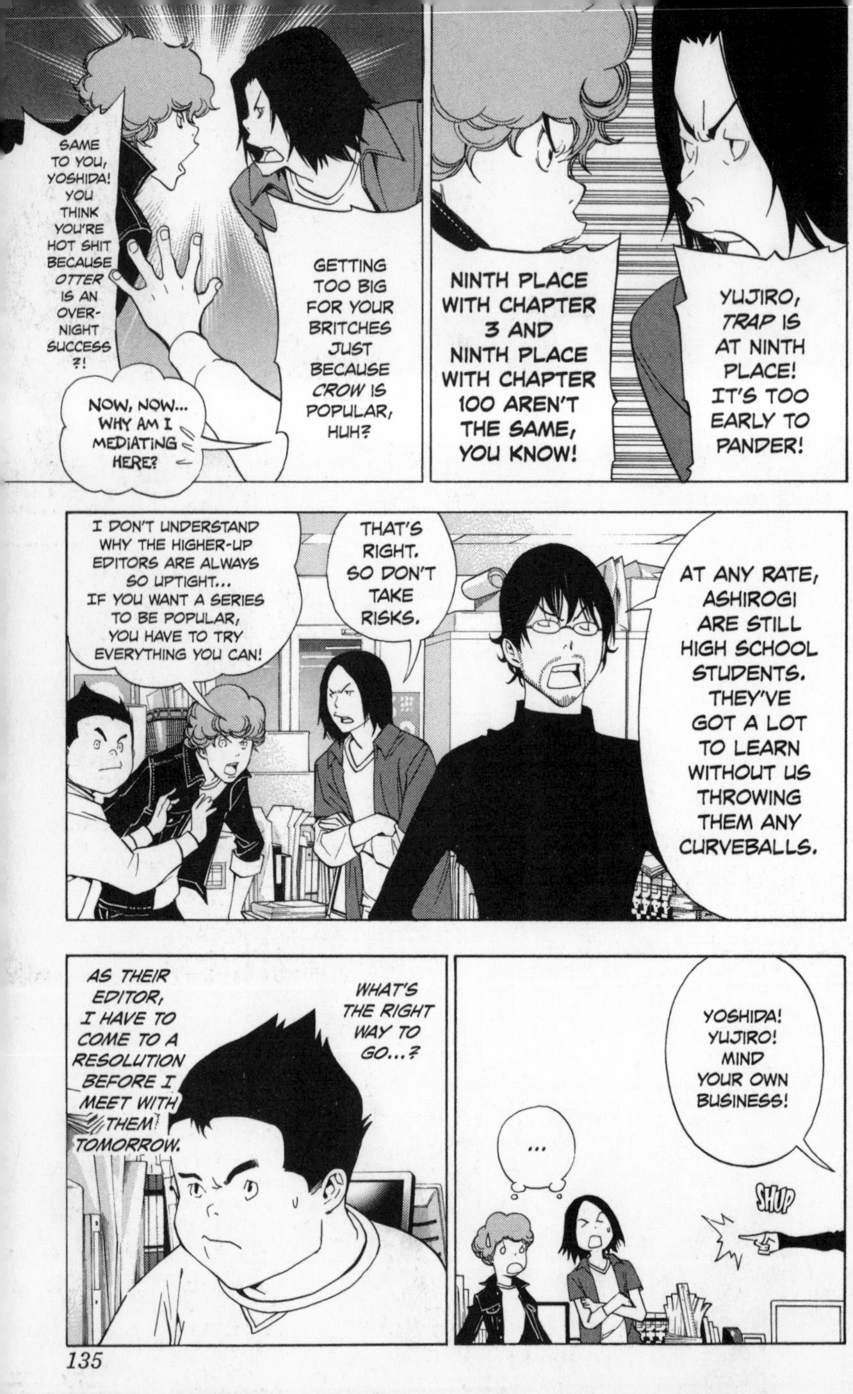
YUJIRO, TRAP IS AT NINTH PLACE! IT'S TOO EARLY TO PANDER!
NINTH PLACE WITH CHAPTER 3 AND NINTH PLACE WITH CHAPTER 100 AREN'T THE SAME, YOU KNOW!
GETTING TOO BIG FOR YOUR BRITCHES JUST BECAUSE CROW IS POPULAR, HUH?
SAME TO YOU, YOSHIDA! YOU THINK YOU'RE HOT SHIT BECAUSE OTTER IS AN OVERNIGHT SUCCESS?!
NOW, NOW... WHY AM I MEDIATING HERE?
AT ANY RATE, ASHIROGI ARE STILL HIGH SCHOOL STUDENTS. THEY'VE GOT A LOT TO LEARN WITHOUT US THROWING THEM ANY CURVEBALLS.
THAT'S RIGHT. SO DON'T TAKE RISKS.
I DON'T UNDERSTAND WHY THE HIGHER-UP EDITORS ARE ALWAYS SO UPTIGHT... IF YOU WANT A SERIES TO BE POPULAR, YOU HAVE TO TRY EVERYTHING YOU CAN!
YOSHIDA! YUJIRO! MIND YOUR OWN BUSINESS!
SHUP
...
WHAT'S THE RIGHT WAY TO GO...?
AS THEIR EDITOR, I HAVE TO COME TO A RESOLUTION BEFORE I MEET WITH THEM TOMORROW.

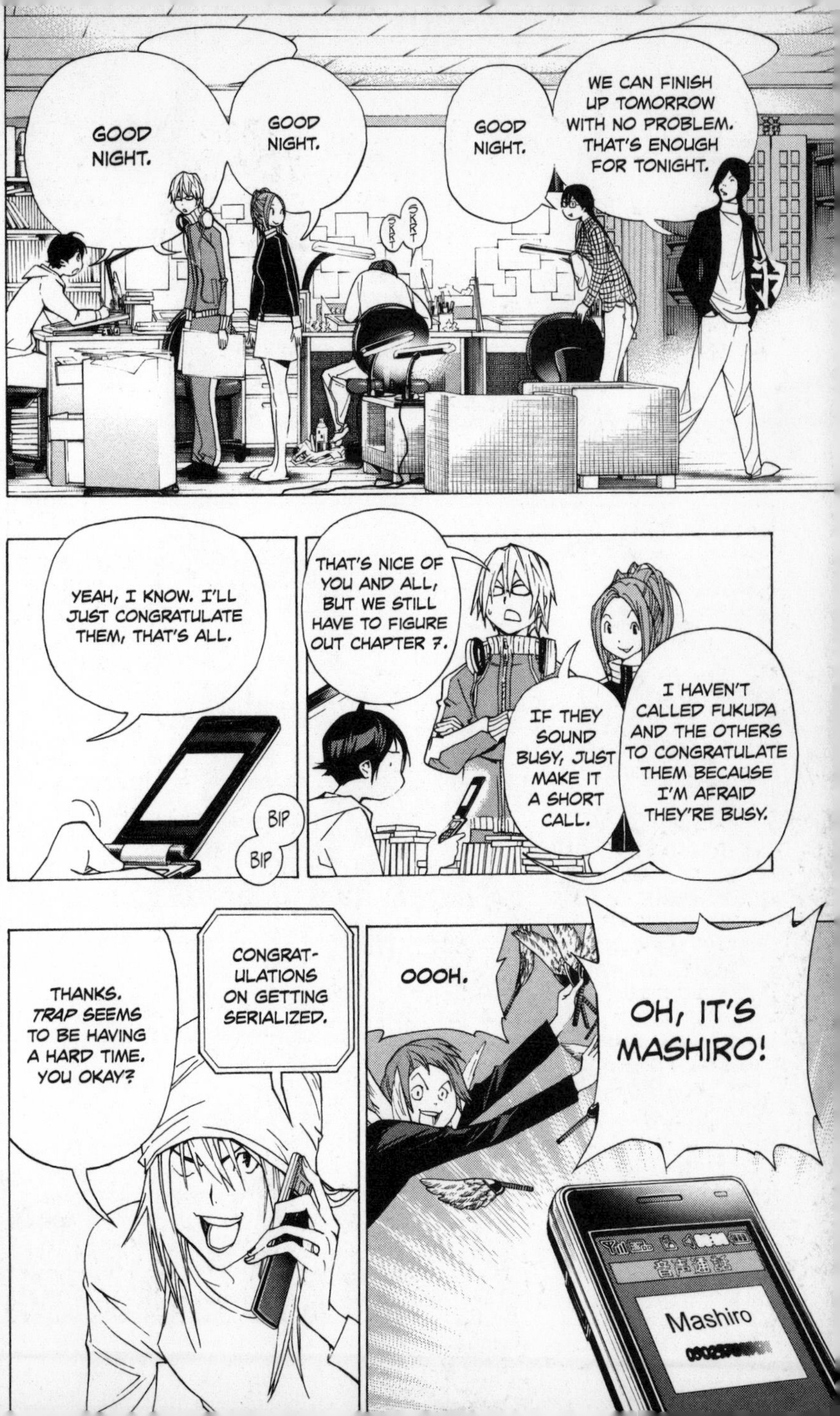
WE CAN FINISH UP TOMORROW WITH NO PROBLEM. THAT'S ENOUGH FOR TONIGHT.
GOOD NIGHT.
SKRT
SKRT
GOOD NIGHT.
GOOD NIGHT.
I HAVEN'T CALLED FUKUDA AND THE OTHERS TO CONGRATULATE THEM BECAUSE I'M AFRAID THEY'RE BUSY.
IF THEY SOUND BUSY, JUST MAKE IT A SHORT CALL.
THAT'S NICE OF YOU AND ALL, BUT WE STILL HAVE TO FIGURE OUT CHAPTER 7.
BIP
BIP
YEAH, I KNOW. I'LL JUST CONGRATULATE THEM, THAT'S ALL.
OH, IT'S MASHIRO!
OOOH.
Mashiro
CONGRAT-ULATIONS ON GETTING SERIALIZED.
THANKS. *TRAP* SEEMS TO BE HAVING A HARD TIME. YOU OKAY?

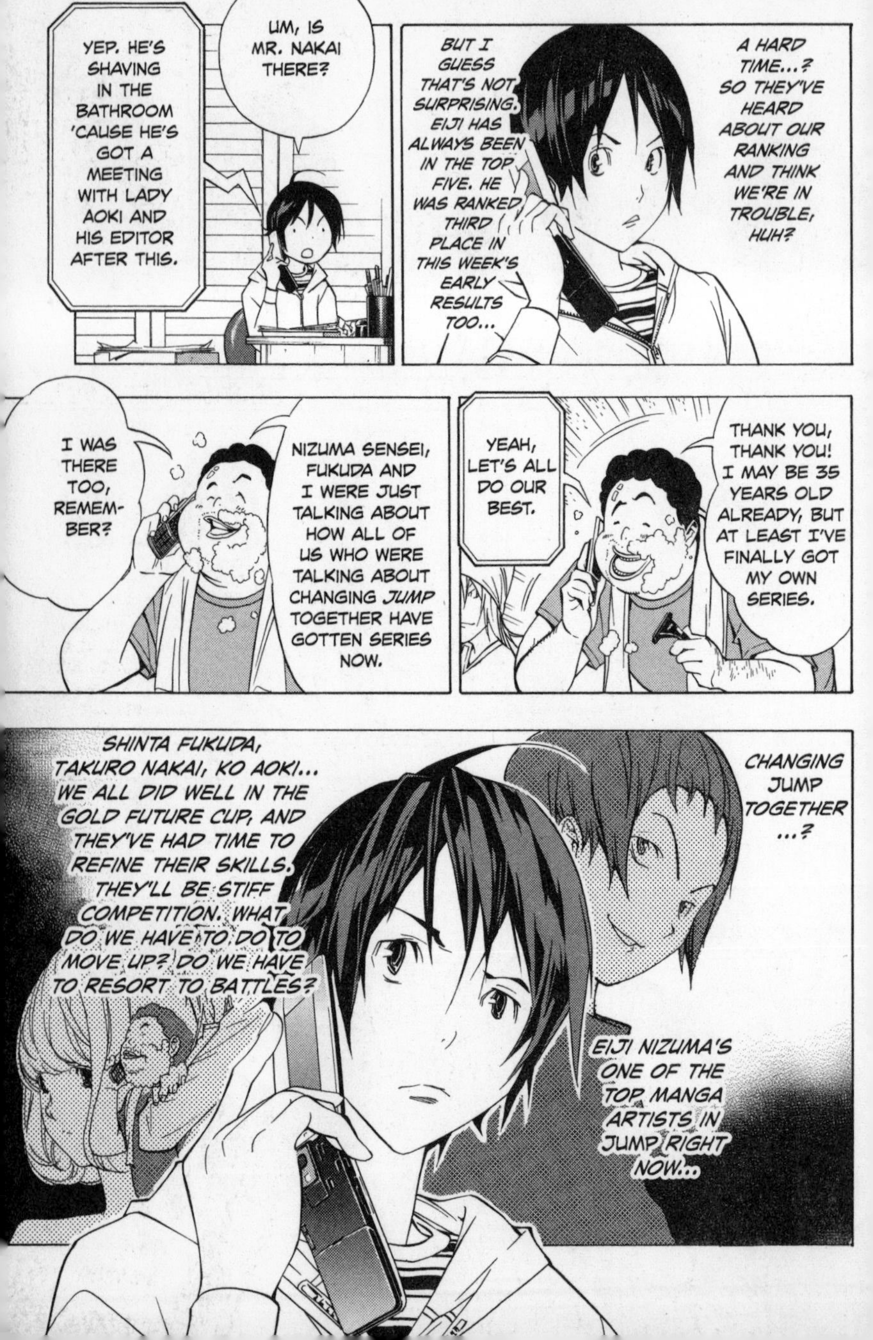
A HARD TIME...? SO THEY'VE HEARD ABOUT OUR RANKING AND THINK WE'RE IN TROUBLE, HUH?
BUT I GUESS THAT'S NOT SURPRISING. EIJI HAS ALWAYS BEEN IN THE TOP FIVE. HE WAS RANKED THIRD PLACE IN THIS WEEK'S EARLY RESULTS TOO...
UM, IS MR. NAKAI THERE?
YEP. HE'S SHAVING IN THE BATHROOM 'CAUSE HE'S GOT A MEETING WITH LADY AOKI AND HIS EDITOR AFTER THIS.
THANK YOU, THANK YOU! I MAY BE 35 YEARS OLD ALREADY, BUT AT LEAST I'VE FINALLY GOT MY OWN SERIES.
YEAH, LET'S ALL DO OUR BEST.
NIZUMA SENSEI, FUKUDA AND I WERE JUST TALKING ABOUT HOW ALL OF US WHO WERE TALKING ABOUT CHANGING *JUMP* TOGETHER HAVE GOTTEN SERIES NOW.
I WAS THERE TOO, REMEMBER?
CHANGING JUMP TOGETHER ...?
SHINTA FUKUDA, TAKURO NAKAI, KO AOKI... WE ALL DID WELL IN THE GOLD FUTURE CUP, AND THEY'VE HAD TIME TO REFINE THEIR SKILLS. THEY'LL BE STIFF COMPETITION. WHAT DO WE HAVE TO DO TO MOVE UP? DO WE HAVE TO RESORT TO BATTLES?
EIJI NIZUMA'S ONE OF THE TOP MANGA ARTISTS IN JUMP RIGHT NOW...

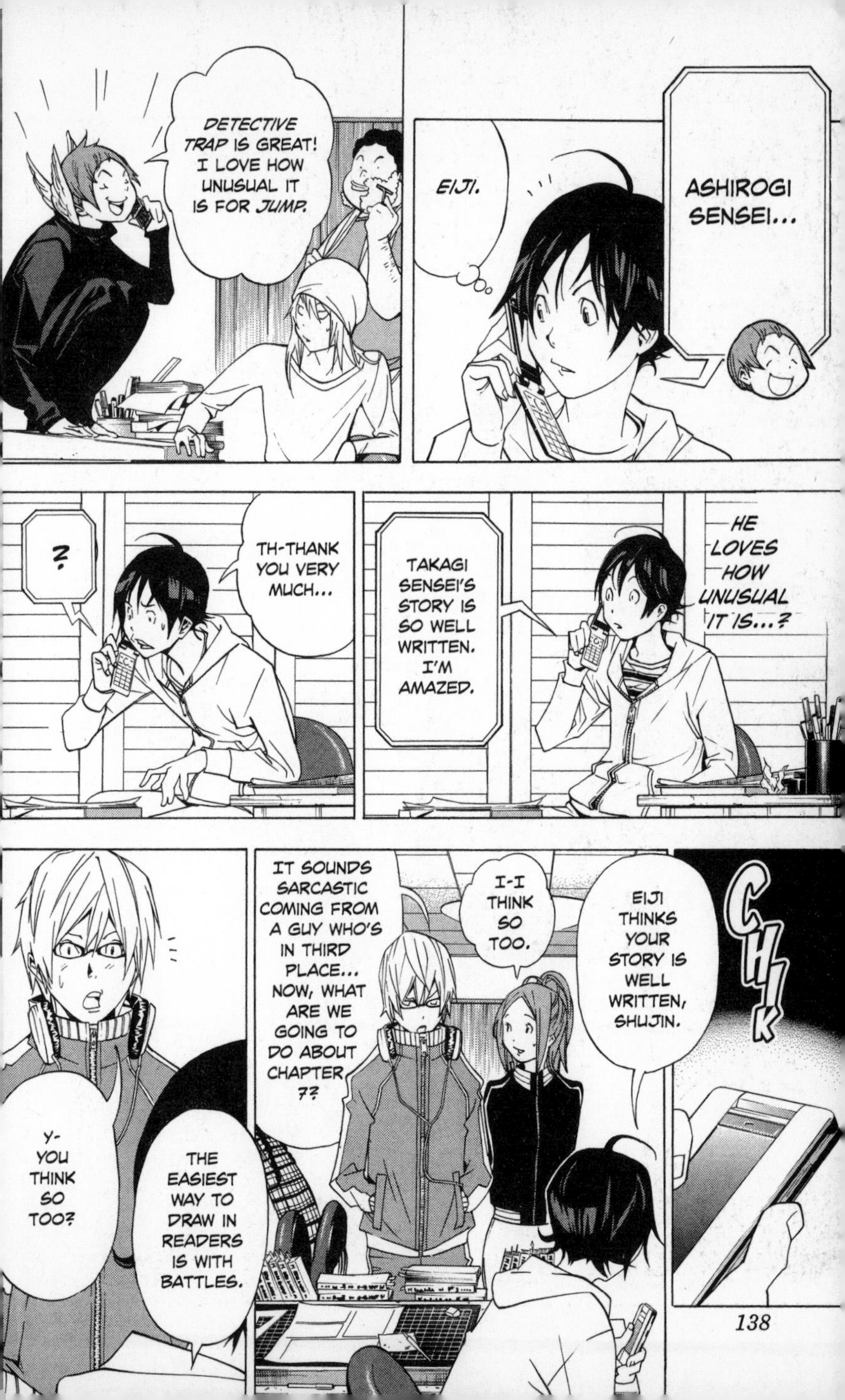
ASHIROGI SENSEI...
EIJI.
DETECTIVE TRAP IS GREAT! I LOVE HOW UNUSUAL IT IS FOR JUMP.
TAKAGI SENSEI'S STORY IS SO WELL WRITTEN. I'M AMAZED.
HE LOVES HOW UNUSUAL IT IS...?
TH-THANK YOU VERY MUCH...
?
CHK
EIJI THINKS YOUR STORY IS WELL WRITTEN, SHUJIN.
I-I THINK SO TOO.
IT SOUNDS SARCASTIC COMING FROM A GUY WHO'S IN THIRD PLACE... NOW, WHAT ARE WE GOING TO DO ABOUT CHAPTER 7?
THE EASIEST WAY TO DRAW IN READERS IS WITH BATTLES.
Y-YOU THINK SO TOO?

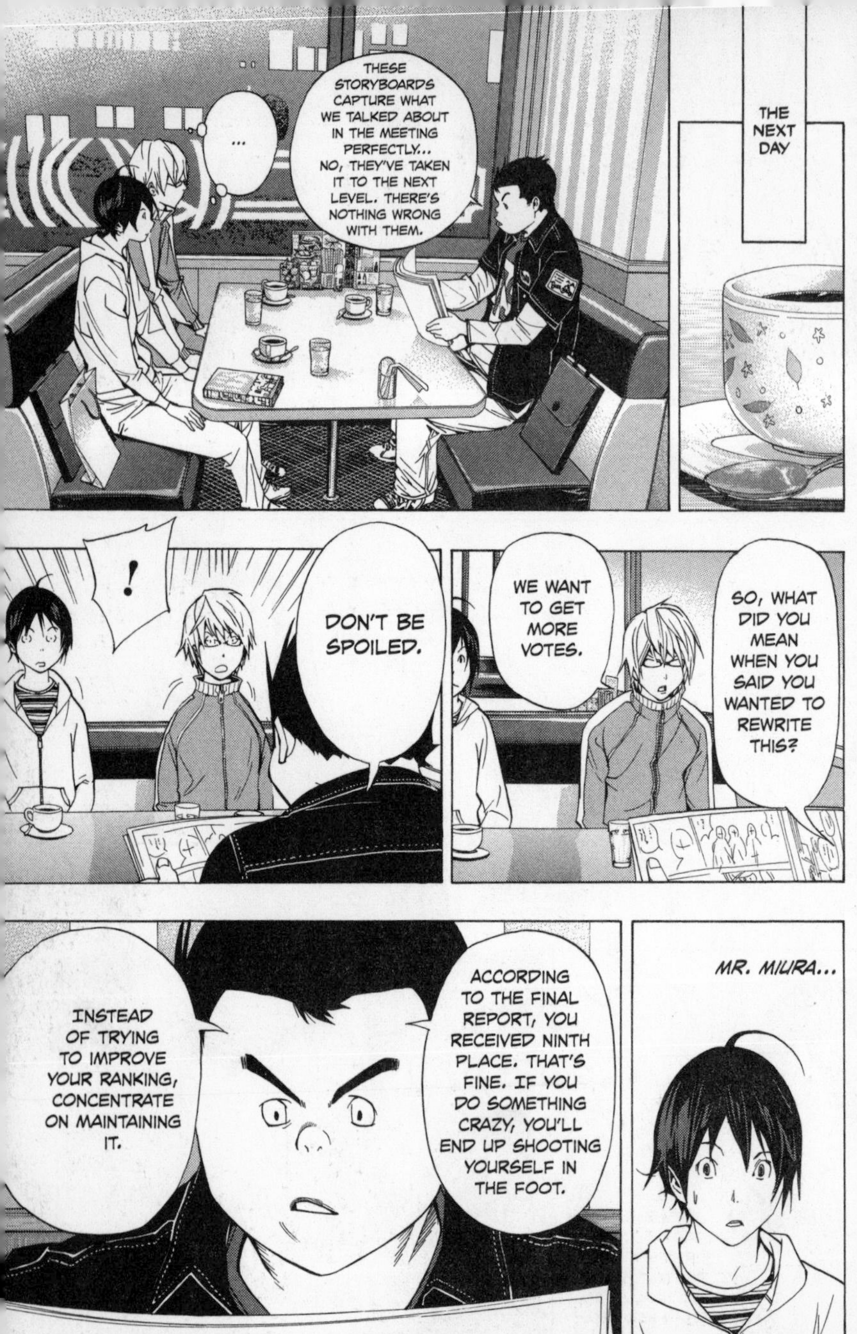
THE NEXT DAY
THESE STORYBOARDS CAPTURE WHAT WE TALKED ABOUT IN THE MEETING PERFECTLY... NO, THEY'VE TAKEN IT TO THE NEXT LEVEL. THERE'S NOTHING WRONG WITH THEM.
...
SO, WHAT DID YOU MEAN WHEN YOU SAID YOU WANTED TO REWRITE THIS?
WE WANT TO GET MORE VOTES.
DON'T BE SPOILED.
!
MR. MIURA...
ACCORDING TO THE FINAL REPORT, YOU RECEIVED NINTH PLACE. THAT'S FINE. IF YOU DO SOMETHING CRAZY, YOU'LL END UP SHOOTING YOURSELF IN THE FOOT.
INSTEAD OF TRYING TO IMPROVE YOUR RANKING, CONCENTRATE ON MAINTAINING IT.

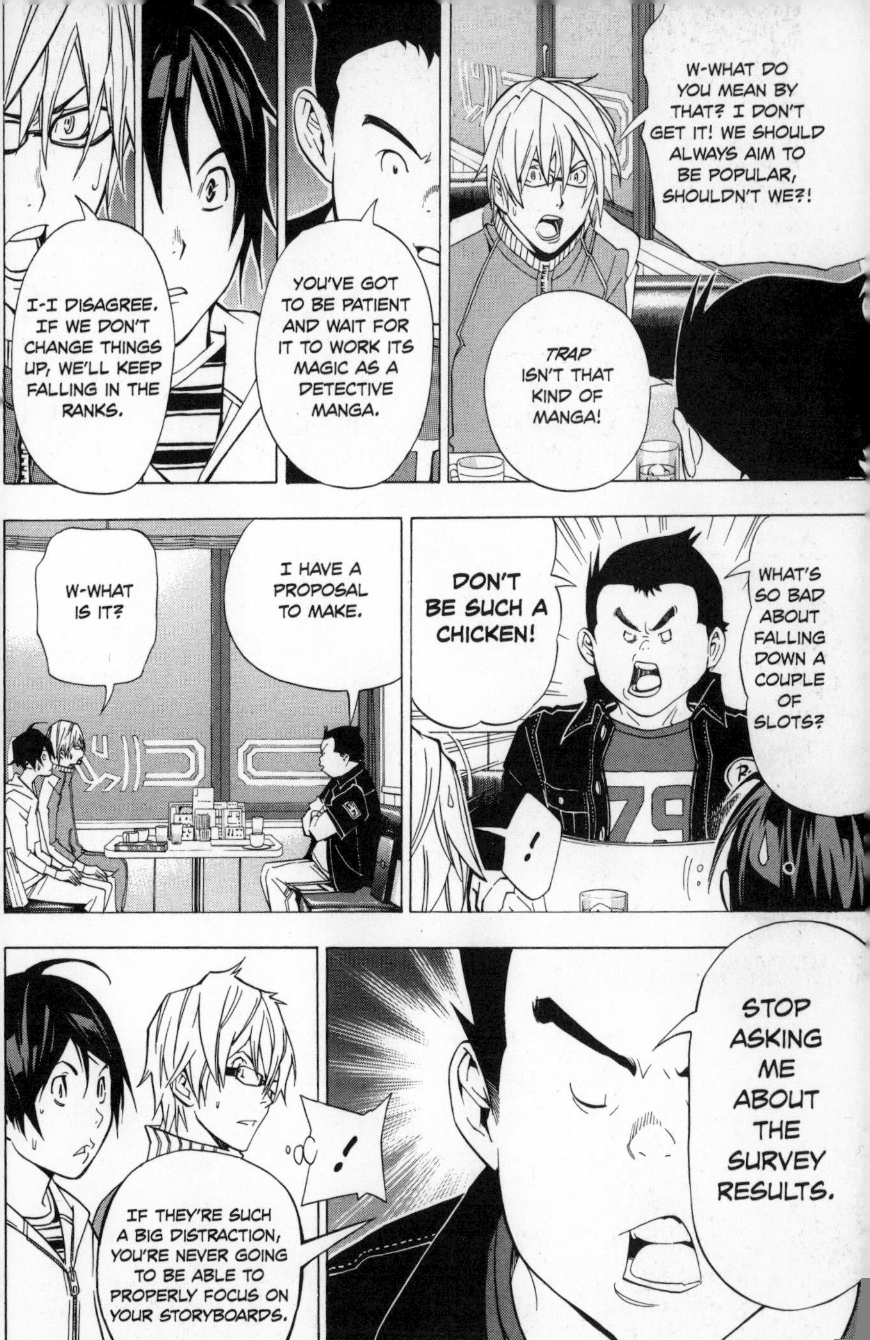
W-WHAT DO YOU MEAN BY THAT? I DON'T GET IT! WE SHOULD ALWAYS AIM TO BE POPULAR, SHOULDN'T WE?!
TRAP ISN'T THAT KIND OF MANGA!
YOU'VE GOT TO BE PATIENT AND WAIT FOR IT TO WORK ITS MAGIC AS A DETECTIVE MANGA.
I-I DISAGREE. IF WE DON'T CHANGE THINGS UP, WE'LL KEEP FALLING IN THE RANKS.
WHAT'S SO BAD ABOUT FALLING DOWN A COUPLE OF SLOTS?
DON'T BE SUCH A CHICKEN!
!
I HAVE A PROPOSAL TO MAKE.
W-WHAT IS IT?
STOP ASKING ME ABOUT THE SURVEY RESULTS.
!
IF THEY'RE SUCH A BIG DISTRACTION, YOU'RE NEVER GOING TO BE ABLE TO PROPERLY FOCUS ON YOUR STORYBOARDS.

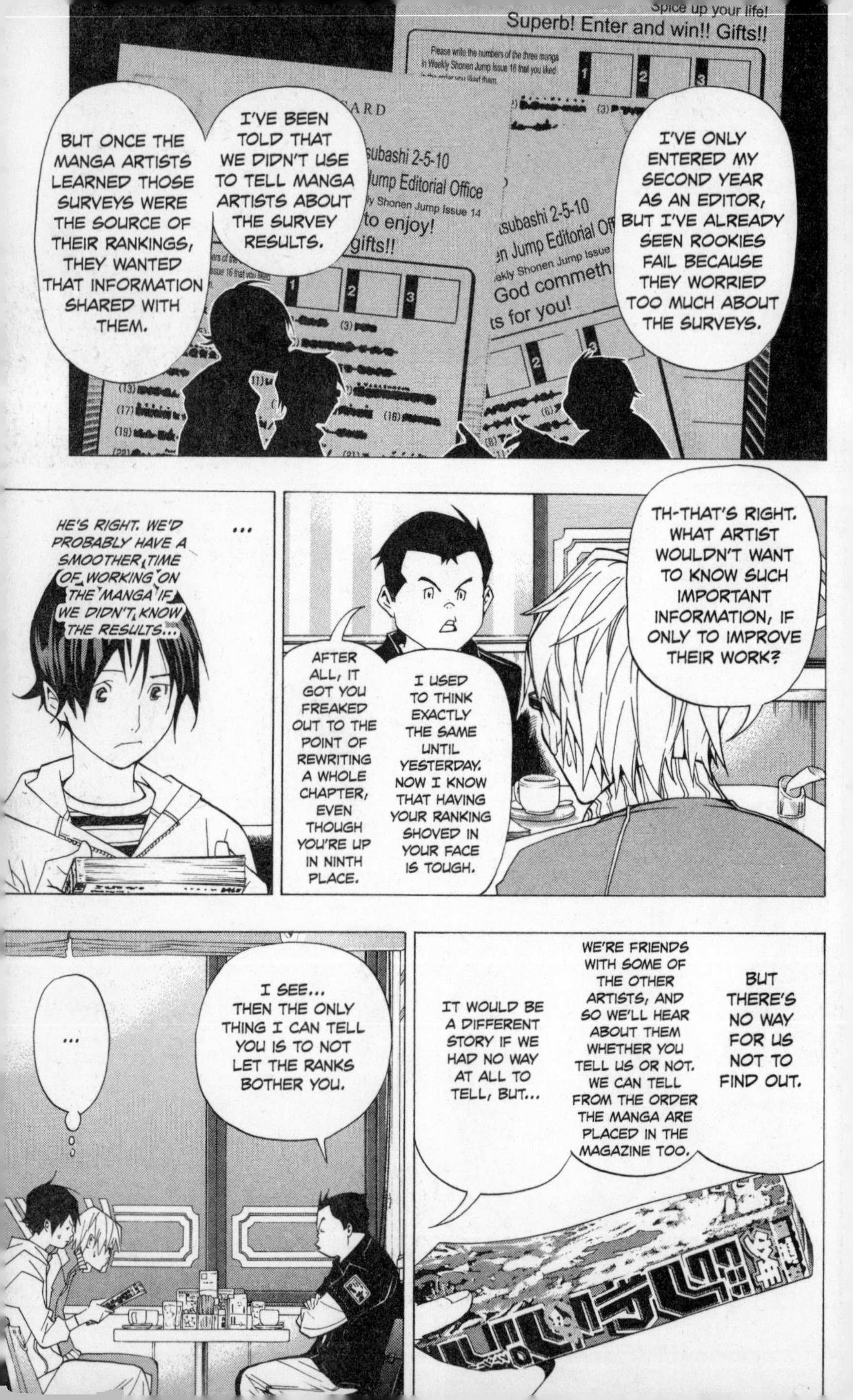
Spice up your life!
Superb! Enter and win!! Gifts!!
I'VE ONLY ENTERED MY SECOND YEAR AS AN EDITOR, BUT I'VE ALREADY SEEN ROOKIES FAIL BECAUSE THEY WORRIED TOO MUCH ABOUT THE SURVEYS.
I'VE BEEN TOLD THAT WE DIDN'T USE TO TELL MANGA ARTISTS ABOUT THE SURVEY RESULTS.
BUT ONCE THE MANGA ARTISTS LEARNED THOSE SURVEYS WERE THE SOURCE OF THEIR RANKINGS, THEY WANTED THAT INFORMATION SHARED WITH THEM.
TH-THAT'S RIGHT. WHAT ARTIST WOULDN'T WANT TO KNOW SUCH IMPORTANT INFORMATION, IF ONLY TO IMPROVE THEIR WORK?
I USED TO THINK EXACTLY THE SAME UNTIL YESTERDAY. NOW I KNOW THAT HAVING YOUR RANKING SHOVED IN YOUR FACE IS TOUGH.
AFTER ALL, IT GOT YOU FREAKED OUT TO THE POINT OF REWRITING A WHOLE CHAPTER, EVEN THOUGH YOU'RE UP IN NINTH PLACE.
...
HE'S RIGHT. WE'D PROBABLY HAVE A SMOOTHER TIME OF WORKING ON THE MANGA IF WE DIDN'T KNOW THE RESULTS...
BUT THERE'S NO WAY FOR US NOT TO FIND OUT.
WE'RE FRIENDS WITH SOME OF THE OTHER ARTISTS, AND SO WE'LL HEAR ABOUT THEM WHETHER YOU TELL US OR NOT. WE CAN TELL FROM THE ORDER THE MANGA ARE PLACED IN THE MAGAZINE TOO.
IT WOULD BE A DIFFERENT STORY IF WE HAD NO WAY AT ALL TO TELL, BUT...
I SEE... THEN THE ONLY THING I CAN TELL YOU IS TO NOT LET THE RANKS BOTHER YOU.
...

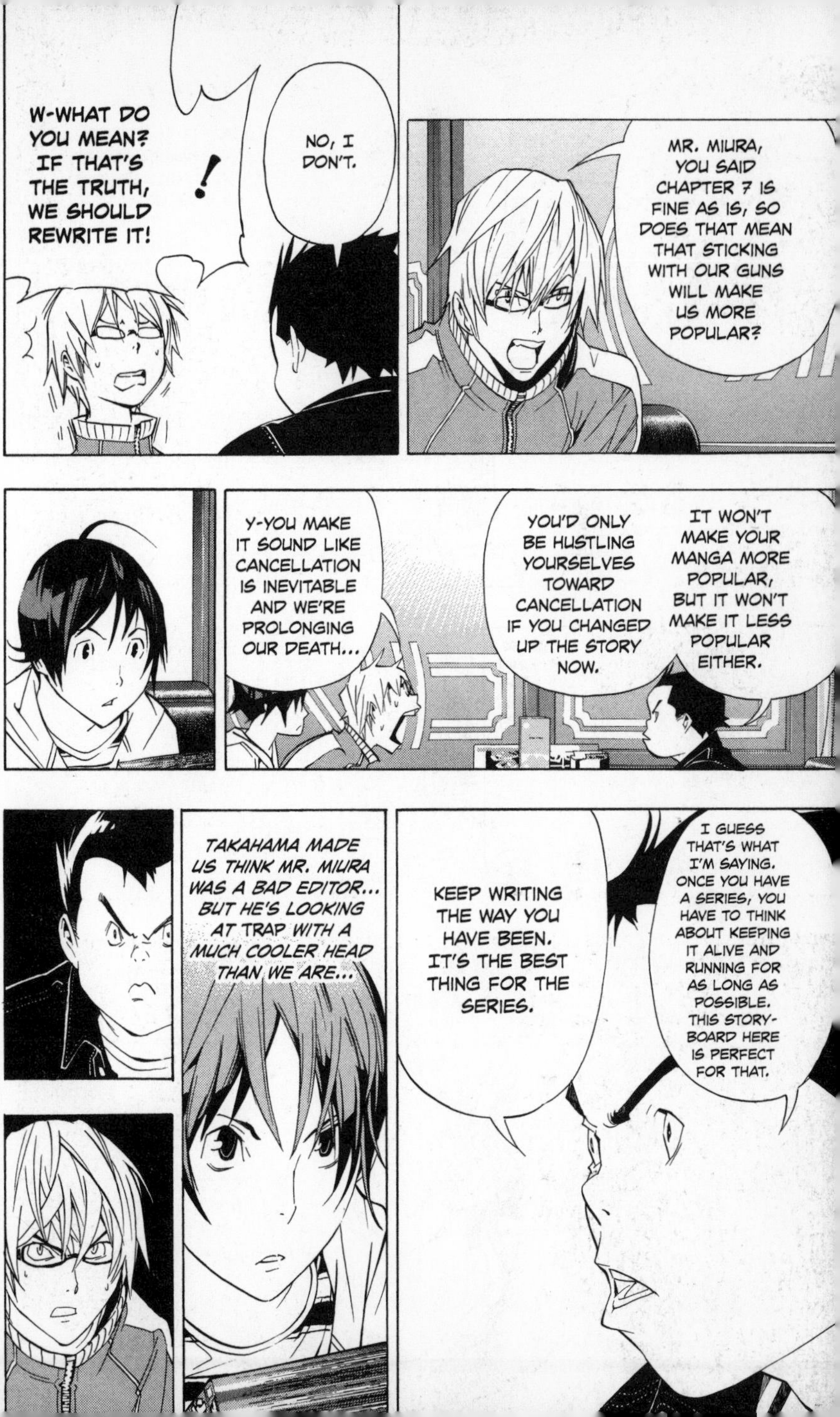
MR. MIURA, YOU SAID CHAPTER 7 IS FINE AS IS, SO DOES THAT MEAN THAT STICKING WITH OUR GUNS WILL MAKE US MORE POPULAR?
NO, I DON'T.
!
W-WHAT DO YOU MEAN? IF THAT'S THE TRUTH, WE SHOULD REWRITE IT!
IT WON'T MAKE YOUR MANGA MORE POPULAR, BUT IT WON'T MAKE IT LESS POPULAR EITHER.
YOU'D ONLY BE HUSTLING YOURSELVES TOWARD CANCELLATION IF YOU CHANGED UP THE STORY NOW.
Y-YOU MAKE IT SOUND LIKE CANCELLATION IS INEVITABLE AND WE'RE PROLONGING OUR DEATH...
I GUESS THAT'S WHAT I'M SAYING. ONCE YOU HAVE A SERIES, YOU HAVE TO THINK ABOUT KEEPING IT ALIVE AND RUNNING FOR AS LONG AS POSSIBLE. THIS STORY-BOARD HERE IS PERFECT FOR THAT.
KEEP WRITING THE WAY YOU HAVE BEEN. IT'S THE BEST THING FOR THE SERIES.
TAKAHAMA MADE US THINK MR. MIURA WAS A BAD EDITOR... BUT HE'S LOOKING AT TRAP WITH A MUCH COOLER HEAD THAN WE ARE...

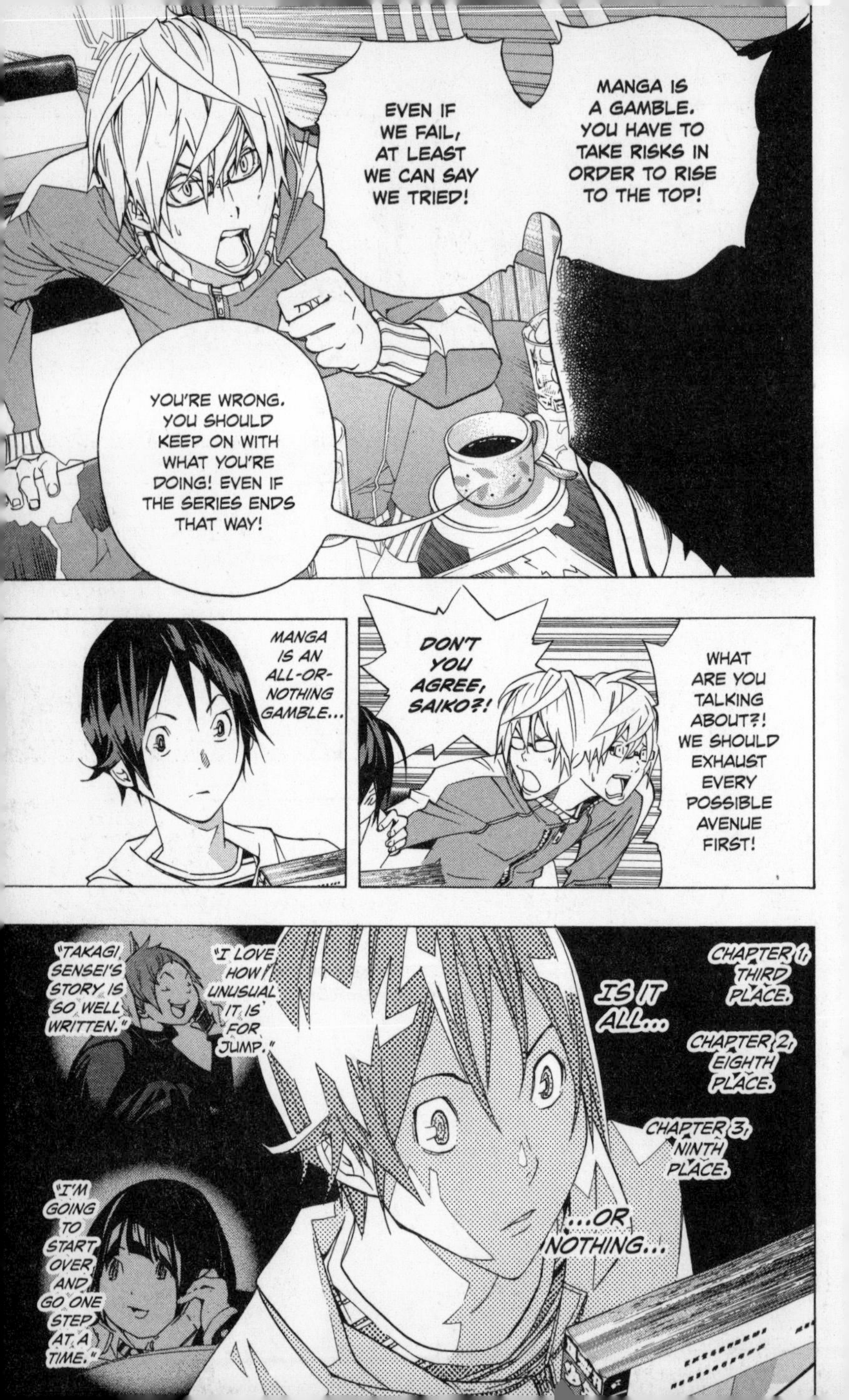
MANGA IS A GAMBLE. YOU HAVE TO TAKE RISKS IN ORDER TO RISE TO THE TOP!
EVEN IF WE FAIL, AT LEAST WE CAN SAY WE TRIED!
YOU'RE WRONG. YOU SHOULD KEEP ON WITH WHAT YOU'RE DOING! EVEN IF THE SERIES ENDS THAT WAY!
WHAT ARE YOU TALKING ABOUT?! WE SHOULD EXHAUST EVERY POSSIBLE AVENUE FIRST!
DON'T YOU AGREE, SAIKO?!
MANGA IS AN ALL-OR-NOTHING GAMBLE...
CHAPTER 1, THIRD PLACE.
CHAPTER 2, EIGHTH PLACE.
CHAPTER 3, NINTH PLACE.
IS IT ALL...
"I LOVE HOW UNUSUAL IT IS FOR JUMP."
"TAKAGI SENSEI'S STORY IS SO WELL WRITTEN."
...OR NOTHING...
"I'M GOING TO START OVER AND GO ONE STEP AT A TIME."

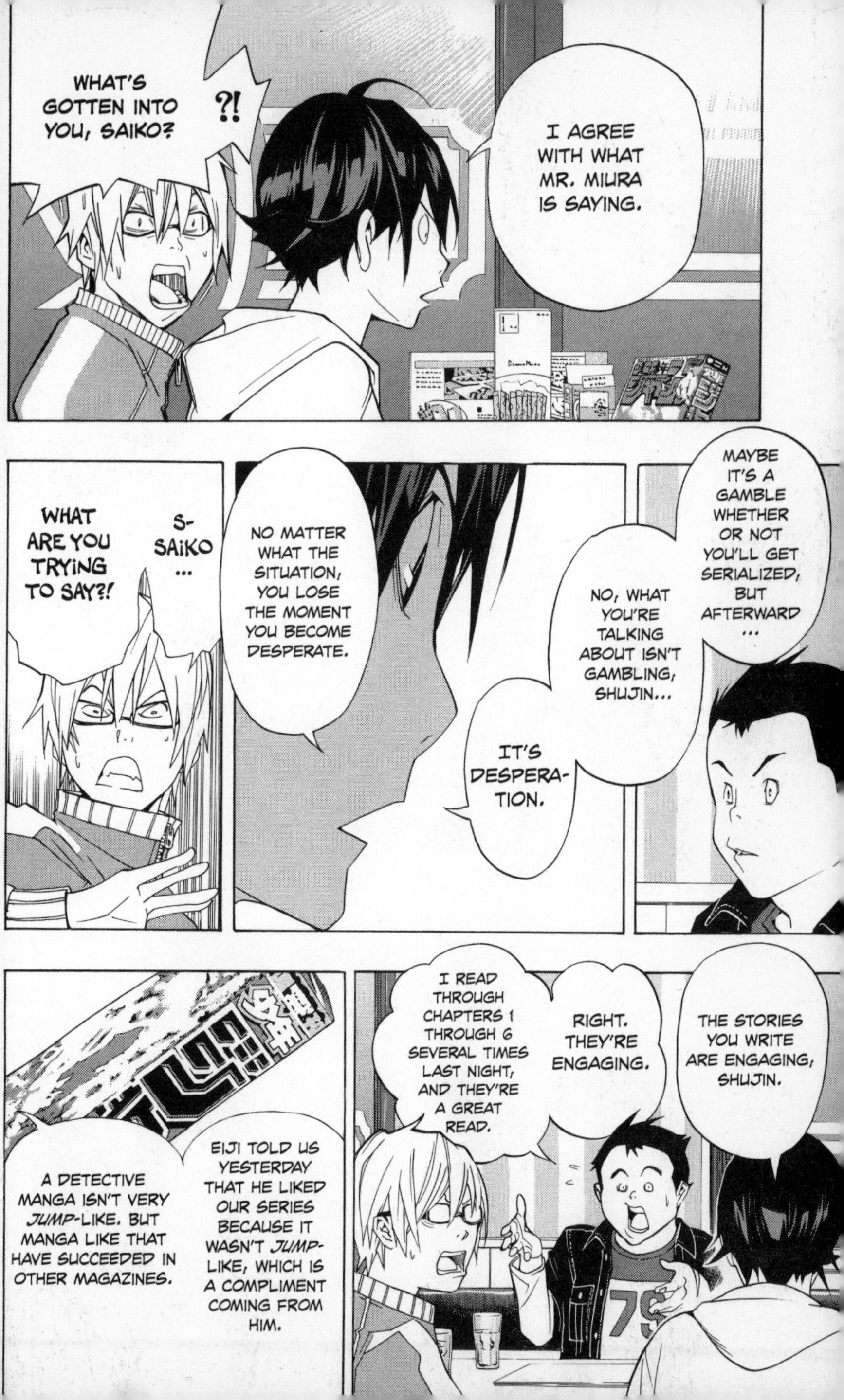
I AGREE WITH WHAT MR. MIURA IS SAYING.
?!
WHAT'S GOTTEN INTO YOU, SAIKO?
MAYBE IT'S A GAMBLE WHETHER OR NOT YOU'LL GET SERIALIZED, BUT AFTERWARD...
NO, WHAT YOU'RE TALKING ABOUT ISN'T GAMBLING, SHUJIN...
IT'S DESPERATION.
NO MATTER WHAT THE SITUATION, YOU LOSE THE MOMENT YOU BECOME DESPERATE.
S-SAIKO...
WHAT ARE YOU TRYING TO SAY?!
THE STORIES YOU WRITE ARE ENGAGING, SHUJIN.
RIGHT. THEY'RE ENGAGING.
I READ THROUGH CHAPTERS 1 THROUGH 6 SEVERAL TIMES LAST NIGHT, AND THEY'RE A GREAT READ.
EIJI TOLD US YESTERDAY THAT HE LIKED OUR SERIES BECAUSE IT WASN'T *JUMP*-LIKE, WHICH IS A COMPLIMENT COMING FROM HIM.
A DETECTIVE MANGA ISN'T VERY *JUMP*-LIKE. BUT MANGA LIKE THAT HAVE SUCCEEDED IN OTHER MAGAZINES.

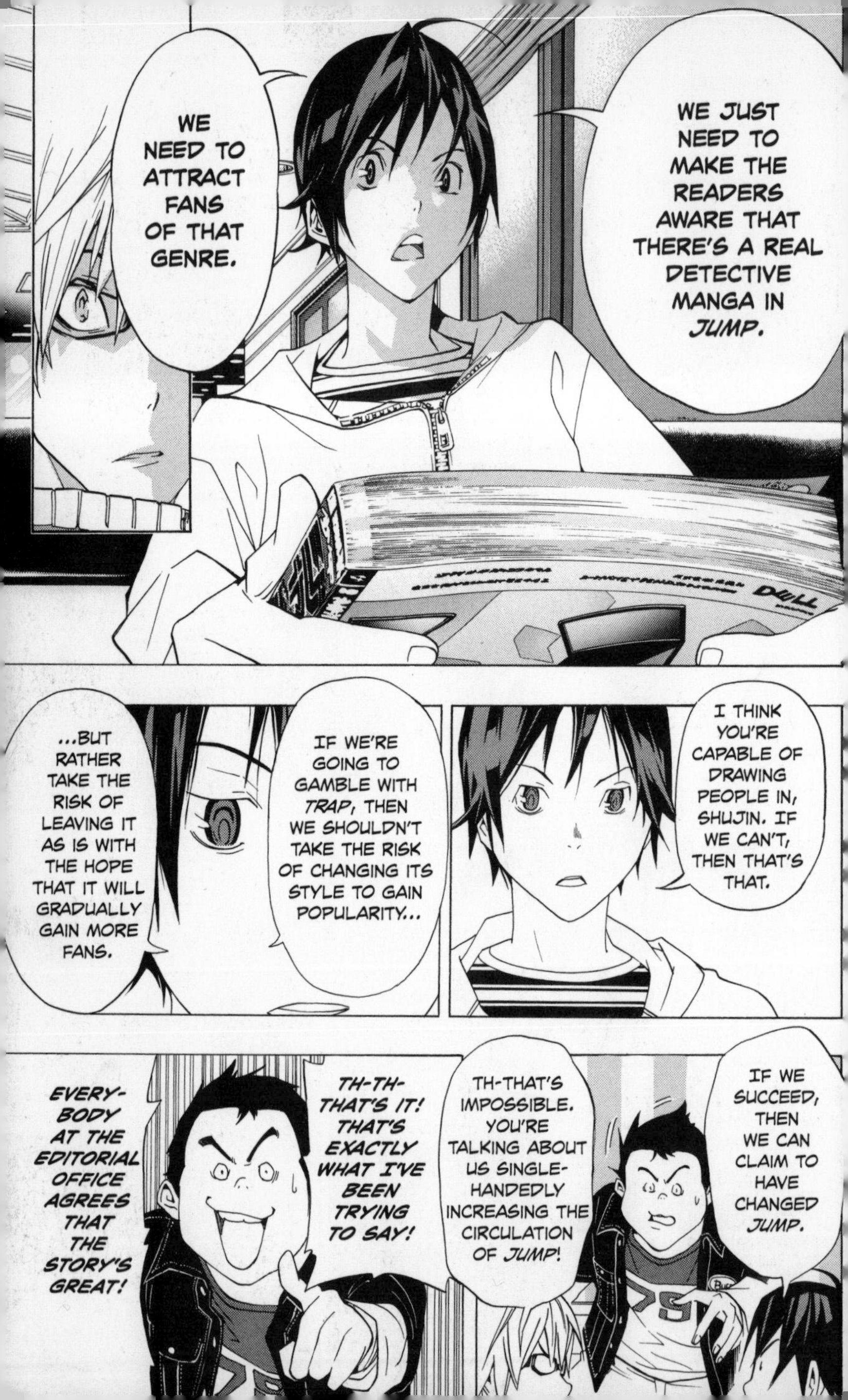
WE JUST NEED TO MAKE THE READERS AWARE THAT THERE'S A REAL DETECTIVE MANGA IN *JUMP*.
WE NEED TO ATTRACT FANS OF THAT GENRE.
I THINK YOU'RE CAPABLE OF DRAWING PEOPLE IN, SHUJIN. IF WE CAN'T, THEN THAT'S THAT.
IF WE'RE GOING TO GAMBLE WITH *TRAP*, THEN WE SHOULDN'T TAKE THE RISK OF CHANGING ITS STYLE TO GAIN POPULARITY...
...BUT RATHER TAKE THE RISK OF LEAVING IT AS IS WITH THE HOPE THAT IT WILL GRADUALLY GAIN MORE FANS.
IF WE SUCCEED, THEN WE CAN CLAIM TO HAVE CHANGED *JUMP*.
TH-THAT'S IMPOSSIBLE. YOU'RE TALKING ABOUT US SINGLE-HANDEDLY INCREASING THE CIRCULATION OF *JUMP*!
TH-TH-THAT'S IT! THAT'S EXACTLY WHAT I'VE BEEN TRYING TO SAY!
EVERYBODY AT THE EDITORIAL OFFICE AGREES THAT THE STORY'S GREAT!

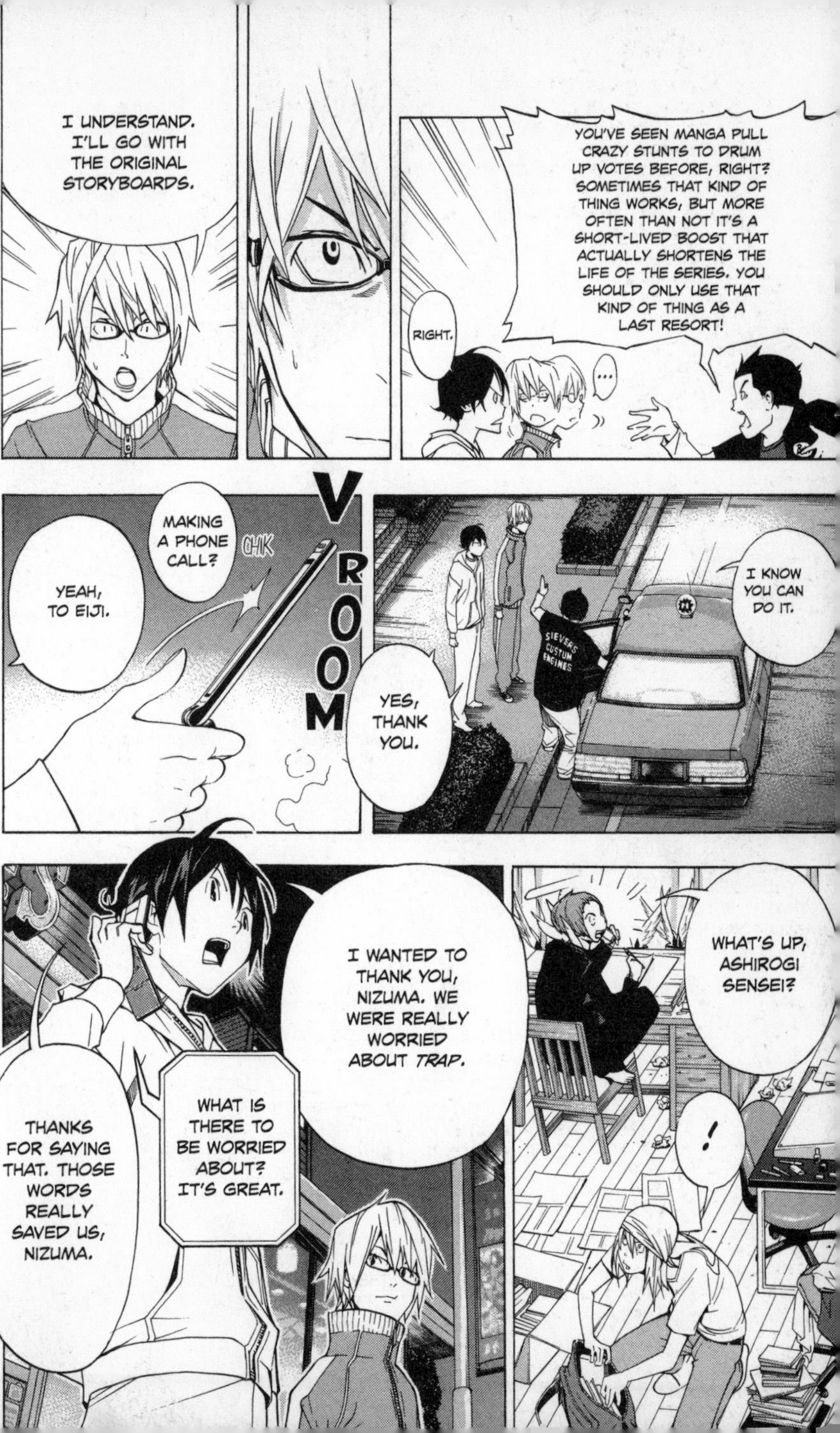
YOU'VE SEEN MANGA PULL CRAZY STUNTS TO DRUM UP VOTES BEFORE, RIGHT? SOMETIMES THAT KIND OF THING WORKS, BUT MORE OFTEN THAN NOT IT'S A SHORT-LIVED BOOST THAT ACTUALLY SHORTENS THE LIFE OF THE SERIES. YOU SHOULD ONLY USE THAT KIND OF THING AS A LAST RESORT!
RIGHT.
...
I UNDERSTAND. I'LL GO WITH THE ORIGINAL STORYBOARDS.
I KNOW YOU CAN DO IT.
YES, THANK YOU.
VROOM
MAKING A PHONE CALL?
CHIK
YEAH, TO EIJI.
WHAT'S UP, ASHIROGI SENSEI?
!
I WANTED TO THANK YOU, NIZUMA. WE WERE REALLY WORRIED ABOUT *TRAP*.
WHAT IS THERE TO BE WORRIED ABOUT? IT'S GREAT.
THANKS FOR SAYING THAT. THOSE WORDS REALLY SAVED US, NIZUMA.

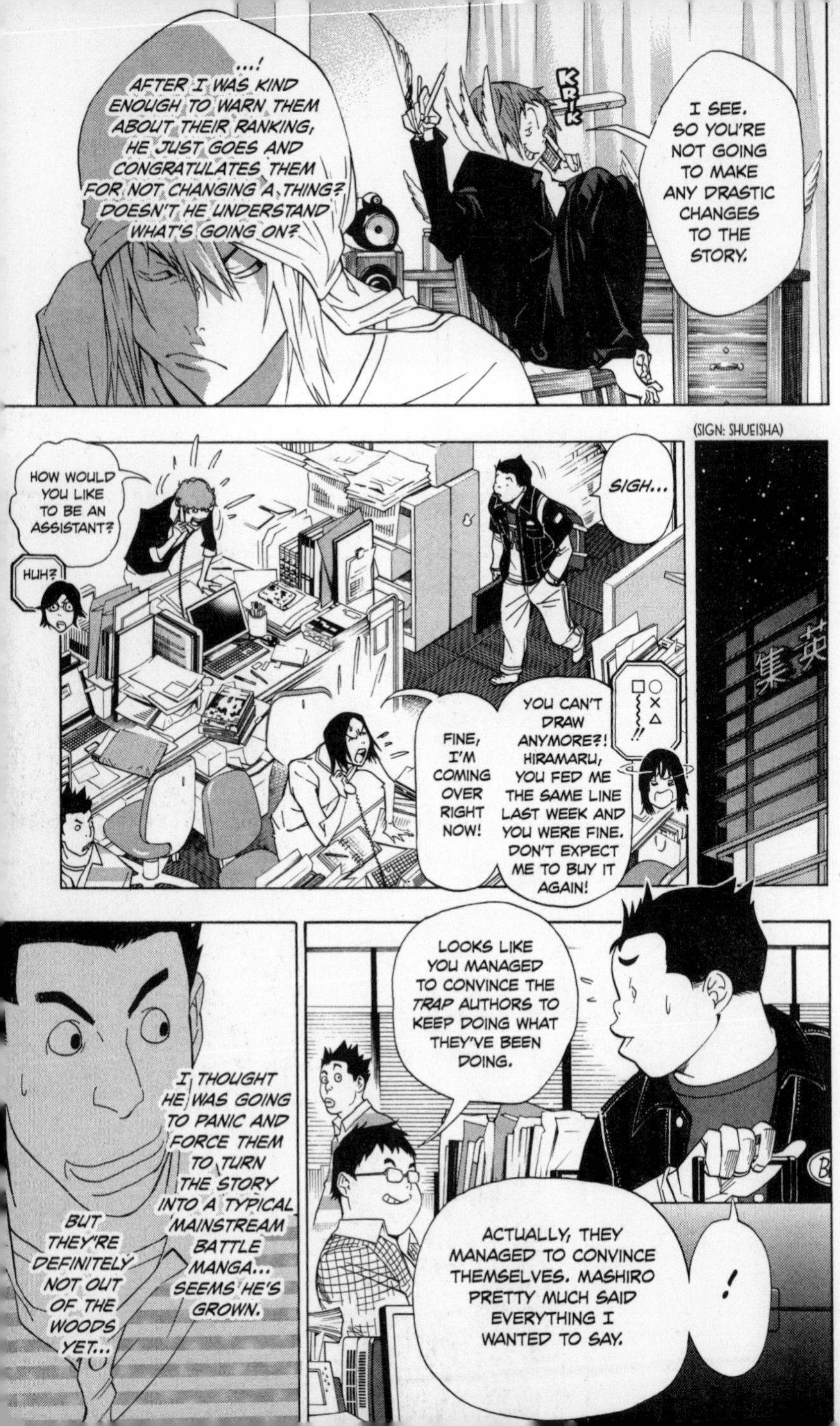
KRIK
I SEE. SO YOU'RE NOT GOING TO MAKE ANY DRASTIC CHANGES TO THE STORY.
...! AFTER I WAS KIND ENOUGH TO WARN THEM ABOUT THEIR RANKING, HE JUST GOES AND CONGRATULATES THEM FOR NOT CHANGING A THING? DOESN'T HE UNDERSTAND WHAT'S GOING ON?
(SIGN: SHUEISHA)
集英
SIGH...
□○×△!!
YOU CAN'T DRAW ANYMORE?! HIRAMARU, YOU FED ME THE SAME LINE LAST WEEK AND YOU WERE FINE. DON'T EXPECT ME TO BUY IT AGAIN!
FINE, I'M COMING OVER RIGHT NOW!
HOW WOULD YOU LIKE TO BE AN ASSISTANT?
HUH?
LOOKS LIKE YOU MANAGED TO CONVINCE THE TRAP AUTHORS TO KEEP DOING WHAT THEY'VE BEEN DOING.
ACTUALLY, THEY MANAGED TO CONVINCE THEMSELVES. MASHIRO PRETTY MUCH SAID EVERYTHING I WANTED TO SAY.
!
I THOUGHT HE WAS GOING TO PANIC AND FORCE THEM TO TURN THE STORY INTO A TYPICAL MAINSTREAM BATTLE MANGA... SEEMS HE'S GROWN.
BUT THEY'RE DEFINITELY NOT OUT OF THE WOODS YET...

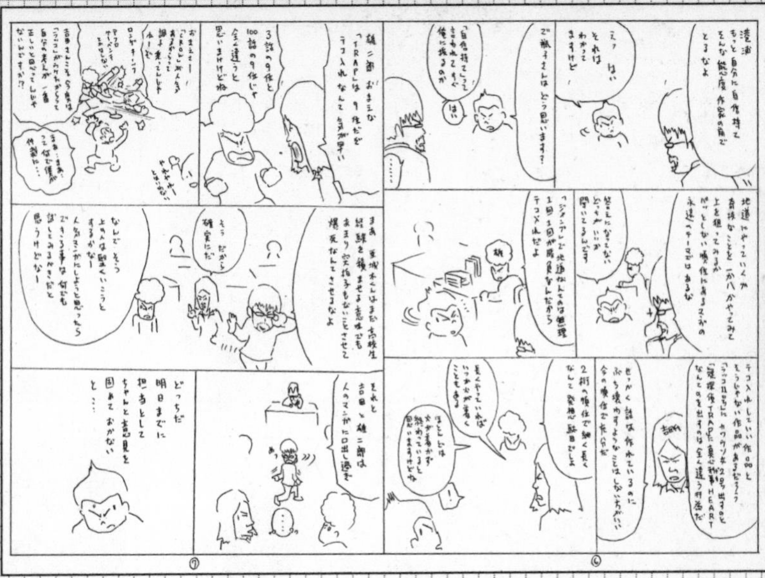
浅浦 もっと自分に自信持て そんな態度 作家の前でとるなよ
えっ はい それはわかってますけど
ご瓶子さんはどう思います?
「自信持て」って言われてすぐ俺に振るのか
はい
地道にやっていくか 奇抜なことを一か八かやってみて 上を狙ってみるか パッとしない連載作家にありがちの永遠のテーマではあるな
どっちがいいか聞いてるんだ
マジシャンで地道なんてのは無理 1回1回が勝負なんだから テコ入れだよ
せっかく話を作れているのに ぶち壊すような事はしない方がいい
2作の連載で細く長くなんて発想駄目だよ
長くやっていればいつか火が着くこともある
ほとんどは火が着かず終わっていると思いますけどね
雄二郎 おまえな「TRAP」は9位だぞ テコ入れなんて気が早い
3話の9位と100話の9位じゃ全く違うと思いますけどね
まあまあ
まあ 亜城木くんはまだ高校生 経験を積ませる意味でもあまり突拍子もないことさせて爆死なんてさせるなよ
そう だから確実にだ
それと吉田と雄二郎は人のマンガに口出し過ぎ
あっ
どっちだ 明日までに担当としてちゃんと意見を固めておかないと…

OHBA'S STORYBOARD

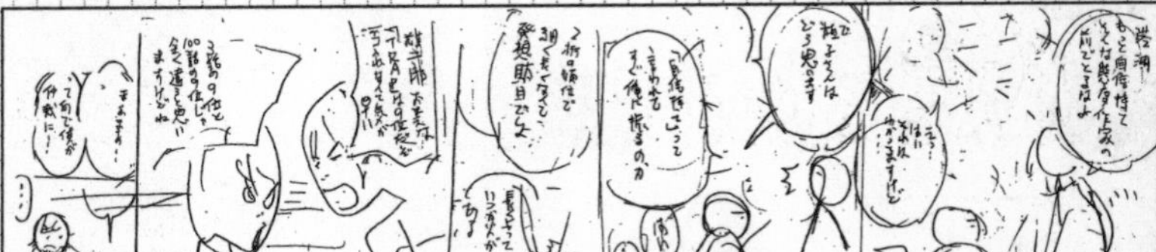

OBATA'S STORYBOARD

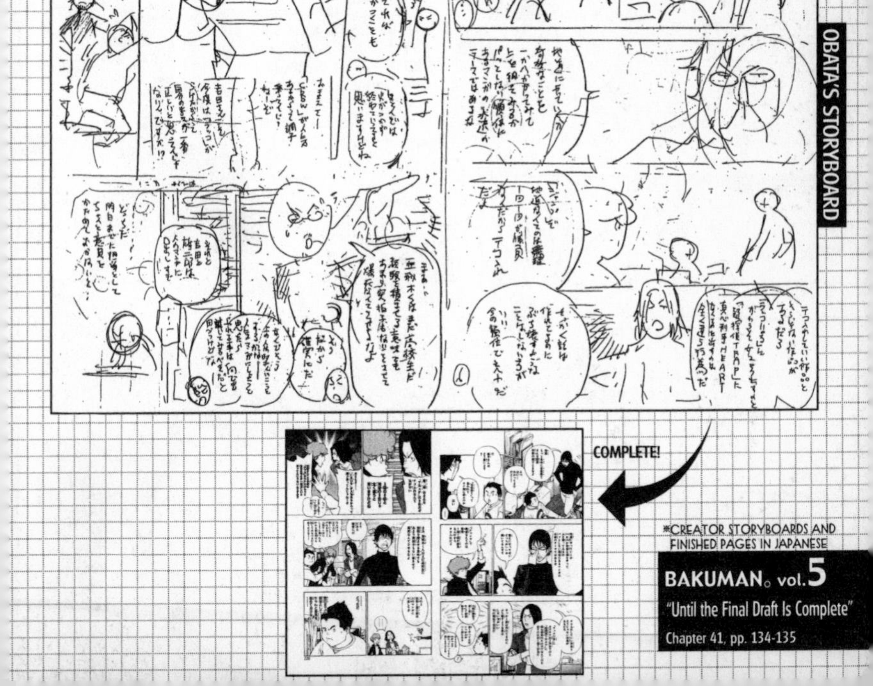

COMPLETE!

*CREATOR STORYBOARDS AND FINISHED PAGES IN JAPANESE

BAKUMAN。 vol.5

"Until the Final Draft Is Complete"

Chapter 41, pp. 134-135

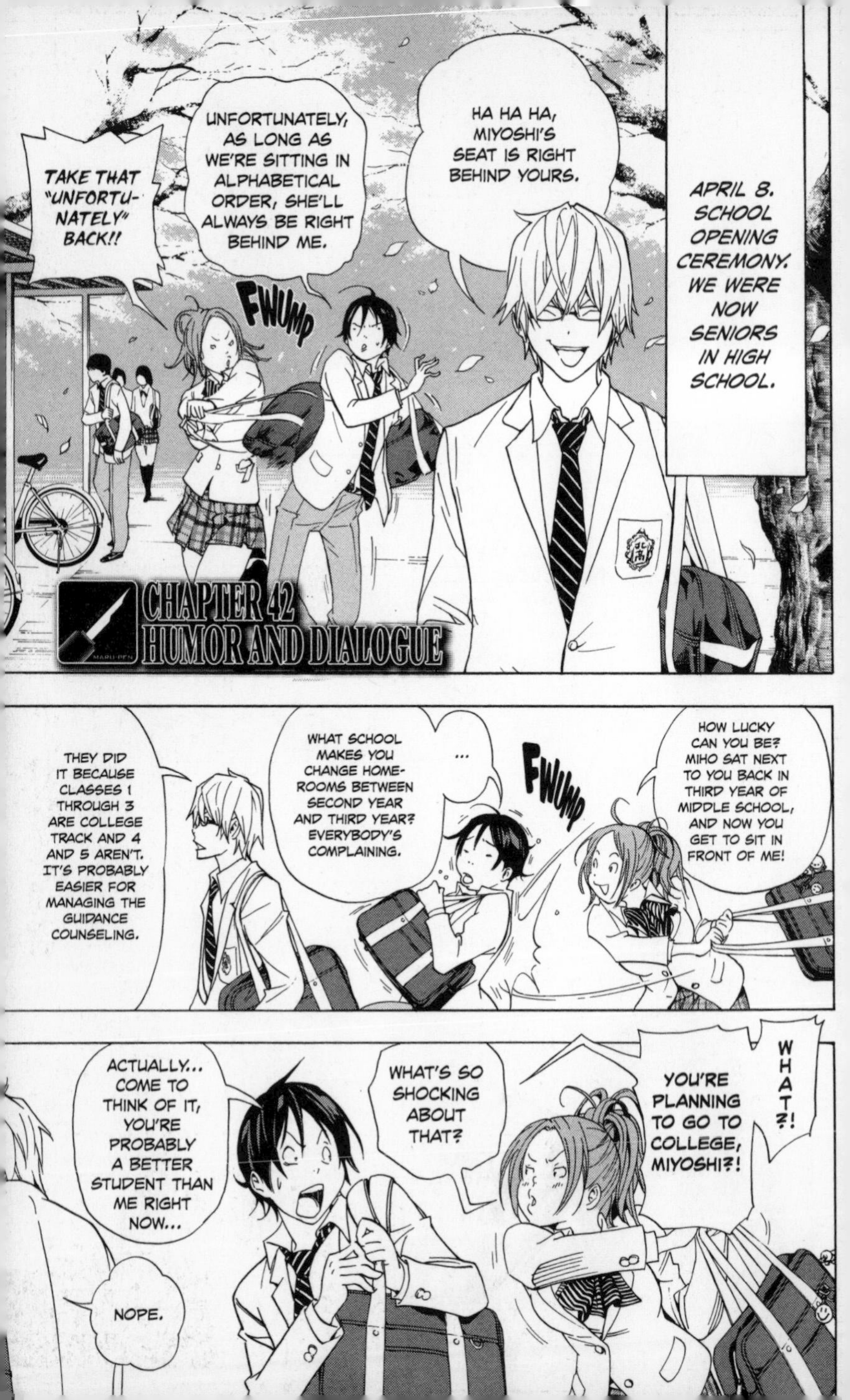
APRIL 8. SCHOOL OPENING CEREMONY. WE WERE NOW SENIORS IN HIGH SCHOOL.
HA HA HA, MIYOSHI'S SEAT IS RIGHT BEHIND YOURS.
UNFORTUNATELY, AS LONG AS WE'RE SITTING IN ALPHABETICAL ORDER, SHE'LL ALWAYS BE RIGHT BEHIND ME.
FWUMP
TAKE THAT "UNFORTU-NATELY" BACK!!
CHAPTER 42 HUMOR AND DIALOGUE
HOW LUCKY CAN YOU BE? MIHO SAT NEXT TO YOU BACK IN THIRD YEAR OF MIDDLE SCHOOL, AND NOW YOU GET TO SIT IN FRONT OF ME!
FWUMP
...
WHAT SCHOOL MAKES YOU CHANGE HOME-ROOMS BETWEEN SECOND YEAR AND THIRD YEAR? EVERYBODY'S COMPLAINING.
THEY DID IT BECAUSE CLASSES 1 THROUGH 3 ARE COLLEGE TRACK AND 4 AND 5 AREN'T. IT'S PROBABLY EASIER FOR MANAGING THE GUIDANCE COUNSELING.
WHAT?!
YOU'RE PLANNING TO GO TO COLLEGE, MIYOSHI?!
WHAT'S SO SHOCKING ABOUT THAT?
ACTUALLY... COME TO THINK OF IT, YOU'RE PROBABLY A BETTER STUDENT THAN ME RIGHT NOW...
NOPE.

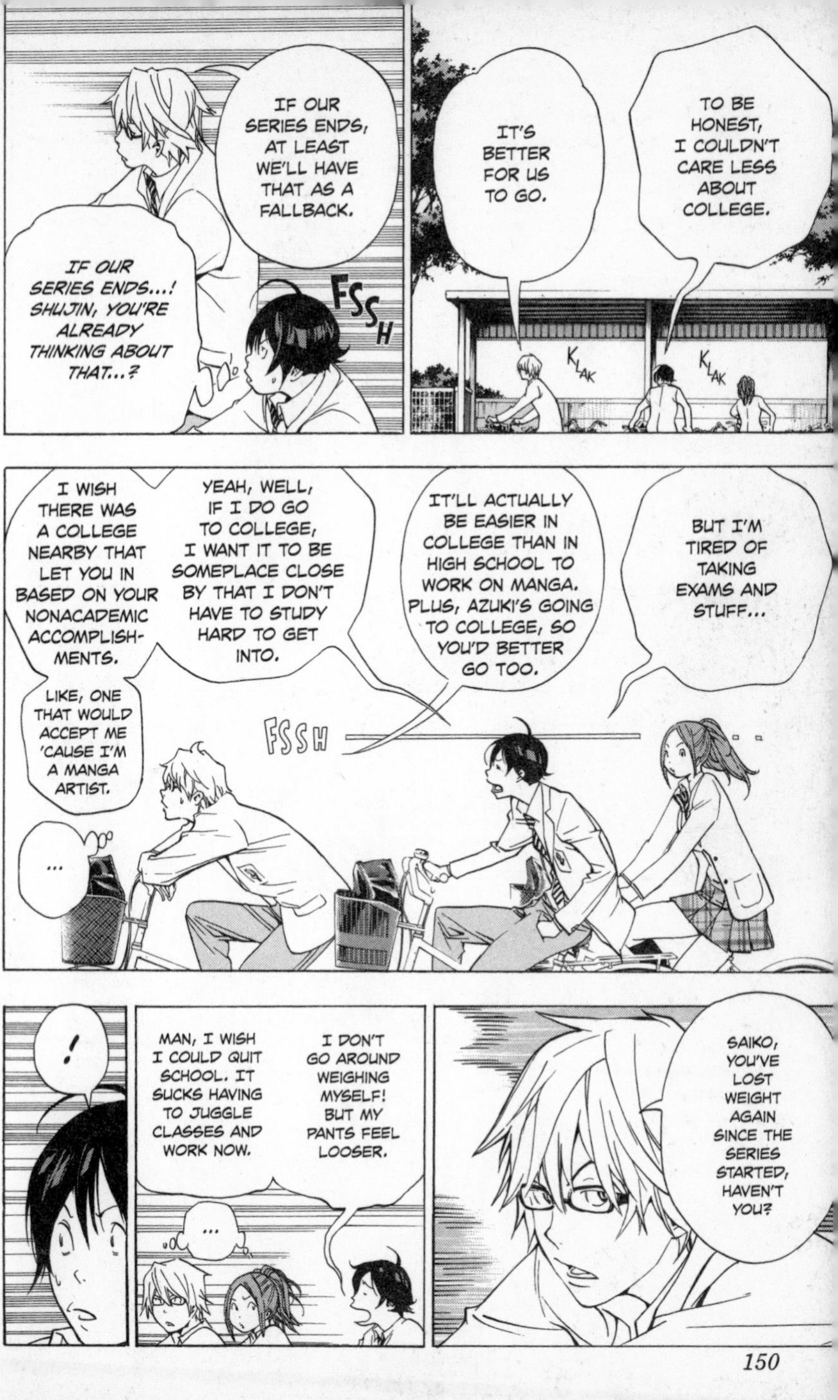
TO BE HONEST, I COULDN'T CARE LESS ABOUT COLLEGE.
IT'S BETTER FOR US TO GO.
KLAK
KLAK
IF OUR SERIES ENDS, AT LEAST WE'LL HAVE THAT AS A FALLBACK.
FSSH
IF OUR SERIES ENDS...! SHUJIN, YOU'RE ALREADY THINKING ABOUT THAT...?
BUT I'M TIRED OF TAKING EXAMS AND STUFF...
IT'LL ACTUALLY BE EASIER IN COLLEGE THAN IN HIGH SCHOOL TO WORK ON MANGA. PLUS, AZUKI'S GOING TO COLLEGE, SO YOU'D BETTER GO TOO.
YEAH, WELL, IF I DO GO TO COLLEGE, I WANT IT TO BE SOMEPLACE CLOSE BY THAT I DON'T HAVE TO STUDY HARD TO GET INTO.
I WISH THERE WAS A COLLEGE NEARBY THAT LET YOU IN BASED ON YOUR NONACADEMIC ACCOMPLISH-MENTS.
LIKE, ONE THAT WOULD ACCEPT ME 'CAUSE I'M A MANGA ARTIST.
FSSH
...
SAIKO, YOU'VE LOST WEIGHT AGAIN SINCE THE SERIES STARTED, HAVEN'T YOU?
I DON'T GO AROUND WEIGHING MYSELF! BUT MY PANTS FEEL LOOSER.
MAN, I WISH I COULD QUIT SCHOOL. IT SUCKS HAVING TO JUGGLE CLASSES AND WORK NOW.
...
!

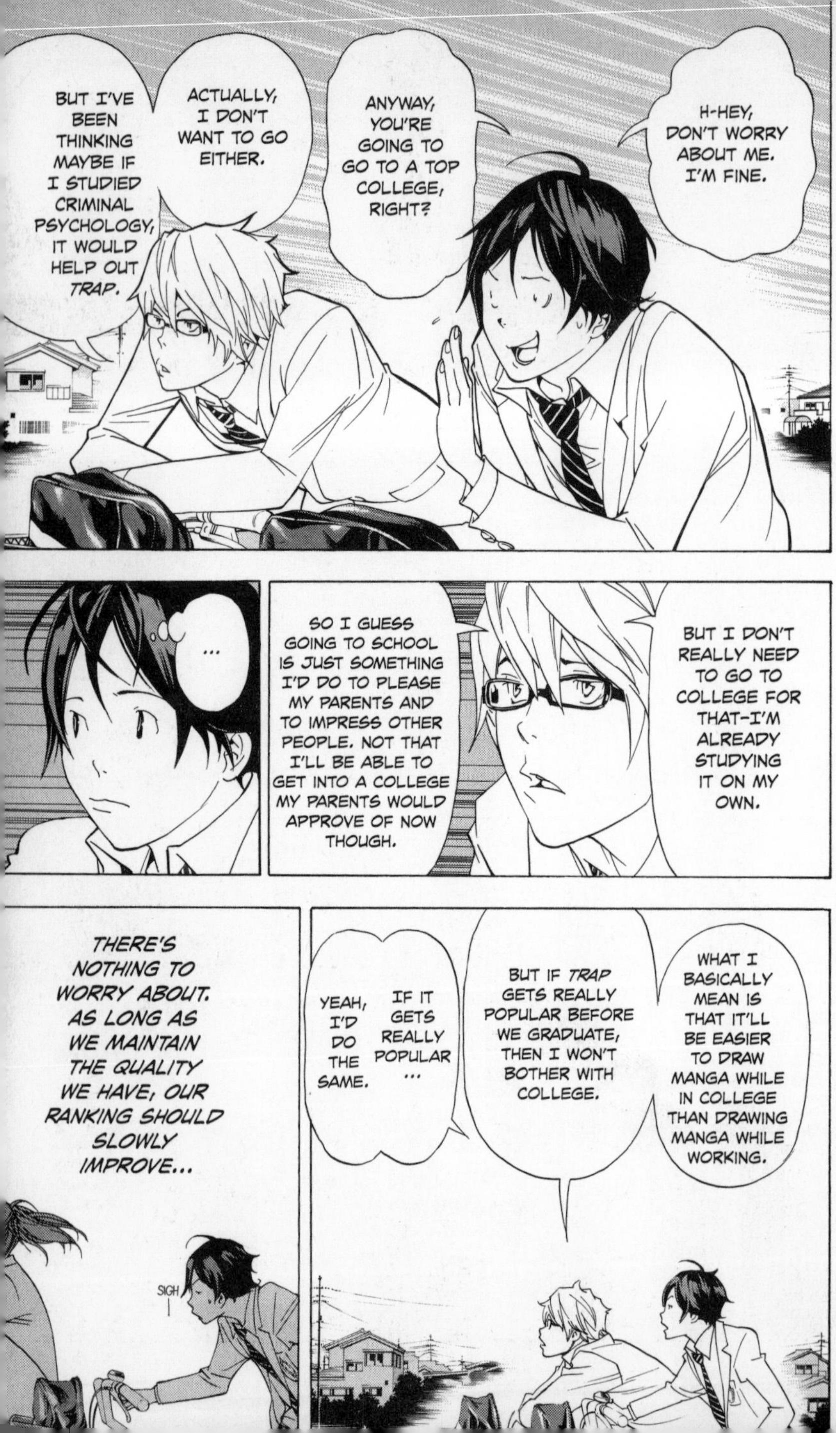
H-HEY, DON'T WORRY ABOUT ME. I'M FINE.
ANYWAY, YOU'RE GOING TO GO TO A TOP COLLEGE, RIGHT?
ACTUALLY, I DON'T WANT TO GO EITHER.
BUT I'VE BEEN THINKING MAYBE IF I STUDIED CRIMINAL PSYCHOLOGY, IT WOULD HELP OUT *TRAP*.
BUT I DON'T REALLY NEED TO GO TO COLLEGE FOR THAT–I'M ALREADY STUDYING IT ON MY OWN.
SO I GUESS GOING TO SCHOOL IS JUST SOMETHING I'D DO TO PLEASE MY PARENTS AND TO IMPRESS OTHER PEOPLE. NOT THAT I'LL BE ABLE TO GET INTO A COLLEGE MY PARENTS WOULD APPROVE OF NOW THOUGH.
...
WHAT I BASICALLY MEAN IS THAT IT'LL BE EASIER TO DRAW MANGA WHILE IN COLLEGE THAN DRAWING MANGA WHILE WORKING.
BUT IF *TRAP* GETS REALLY POPULAR BEFORE WE GRADUATE, THEN I WON'T BOTHER WITH COLLEGE.
IF IT GETS REALLY POPULAR ...
YEAH, I'D DO THE SAME.
THERE'S NOTHING TO WORRY ABOUT. AS LONG AS WE MAINTAIN THE QUALITY WE HAVE, OUR RANKING SHOULD SLOWLY IMPROVE...
SIGH

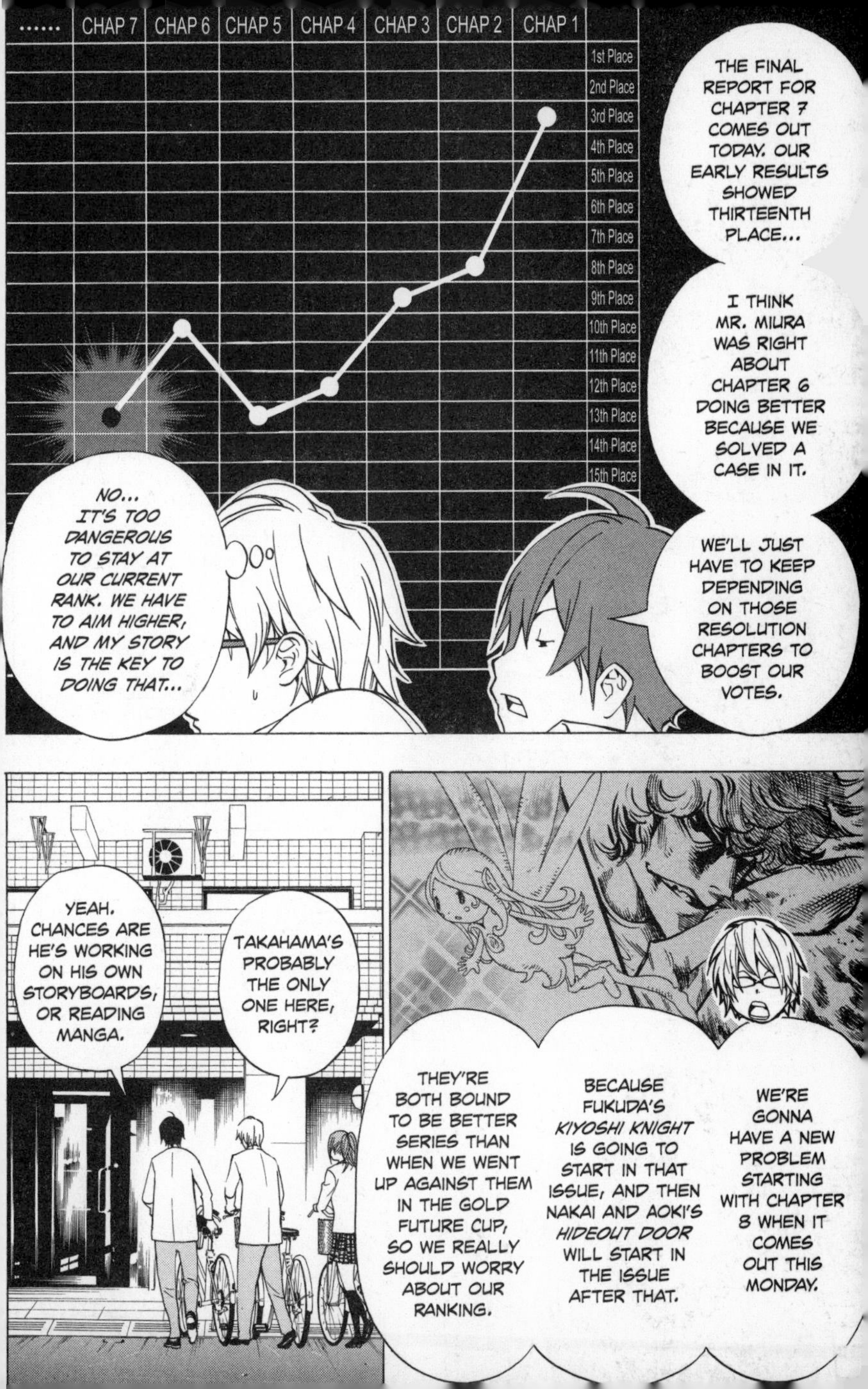
CHAP 1
CHAP 2
CHAP 3
CHAP 4
CHAP 5
CHAP 6
CHAP 7
......
1st Place
2nd Place
3rd Place
4th Place
5th Place
6th Place
7th Place
8th Place
9th Place
10th Place
11th Place
12th Place
13th Place
14th Place
15th Place
THE FINAL REPORT FOR CHAPTER 7 COMES OUT TODAY. OUR EARLY RESULTS SHOWED THIRTEENTH PLACE...
I THINK MR. MIURA WAS RIGHT ABOUT CHAPTER 6 DOING BETTER BECAUSE WE SOLVED A CASE IN IT.
WE'LL JUST HAVE TO KEEP DEPENDING ON THOSE RESOLUTION CHAPTERS TO BOOST OUR VOTES.
NO... IT'S TOO DANGEROUS TO STAY AT OUR CURRENT RANK. WE HAVE TO AIM HIGHER, AND MY STORY IS THE KEY TO DOING THAT...
WE'RE GONNA HAVE A NEW PROBLEM STARTING WITH CHAPTER 8 WHEN IT COMES OUT THIS MONDAY.
BECAUSE FUKUDA'S *KIYOSHI KNIGHT* IS GOING TO START IN THAT ISSUE, AND THEN NAKAI AND AOKI'S *HIDEOUT DOOR* WILL START IN THE ISSUE AFTER THAT.
THEY'RE BOTH BOUND TO BE BETTER SERIES THAN WHEN WE WENT UP AGAINST THEM IN THE GOLD FUTURE CUP, SO WE REALLY SHOULD WORRY ABOUT OUR RANKING.
TAKAHAMA'S PROBABLY THE ONLY ONE HERE, RIGHT?
YEAH. CHANCES ARE HE'S WORKING ON HIS OWN STORYBOARDS, OR READING MANGA.

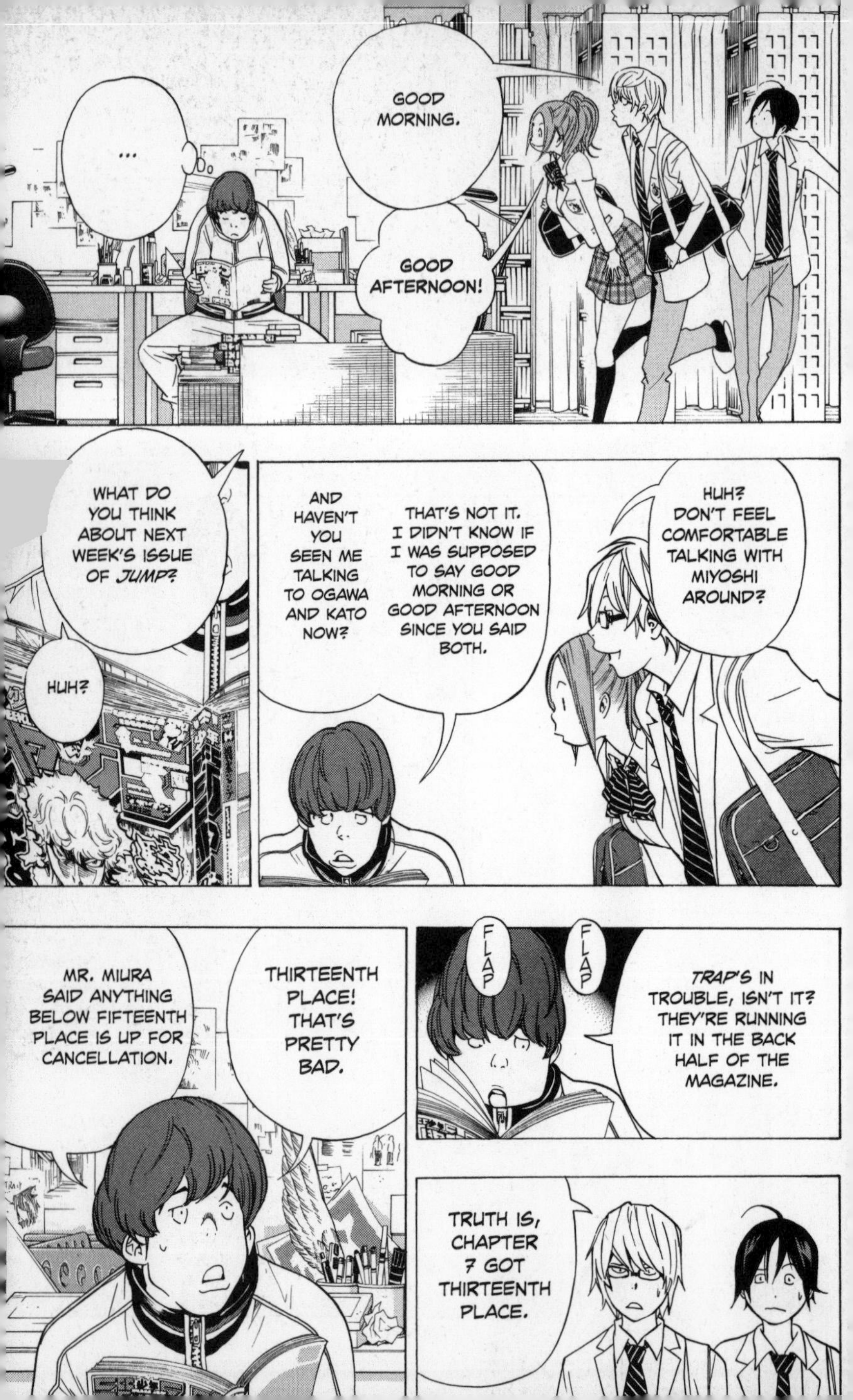
GOOD MORNING.
GOOD AFTERNOON!
...
HUH? DON'T FEEL COMFORTABLE TALKING WITH MIYOSHI AROUND?
THAT'S NOT IT. I DIDN'T KNOW IF I WAS SUPPOSED TO SAY GOOD MORNING OR GOOD AFTERNOON SINCE YOU SAID BOTH.
AND HAVEN'T YOU SEEN ME TALKING TO OGAWA AND KATO NOW?
WHAT DO YOU THINK ABOUT NEXT WEEK'S ISSUE OF *JUMP*?
HUH?
FLAP
FLAP
TRAP'S IN TROUBLE, ISN'T IT? THEY'RE RUNNING IT IN THE BACK HALF OF THE MAGAZINE.
TRUTH IS, CHAPTER 7 GOT THIRTEENTH PLACE.
THIRTEENTH PLACE! THAT'S PRETTY BAD.
MR. MIURA SAID ANYTHING BELOW FIFTEENTH PLACE IS UP FOR CANCELLATION.

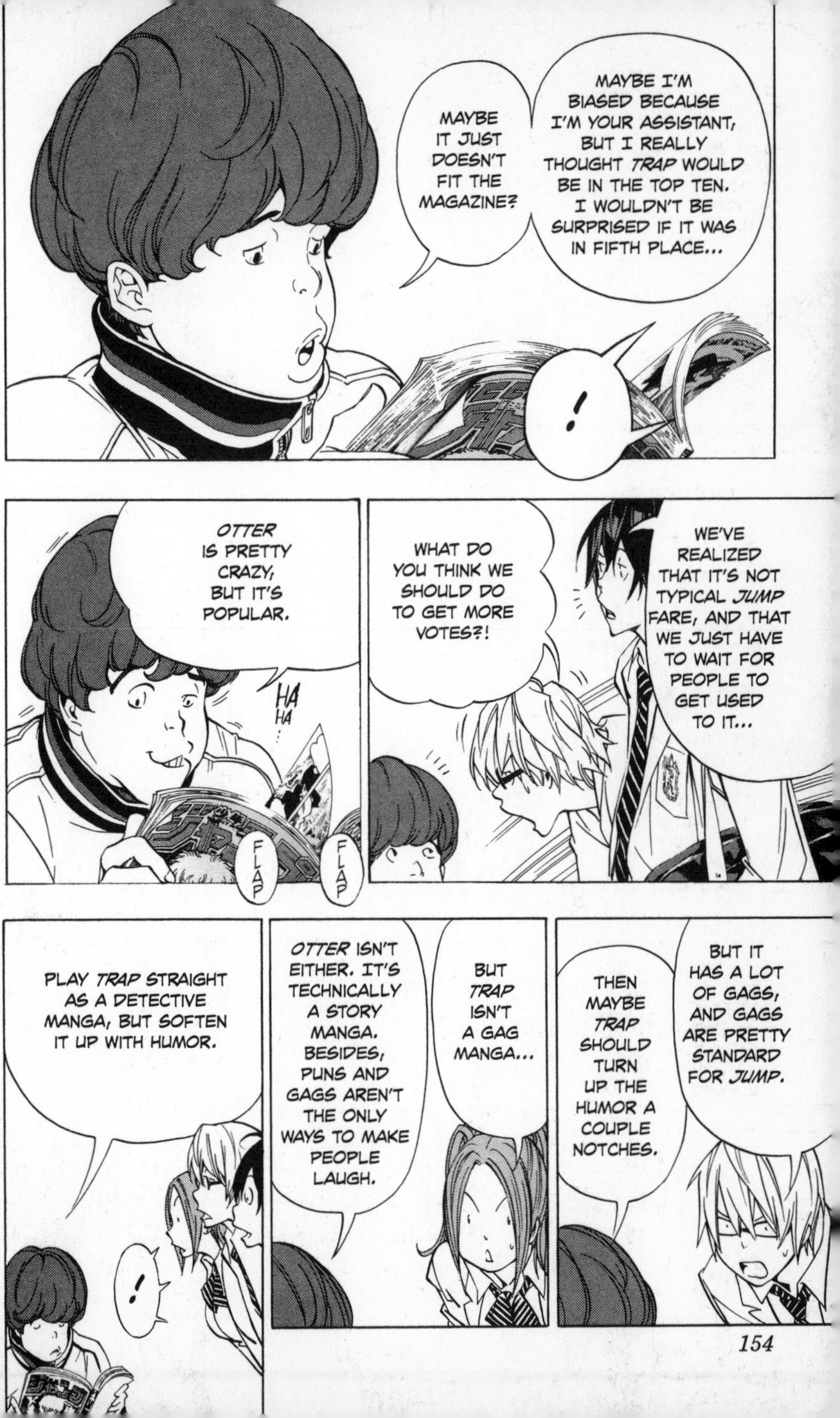
MAYBE I'M BIASED BECAUSE I'M YOUR ASSISTANT, BUT I REALLY THOUGHT *TRAP* WOULD BE IN THE TOP TEN. I WOULDN'T BE SURPRISED IF IT WAS IN FIFTH PLACE...
MAYBE IT JUST DOESN'T FIT THE MAGAZINE?
!
WE'VE REALIZED THAT IT'S NOT TYPICAL *JUMP* FARE, AND THAT WE JUST HAVE TO WAIT FOR PEOPLE TO GET USED TO IT...
WHAT DO YOU THINK WE SHOULD DO TO GET MORE VOTES?!
OTTER IS PRETTY CRAZY, BUT IT'S POPULAR.
HA HA...
FLAP
FLAP
BUT IT HAS A LOT OF GAGS, AND GAGS ARE PRETTY STANDARD FOR *JUMP*.
THEN MAYBE *TRAP* SHOULD TURN UP THE HUMOR A COUPLE NOTCHES.
BUT *TRAP* ISN'T A GAG MANGA...
OTTER ISN'T EITHER. IT'S TECHNICALLY A STORY MANGA. BESIDES, PUNS AND GAGS AREN'T THE ONLY WAYS TO MAKE PEOPLE LAUGH.
PLAY *TRAP* STRAIGHT AS A DETECTIVE MANGA, BUT SOFTEN IT UP WITH HUMOR.
!

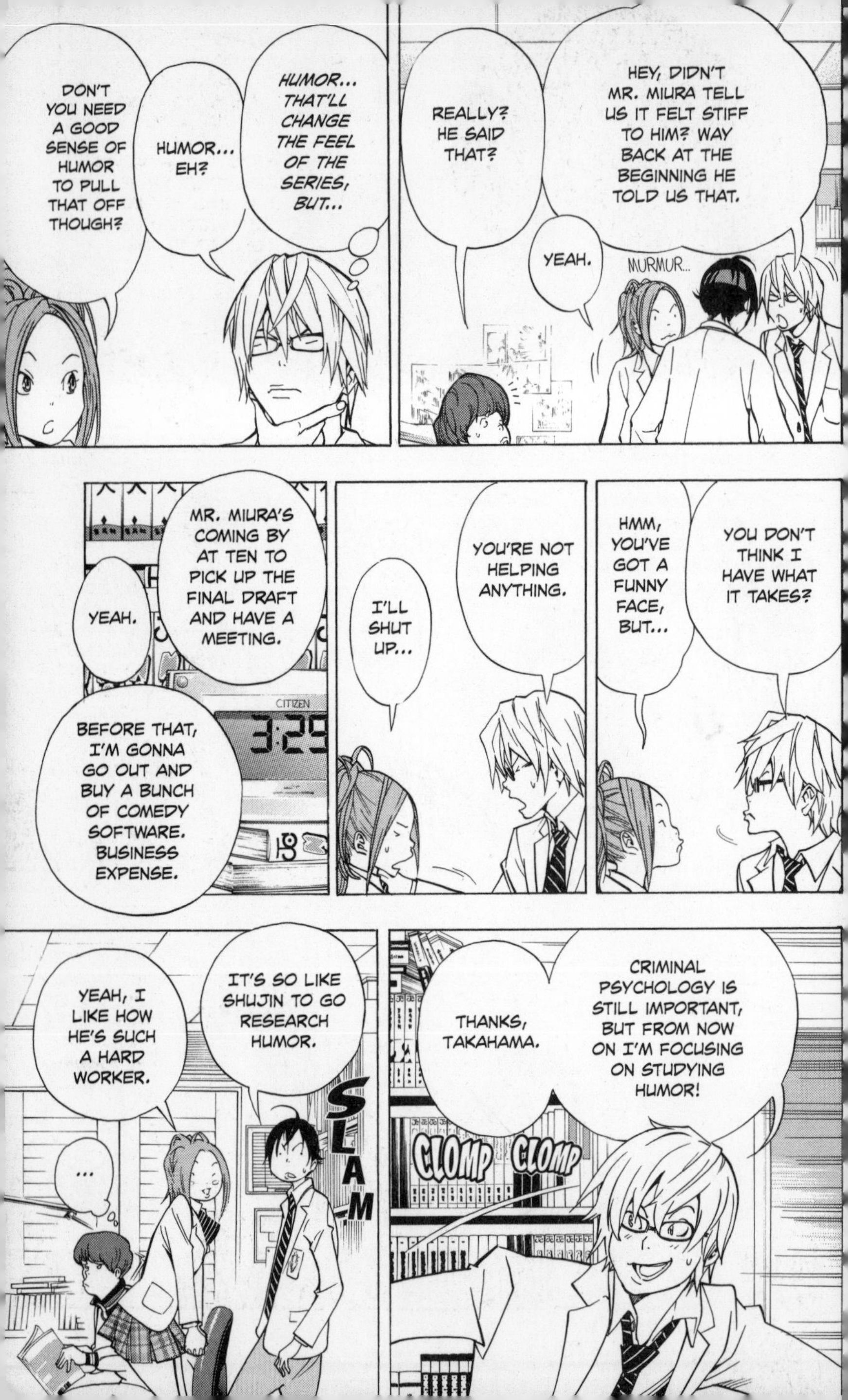
HEY, DIDN'T MR. MIURA TELL US IT FELT STIFF TO HIM? WAY BACK AT THE BEGINNING HE TOLD US THAT.
REALLY? HE SAID THAT?
YEAH.
MURMUR...
HUMOR... THAT'LL CHANGE THE FEEL OF THE SERIES, BUT...
HUMOR... EH?
DON'T YOU NEED A GOOD SENSE OF HUMOR TO PULL THAT OFF THOUGH?
YOU DON'T THINK I HAVE WHAT IT TAKES?
HMM, YOU'VE GOT A FUNNY FACE, BUT...
YOU'RE NOT HELPING ANYTHING.
I'LL SHUT UP...
MR. MIURA'S COMING BY AT TEN TO PICK UP THE FINAL DRAFT AND HAVE A MEETING.
YEAH.
CITIZEN
3:29
BEFORE THAT, I'M GONNA GO OUT AND BUY A BUNCH OF COMEDY SOFTWARE. BUSINESS EXPENSE.
CRIMINAL PSYCHOLOGY IS STILL IMPORTANT, BUT FROM NOW ON I'M FOCUSING ON STUDYING HUMOR!
THANKS, TAKAHAMA.
CLOMP CLOMP
SLAM
IT'S SO LIKE SHUJIN TO GO RESEARCH HUMOR.
YEAH, I LIKE HOW HE'S SUCH A HARD WORKER.
...

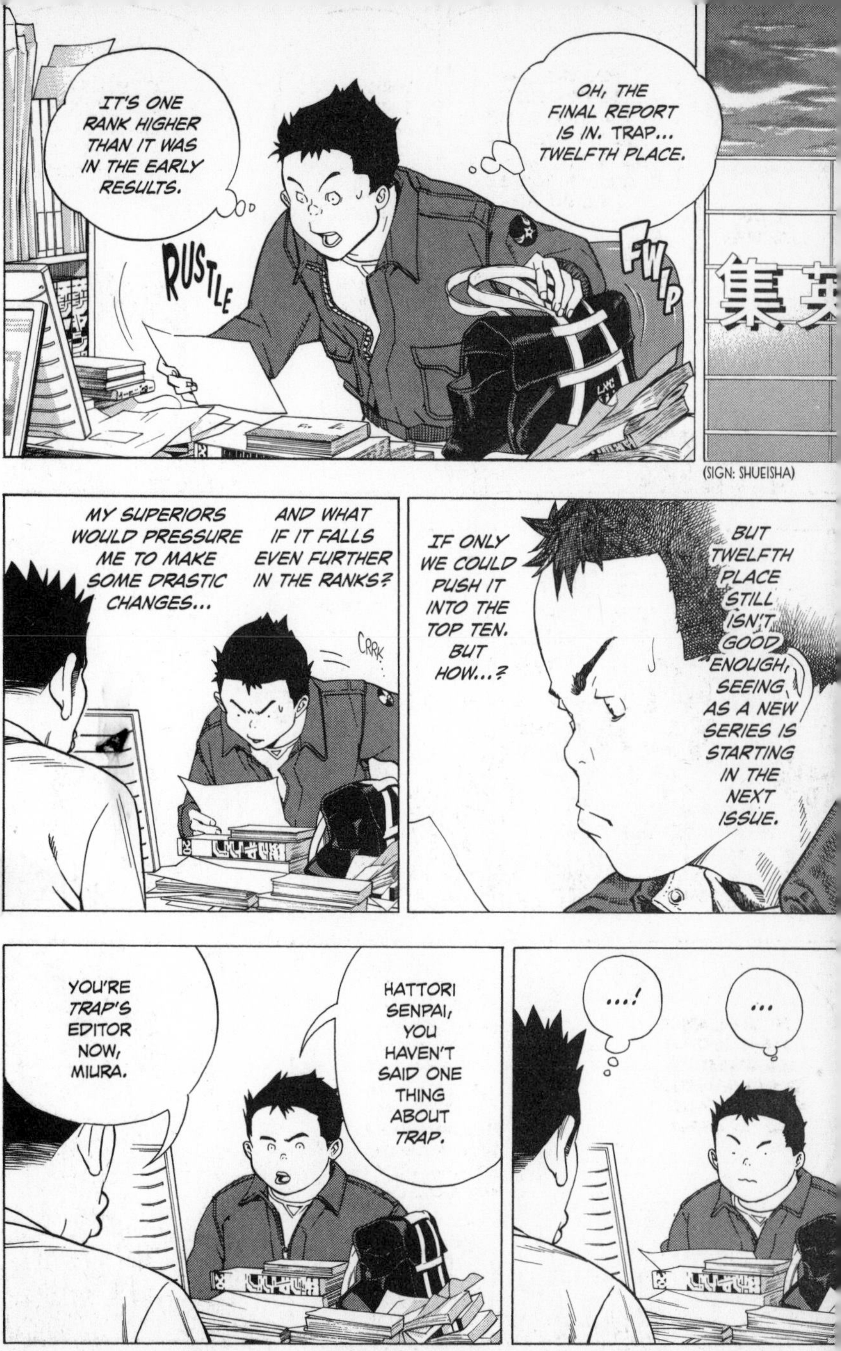
集英
(SIGN: SHUEISHA)
OH, THE FINAL REPORT IS IN. TRAP... TWELFTH PLACE.
FWIP
IT'S ONE RANK HIGHER THAN IT WAS IN THE EARLY RESULTS.
RUSTLE
BUT TWELFTH PLACE STILL ISN'T GOOD ENOUGH, SEEING AS A NEW SERIES IS STARTING IN THE NEXT ISSUE.
IF ONLY WE COULD PUSH IT INTO THE TOP TEN. BUT HOW...?
AND WHAT IF IT FALLS EVEN FURTHER IN THE RANKS?
MY SUPERIORS WOULD PRESSURE ME TO MAKE SOME DRASTIC CHANGES...
CRRK
...
...!
HATTORI SENPAI, YOU HAVEN'T SAID ONE THING ABOUT *TRAP*.
YOU'RE *TRAP'S* EDITOR NOW, MIURA.

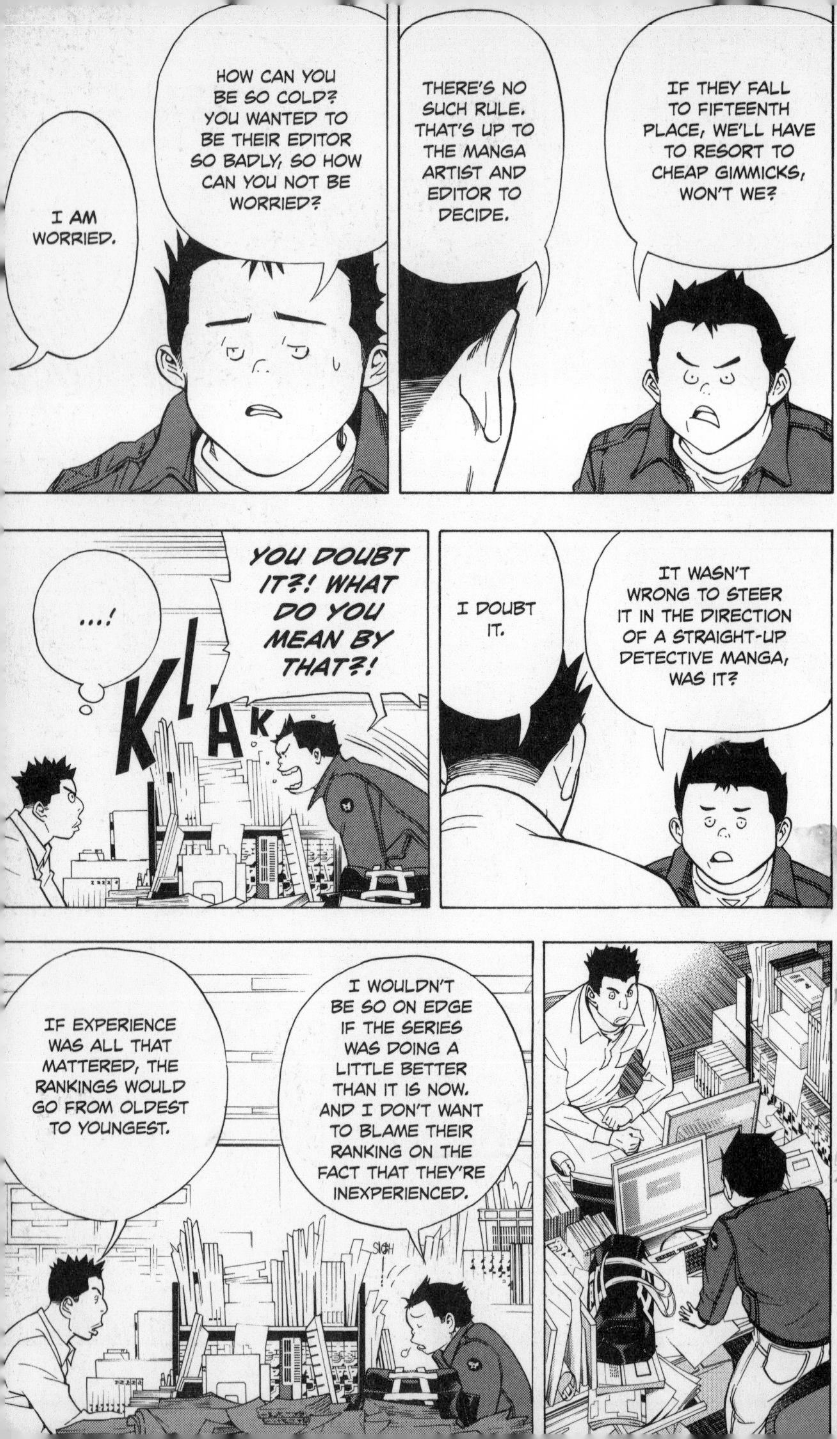
IF THEY FALL TO FIFTEENTH PLACE, WE'LL HAVE TO RESORT TO CHEAP GIMMICKS, WON'T WE?
THERE'S NO SUCH RULE. THAT'S UP TO THE MANGA ARTIST AND EDITOR TO DECIDE.
HOW CAN YOU BE SO COLD? YOU WANTED TO BE THEIR EDITOR SO BADLY, SO HOW CAN YOU NOT BE WORRIED?
I AM WORRIED.
IT WASN'T WRONG TO STEER IT IN THE DIRECTION OF A STRAIGHT-UP DETECTIVE MANGA, WAS IT?
I DOUBT IT.
YOU DOUBT IT?! WHAT DO YOU MEAN BY THAT?!
KLAK
...!
I WOULDN'T BE SO ON EDGE IF THE SERIES WAS DOING A LITTLE BETTER THAN IT IS NOW. AND I DON'T WANT TO BLAME THEIR RANKING ON THE FACT THAT THEY'RE INEXPERIENCED.
SIGH
IF EXPERIENCE WAS ALL THAT MATTERED, THE RANKINGS WOULD GO FROM OLDEST TO YOUNGEST.

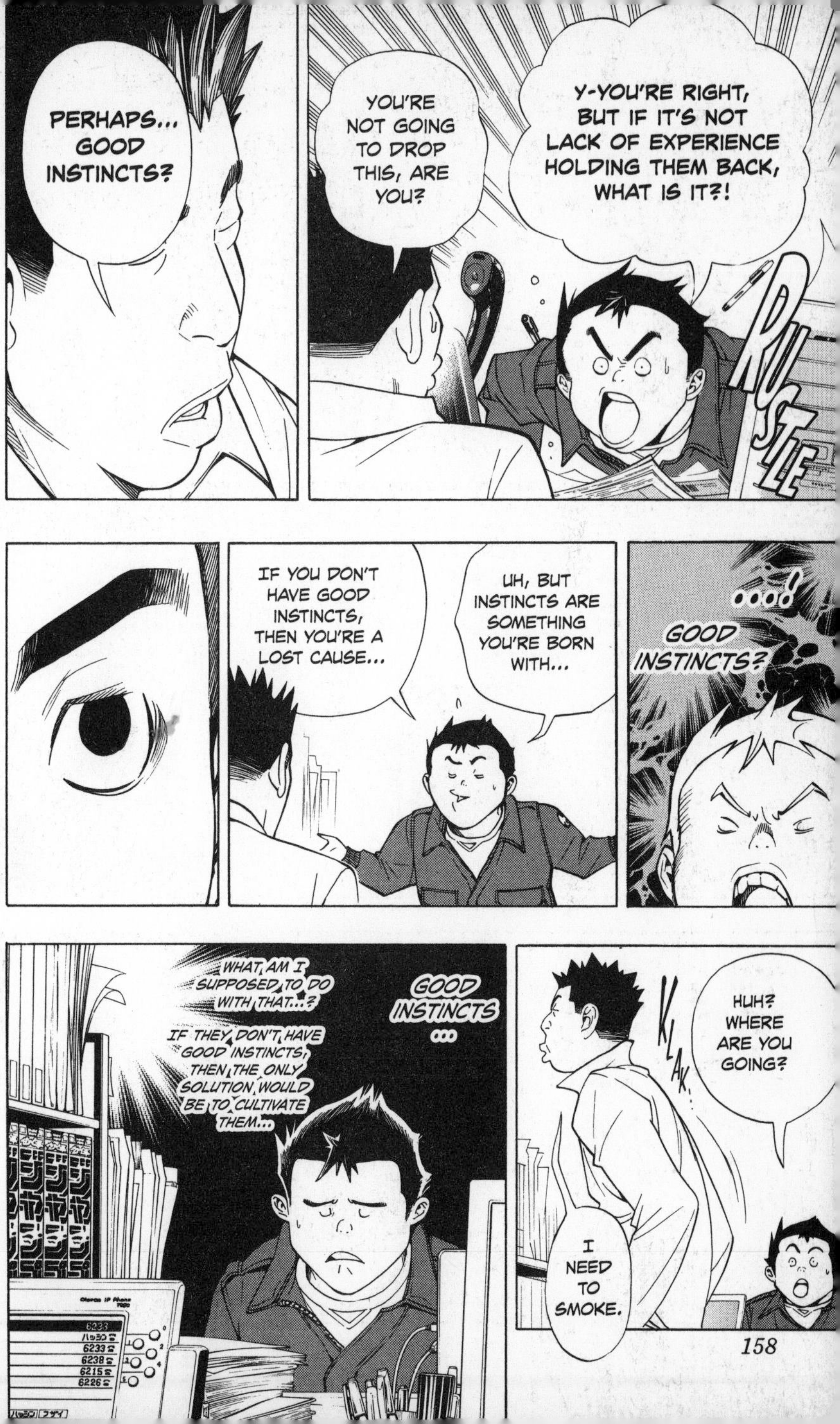
Y-YOU'RE RIGHT, BUT IF IT'S NOT LACK OF EXPERIENCE HOLDING THEM BACK, WHAT IS IT?!
RUSTLE
YOU'RE NOT GOING TO DROP THIS, ARE YOU?
PERHAPS... GOOD INSTINCTS?
...!
GOOD INSTINCTS?
UH, BUT INSTINCTS ARE SOMETHING YOU'RE BORN WITH...
IF YOU DON'T HAVE GOOD INSTINCTS, THEN YOU'RE A LOST CAUSE...
HUH? WHERE ARE YOU GOING?
KLAK...
I NEED TO SMOKE.
GOOD INSTINCTS...
WHAT AM I SUPPOSED TO DO WITH THAT...?
IF THEY DON'T HAVE GOOD INSTINCTS, THEN THE ONLY SOLUTION WOULD BE TO CULTIVATE THEM...

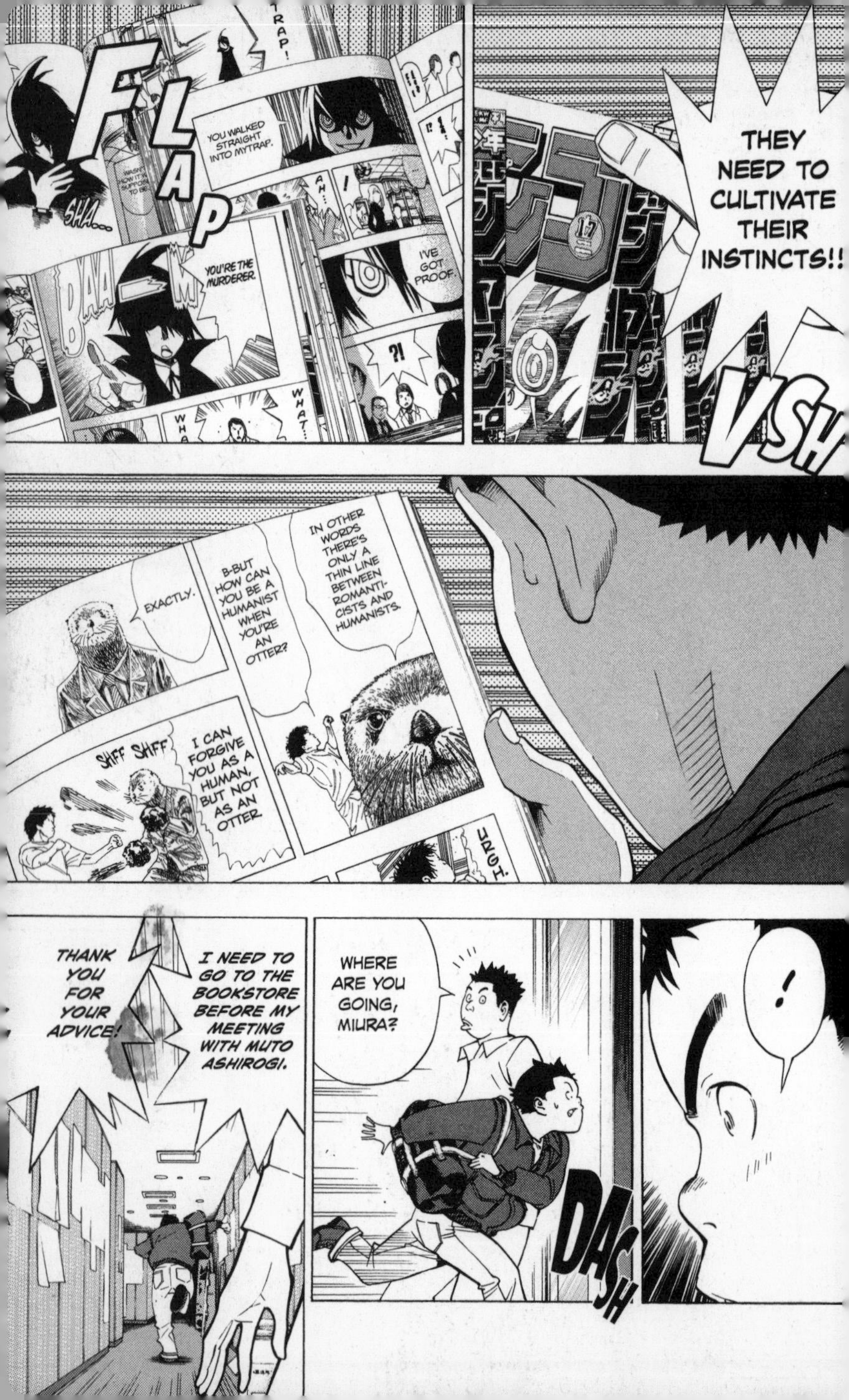
THEY NEED TO CULTIVATE THEIR INSTINCTS!!
VSH
FLAP
TRAP!
YOU WALKED STRAIGHT INTO MYTRAP.
AH...
!
SHA...
I'VE GOT PROOF.
YOU'RE THE MURDERER.
BAAM
?!
WHAT...
WHA
IN OTHER WORDS THERE'S ONLY A THIN LINE BETWEEN ROMANTI-CISTS AND HUMANISTS.
B-BUT HOW CAN YOU BE A HUMANIST WHEN YOU'RE AN OTTER?
EXACTLY.
URGH.
I CAN FORGIVE YOU AS A HUMAN, BUT NOT AS AN OTTER
SHFF SHFF
!
WHERE ARE YOU GOING, MIURA?
DASH
I NEED TO GO TO THE BOOKSTORE BEFORE MY MEETING WITH MUTO ASHIROGI.
THANK YOU FOR YOUR ADVICE!

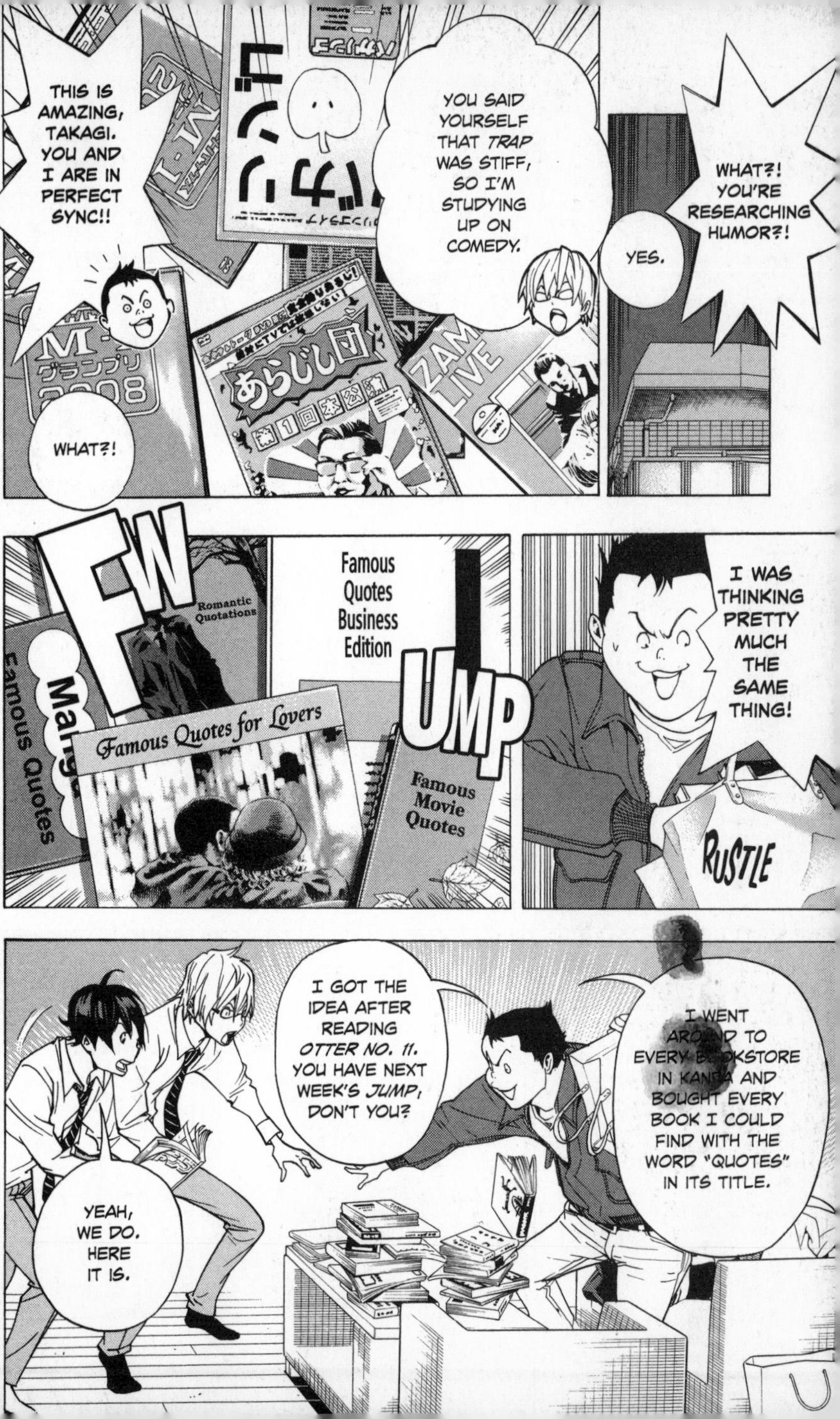
WHAT?! YOU'RE RESEARCHING HUMOR?!
YES.
YOU SAID YOURSELF THAT *TRAP* WAS STIFF, SO I'M STUDYING UP ON COMEDY.
ZAM LIVE
THIS IS AMAZING, TAKAGI. YOU AND I ARE IN PERFECT SYNC!!
M-1 グランプリ 2008
あらじし団
WHAT?!
I WAS THINKING PRETTY MUCH THE SAME THING!
RUSTLE
FWUMP
Famous Quotes Business Edition
Romantic Quotations
Famous Quotes for Lovers
Famous Movie Quotes
Famous Quotes
I WENT AROUND TO EVERY BOOKSTORE IN KANDA AND BOUGHT EVERY BOOK I COULD FIND WITH THE WORD "QUOTES" IN ITS TITLE.
I GOT THE IDEA AFTER READING *OTTER NO. 11*. YOU HAVE NEXT WEEK'S *JUMP*, DON'T YOU?
YEAH, WE DO. HERE IT IS.

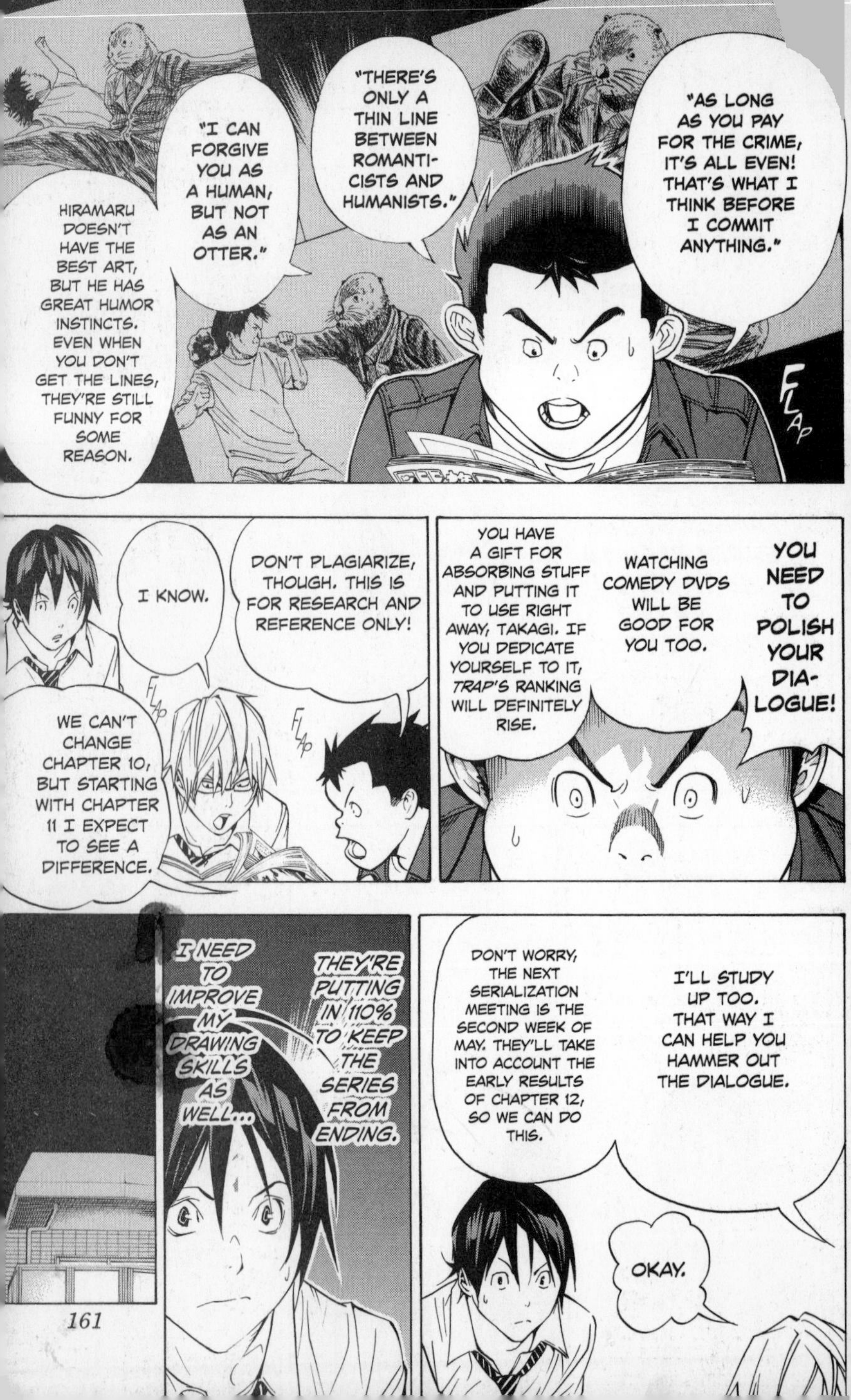
"AS LONG AS YOU PAY FOR THE CRIME, IT'S ALL EVEN! THAT'S WHAT I THINK BEFORE I COMMIT ANYTHING."
"THERE'S ONLY A THIN LINE BETWEEN ROMANTICISTS AND HUMANISTS."
"I CAN FORGIVE YOU AS A HUMAN, BUT NOT AS AN OTTER."
HIRAMARU DOESN'T HAVE THE BEST ART, BUT HE HAS GREAT HUMOR INSTINCTS. EVEN WHEN YOU DON'T GET THE LINES, THEY'RE STILL FUNNY FOR SOME REASON.
FLAP
YOU NEED TO POLISH YOUR DIALOGUE!
WATCHING COMEDY DVDS WILL BE GOOD FOR YOU TOO.
YOU HAVE A GIFT FOR ABSORBING STUFF AND PUTTING IT TO USE RIGHT AWAY, TAKAGI. IF YOU DEDICATE YOURSELF TO IT, *TRAP*'S RANKING WILL DEFINITELY RISE.
DON'T PLAGIARIZE, THOUGH. THIS IS FOR RESEARCH AND REFERENCE ONLY!
I KNOW.
FLAP
FLAP
WE CAN'T CHANGE CHAPTER 10, BUT STARTING WITH CHAPTER 11 I EXPECT TO SEE A DIFFERENCE.
I'LL STUDY UP TOO. THAT WAY I CAN HELP YOU HAMMER OUT THE DIALOGUE.
DON'T WORRY, THE NEXT SERIALIZATION MEETING IS THE SECOND WEEK OF MAY. THEY'LL TAKE INTO ACCOUNT THE EARLY RESULTS OF CHAPTER 12, SO WE CAN DO THIS.
OKAY.
THEY'RE PUTTING IN 110% TO KEEP THE SERIES FROM ENDING.
I NEED TO IMPROVE MY DRAWING SKILLS AS WELL...

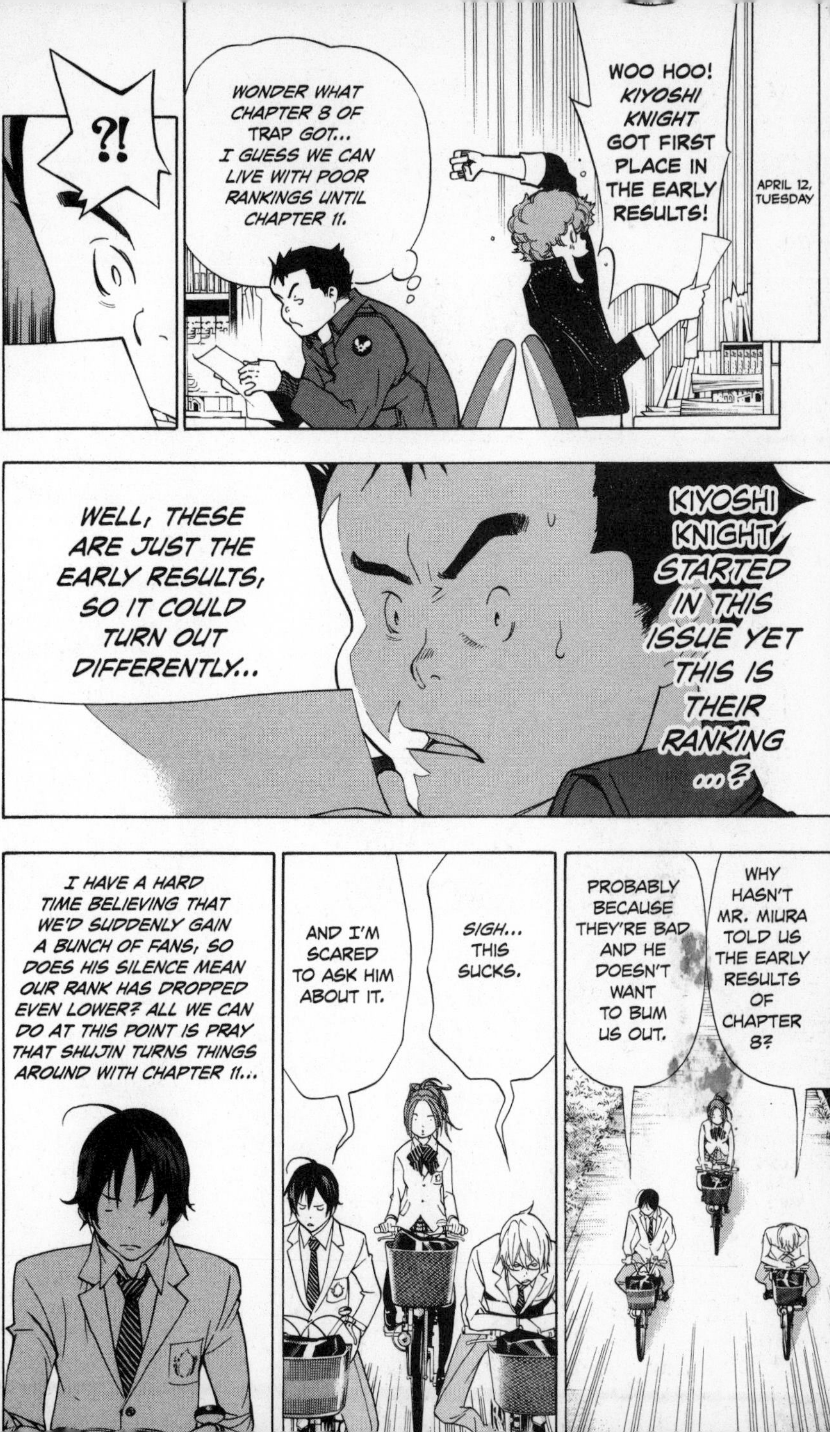
APRIL 12, TUESDAY
WOO HOO! KIYOSHI KNIGHT GOT FIRST PLACE IN THE EARLY RESULTS!
WONDER WHAT CHAPTER 8 OF TRAP GOT... I GUESS WE CAN LIVE WITH POOR RANKINGS UNTIL CHAPTER 11.
?!
KIYOSHI KNIGHT STARTED IN THIS ISSUE YET THIS IS THEIR RANKING...?
WELL, THESE ARE JUST THE EARLY RESULTS, SO IT COULD TURN OUT DIFFERENTLY...
WHY HASN'T MR. MIURA TOLD US THE EARLY RESULTS OF CHAPTER 8?
PROBABLY BECAUSE THEY'RE BAD AND HE DOESN'T WANT TO BUM US OUT.
SIGH... THIS SUCKS.
AND I'M SCARED TO ASK HIM ABOUT IT.
I HAVE A HARD TIME BELIEVING THAT WE'D SUDDENLY GAIN A BUNCH OF FANS, SO DOES HIS SILENCE MEAN OUR RANK HAS DROPPED EVEN LOWER? ALL WE CAN DO AT THIS POINT IS PRAY THAT SHUJIN TURNS THINGS AROUND WITH CHAPTER 11...

READ THIS WAY

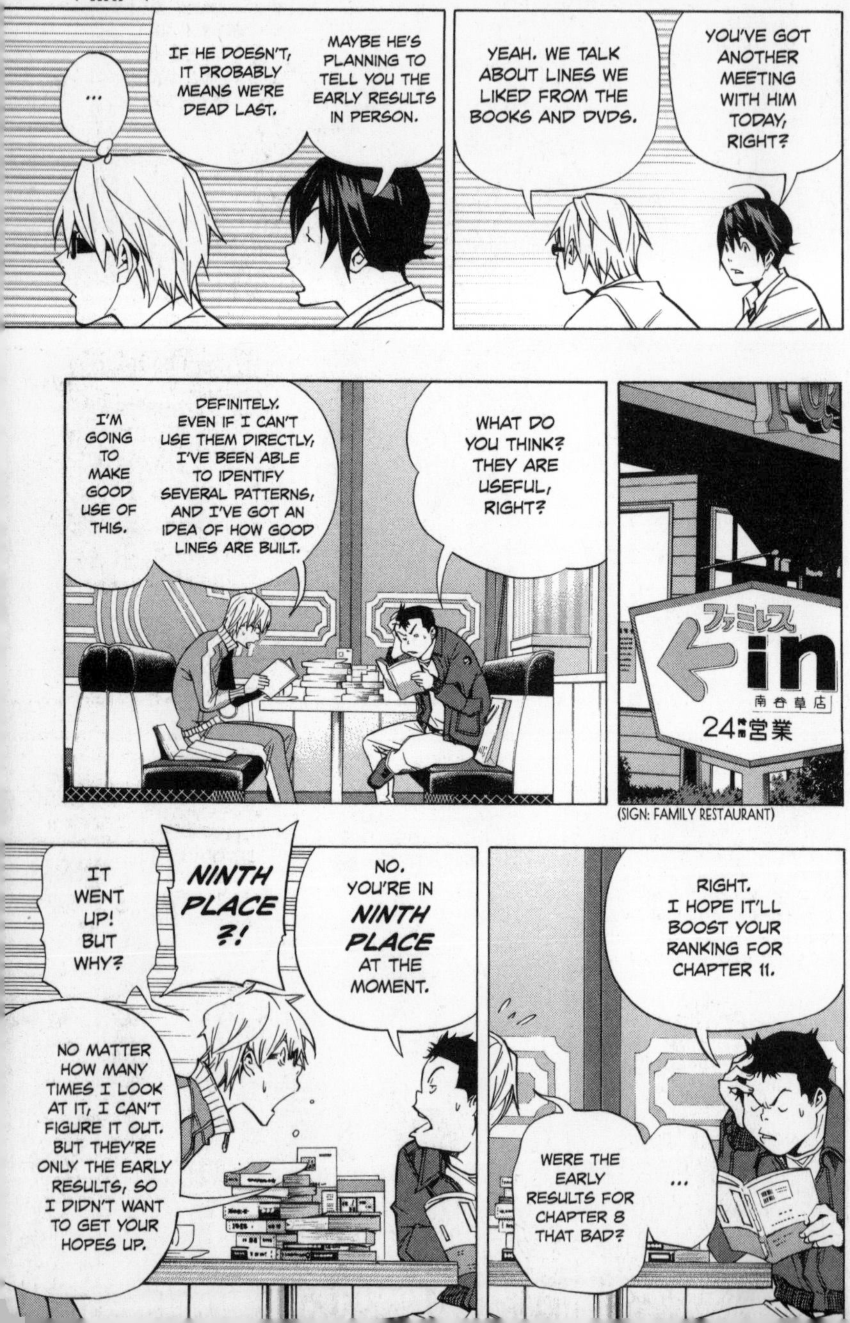
YOU'VE GOT ANOTHER MEETING WITH HIM TODAY, RIGHT?
YEAH. WE TALK ABOUT LINES WE LIKED FROM THE BOOKS AND DVDS.
MAYBE HE'S PLANNING TO TELL YOU THE EARLY RESULTS IN PERSON.
IF HE DOESN'T, IT PROBABLY MEANS WE'RE DEAD LAST.
...
ファミレス
in
南谷草店
24時間営業
(SIGN: FAMILY RESTAURANT)
WHAT DO YOU THINK? THEY ARE USEFUL, RIGHT?
DEFINITELY. EVEN IF I CAN'T USE THEM DIRECTLY, I'VE BEEN ABLE TO IDENTIFY SEVERAL PATTERNS, AND I'VE GOT AN IDEA OF HOW GOOD LINES ARE BUILT.
I'M GOING TO MAKE GOOD USE OF THIS.
RIGHT. I HOPE IT'LL BOOST YOUR RANKING FOR CHAPTER 11.
...
WERE THE EARLY RESULTS FOR CHAPTER 8 THAT BAD?
NO. YOU'RE IN NINTH PLACE AT THE MOMENT.
NINTH PLACE?!
IT WENT UP! BUT WHY?
NO MATTER HOW MANY TIMES I LOOK AT IT, I CAN'T FIGURE IT OUT. BUT THEY'RE ONLY THE EARLY RESULTS, SO I DIDN'T WANT TO GET YOUR HOPES UP.

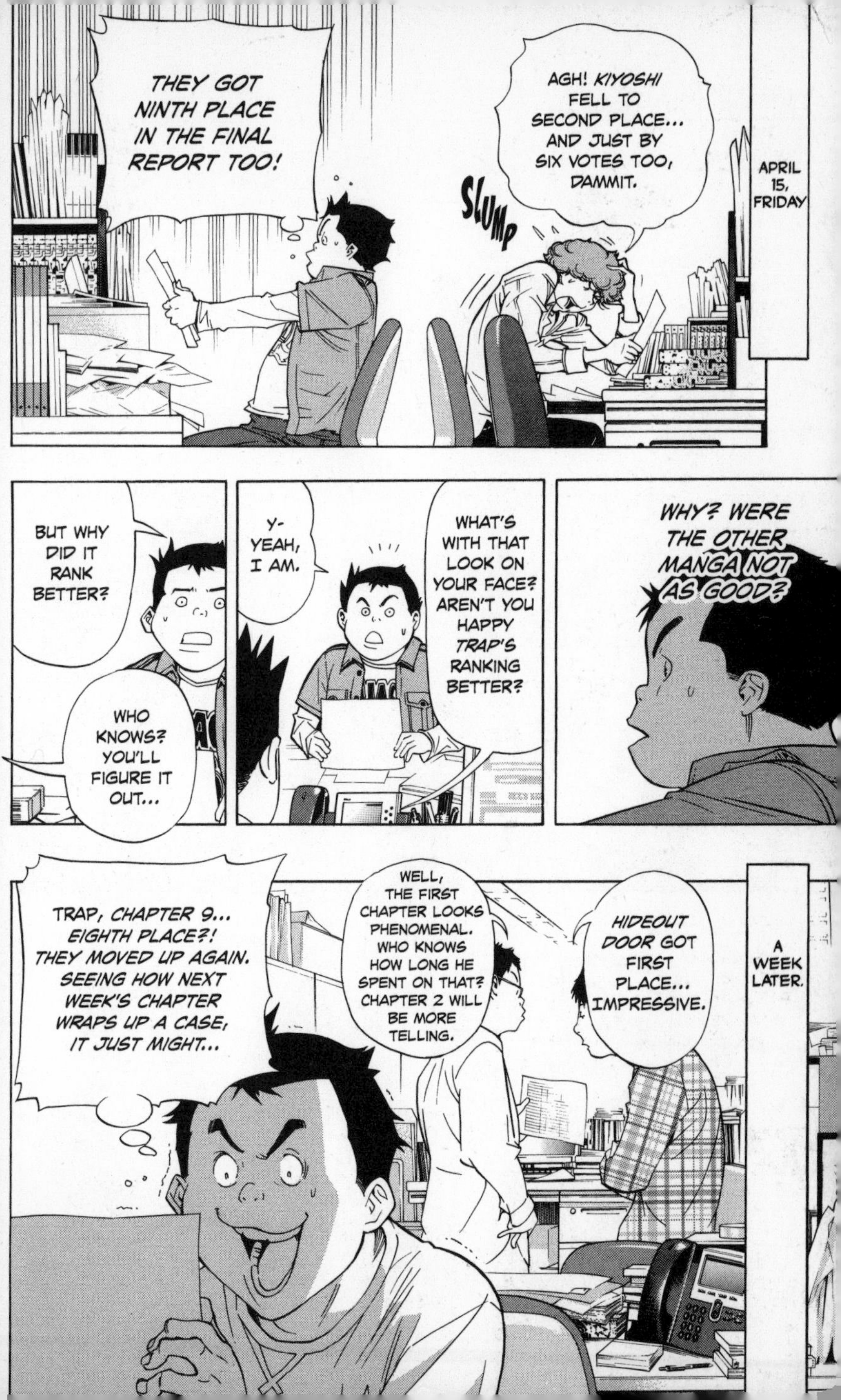
APRIL 15, FRIDAY
AGH! KIYOSHI FELL TO SECOND PLACE... AND JUST BY SIX VOTES TOO, DAMMIT.
SLUMP
THEY GOT NINTH PLACE IN THE FINAL REPORT TOO!
WHY? WERE THE OTHER MANGA NOT AS GOOD?
WHAT'S WITH THAT LOOK ON YOUR FACE? AREN'T YOU HAPPY TRAP'S RANKING BETTER?
Y-YEAH, I AM.
BUT WHY DID IT RANK BETTER?
WHO KNOWS? YOU'LL FIGURE IT OUT...
A WEEK LATER.
HIDEOUT DOOR GOT FIRST PLACE... IMPRESSIVE.
WELL, THE FIRST CHAPTER LOOKS PHENOMENAL. WHO KNOWS HOW LONG HE SPENT ON THAT? CHAPTER 2 WILL BE MORE TELLING.
TRAP, CHAPTER 9... EIGHTH PLACE?! THEY MOVED UP AGAIN. SEEING HOW NEXT WEEK'S CHAPTER WRAPS UP A CASE, IT JUST MIGHT...

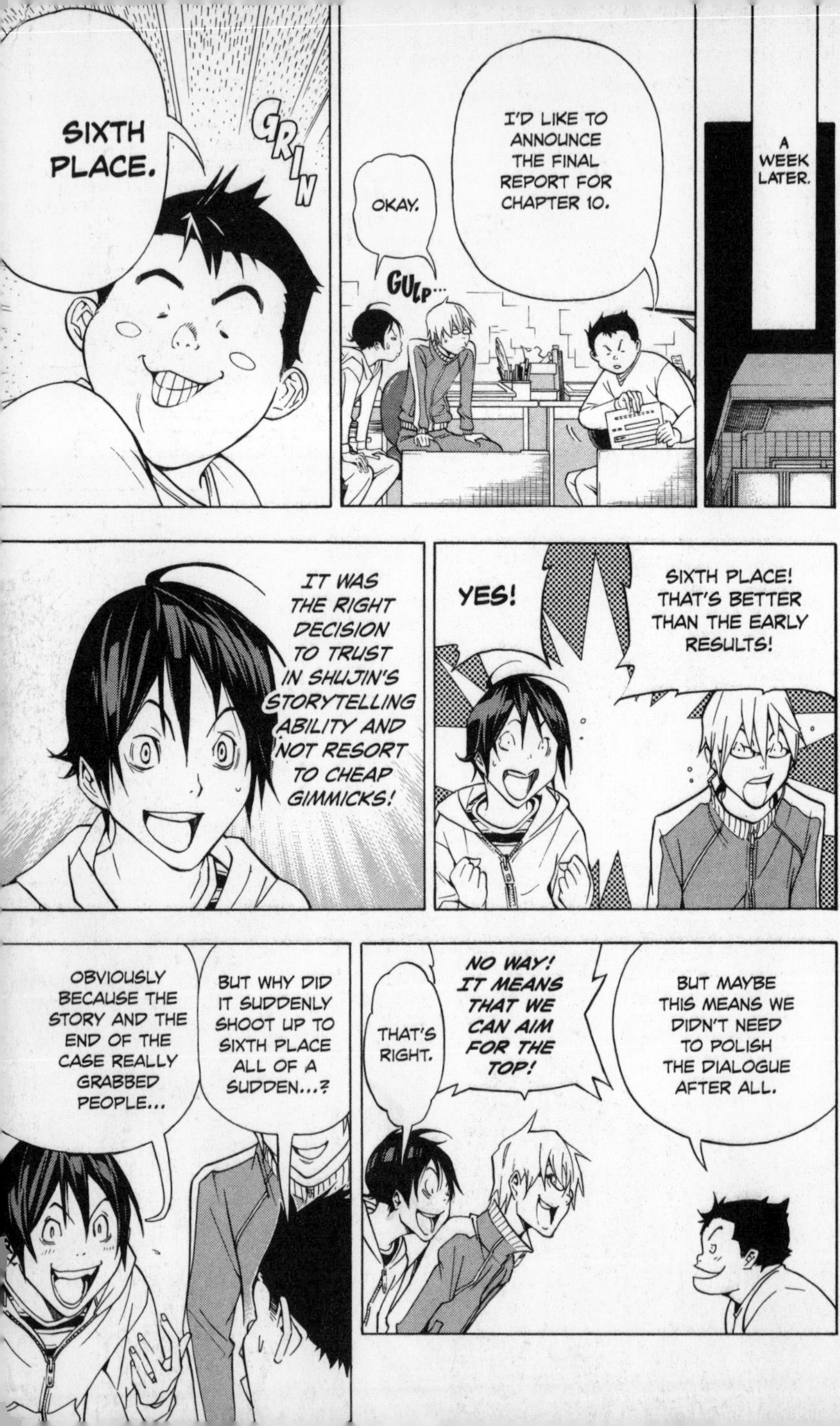
A WEEK LATER.
I'D LIKE TO ANNOUNCE THE FINAL REPORT FOR CHAPTER 10.
OKAY.
GULP...
GRIN
SIXTH PLACE.
SIXTH PLACE! THAT'S BETTER THAN THE EARLY RESULTS!
YES!
IT WAS THE RIGHT DECISION TO TRUST IN SHUJIN'S STORYTELLING ABILITY AND NOT RESORT TO CHEAP GIMMICKS!
BUT MAYBE THIS MEANS WE DIDN'T NEED TO POLISH THE DIALOGUE AFTER ALL.
NO WAY! IT MEANS THAT WE CAN AIM FOR THE TOP!
THAT'S RIGHT.
BUT WHY DID IT SUDDENLY SHOOT UP TO SIXTH PLACE ALL OF A SUDDEN...?
OBVIOUSLY BECAUSE THE STORY AND THE END OF THE CASE REALLY GRABBED PEOPLE...

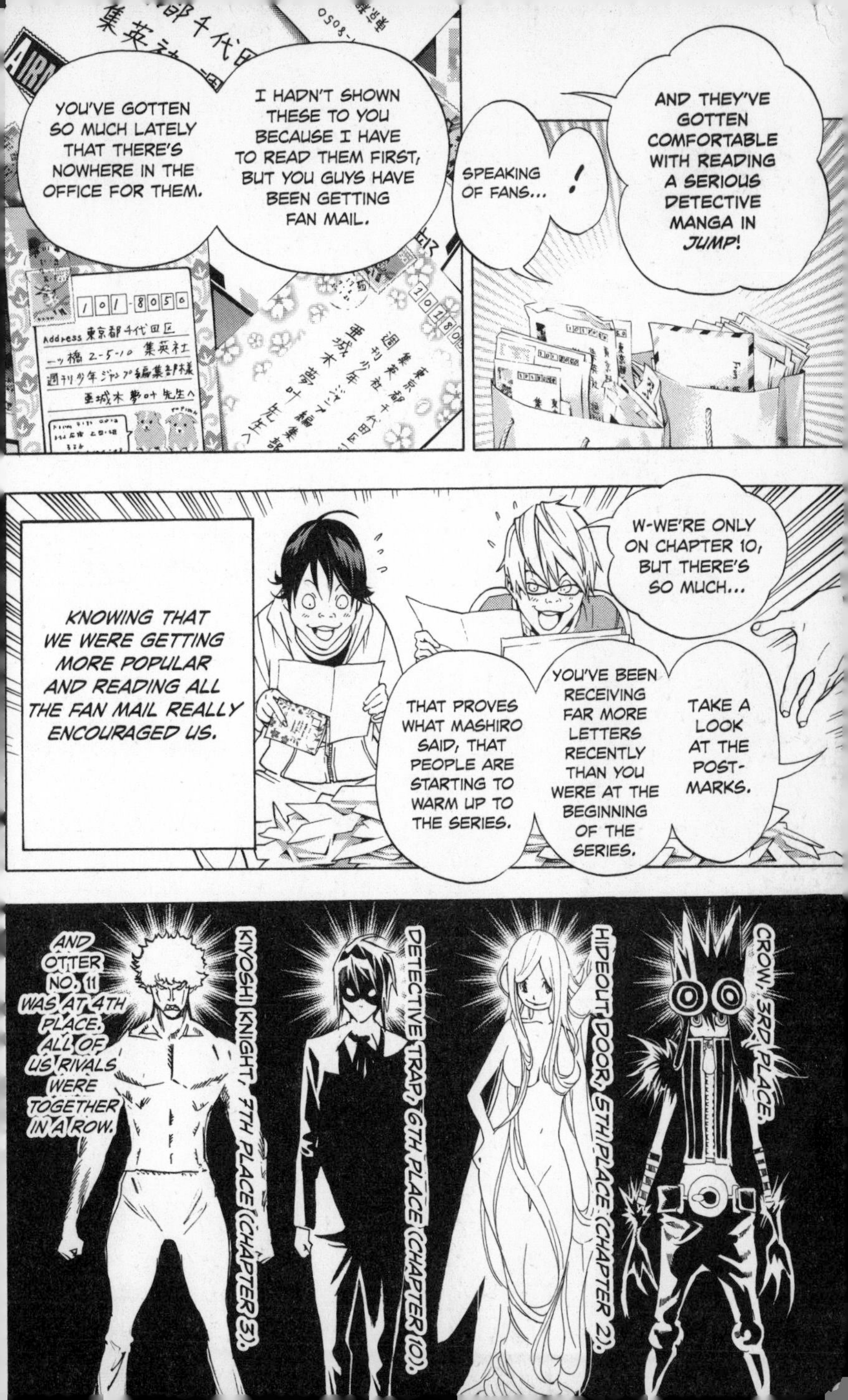
AND THEY'VE GOTTEN COMFORTABLE WITH READING A SERIOUS DETECTIVE MANGA IN *JUMP*!
!
SPEAKING OF FANS...
I HADN'T SHOWN THESE TO YOU BECAUSE I HAVE TO READ THEM FIRST, BUT YOU GUYS HAVE BEEN GETTING FAN MAIL.
YOU'VE GOTTEN SO MUCH LATELY THAT THERE'S NOWHERE IN THE OFFICE FOR THEM.
101-8050
Address 東京都千代田区
一ツ橋 2-5-10 集英社
週刊少年ジャンプ編集部様
亜城木夢叶 先生へ
W-WE'RE ONLY ON CHAPTER 10, BUT THERE'S SO MUCH...
TAKE A LOOK AT THE POST-MARKS.
YOU'VE BEEN RECEIVING FAR MORE LETTERS RECENTLY THAN YOU WERE AT THE BEGINNING OF THE SERIES.
THAT PROVES WHAT MASHIRO SAID, THAT PEOPLE ARE STARTING TO WARM UP TO THE SERIES.
KNOWING THAT WE WERE GETTING MORE POPULAR AND READING ALL THE FAN MAIL REALLY ENCOURAGED US.
CROW, 3RD PLACE.
HIDEOUT DOOR, 5TH PLACE (CHAPTER 2).
DETECTIVE TRAP, 6TH PLACE (CHAPTER 10).
KIYOSHI KNIGHT, 7TH PLACE (CHAPTER 3).
AND OTTER NO. 11 WAS AT 4TH PLACE. ALL OF US RIVALS WERE TOGETHER IN A ROW.

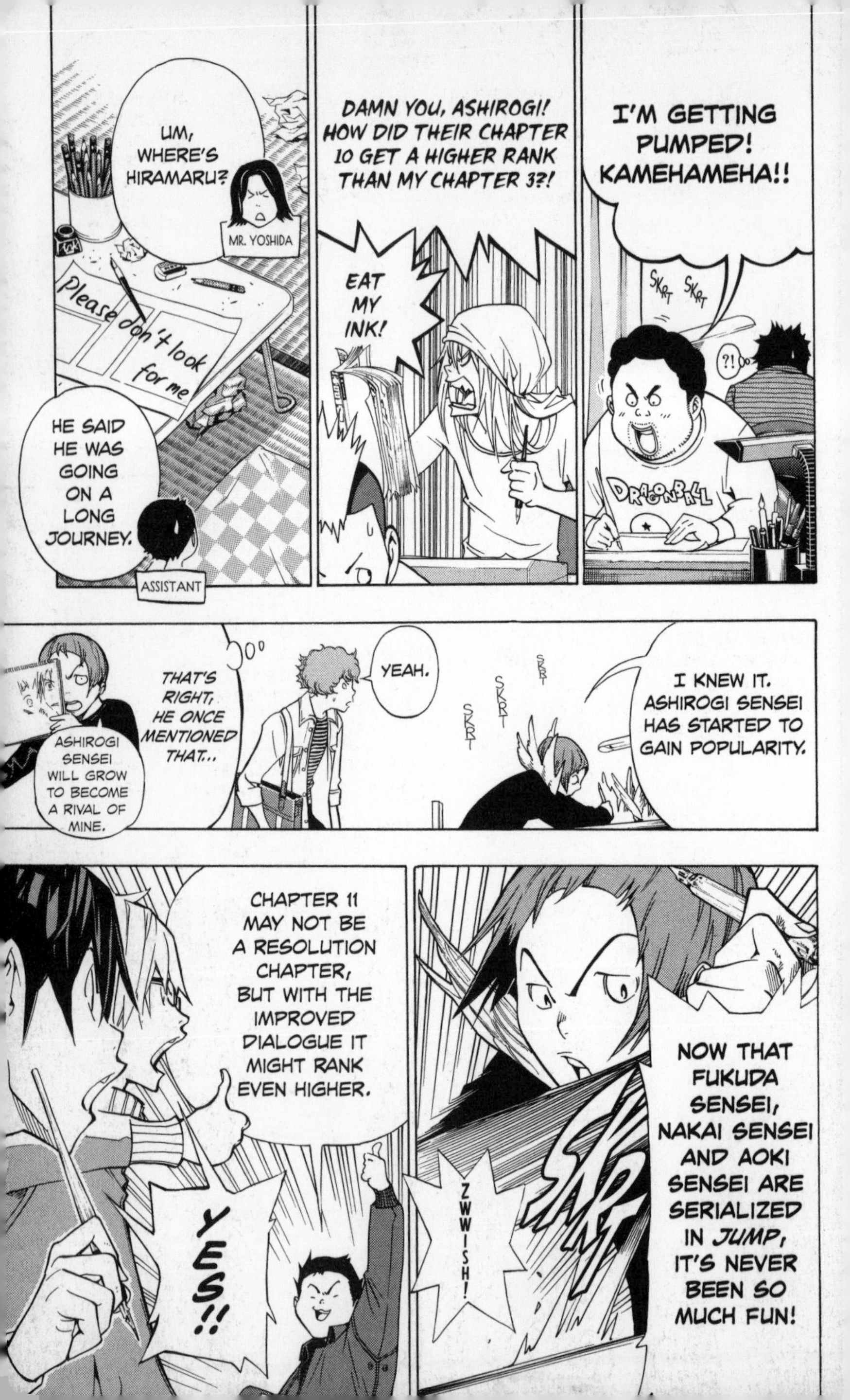

I'M GETTING PUMPED! KAMEHAMEHA!!
SKRT SKRT
?!
DRAGON BALL
DAMN YOU, ASHIROGI! HOW DID THEIR CHAPTER 10 GET A HIGHER RANK THAN MY CHAPTER 3?!
EAT MY INK!
UM, WHERE'S HIRAMARU?
MR. YOSHIDA
Please don't look for me
HE SAID HE WAS GOING ON A LONG JOURNEY.
ASSISTANT
I KNEW IT. ASHIROGI SENSEI HAS STARTED TO GAIN POPULARITY.
SKRT SKRT SKRT
YEAH.
THAT'S RIGHT, HE ONCE MENTIONED THAT...
ASHIROGI SENSEI WILL GROW TO BECOME A RIVAL OF MINE.
NOW THAT FUKUDA SENSEI, NAKAI SENSEI AND AOKI SENSEI ARE SERIALIZED IN *JUMP*, IT'S NEVER BEEN SO MUCH FUN!
ZWWISH!
CHAPTER 11 MAY NOT BE A RESOLUTION CHAPTER, BUT WITH THE IMPROVED DIALOGUE IT MIGHT RANK EVEN HIGHER.
YES!!

OHBA'S STORYBOARD

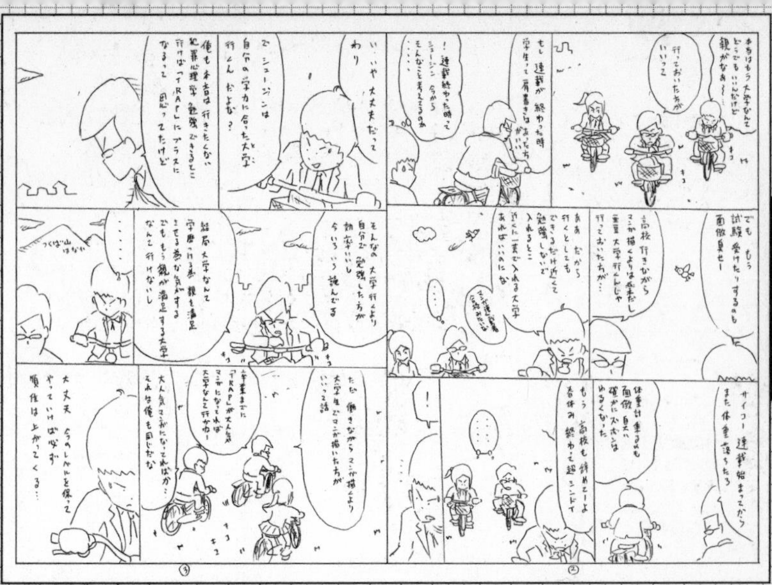
本当はもう大学なんてどうでもいいんだけど親がなぁ～
行っておいたほうがいいって
もし連載が終わった時学生って肩書きはあったほうがいい
!連載終わった時てシュージン今からそんなこと考えてるのか
でももう試験受けたりするのも面倒臭せー
……
サイコー連載始まってからまた体重落ちたろ
……
!
いいや大丈夫だって
わり
でシュージンは自分の学力に合った大学行くんだよな?
俺も本音は行きたくない 犯罪心理学勉強できるとこ行けば「TRAP」にプラスになるって思ってたけど
そんなの大学行くより自分で勉強した方が効率いいし今いろいろ読んでる
……
結局大学なんて学歴つける為親を満足させる為な気がする でももう親が満足する大学なんて行けないし
ただ働きながらマンガ描くより大学生でマンガ描いた方がいいって話
卒業までに「TRAP」が大人気マンガになってれば大学なんて行かねー
大人気マンガになってればか… それは俺も同じだな
大丈夫 今のレベルを保ってやっていけば必ず順位は上がってくる…

OBATA'S STORYBOARD

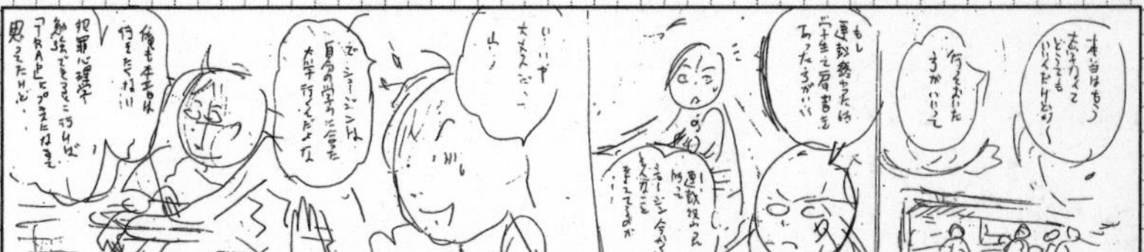
行っておいたほうがいいって
でももう試験受けたりするのも面倒臭せー
……
いいや大丈夫だって
でシュージンは自分の学力に合った大学行くんだよな
……
大丈夫 今のレベルを保ってやっていけば必ず順位は上がってくる…

COMPLETE!

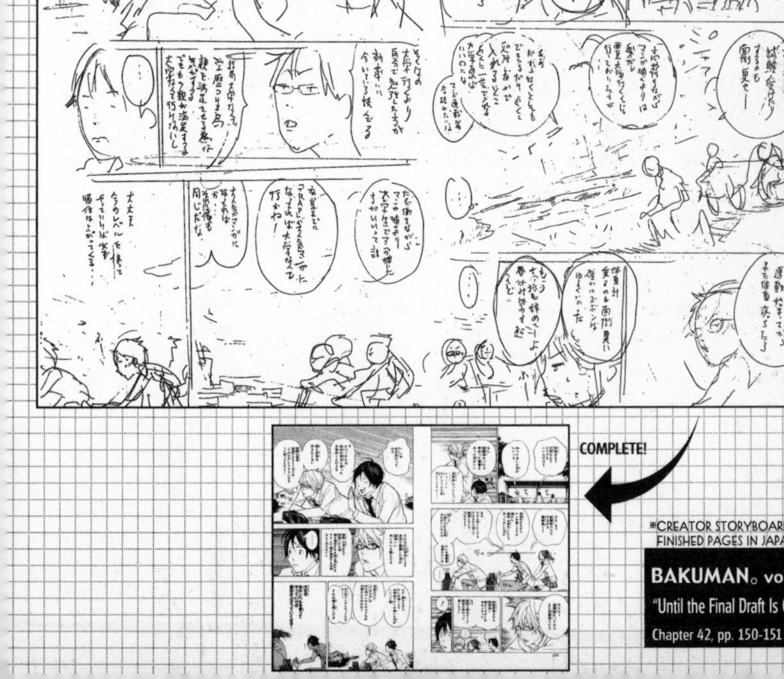

*CREATOR STORYBOARDS AND FINISHED PAGES IN JAPANESE

BAKUMAN。 vol.5

"Until the Final Draft Is Complete"

Chapter 42, pp. 150-151

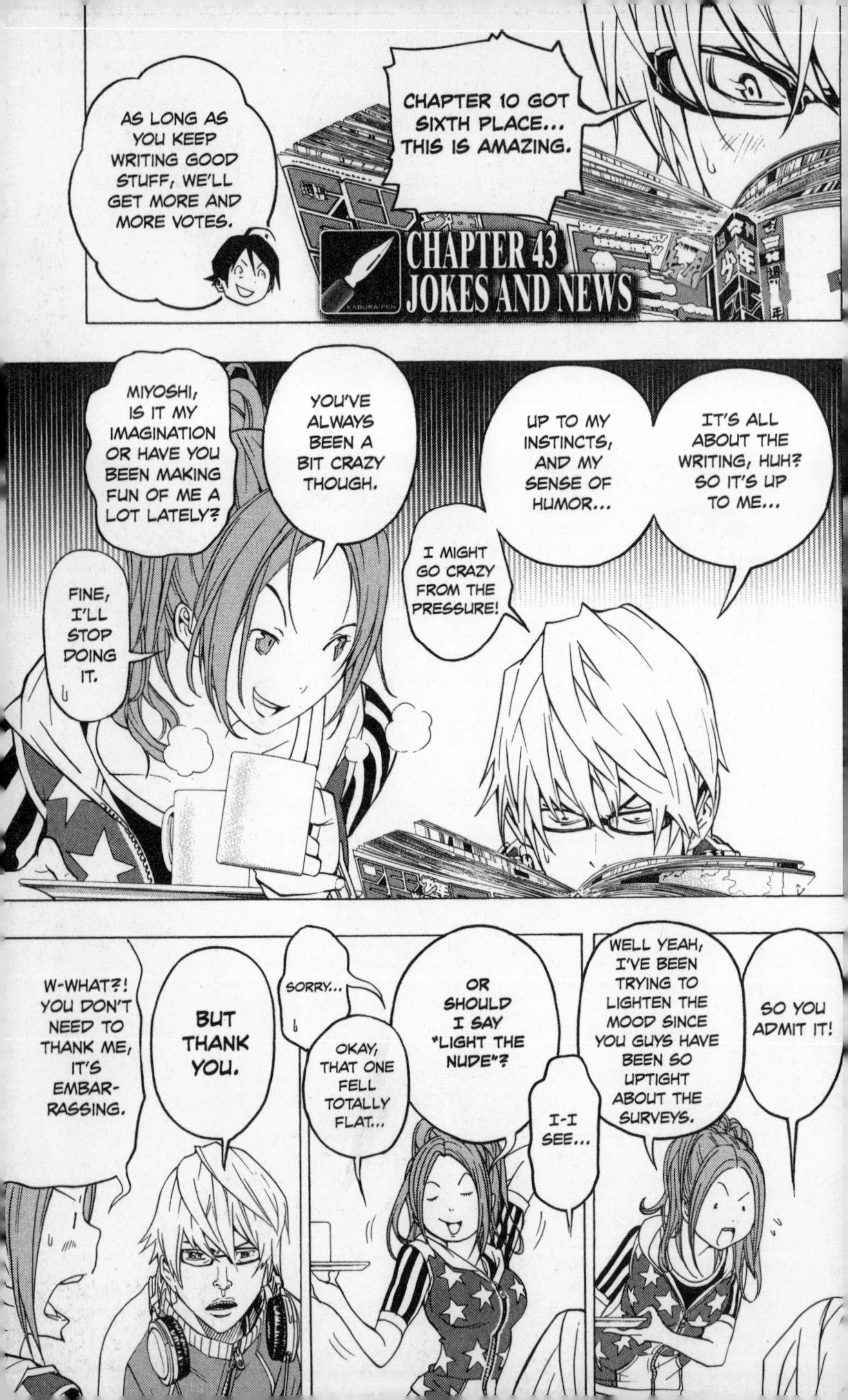
CHAPTER 10 GOT SIXTH PLACE... THIS IS AMAZING.
AS LONG AS YOU KEEP WRITING GOOD STUFF, WE'LL GET MORE AND MORE VOTES.
CHAPTER 43 JOKES AND NEWS
IT'S ALL ABOUT THE WRITING, HUH? SO IT'S UP TO ME...
UP TO MY INSTINCTS, AND MY SENSE OF HUMOR...
I MIGHT GO CRAZY FROM THE PRESSURE!
YOU'VE ALWAYS BEEN A BIT CRAZY THOUGH.
MIYOSHI, IS IT MY IMAGINATION OR HAVE YOU BEEN MAKING FUN OF ME A LOT LATELY?
FINE, I'LL STOP DOING IT.
SO YOU ADMIT IT!
WELL YEAH, I'VE BEEN TRYING TO LIGHTEN THE MOOD SINCE YOU GUYS HAVE BEEN SO UPTIGHT ABOUT THE SURVEYS.
I-I SEE...
OR SHOULD I SAY "LIGHT THE NUDE"?
OKAY, THAT ONE FELL TOTALLY FLAT...
SORRY...
BUT THANK YOU.
W-WHAT?! YOU DON'T NEED TO THANK ME, IT'S EMBARRASSING.

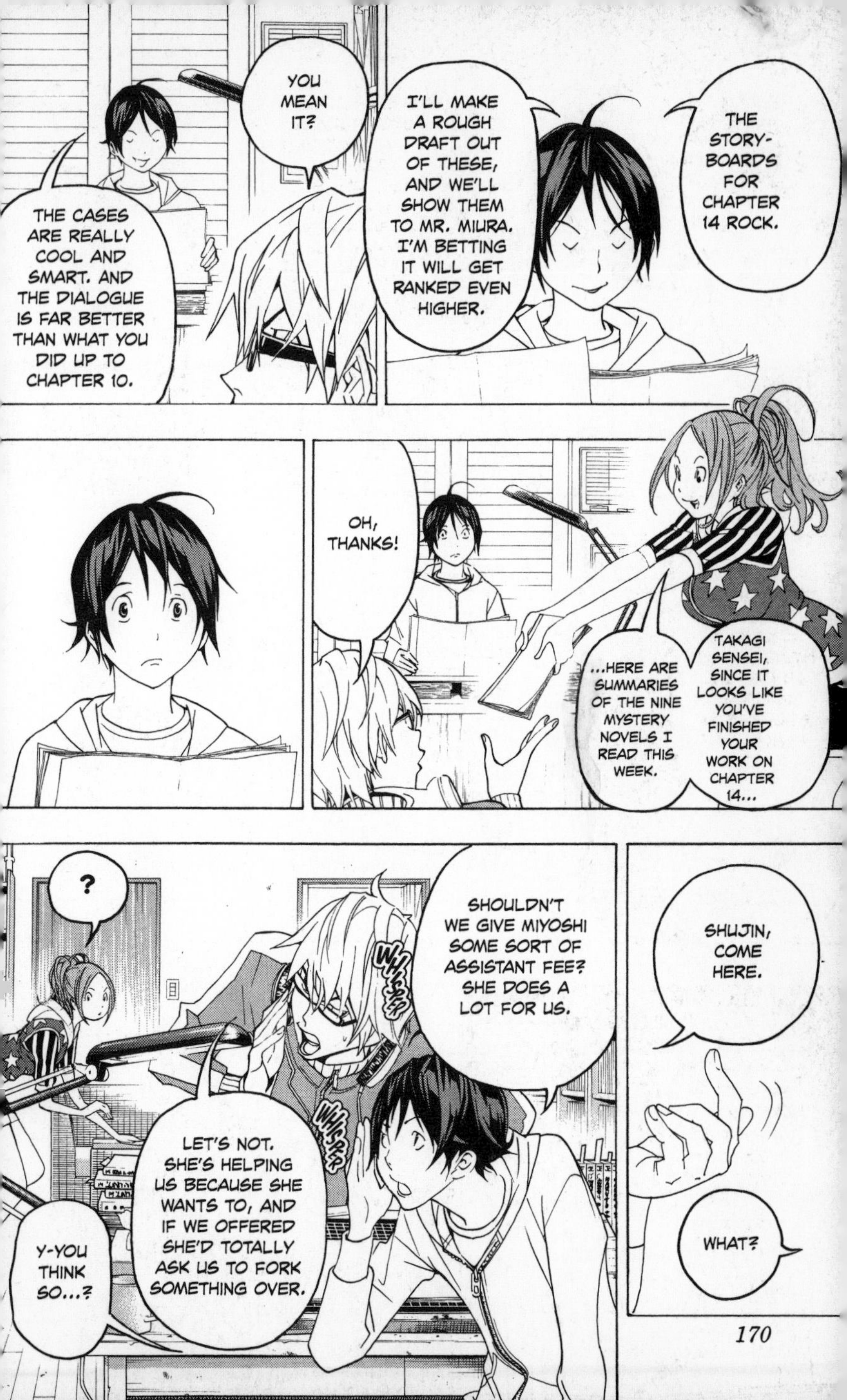
THE STORY-BOARDS FOR CHAPTER 14 ROCK.
I'LL MAKE A ROUGH DRAFT OUT OF THESE, AND WE'LL SHOW THEM TO MR. MIURA. I'M BETTING IT WILL GET RANKED EVEN HIGHER.
YOU MEAN IT?
THE CASES ARE REALLY COOL AND SMART. AND THE DIALOGUE IS FAR BETTER THAN WHAT YOU DID UP TO CHAPTER 10.
TAKAGI SENSEI, SINCE IT LOOKS LIKE YOU'VE FINISHED YOUR WORK ON CHAPTER 14...
...HERE ARE SUMMARIES OF THE NINE MYSTERY NOVELS I READ THIS WEEK.
OH, THANKS!
SHUJIN, COME HERE.
WHAT?
SHOULDN'T WE GIVE MIYOSHI SOME SORT OF ASSISTANT FEE? SHE DOES A LOT FOR US.
WHISPER
WHISPER
?
LET'S NOT. SHE'S HELPING US BECAUSE SHE WANTS TO, AND IF WE OFFERED SHE'D TOTALLY ASK US TO FORK SOMETHING OVER.
Y-YOU THINK SO...?

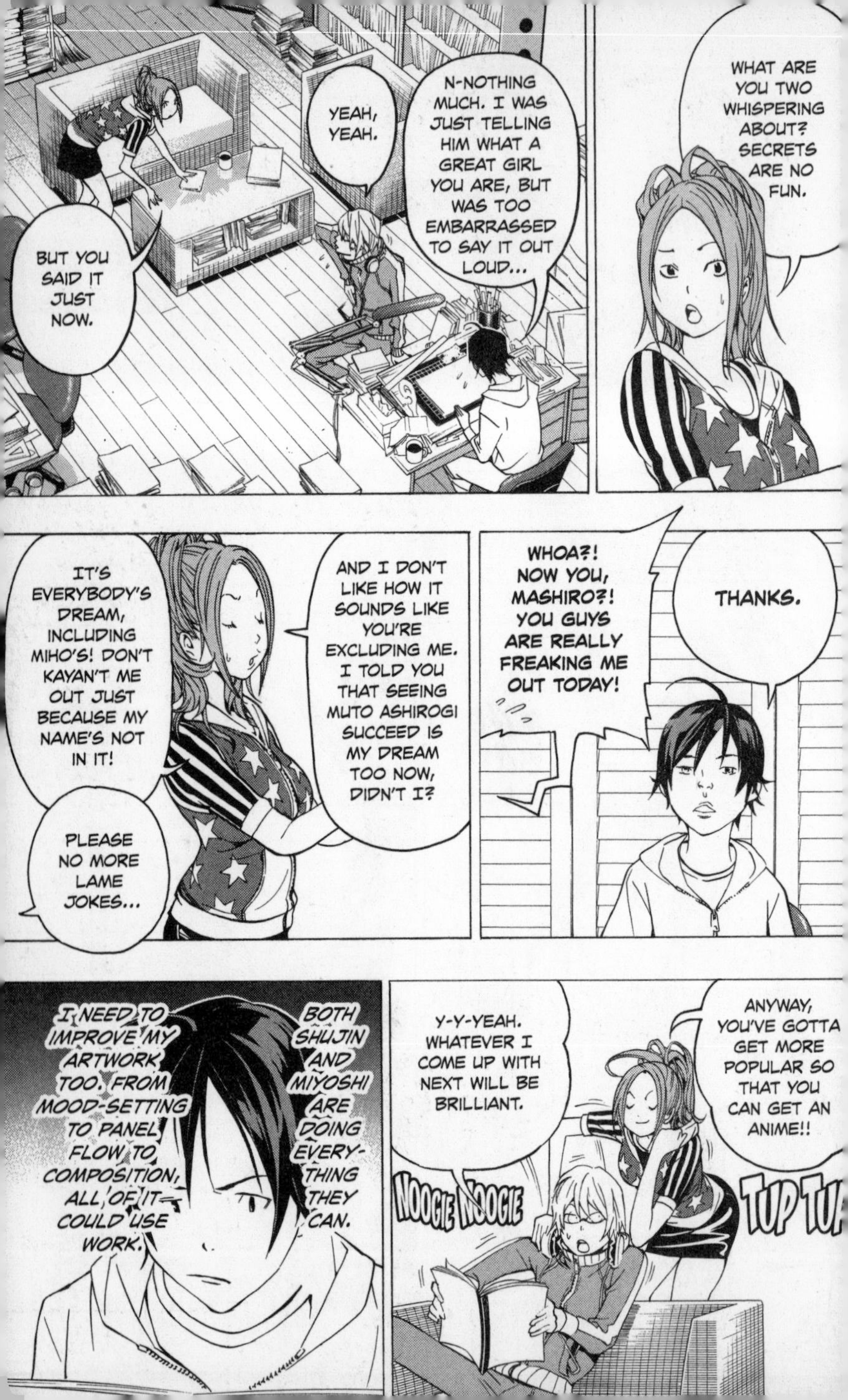
WHAT ARE YOU TWO WHISPERING ABOUT? SECRETS ARE NO FUN.
N-NOTHING MUCH. I WAS JUST TELLING HIM WHAT A GREAT GIRL YOU ARE, BUT WAS TOO EMBARRASSED TO SAY IT OUT LOUD...
YEAH, YEAH.
BUT YOU SAID IT JUST NOW.
THANKS.
WHOA?! NOW YOU, MASHIRO?! YOU GUYS ARE REALLY FREAKING ME OUT TODAY!
AND I DON'T LIKE HOW IT SOUNDS LIKE YOU'RE EXCLUDING ME. I TOLD YOU THAT SEEING MUTO ASHIROGI SUCCEED IS MY DREAM TOO NOW, DIDN'T I?
IT'S EVERYBODY'S DREAM, INCLUDING MIHO'S! DON'T KAYAN'T ME OUT JUST BECAUSE MY NAME'S NOT IN IT!
PLEASE NO MORE LAME JOKES...
ANYWAY, YOU'VE GOTTA GET MORE POPULAR SO THAT YOU CAN GET AN ANIME!!
TUP TU
Y-Y-YEAH. WHATEVER I COME UP WITH NEXT WILL BE BRILLIANT.
NOOGIE NOOGIE
BOTH SHUJIN AND MIYOSHI ARE DOING EVERYTHING THEY CAN.
I NEED TO IMPROVE MY ARTWORK TOO. FROM MOOD-SETTING TO PANEL FLOW TO COMPOSITION, ALL OF IT COULD USE WORK.

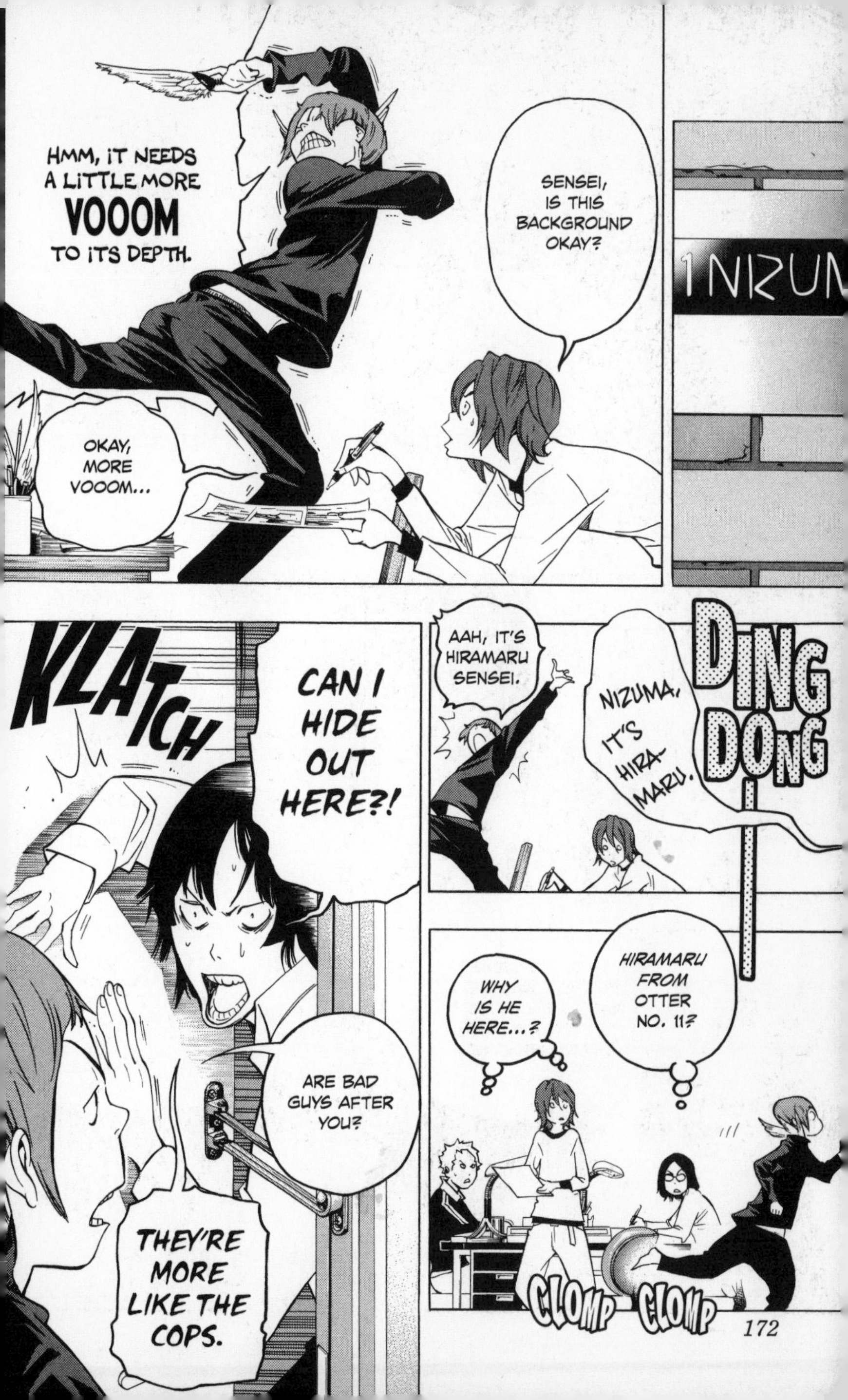
1 NIZUM
SENSEI, IS THIS BACKGROUND OKAY?
HMM, IT NEEDS A LITTLE MORE VOOOM TO ITS DEPTH.
OKAY, MORE VOOOM...
DING DONG
NIZUMA, IT'S HIRAMARU.
AAH, IT'S HIRAMARU SENSEI.
HIRAMARU FROM OTTER NO. 11?
WHY IS HE HERE...?
CLOMP CLOMP
KLATCH
CAN I HIDE OUT HERE?!
ARE BAD GUYS AFTER YOU?
THEY'RE MORE LIKE THE COPS.

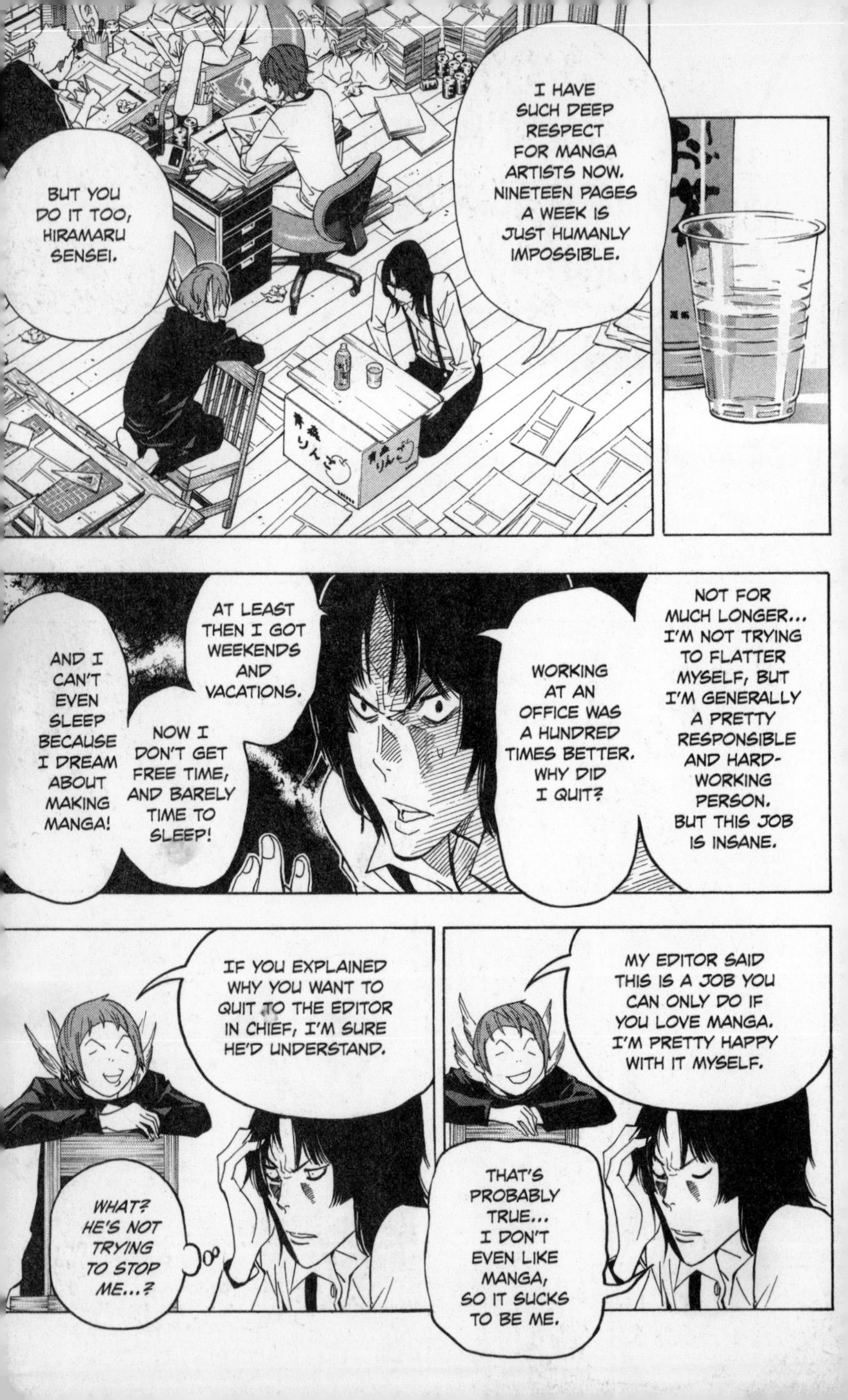
I HAVE SUCH DEEP RESPECT FOR MANGA ARTISTS NOW. NINETEEN PAGES A WEEK IS JUST HUMANLY IMPOSSIBLE.
BUT YOU DO IT TOO, HIRAMARU SENSEI.
NOT FOR MUCH LONGER... I'M NOT TRYING TO FLATTER MYSELF, BUT I'M GENERALLY A PRETTY RESPONSIBLE AND HARD-WORKING PERSON. BUT THIS JOB IS INSANE.
WORKING AT AN OFFICE WAS A HUNDRED TIMES BETTER. WHY DID I QUIT?
AT LEAST THEN I GOT WEEKENDS AND VACATIONS.
NOW I DON'T GET FREE TIME, AND BARELY TIME TO SLEEP!
AND I CAN'T EVEN SLEEP BECAUSE I DREAM ABOUT MAKING MANGA!
MY EDITOR SAID THIS IS A JOB YOU CAN ONLY DO IF YOU LOVE MANGA. I'M PRETTY HAPPY WITH IT MYSELF.
THAT'S PROBABLY TRUE... I DON'T EVEN LIKE MANGA, SO IT SUCKS TO BE ME.
IF YOU EXPLAINED WHY YOU WANT TO QUIT TO THE EDITOR IN CHIEF, I'M SURE HE'D UNDERSTAND.
WHAT? HE'S NOT TRYING TO STOP ME...?

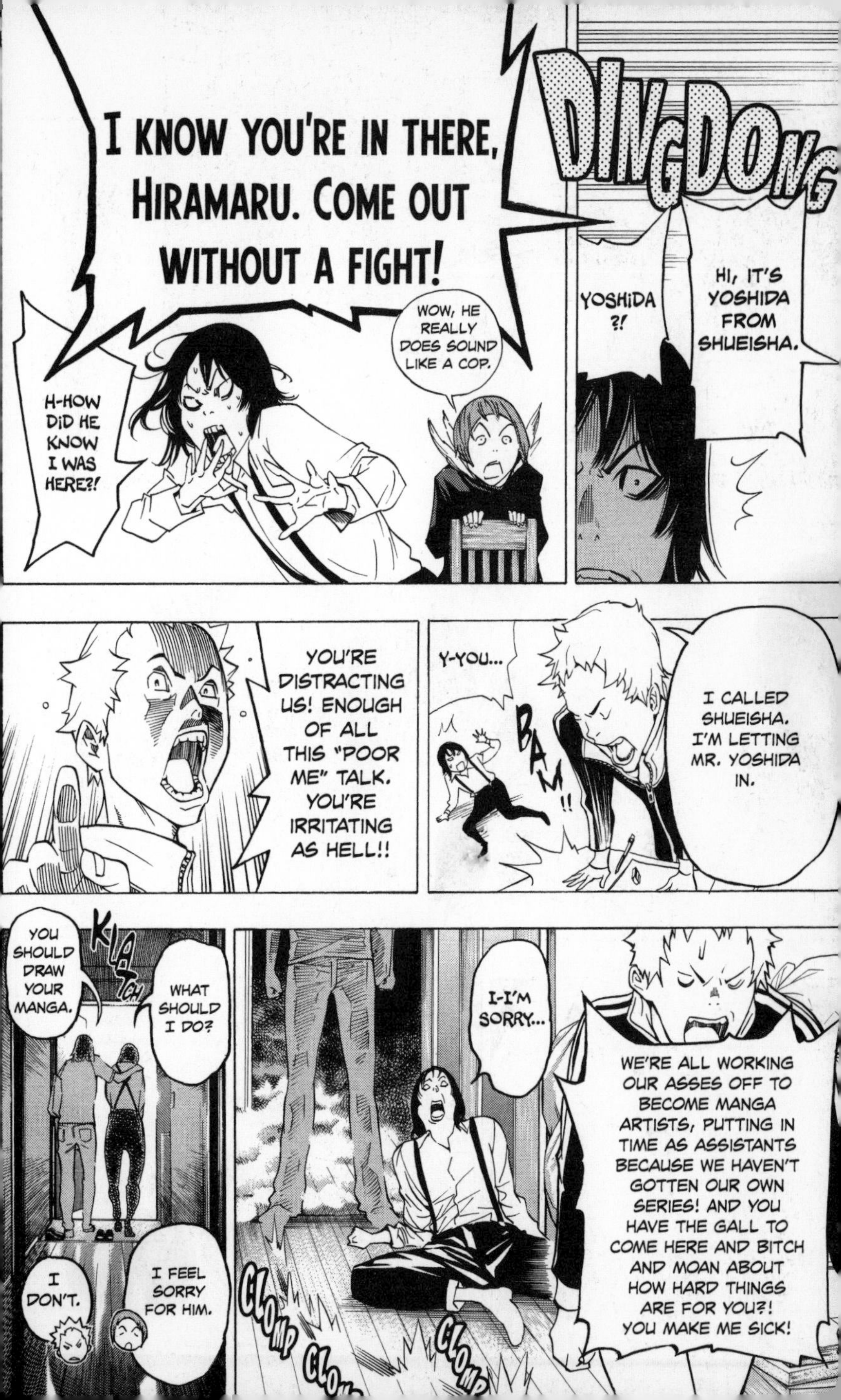
DINGDONG
HI, IT'S YOSHIDA FROM SHUEISHA.
YOSHIDA?!
I KNOW YOU'RE IN THERE, HIRAMARU. COME OUT WITHOUT A FIGHT!
WOW, HE REALLY DOES SOUND LIKE A COP.
H-HOW DID HE KNOW I WAS HERE?!
I CALLED SHUEISHA. I'M LETTING MR. YOSHIDA IN.
BAM!!
Y-YOU...
YOU'RE DISTRACTING US! ENOUGH OF ALL THIS "POOR ME" TALK. YOU'RE IRRITATING AS HELL!!
WE'RE ALL WORKING OUR ASSES OFF TO BECOME MANGA ARTISTS, PUTTING IN TIME AS ASSISTANTS BECAUSE WE HAVEN'T GOTTEN OUR OWN SERIES! AND YOU HAVE THE GALL TO COME HERE AND BITCH AND MOAN ABOUT HOW HARD THINGS ARE FOR YOU?! YOU MAKE ME SICK!
I-I'M SORRY...
CLOMP
CLOMP
CLOMP
KLATCH
WHAT SHOULD I DO?
YOU SHOULD DRAW YOUR MANGA.
I FEEL SORRY FOR HIM.
I DON'T.

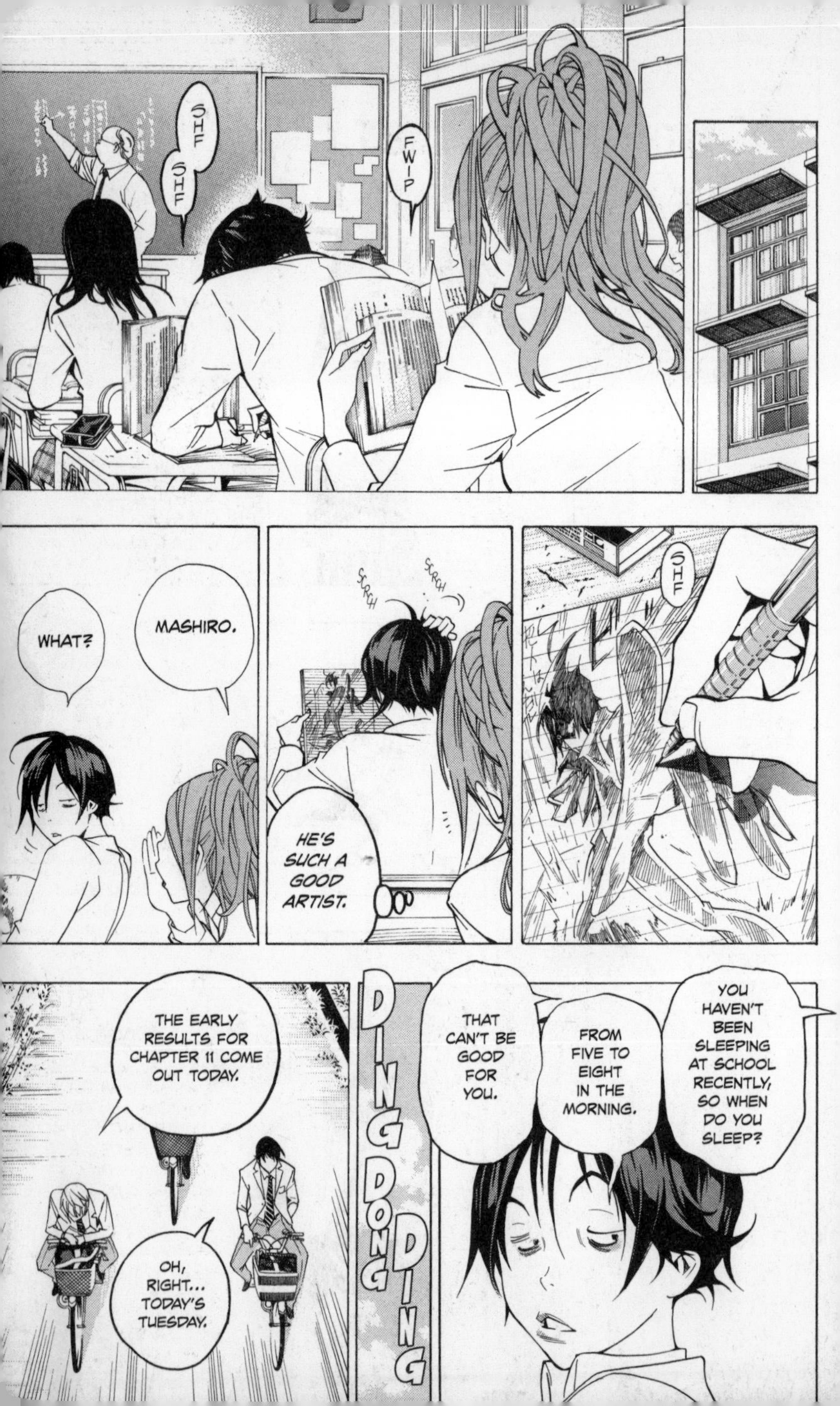
FWIP
SHF SHF
SHF
SCRCH SCRCH
HE'S SUCH A GOOD ARTIST.
MASHIRO.
WHAT?
YOU HAVEN'T BEEN SLEEPING AT SCHOOL RECENTLY, SO WHEN DO YOU SLEEP?
FROM FIVE TO EIGHT IN THE MORNING.
THAT CAN'T BE GOOD FOR YOU.
DING DONG DING
THE EARLY RESULTS FOR CHAPTER 11 COME OUT TODAY.
OH, RIGHT... TODAY'S TUESDAY.

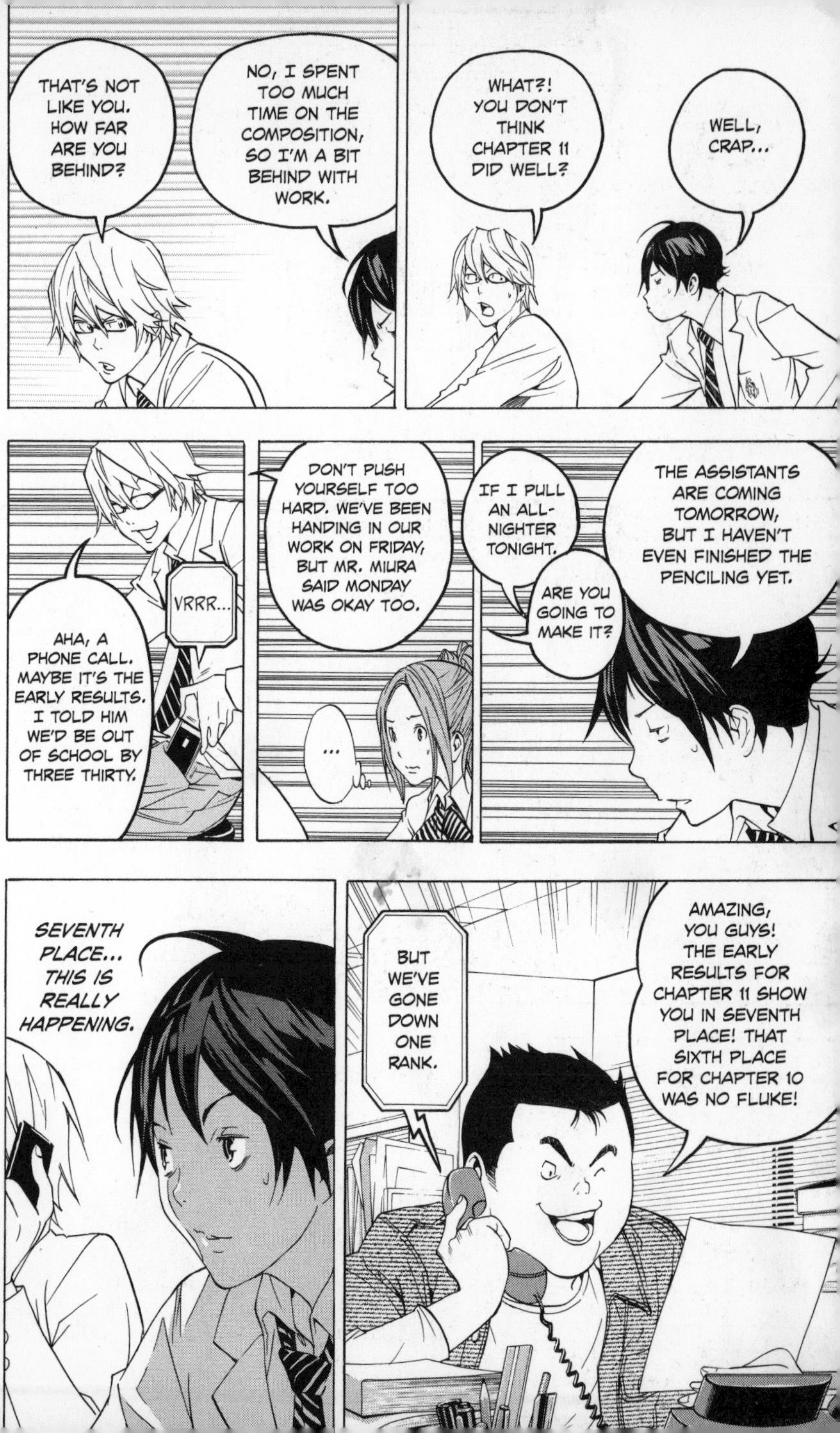
WELL, CRAP...
WHAT?! YOU DON'T THINK CHAPTER 11 DID WELL?
NO, I SPENT TOO MUCH TIME ON THE COMPOSITION, SO I'M A BIT BEHIND WITH WORK.
THAT'S NOT LIKE YOU. HOW FAR ARE YOU BEHIND?
THE ASSISTANTS ARE COMING TOMORROW, BUT I HAVEN'T EVEN FINISHED THE PENCILING YET.
IF I PULL AN ALL-NIGHTER TONIGHT.
ARE YOU GOING TO MAKE IT?
DON'T PUSH YOURSELF TOO HARD. WE'VE BEEN HANDING IN OUR WORK ON FRIDAY, BUT MR. MIURA SAID MONDAY WAS OKAY TOO.
...
VRRR...
AHA, A PHONE CALL. MAYBE IT'S THE EARLY RESULTS. I TOLD HIM WE'D BE OUT OF SCHOOL BY THREE THIRTY.
AMAZING, YOU GUYS! THE EARLY RESULTS FOR CHAPTER 11 SHOW YOU IN SEVENTH PLACE! THAT SIXTH PLACE FOR CHAPTER 10 WAS NO FLUKE!
BUT WE'VE GONE DOWN ONE RANK.
SEVENTH PLACE... THIS IS REALLY HAPPENING.

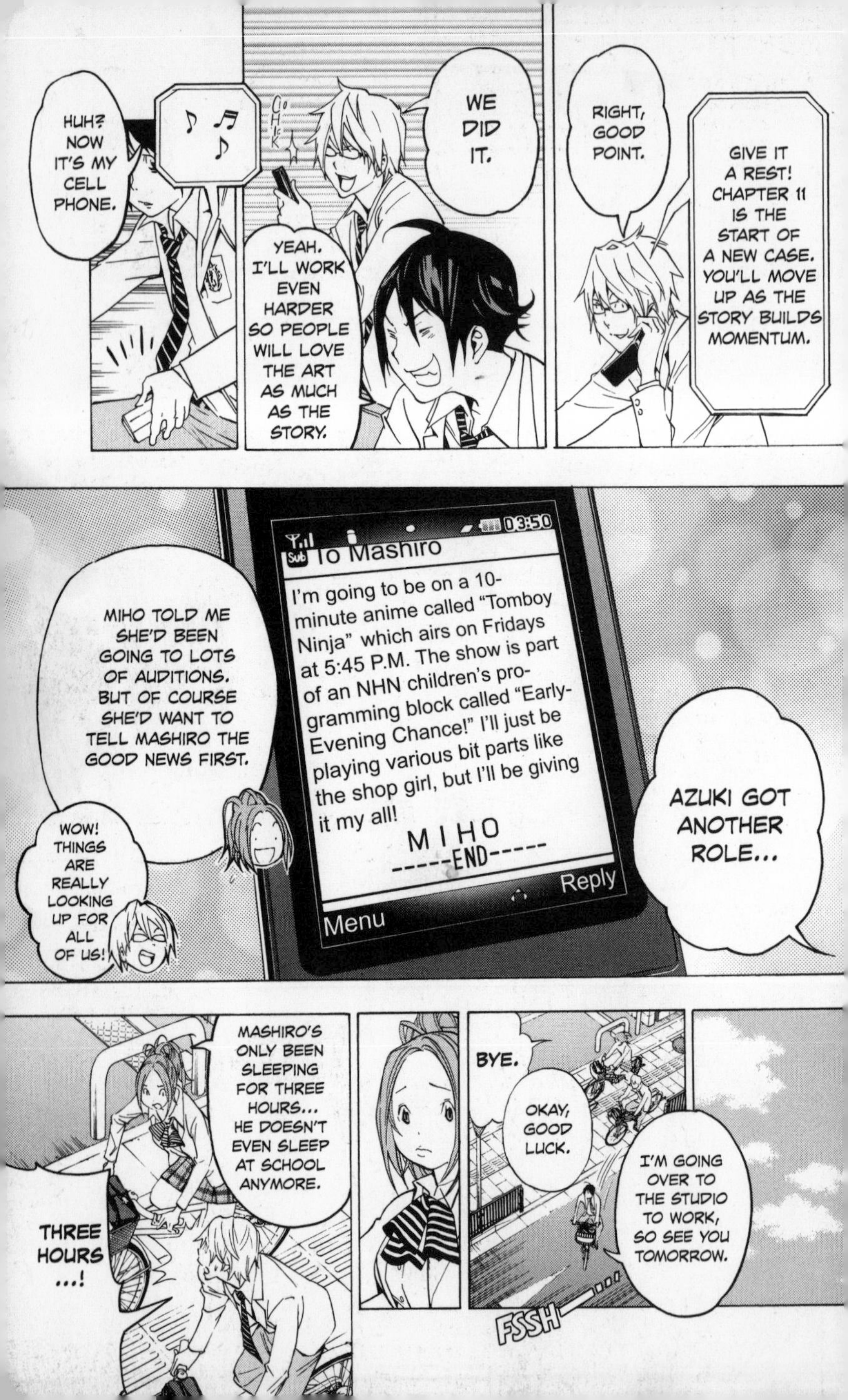

GIVE IT A REST! CHAPTER 11 IS THE START OF A NEW CASE. YOU'LL MOVE UP AS THE STORY BUILDS MOMENTUM.
RIGHT, GOOD POINT.
WE DID IT.
YEAH. I'LL WORK EVEN HARDER SO PEOPLE WILL LOVE THE ART AS MUCH AS THE STORY.
HUH? NOW IT'S MY CELL PHONE.
AZUKI GOT ANOTHER ROLE...
03:50
To Mashiro
I'm going to be on a 10-minute anime called "Tomboy Ninja" which airs on Fridays at 5:45 P.M. The show is part of an NHN children's programming block called "Early-Evening Chance!" I'll just be playing various bit parts like the shop girl, but I'll be giving it my all!
MIHO
-----END-----
Reply
Menu
MIHO TOLD ME SHE'D BEEN GOING TO LOTS OF AUDITIONS. BUT OF COURSE SHE'D WANT TO TELL MASHIRO THE GOOD NEWS FIRST.
WOW! THINGS ARE REALLY LOOKING UP FOR ALL OF US!
I'M GOING OVER TO THE STUDIO TO WORK, SO SEE YOU TOMORROW.
OKAY, GOOD LUCK.
BYE.
FSSH
MASHIRO'S ONLY BEEN SLEEPING FOR THREE HOURS... HE DOESN'T EVEN SLEEP AT SCHOOL ANYMORE.
THREE HOURS...!

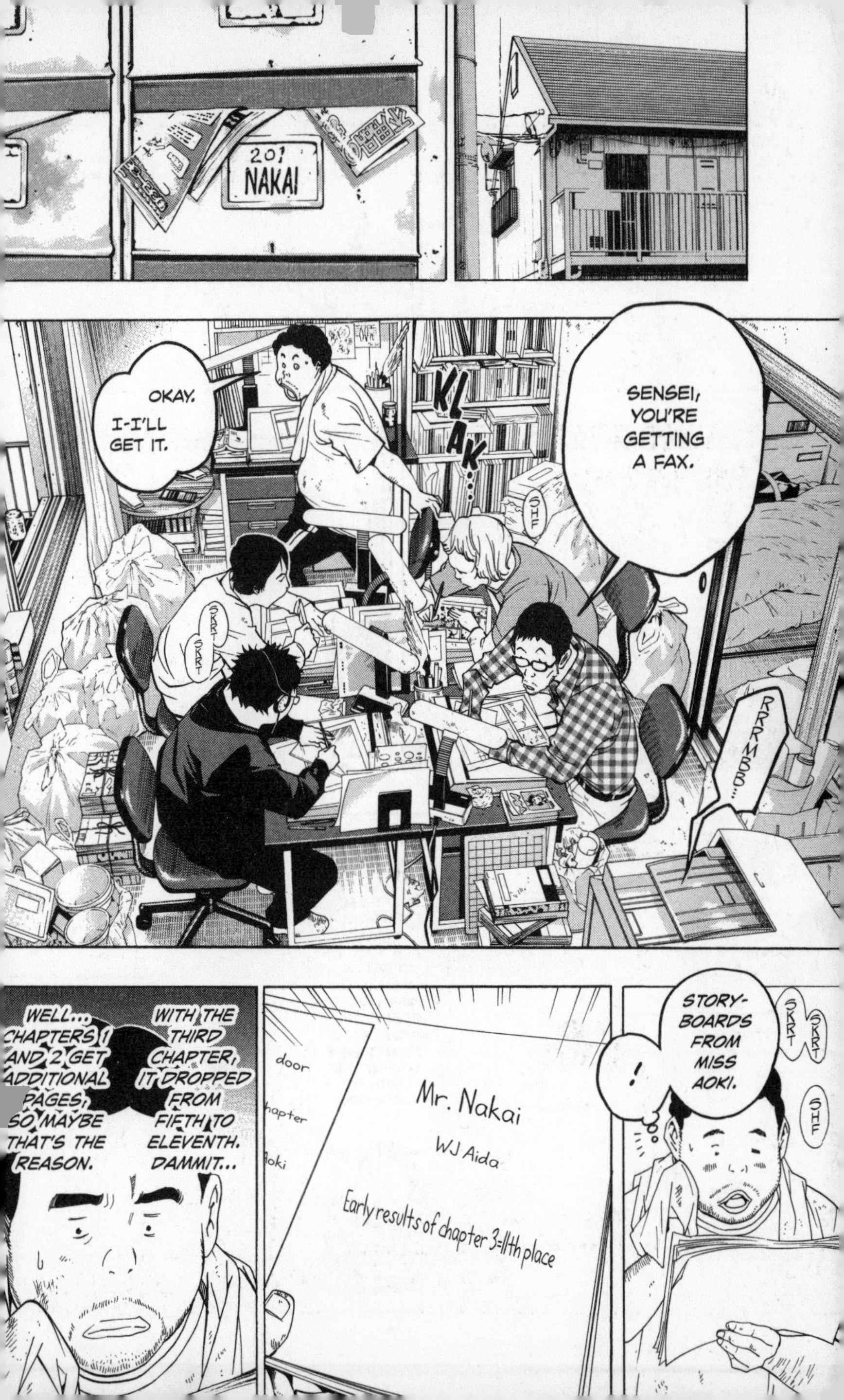
201 NAKAI
SENSEI, YOU'RE GETTING A FAX.
RRRMBB...
KLAK...
SHF
OKAY. I-I'LL GET IT.
SKRT SKRT
STORY-BOARDS FROM MISS AOKI.
SKRT SKRT
SHF
!
door
hapter
oki
Mr. Nakai
WJ Aida
Early results of chapter 3=11th place
WITH THE THIRD CHAPTER, IT DROPPED FROM FIFTH TO ELEVENTH. DAMMIT...
WELL... CHAPTERS 1 AND 2 GET ADDITIONAL PAGES, SO MAYBE THAT'S THE REASON.

READ THIS WAY

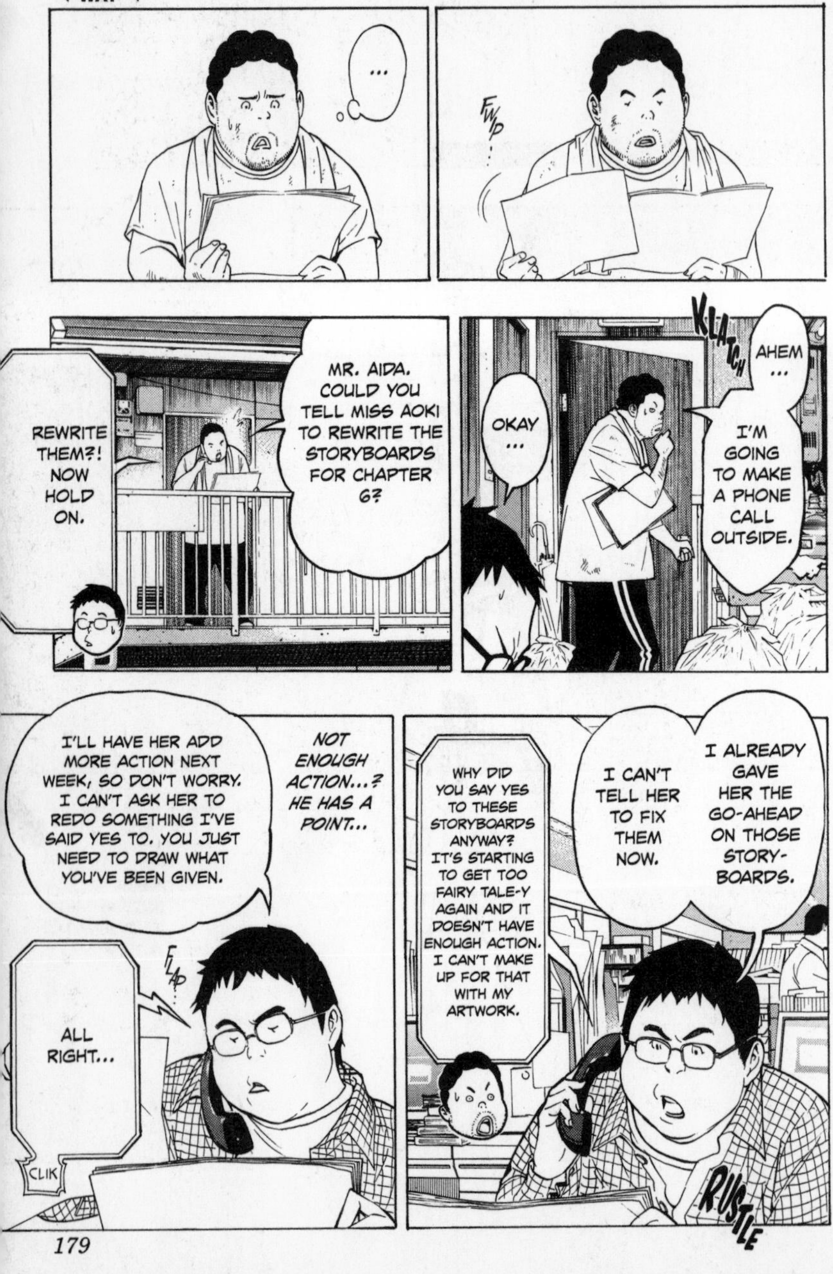
FWIP
...
K-LATCH
AHEM ...
I'M GOING TO MAKE A PHONE CALL OUTSIDE.
OKAY ...
MR. AIDA. COULD YOU TELL MISS AOKI TO REWRITE THE STORYBOARDS FOR CHAPTER 6?
REWRITE THEM?! NOW HOLD ON.
I ALREADY GAVE HER THE GO-AHEAD ON THOSE STORY-BOARDS.
I CAN'T TELL HER TO FIX THEM NOW.
WHY DID YOU SAY YES TO THESE STORYBOARDS ANYWAY? IT'S STARTING TO GET TOO FAIRY TALE-Y AGAIN AND IT DOESN'T HAVE ENOUGH ACTION. I CAN'T MAKE UP FOR THAT WITH MY ARTWORK.
RUSTLE
NOT ENOUGH ACTION...? HE HAS A POINT...
I'LL HAVE HER ADD MORE ACTION NEXT WEEK, SO DON'T WORRY. I CAN'T ASK HER TO REDO SOMETHING I'VE SAID YES TO. YOU JUST NEED TO DRAW WHAT YOU'VE BEEN GIVEN.
FLAP
ALL RIGHT...
CLIK

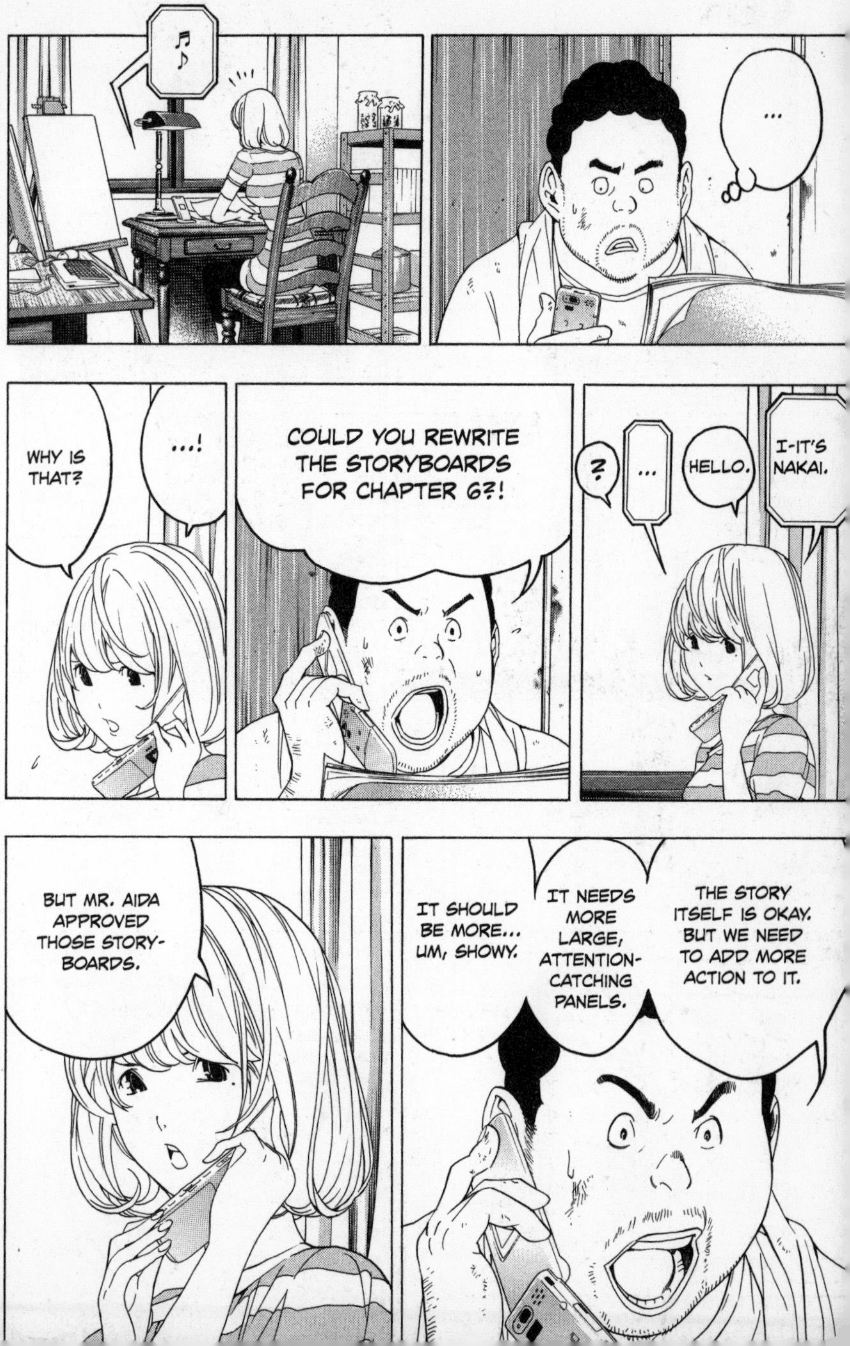
...
♪
I-IT'S NAKAI.
HELLO.
...
?
COULD YOU REWRITE THE STORYBOARDS FOR CHAPTER 6?!
...!
WHY IS THAT?
THE STORY ITSELF IS OKAY. BUT WE NEED TO ADD MORE ACTION TO IT.
IT NEEDS MORE LARGE, ATTENTION-CATCHING PANELS.
IT SHOULD BE MORE... UM, SHOWY.
BUT MR. AIDA APPROVED THOSE STORY-BOARDS.

READ THIS WAY

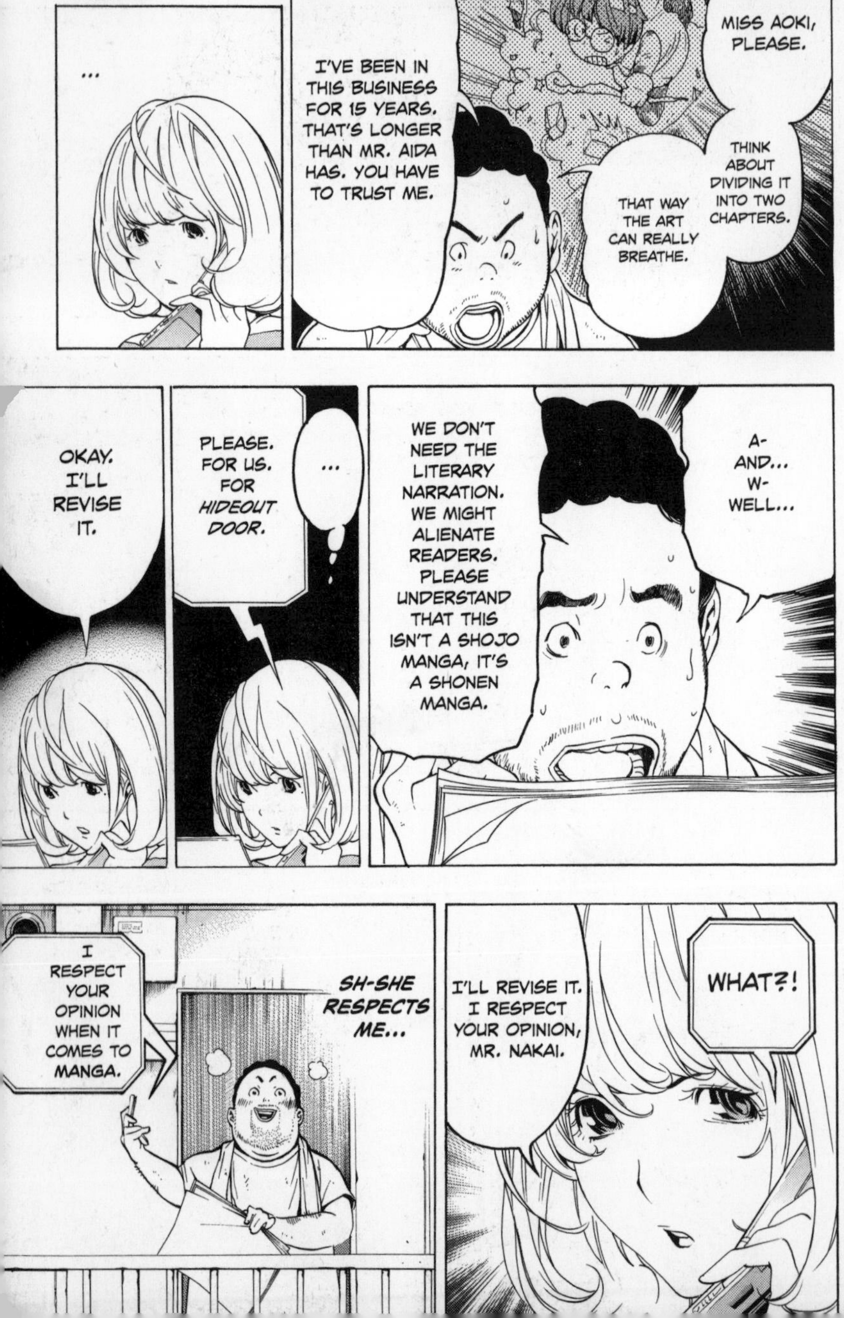

MISS AOKI, PLEASE.
THINK ABOUT DIVIDING IT INTO TWO CHAPTERS.
THAT WAY THE ART CAN REALLY BREATHE.
I'VE BEEN IN THIS BUSINESS FOR 15 YEARS. THAT'S LONGER THAN MR. AIDA HAS. YOU HAVE TO TRUST ME.
...
A- AND... W- WELL...
WE DON'T NEED THE LITERARY NARRATION. WE MIGHT ALIENATE READERS. PLEASE UNDERSTAND THAT THIS ISN'T A SHOJO MANGA, IT'S A SHONEN MANGA.
...
PLEASE. FOR US. FOR *HIDEOUT DOOR*.
OKAY. I'LL REVISE IT.
WHAT?!
I'LL REVISE IT. I RESPECT YOUR OPINION, MR. NAKAI.
SH-SHE RESPECTS ME...
I RESPECT YOUR OPINION WHEN IT COMES TO MANGA.

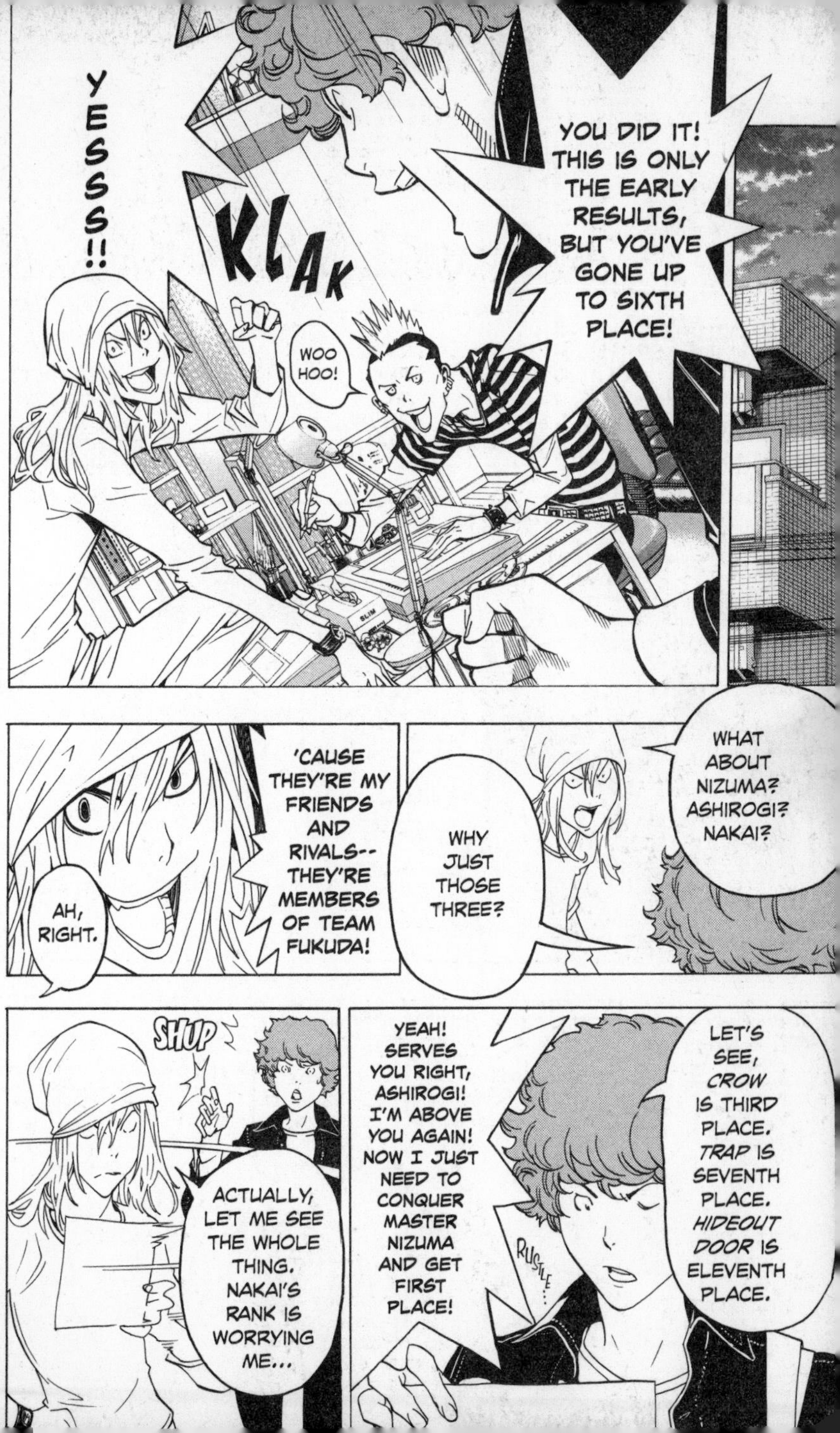
YOU DID IT! THIS IS ONLY THE EARLY RESULTS, BUT YOU'VE GONE UP TO SIXTH PLACE!
KLAK
YESSS!!
WOO HOO!
WHAT ABOUT NIZUMA? ASHIROGI? NAKAI?
WHY JUST THOSE THREE?
'CAUSE THEY'RE MY FRIENDS AND RIVALS--THEY'RE MEMBERS OF TEAM FUKUDA!
AH, RIGHT.
LET'S SEE, *CROW* IS THIRD PLACE. *TRAP* IS SEVENTH PLACE. *HIDEOUT DOOR* IS ELEVENTH PLACE.
YEAH! SERVES YOU RIGHT, ASHIROGI! I'M ABOVE YOU AGAIN! NOW I JUST NEED TO CONQUER MASTER NIZUMA AND GET FIRST PLACE!
RUSTLE...
SHUP
ACTUALLY, LET ME SEE THE WHOLE THING. NAKAI'S RANK IS WORRYING ME...

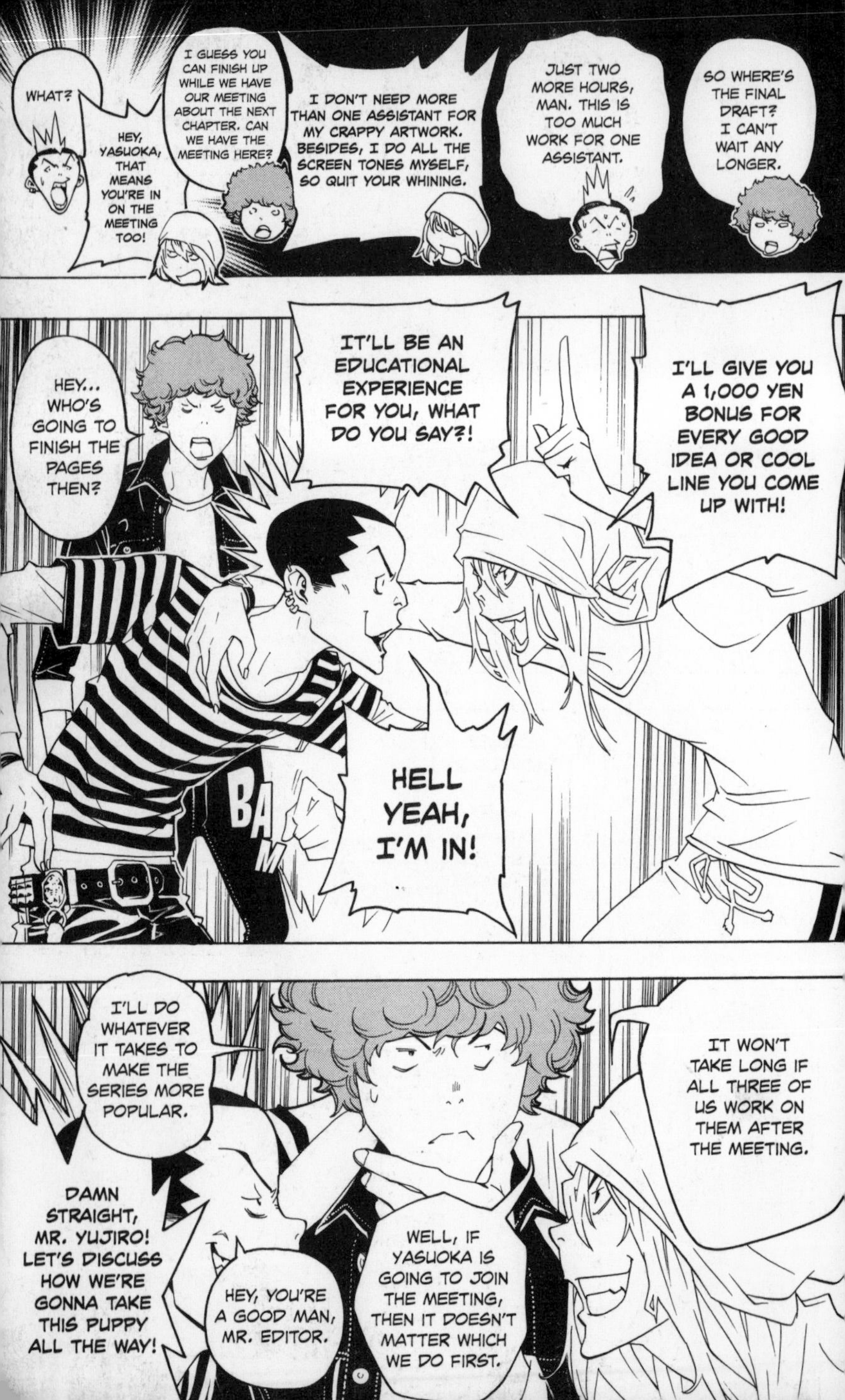
SO WHERE'S THE FINAL DRAFT? I CAN'T WAIT ANY LONGER.
JUST TWO MORE HOURS, MAN. THIS IS TOO MUCH WORK FOR ONE ASSISTANT.
I DON'T NEED MORE THAN ONE ASSISTANT FOR MY CRAPPY ARTWORK. BESIDES, I DO ALL THE SCREEN TONES MYSELF, SO QUIT YOUR WHINING.
I GUESS YOU CAN FINISH UP WHILE WE HAVE OUR MEETING ABOUT THE NEXT CHAPTER. CAN WE HAVE THE MEETING HERE?
HEY, YASUOKA, THAT MEANS YOU'RE IN ON THE MEETING TOO!
WHAT?
I'LL GIVE YOU A 1,000 YEN BONUS FOR EVERY GOOD IDEA OR COOL LINE YOU COME UP WITH!
IT'LL BE AN EDUCATIONAL EXPERIENCE FOR YOU, WHAT DO YOU SAY?!
HELL YEAH, I'M IN!
BAM
HEY... WHO'S GOING TO FINISH THE PAGES THEN?
IT WON'T TAKE LONG IF ALL THREE OF US WORK ON THEM AFTER THE MEETING.
WELL, IF YASUOKA IS GOING TO JOIN THE MEETING, THEN IT DOESN'T MATTER WHICH WE DO FIRST.
HEY, YOU'RE A GOOD MAN, MR. EDITOR.
I'LL DO WHATEVER IT TAKES TO MAKE THE SERIES MORE POPULAR.
DAMN STRAIGHT, MR. YUJIRO! LET'S DISCUSS HOW WE'RE GONNA TAKE THIS PUPPY ALL THE WAY!

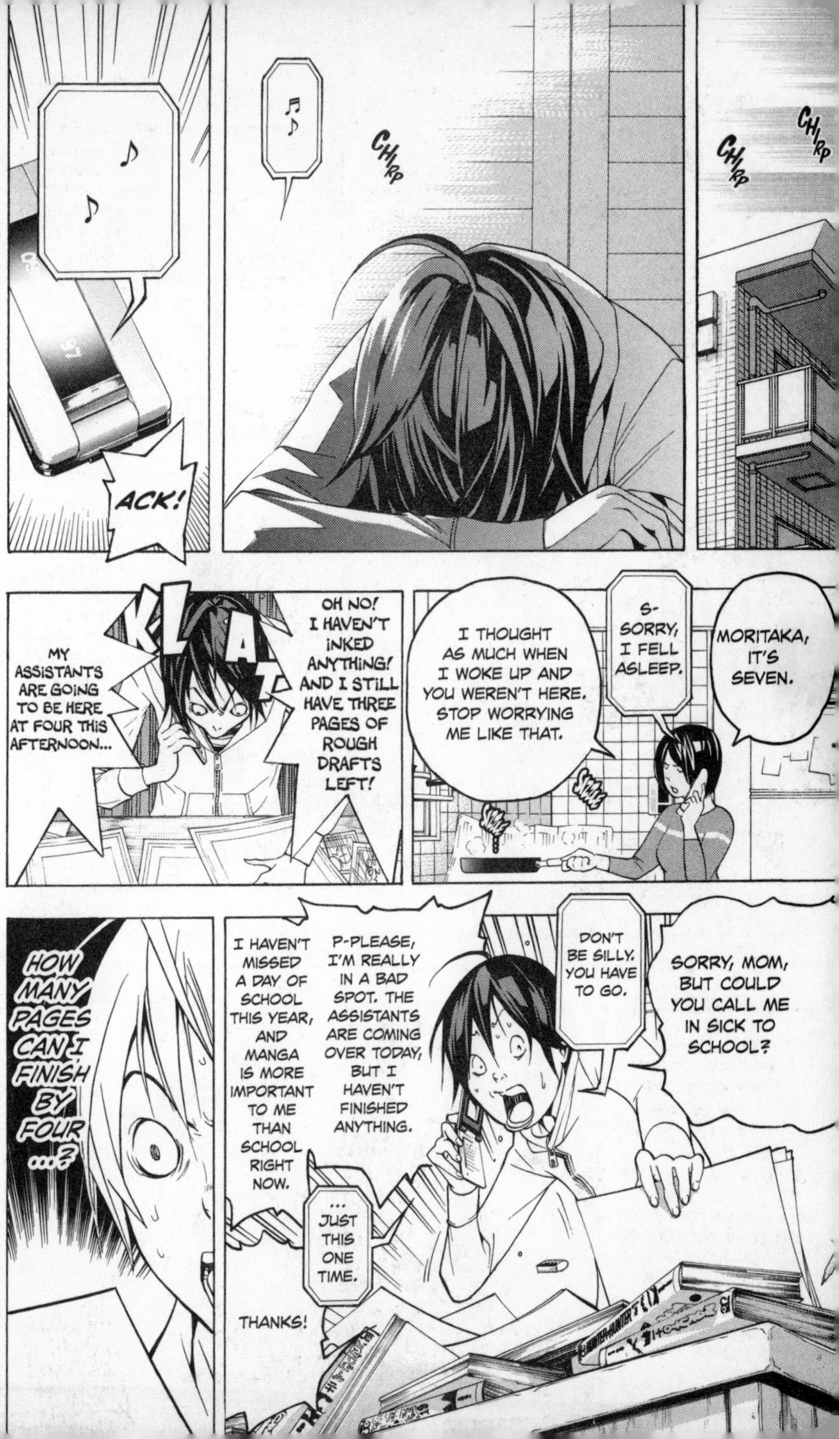
CHIRP
CHIRP
♬ ♪
CHIRP
♪ ♪
ACK!
MORITAKA, IT'S SEVEN.
S-SORRY, I FELL ASLEEP.
I THOUGHT AS MUCH WHEN I WOKE UP AND YOU WEREN'T HERE. STOP WORRYING ME LIKE THAT.
OH NO! I HAVEN'T INKED ANYTHING! AND I STILL HAVE THREE PAGES OF ROUGH DRAFTS LEFT!
KLAT
MY ASSISTANTS ARE GOING TO BE HERE AT FOUR THIS AFTERNOON...
SORRY, MOM, BUT COULD YOU CALL ME IN SICK TO SCHOOL?
DON'T BE SILLY. YOU HAVE TO GO.
P-PLEASE, I'M REALLY IN A BAD SPOT. THE ASSISTANTS ARE COMING OVER TODAY, BUT I HAVEN'T FINISHED ANYTHING.
I HAVEN'T MISSED A DAY OF SCHOOL THIS YEAR, AND MANGA IS MORE IMPORTANT TO ME THAN SCHOOL RIGHT NOW.
...JUST THIS ONE TIME.
THANKS!
HOW MANY PAGES CAN I FINISH BY FOUR...?

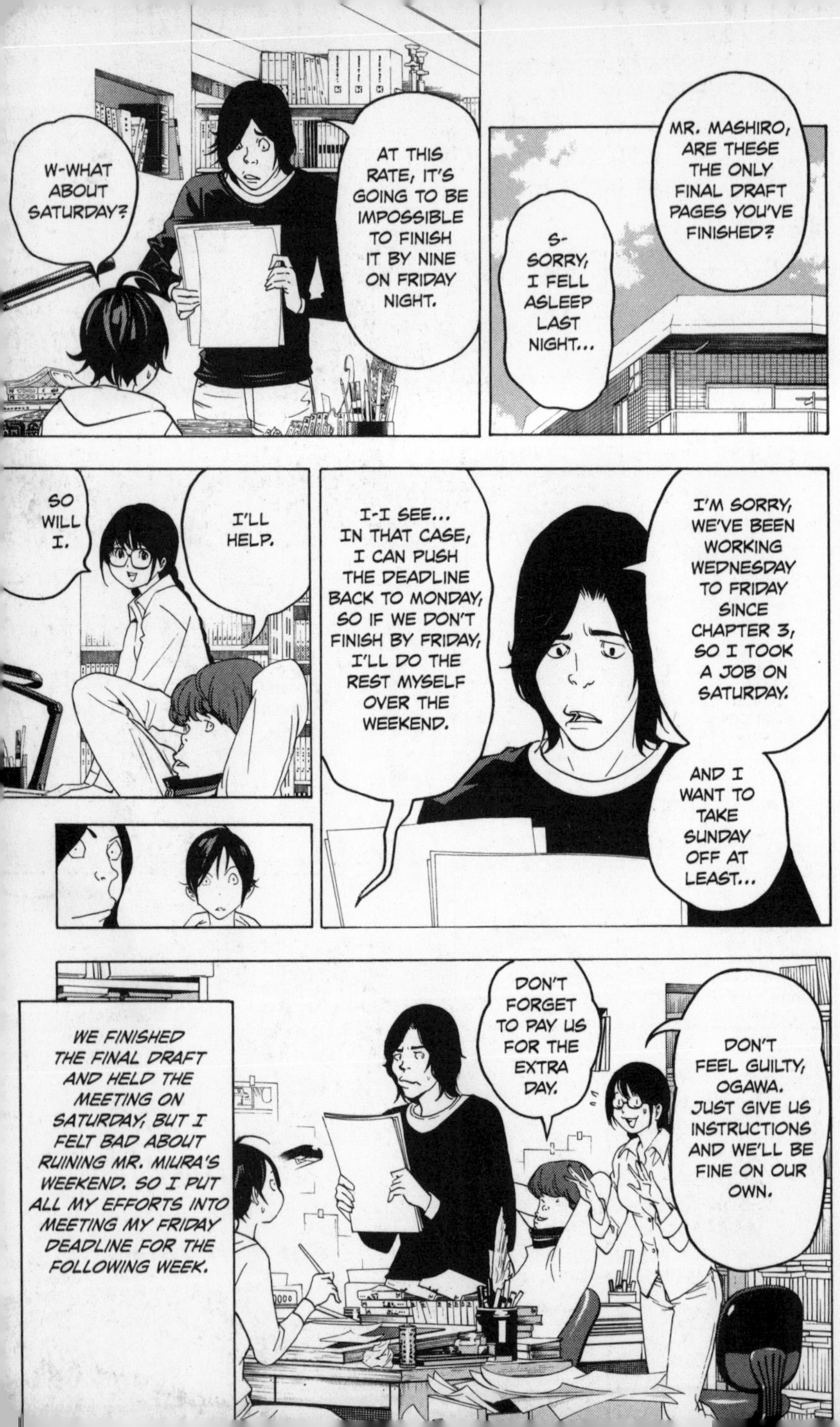
MR. MASHIRO, ARE THESE THE ONLY FINAL DRAFT PAGES YOU'VE FINISHED?
S-SORRY, I FELL ASLEEP LAST NIGHT...
AT THIS RATE, IT'S GOING TO BE IMPOSSIBLE TO FINISH IT BY NINE ON FRIDAY NIGHT.
W-WHAT ABOUT SATURDAY?
I'M SORRY, WE'VE BEEN WORKING WEDNESDAY TO FRIDAY SINCE CHAPTER 3, SO I TOOK A JOB ON SATURDAY.
AND I WANT TO TAKE SUNDAY OFF AT LEAST...
I-I SEE... IN THAT CASE, I CAN PUSH THE DEADLINE BACK TO MONDAY, SO IF WE DON'T FINISH BY FRIDAY, I'LL DO THE REST MYSELF OVER THE WEEKEND.
I'LL HELP.
SO WILL I.
DON'T FEEL GUILTY, OGAWA. JUST GIVE US INSTRUCTIONS AND WE'LL BE FINE ON OUR OWN.
DON'T FORGET TO PAY US FOR THE EXTRA DAY.
WE FINISHED THE FINAL DRAFT AND HELD THE MEETING ON SATURDAY, BUT I FELT BAD ABOUT RUINING MR. MIURA'S WEEKEND. SO I PUT ALL MY EFFORTS INTO MEETING MY FRIDAY DEADLINE FOR THE FOLLOWING WEEK.

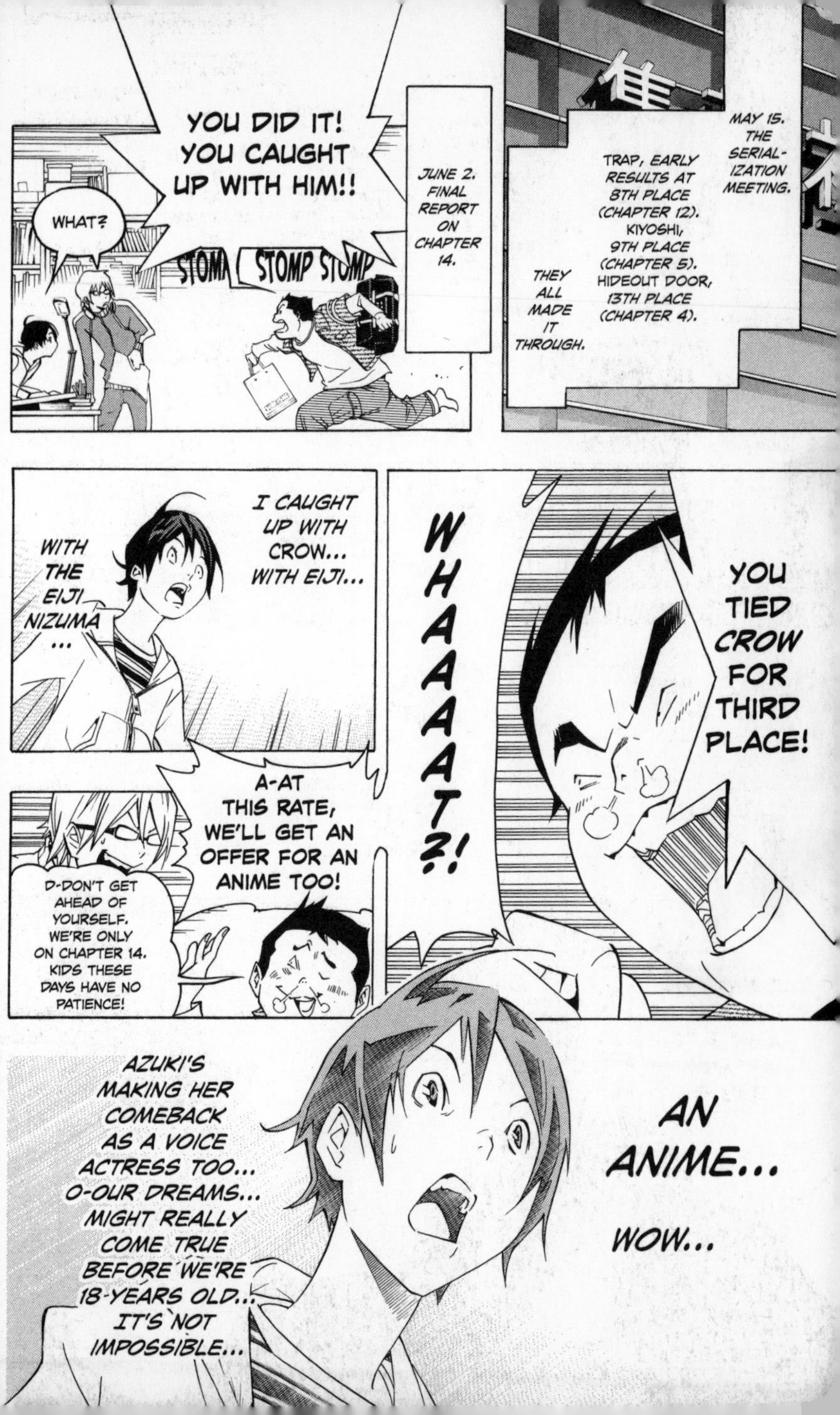
MAY 15. THE SERIALIZATION MEETING.
TRAP, EARLY RESULTS AT 8TH PLACE (CHAPTER 12). KIYOSHI, 9TH PLACE (CHAPTER 5). HIDEOUT DOOR, 13TH PLACE (CHAPTER 4).
THEY ALL MADE IT THROUGH.
JUNE 2. FINAL REPORT ON CHAPTER 14.
YOU DID IT! YOU CAUGHT UP WITH HIM!!
STOMP STOMP STOMP
WHAT?
YOU TIED CROW FOR THIRD PLACE!
WHAAAAAT?!
I CAUGHT UP WITH CROW... WITH EIJI...
WITH THE EIJI NIZUMA...
A-AT THIS RATE, WE'LL GET AN OFFER FOR AN ANIME TOO!
D-DON'T GET AHEAD OF YOURSELF. WE'RE ONLY ON CHAPTER 14. KIDS THESE DAYS HAVE NO PATIENCE!
AN ANIME...
WOW...
AZUKI'S MAKING HER COMEBACK AS A VOICE ACTRESS TOO... O-OUR DREAMS... MIGHT REALLY COME TRUE BEFORE WE'RE 18-YEARS OLD... IT'S NOT IMPOSSIBLE...

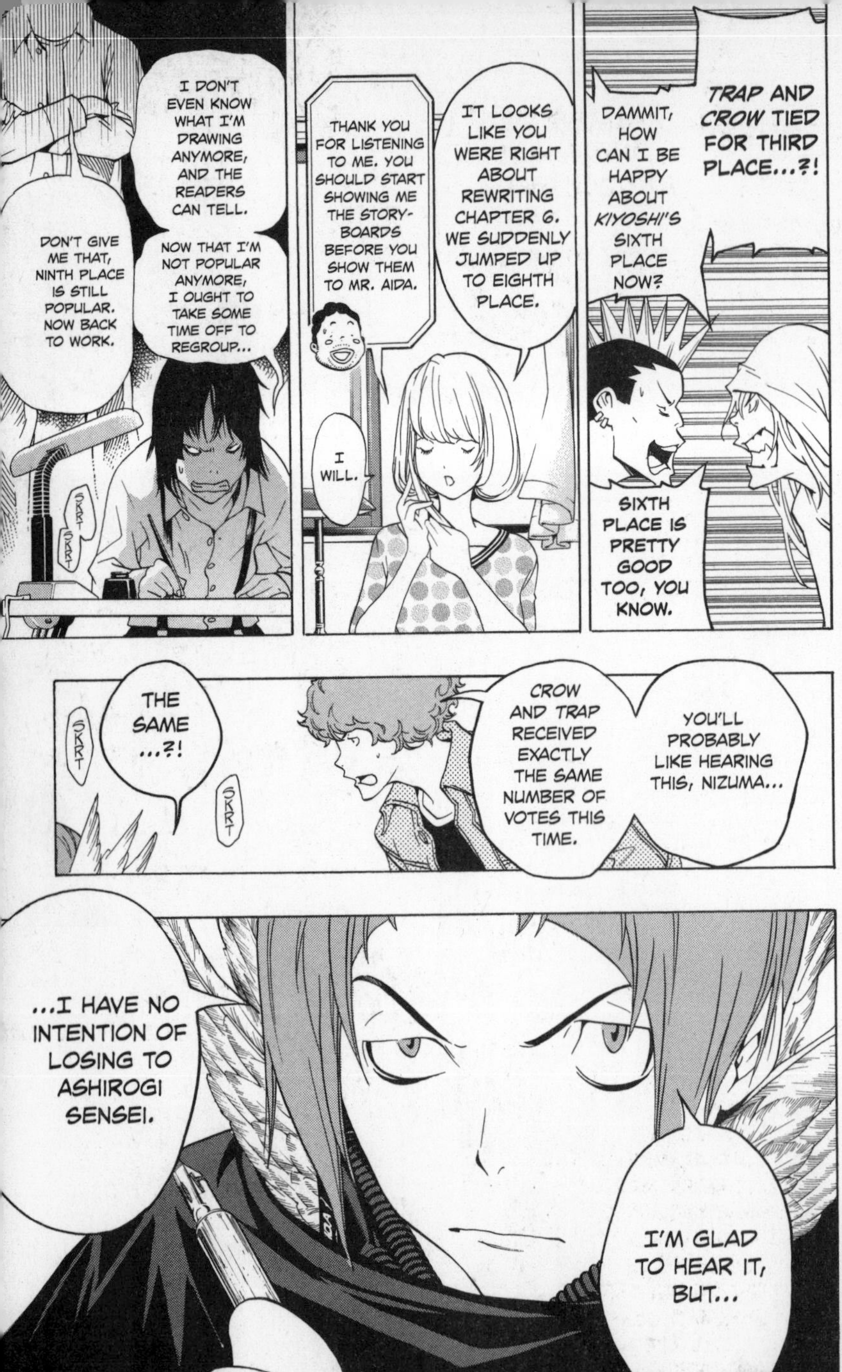
TRAP AND CROW TIED FOR THIRD PLACE...?!
DAMMIT, HOW CAN I BE HAPPY ABOUT KIYOSHI'S SIXTH PLACE NOW?
SIXTH PLACE IS PRETTY GOOD TOO, YOU KNOW.
IT LOOKS LIKE YOU WERE RIGHT ABOUT REWRITING CHAPTER 6. WE SUDDENLY JUMPED UP TO EIGHTH PLACE.
THANK YOU FOR LISTENING TO ME. YOU SHOULD START SHOWING ME THE STORY-BOARDS BEFORE YOU SHOW THEM TO MR. AIDA.
I WILL.
I DON'T EVEN KNOW WHAT I'M DRAWING ANYMORE, AND THE READERS CAN TELL.
NOW THAT I'M NOT POPULAR ANYMORE, I OUGHT TO TAKE SOME TIME OFF TO REGROUP...
DON'T GIVE ME THAT, NINTH PLACE IS STILL POPULAR. NOW BACK TO WORK.
SKRT SKRT
YOU'LL PROBABLY LIKE HEARING THIS, NIZUMA...
CROW AND TRAP RECEIVED EXACTLY THE SAME NUMBER OF VOTES THIS TIME.
SKRT
THE SAME...?!
SKRT
I'M GLAD TO HEAR IT, BUT...
...I HAVE NO INTENTION OF LOSING TO ASHIROGI SENSEI.

5 Yearbook and Photobook (The End)

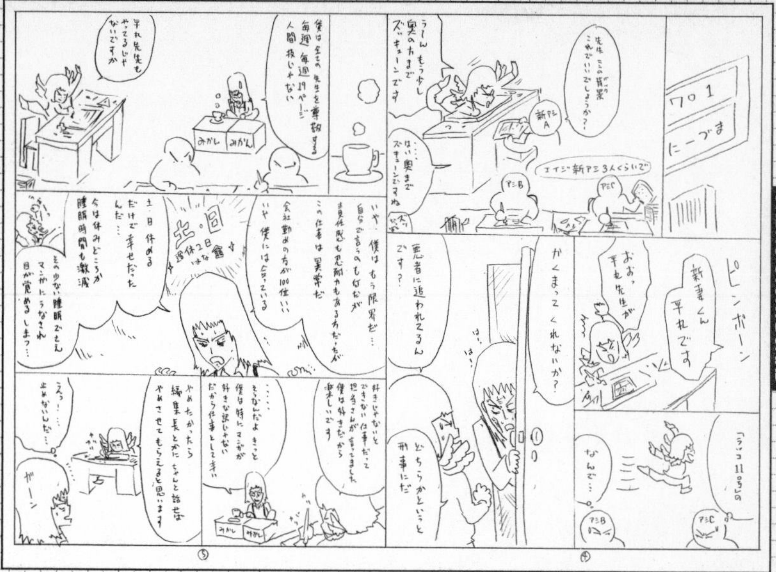
ワロ1 にーづま
先生 この背景 これでいいでしょうか?
新アシA
うーん もう少し 奥の方まで ズッキューンです
はい 奥まで ズキューンですね
エイジ新アシ3人くらいで
アシB
アシC
ピンポーン
新妻くん 平丸です
おお 平丸先生が
かくまってくれないか?
悪者に追われてるんです?
は! は!
「ラッコ11号」の
なんで…
どちらかというと 刑事にだ
僕は全ての先生を尊敬する 毎週 毎週19ページ 人間技じゃない
平丸先生も やってるじゃ ないですか
みかん
みかん
いや 僕はもう限界だ… 自分で言うのもなんだが 責任感も忍耐力もある方だ ただ この仕事は異常だ
会社勤めの方が100倍いい いや 僕には合っている
土・日 週休2日
土・日 休める だけで幸せだったんだ…
今は休みどころか 睡眠時間も激減
その少ない睡眠でさえ マンガにうなされ 目が覚めるしまつ…
好きじゃないと 出来ない仕事だって 担当さんが言ってました 僕は好きだから 楽しいです
そんなことないよ きっと 僕は特にマンガが 好きな訳じゃない だから仕事として辛い
やめたかったら 編集長とかにちゃんと話せ やめさせてもらえると思います
えっ… 止めないんだ…
ガーン

OHBA'S STORYBOARD

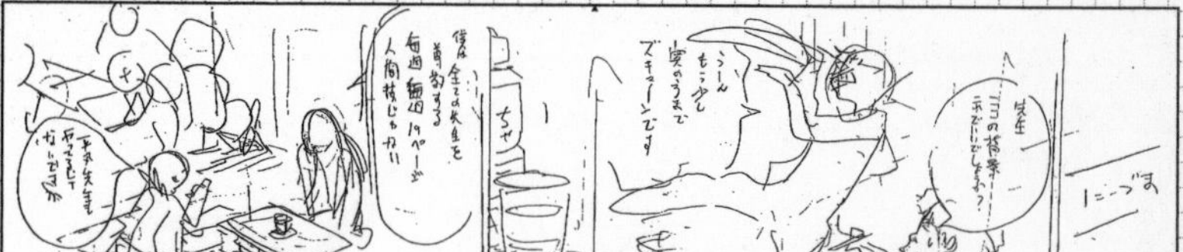

OBATA'S STORYBOARD

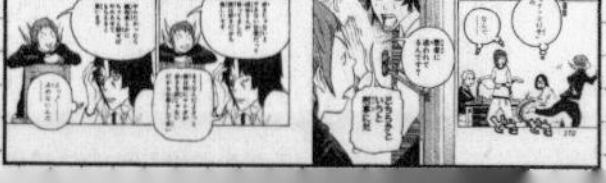

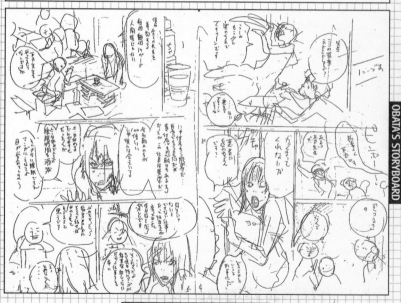

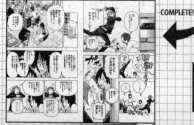

COMPLETE!

*CREATOR STORYBOARDS AND FINISHED PAGES IN JAPANESE

BAKUMAN。 vol.5

"Until the Final Draft Is Complete"

Chapter 43, pp. 172-173

BAKUMAN。

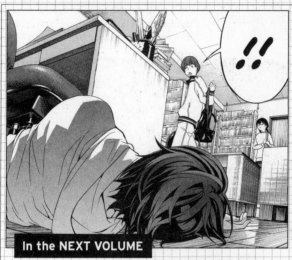

In the NEXT VOLUME

With a successful series now in *Shonen Jump* magazine, Moritaka and Akito keep working harder and harder to retain their newfound popularity. But all their dreams may go up in smoke when one member of the team can't take the pressure.

Available August 2011!

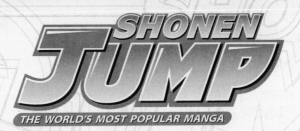
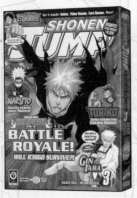
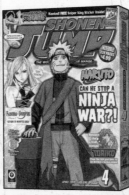
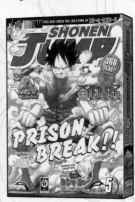

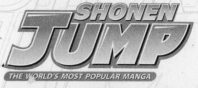

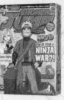